Democratization of Indian Christianity

This book highlights the transformative potential of democratic Church and Christian community in India. In the light of both ongoing and, also to some extent, foregone sociopolitical and theological challenges confronting Indian Christianity, this book invokes the need to democratize Indian Christianity in terms of its theology, liturgy, teachings, practices, resources, leadership roles, and institutional power relations/sharing by keeping contemporary "social realities" of Indian Christians at the core of its approach and discourse. It explores internal challenges – of caste, class, gender, and regional contestations – and external forces of communalism and majoritarianism confronting Indian Christianity today. Further, it underlines the importance of dignity, equality, fraternity, freedom, and responsibility emerging at an organizational level through strong mechanisms of deliberation, decision-making, and execution. A major contribution to religious studies in India, this book will be of great interest to scholars and researchers of religion, especially Christian theology, South Asian studies, politics, and sociology.

Ashok Kumar Mocherla is a Yang Scholar (2022-23) in World Christianity at the Harvard Divinity School, Harvard University, USA. He is Associate professor of Sociology at the Indian Institute of Technology (IIT), Indore. His academic interests include sociology of religion, caste, Indian Christianity, missionary medicine, public health, and minority studies. He is the author of *Dalit Christians in South India: Caste, Ideology and Lived Religion* (Routledge 2020). His research has been funded by the AHRC (Arts and Humanities Research Council), UK; ICSSR (Indian Council for Social Science Research); and INSA (Indian National Science Academy), New Delhi.

James Ponniah is Assistant Professor and Head i/c of Christian Studies at the University of Madras, India. He was formerly the Dean of the Faculty of Philosophy at Jnana Deepa, Pontifical Institute of Philosophy and Religion, Pune. He has authored, edited, or coedited several books: *The Dynamics of Folk Religion in Society: Pericentralisation as Deconstruction of Sanskritisation* (2011), *Dancing Peacock: Indian Insight into Religion and Redevelopment* (2010), *Identity, Difference and Conflict: Postcolonial Critique* (2013), *Committed to the Church and the Country* (2013), *Psycho-Spiritual Mentoring of Adolescents* (2019), and *Culture, Religion and Home-Making in and beyond South Asia* (2020).

"Essays in this volume skillfully contextualize complex challenges, both internal and external, that confront India's Christian institutions' journey in democracy. With penetrating insight and sophistication, each author interrogates issues being faced in a different cultural region or on a different societal level. Readers soon become acutely aware of threats and challenges coming from within and without Indian Christianity to engage in democratic practices and processes. In short, this work makes a remarkable contribution to our understandings of Christianity in India."

    Prof. Robert Eric Frykenberg, *University of Wisconsin – Madison*

"At a time when political democracy appears to be in grave crisis across the world this volume makes a case for democracy as a way of life that could foster what Dr Ambedkar described as 'social endosmosis'. Comprising studies of everyday Christian endeavors as these are undertaken by women and Dalit and Adivasi Christians in India, as well as thoughtful and self critical reflections on doctrine, faith and the church structures, the essays in this book point to both productive changes that have taken place in subaltern Christian communities as well as to conflicts and questions to do with hierarchy and authority which remain unresolved. Importantly, the book makes a case for rendering lived democracy a measure of the good and just Christian life. The point is made that it is not enough to bear witness to the truth of the cross and gospel but realise its meaning in and through everyday practices of equality and fraternity."

    V Geetha, *Independent Scholar, Chennai*

"It is to the credit of the co-editors and contributors to this impressive book that taken-for-granted and over-simplified terms are problematized, interrogated, and evaluated from a variety of perspectives, including the terms "democracy" and "Christianity", not to say anything about the understandings of religion in India. Is there anything particularly democratic in the way Indian Christianity is practiced and how do adherents of various Christian traditions negotiate this? How has the long-convoluted history of Christianity in India been shaped by various missions down the centuries, and what about indigenous agency? Has the seemingly secular nature of the Indian Constitution impacted issues that continue to bedevil Indian Christianity like pervasive patriarchy, unproblematized acceptance of hierarchy, and interfaith interactions which are lived out in the places where people live, work, and worship? What about the persistence of caste oppression within the framework of a religion that prides itself on equality? Can certain forms of worship and prayer be seen as a protest against

all manner of injustice and oppression? All these questions and more are thoroughly and frankly addressed in this splendid volume that will be a touchstone in understanding Christianity in India for decades to come."
Rev. Dr. J. Jayakiran Sebastian, Dean and H. George Anderson
*Professor of Mission and Cultures, United Lutheran Seminary
| Gettysburg + Philadelphia*

Democratization of Indian Christianity
Hegemony, Accessibility, and Resistance

Edited by Ashok Kumar Mocherla and James Ponniah

LONDON AND NEW YORK

First published 2024
by Routledge
4 Park Square, Milton Park, Abingdon, Oxon OX14 4RN

and by Routledge
605 Third Avenue, New York, NY 10158

Routledge is an imprint of the Taylor & Francis Group, an informa business

© 2024 Ashok Kumar Mocherla and James Ponniah

The right of Ashok Kumar Mocherla and James Ponniah to be identified as the authors of the editorial material, and of the authors for their individual chapters, has been asserted in accordance with sections 77 and 78 of the Copyright, Designs and Patents Act 1988.

All rights reserved. No part of this book may be reprinted or reproduced or utilised in any form or by any electronic, mechanical, or other means, now known or hereafter invented, including photocopying and recording, or in any information storage or retrieval system, without permission in writing from the publishers.

Trademark notice: Product or corporate names may be trademarks or registered trademarks, and are used only for identification and explanation without intent to infringe.

British Library Cataloguing-in-Publication Data
A catalogue record for this book is available from the British Library

ISBN: 978-1-032-00707-6 (hbk)
ISBN: 978-1-032-54661-2 (pbk)
ISBN: 978-1-003-42603-5 (ebk)

DOI: 10.4324/9781003426035

Typeset in Sabon
by SPi Technologies India Pvt Ltd (Straive)

This volume is dedicated to all the Indian Women and Men (including reputed personalities like **Fr. Stan Swamy** *and the hundreds of unsung heroes) who dedicated and sacrificed their lives to further the cause of democratic values and fought in defense of justice and self-dignity on behalf of the oppressed and the marginalized.*

Contents

List of Contributors	*xii*
Foreword	*xvi*
ROWENA ROBINSON	

Introduction: Indian Christianity, Categorical Inequalities, and the Need for Democratization   1
ASHOK KUMAR MOCHERLA AND JAMES PONNIAH

SECTION I
Indian Christianity, Democratization, and Modernity – Past to Future   29

1 Indian Catholicism and Democratization   31
 FELIX WILFRED

2 Modernity, Democracy, and Christianity in India   51
 GNANA PATRICK

3 Democratization of Indian Christianity: Reclaiming Church in the Context of Empire   66
 Y. T. VINAYARAJ

SECTION II
Gender and Democratization – Forms of Resistance against Hegemony   75

4 The Feminization of Telugu Christianity: An Instance of Democratization of Indian Christianity   77
 JAMES ELISHA TANETI

5 Shifting Power Equations for Women in the Catholic
   Charismatic Renewal   91
   SAVIO ABREU S. J.

6 Can Catholic Religious Women Democratize the Indian
   Church?   106
   PUSHPA JOSEPH

SECTION III
Democratization and the Marginalized – Politics of
Accessibility and Hegemony   127

7 The Christian Churches, Democratic Developments, and People
   at the Margins: Case Studies from Rajasthan and Odisha   129
   SARBESWAR SAHOO AND JAMES PONNIAH

8 Divided Church as a Democratizing Space: Contending
   Hegemonic Practices in a Village in Northeast India   153
   WATI WALLING

9 Divided Churchyards as Contested Democratic Space in
   Tamil Christianity: A Sociology of Caste Geography and
   Social Stigma in Southern India   168
   M. R. PREMRAM AND ASHOK KUMAR MOCHERLA

SECTION IV
Everyday Life, Democratization, and Indian Christianity –
Unfolding Prospects and Challenges   187

10 Prayer as an Instrument of Resistance: Contextualizing Prayer
    and Everyday Life of Dalit Christians in Kerala   189
    P. SANAL MOHAN

11 Via Food Ways: Challenging Ideas of Christian Equality and
    Democratization   210
    MIRIAM BENTELER

12 Naming the Unspoken: Domestic Violence and the Church   224
    BHARATHI NUTHALAPATI

    Afterword: Christianity, Democratization, and Indian Culture   241
    CHAD M. BAUMAN

    Index   *250*

Contributors

Savio Abreu S. J. has his Master of Arts in Sociology from the University of Pune and completed his PhD in Sociology from the Indian Institute of Technology, Bombay in 2011, which is a sociological study on New Christian movements in contemporary Goa. He has published three books including *Heaven's Gates and Hell's Flames: A Sociological Study of New Christian Movements in Contemporary Goa* (Oxford University Press, 2019). He is presently the Principal of St. Paul's High School and St. Paul's Jesuit School in Belgaum.

Chad M. Bauman is Professor of Religion and Chair of the Department of Philosophy and Religious Studies at Butler University. Dr. Bauman completed his PhD at Princeton Theological Seminary. He is author or coeditor of five books: *Christian Identity and Dalit Religion in Hindu India, 1868-1947* (Eerdmans: 2008), *Constructing Indian Christianities* (Routledge: 2014), *Pentecostals, Proselytization, and anti-Christian Violence in Contemporary India* (Oxford University Press: 2015), *Anti-Christian Violence in India* (Cornell University Press, 2020), and a co-edited volume, *The Routledge Handbook of Hindu-Christian Relations* (Routledge, 2021). A forthcoming co-edited volume, *The Routledge Handbook of Megachurches*, is due out in 2024.

Miriam Benteler studied Anthropology and History of Art in Berlin, Germany, and Leicester, UK, and did her PhD at the Freie Universität of Berlin, Germany. Her dissertation, published under the title "Shared Values: Hierarchy and Affinity in a Latin Catholic Community of South India" (Manohar, 2014), focuses on caste, kinship, and religion. Miriam Benteler published several articles in journals and proceedings and co-edited the special issue *The Gift in India in Theory and Practice* (International Journal of Hindu Studies, 2018, with Antony Cerulli). Currently, she works as Diversity Officer at the Bauhaus-Universität Weimar, Germany.

Pushpa Joseph has a PhD from the University of Madras. She has over 12 years of teaching experience at Madras University and other Universities. Dr. Joseph has served in various leadership roles, including Trustee and

Co-chair of the South Asian Task Force at the United Board of Christian Higher Education. She is currently the Chief Editor of *Magnet*, a monthly magazine published by the Conference of Religious India (CRI), New Delhi, and holds the position of Research and Development Officer, CRI, Delhi. She has published books and articles in Feminism, Hermeneutics, Bioethics, Spirituality, and Theology.

P. Sanal Mohan has been Director of the Kerala Council for Historical Research, India. He has been Professor (Retired) in the School of Social Sciences at Mahatma Gandhi University in Kerala and also held numerous visiting fellowships across the world, including, SSRC New York and Smuts Visiting Fellowship in Commonwealth Studies, University of Cambridge. His research focus is on lower caste histories in Kerala, India.

Bharathi Nuthalapati had her MA from the University of Hyderabad and PhD in Church History from the Fuller Theological Seminary, Pasadena, California. Currently, she is an independent researcher and is involved in Church ministry. Her areas of interest are Indigenous Christianity and Women. She has published several articles in journals and chapters in books, and the book *Bro. Bakht Singh: Theologian and Father of Indian Independent Christian Church Movement*. She lives in Hyderabad with her husband D. Kamalakar.

Gnana Patrick, formerly Head of the Department of Christian Studies, University of Madras, holds a doctorate in Christian Studies. He served the University of Madras as Dean-Research and as Chairperson of the School of Philosophy and Religious Thought. In the year 2013, he was awarded the Fulbright–Nehru Visiting Lecturer Fellowship and taught a course on Public Religion: Learning from Indian and American Experiences at the Divinity School, Harvard University, USA. His published works include *Public Theology – Indian Concerns, Perspectives and Issues* (2020) and *Indian Christianity and Its Public Role* (2019).

M. R. Premram is Assistant Professor in the Crescent School of Law. He has been handling Sociology course for Law graduates. He is partly involved in social activism related to caste, class, and gender-based issues in Tamil Nadu. His research interests include political sociology, process of decolonization, deconstruction of colonial modernity/epistemology, analysis of social stratifications, class and; caste struggles, religionand; rituals, and critical study of theology.

Rowena Robinson is Professor of Sociology at the Department of Humanities and Social Sciences, Indian Institute of Technology, Bombay, and has taught earlier at Delhi University and Jawaharlal Nehru University. Among other publications, she is the author of *Boundaries of Religion* (2013) and *Tremors of Violence* (2005) and editor of *Minority Studies* (2012). She is co-editor with Marianus Joseph Kujur of *Margins of Faith:*

Dalit and tribal Christianity in India (2010) and with Sathianathan Clarke of *Religious conversion in India: modes, motivations and meanings* (2003). She has also published in the areas of ethnic conflict, Christianity, and issues of civil society and constitutional law.

Sarbeswar Sahoo is Professor of Sociology at the Indian Institute of Technology Delhi, India. Currently, he is a Fulbright–Nehru Scholar at the Candler School of Theology, Emory University, Atlanta, USA. He was Charles Wallace Fellow at Queen's University Belfast, UK, and Alexander von Humboldt Postdoctoral Fellow at Max Weber Kolleg, University of Erfurt, Germany. He is the author of *Civil Society and Democratization in India* (2013) and *Pentecostalism and Politics of Conversion in India* (2018). He is also the co-editor of *Godroads: Modalities of Conversion in India* (2020) and *Civil Society and Citizenship in India and Bangladesh* (2021).

James Elisha Taneti is Assistant Professor of World Christianity at Union Presbyterian Seminary in the United States of America. His writings include *Caste, Gender, and Christianity: Telugu Women in Mission* (2013) and *Telugu Christians: A History* (2022).

Y. T. Vinayaraj is the Director of the Christian Institute for the Study of Religion and Society (CISRS). He has authored several books and edited volumes that include *Dalit Theology after Continental Philosophy* (2016); *Intercessions, Theology, Liturgy, and Politics* (2016); *Theology after Spivak* (2016); *Re-claiming Manyness: Re-reading M.M. Thomas in the Light of Indian Christian Theologies* (2017); *Re-imagining Reformation* (2017); *Empire, Multitude and the Church: Theology after Hardt and Negri* (2017); *Church and Empire: Detailing Theological Musings* (2019); and *Faith in the Age of Empire: Christian Doctrines in the Postcolonial Sensibility* (2020); *Political Theology in Transition* (2020); and *Religion and Justice* (2022).

Wati Walling is Associate Professor in the Department of Science and Humanities, National Institute of Technology (NIT), Nagaland since 2010. He received his doctorate in Sociology from IIT Bombay. His research interest includes the interface of culture and religion, political ecology, conflict studies, and tribal studies of northeast India. A few of the latest co-authored publications include *Identity of tribes and the modern state: Contestations in Naga civil society* (Asian Journal of Social Science, 2023) and *Tribalization in civic space: Locating civil society in the Naga context* (Asian Ethnicity, 2023).

Felix Wilfred is Founder-Director of the Asian Centre for Cross-Cultural Studies, Chennai. He was Chair of the School of Philosophy and Religious Thought, State University of Madras. He was the President of the International Theological Review *Concilium* published in seven European languages. He was a visiting professor in several international universities, including the University of Frankfurt, University of Münster, University of Nijmegen, Boston College, Ateneo de Manila University, and Fudan University, China. He edited *The Oxford Handbook of Christianity in Asia*. He is Editor-in-Chief of the *International Journal of Asian Christianity* published by Brill, Leiden.

Volume Editors

Ashok Kumar Mocherla is a Yang Scholar (2022–2023) in World Christianity at the Harvard Divinity School, Harvard University. He is Assoicate Professor of Sociology at the Indian Institute of Technology (IIT), Indore. His academic interests include sociology of religion, caste, Indian Christianity, missionary medicine, public health, and minority studies. He is the author of *Dalit Christians in South India: Caste, Ideology and Lived Religion* (Routledge 2020). His research has been funded by the AHRC (Arts and Humanities Research Council), UK; ICSSR (Indian Council for Social Science Research); and INSA (Indian National Science Academy), New Delhi.

James Ponniah is Assistant Professor and Head i/c of Christian Studies at the University of Madras. He was formerly the Dean of the Faculty of Philosophy at Jnana Deepa, Pontifical Institute of Philosophy and Religion, Pune. He has authored, edited, or coedited several books: *The Dynamics of Folk Religion in Society: Pericentralisation as Deconstruction of Sanskritisation* (2011), *Dancing Peacock: Indian Insight into Religion and Redevelopment* (2010), *Identity, Difference and Conflict: Postcolonial Critique* (2013), *Committed to the Church and the Country* (2013), *Psycho-Spiritual Mentoring of Adolescents* (2019), and *Culture, Religion and Home-Making in and beyond South Asia* (2020).

Foreword

I am delighted to write the foreword to this exciting new book *Democratization of Indian Christianity* edited by Ashok Kumar Mocherla and James Ponniah, and including papers on significant aspects of the central theme from across the country. Bringing together a range of scholars from different disciplines and including both established and emergent voices, the book focuses on an important issue concerning fragmentation, inequalities, and discrimination within Christian communities everywhere against the backdrop of their constitutional and political status as a minority, and the rising sway of majoritarianism along with increasing religious hostility and conflict everywhere. The book's introduction analyzes the meaning, development, and shifts in the idea of democracy from the 19th century onward and sees the different movements as waves, which have over time not been confined to universal suffrage but increasingly encompassed inclusiveness, civil liberties, and tolerance.

Another aspect of research that has gained considerable significance, particularly in Anglo-American scholarship, is the study of multiculturalism and the questioning of notions of democratic citizenship and individual rights, which do not allow for group identities, thereby marginalizing groups with histories of oppression (Kymlicka and Norman 2000; Iris Marion Young 1989, 1990). At the same time, these debates may also potentially concern themselves primarily with the unity and viability of democratic nationhood and the apparent threats posed to citizenship by minority rights and multiculturalism (see Kymlicka and Norman 2000). A further trend in such literature has centered around the notion of religious citizenship (Beaman 2013; Parker and Hoon 2013; Permoser and Rosenberger 2009; Nyhagen 2015). While these are not the central questions debated here, it is within this overall academic scholarship that the subject of this book belongs. At the same time, the research in this book takes a quintessentially grounded perspective bringing into focus the everyday lives of Christian citizens of communities across India.

Thus, some of the significant questions that arise in the book are: who is a democratic citizen, how does Christianity enmesh with the values of democratic citizenship on the ground, and what conundrums do issues of caste, gender, and economic inequalities within community life pose for Christians throughout the country? The chapters in the book take up these central concerns in different ways. Based on the scholarship, the necessity of interpersonal trust for citizenship in a democratic society is pointed out by the editors and that idea is explored in various ways in the book. Also focused on are the civil society associations and activities through which Christian charitable organizations and individuals engage with matters of social justice, human rights, and empowerment for deprived and marginalized groups.

Though scholars in the anthropology of Christianity have pointed out that it is of interest to consider questions of democracy, citizenship, and civil society in relation to the everyday lives of Christians in the countries of the global south (see, for instance, O'Neill 2009, 2010), such studies have only just begun to gain importance. In this context, this book locating itself in the Indian context is important. The editors have considerable research experience in the study of Christianity, and they bring to this project both the insights of sociology and religious studies. Moreover, the contributing scholars draw on the diversity of their academic backgrounds to make this a richer volume. Such productive collaboration holds promise for the future of the study of Christianity in this region of the world and, thus, this book is a welcome addition to the scholarship.

Prof. Rowena Robinson
IIT Bombay

References

Beaman, L. G. (2013). The will to religion: Obligatory religious citizenship. *Critical Research on Religion*, 1(2), 141–157.

Kymlicka, Will, and Norman, Wayne, eds. *Citizenship in Diverse Societies*. New York: Oxford University Press, 2000.

Nyhagen, L., 2015. Conceptualizing lived religious citizenship: a case-study of Christian and Muslim women in Norway and the United Kingdom. *Citizenship Studies* 19(6/7), 768–784.

O'Neill, K. (2010). *City of God: Christian citizenship in postwar Guatemala*. Berkeley: University of California Press.

O'Neill, K. (2009). But our citizenship is in heaven: A proposal for the future study of Christian citizenship in the global south. *Citizenship Studies*, 13(4), 333–348.

Parker, L., & Hoon, C. Y. (2013). Secularity, religion and the possibilities for religious citizenship. *Asian Journal of Social Science*, 41(2), 150–174.

Permoser, J. M., & Rosenberger, S. (2009). Religious citizenship as a substitute for immigrant integration? The governance of diversity in Austria. In E. Guild, K. Groenendijk & S. Carrera (Eds.), *Illiberal liberal states* (pp. 149–166). Aldershot: Ashgate.

Young, Iris M. 1989. 'Polity and group difference: A critique of the ideal of universal citizenship'. *Ethics* 99(2): 250–274.

Young, Iris M. 1990. *Justice and the politics of difference*. Princeton, New Jersey: Princeton University Press.

Introduction: Indian Christianity, Categorical Inequalities, and the Need for Democratization

Ashok Kumar Mocherla and James Ponniah

Introduction

The relationship between religion and democracy has historically been complex, multidimensional, and never been uniform across the world religions. To understand Indian Christianity's janus-faced relationship with democracy, Ambedkar's distinction between political democracy and social democracy comes to help. Political democracy is a sense of equality of all in the political domain, while social democracy is "a way of life which recognizes liberty, equality and fraternity as the principles of life". (Ambedkar, 979). Social democracy is a sense of equality in economic and social life, which is deeply influenced by the system of caste stratification in Indian context. For Ambedkar, Indian society which is based on the principle of graded inequality (which offers elevation for some and produces degradation for others) offers no room for equality among its citizens. Hence, in the Constituent Assembly convened to frame the Constitution of Democratic Republic of India, Ambedkar gave a warning "political democracy cannot last unless there lies at the base of its social democracy". Though promotion of social democracy has been on the agenda of many religious traditions of India such as Buddhism and Bhakti traditions, the tentacles of varnashrama ideology has been so strong and deeply ingrained in Indian collective psyche that the initiatives of the former could not ensure long-enduring sociality of equality neither in their own communities nor in the larger social milieu. Such a situation need not discourage the academic fraternity to retell the complex stories of relationship between democracy and religions of India. In this regard, the present volume starts with the basic question: has Indian Christianity contributed to social democracy? The answer is neither a categorical yes nor an absolute no. It cannot be denied that Indian Christianity made its contribution historically toward sowing the seeds of democratic values in Indian society in terms of condemning practices of untouchability, discouraging multiple caste social stereotypes, encouraging women education, promoting common dining across caste groups, and advancing the ideas of equality, justice, and self-respect in manifest and invisible ways. Further, when the downtrodden and marginalized communities of India, who numerically constitute an overwhelming majority of Indian Christians, were attracted to the values of equality, fraternity, freedom, and justice preached by Christianity, and became Christians, they hoped to enjoy those values of social democracy especially in Indian Christian communities. However, such a hope began to dwindle when the caste ideology and caste elites began to institutionalize caste in Indian Christian churches. As a result, many of those democratic values today remain unachieved goals in Indian society even for Indian Christian communities, let alone for other social groups in India. Yet, democracy remains as an incessant journey and democratization a vibrant process.

Democratization as a normative value, for both Indian Christians as a community and Indian church as an institution, is never more compellingly relevant than it is today in the context of the fast-changing political landscape of India wherein the idea of "minority" has lately been viewed as a problematic social category, particularly against the contemporary conceptualizations of the democratic state in Indian politics. Just as external political forces confront Indian Christianity, internal challenges such as inequality, discrimination, and denial of rights too weaken Indian Christianity as a religion with its distinctive vision and unique ideals. Since there are no comprehensive works that exclusively dealt with these questions/issues of Indian Christianity, especially from the perspectives of Social Sciences and Humanities, this book, in that sense, is a modest attempt to address this largely underrepresented academic area. Taking a cue from Christian Welzel's (2006) argument, it intends to examine the idea of democratization as "essentially an emancipative process", driven by emancipative forces that are reflected in particular mass attitudes, which need to be further deepened in the social milieu of Indian Christianities, and the "lifeworld" of Indian Christians. In the light of both ongoing, and to some extent, foregone sociopolitical and theological challenges confronting Indian Christianity, this book attempts to invoke the need to democratize Indian Christianity in terms of its theology, liturgy, teachings, practices, resource distribution, and institutional power relations/sharing by keeping contemporary "social realities" of Indian Christians at the core of its methodological approach and analytical discourse. The transition from empirical diversity to normative diversity, indeed, could be a value addition with a difference and be a potential driving force to address social inequalities within the fold of Indian Christianity. Before we venture into a discussion on Indian Christianity along the lines of its proclaimed empirical diversity and much desired, and yet to be achieved, normative diversity, at every stage of the church hierarchy, in order to mitigate internal social challenges vis-à-vis external challenges of communalism and majoritarian right-wing nationalism that it confronts in India, let's delve into the larger context in which the study of "democratization of Indian Christianity" would be meaningful academically.

Religion in any society is better understood when not limited to, in terms of, institutions and political parties. Religion invariably carries enduring capabilities to influence the temporal world primarily in two interconnected ways: one, in terms of *what it says* and two, in terms of *what it does*. The first aspect relates to religious doctrines and theologies, belonging to both textual and oral traditions, while the second aspect deals with religion as a social phenomenon and mark of social identity through various modes of institutionalized forms of social expressions. Peter Beyer (1994) also distinguishes between the twin roles religions play in our contemporary society, namely: the *functional role of religion* that refers to religion's capacity to deal with concerns, issues, and situations that arise in the domain of religion and the *performative role of religion* that refers to the power of religion that extends beyond its realm to solve issues and situations that arise in other systems (i.e., politics, economics, law, etc.) but not solved there. One also needs to distinguish between social expressions of religion at the individual and group levels. From the individualist point of view, scholars of religion are contemplating religion's private and spiritual sides, that is, *a set of symbolic forms and acts which relates man to the ultimate conditions of his existence* (Bellah 1964: 359). To derive meanings and make sense of the *politics of religion and society*, in a broader sense of the phrase, it is essential to engage ourselves with group religiosity as it expands the horizons of religion to interact with collective social solidarities of diverse forms and orientations and seeks to wield its performative role by producing intergroup tensions, challenging the established values systems of societies, and triggering competition and conflict. To problematize the subject matter at hand a little further, those social influences of collective solidarities, intergroup tensions, and competition and conflict tend to operate differently with *different temporalities for the same theologically defined religion in different parts of the world* (Moyser 1991: 11). Therefore, it is the group religiosity that facilitates our engagement with questions of how religion is involved in determining how power is exercised in society? How the formations of group identities on religious lines are consolidated and challenged? How the group conflicts emanate within a religious group as well as between two religious groups contextually in contemporary societies? How does religion play its performative role in the emerging sociopolitical contexts? Therefore, the nature of the relationship/interaction between religion, democracy, and the idea of democratization is bound to be interactive, and to some extent dialectical.

To get a sense of the pressing need for the democratization of Indian Christianity in the light of enduring and emerging challenges, both internal and external, that Indian Christianity is confronting today, one needs to have an overview of its history and sociopolitical contexts that determined its growth at different time frames. Having said that, any academic attempt in that direction warrants the usage of a theoretically comprehensive and methodologically sound framework since the growth of Christianity witnessed uneven patterns during the precolonial, colonial, and postcolonial phases. In these three stages of Indian history, the growth of Christianity was under the strong influence of local sociocultural dynamics and ongoing national/

international politics. Christianity in this part of the world closely interacted with Hinduism, Islam, and Buddhism in various historical and cultural contexts, and consequently it underwent a certain degree of indigenization. Over a course of time, Christianity in the subcontinent acquired a fascinating history and practice of its own that speaks volumes about *the Indianness of Indian Christianity* (Young 2009; Frykenberg 2008). At least in the colonial period, Christian missionaries were viewed as active agents of social change, and the future outcomes of such social change might head in the direction of contesting the Colonial political authority. Such views had a direct impact on the growth patterns of Christianity in India; hence, we now have the Christian population representing numerous denominations and unevenly distributed among the Indian states or provinces. Academic scholarship on religious conversions to Christianity in India portrayed no single dominant reason that could cut-across regional and linguistic boundaries. It has always been contextual. In that sense, modes and meanings of conversion to Christianity are thoroughly diverse and highly contextual that fostered new boundaries, identities, beliefs, and practices (Robinson and Clarke: 2003). In such a complex situation, it is perhaps important to understand where and how religion and democracy cross their paths. The following section precisely deals with that subject matter.

Where Does Religion Meet Democracy?

For too long, scholars of democracy – particularly political scientists – have not paid enough attention to religion: treating it as a peripheral concern for the studies of democracy. Of late, scholarly literature on the growing prominence of religion in world politics, both in the global south and global north, seems to be mounting day by day (Berger 1999; Haynes 1998; Moghadam 2003; Thomas 2005). The return of religion to the public sphere or the public visibility of religion certainly casts doubt on the future of democracy. Increased transnational migration, the growth of new religious movements, and the revitalization of religious traditions across the globe seem to be generating enduring impetus for the return of religion into the public domain. This argument holds water even in the context of Europe (Jenkins 2007; Motzkin and Fischer 2008), where scholars began to look beyond the dichotomous relationship between religion and state. Despite many voices arguing that religion will always remain an antidemocratic force, a body of the Western scholarship on democracy explored how religious affiliations are to be viewed as prominent determinants of democracy, more so by treating some religions as being more compatible with democracy than others (Huntington 1991; Fukuyama 2001; Lipset 1994).

In the western context, it is argued that "democracy is not attained simply by making institutional changes through elite level maneuvering. Its survival apparently depends also on the values and beliefs of ordinary citizens" (Inglehart 2000: 96). Therefore, certain values or attitudes such as individual autonomy, tolerance, free choice, popular participation, interpersonal trust, and skepticism with respect to authority could be seen either as preconditions for the establishment of a democratic regime or as consequent aspects of the democratic transition. On similar lines, high levels of tolerance and interpersonal trust are seen as fundamental for the functioning of democratic regimes (Fukuyama 1995; Putnam 1991). For Gibson, a democratic citizen is one who

> believes in individual liberty and is politically tolerant, has a certain distrust of political authority but at the same time is trusting of fellow citizens, is obedient but nonetheless willing to assert rights against the state, and views that state as constrained by legality.
> (Gibson 1995: 55)

Besides these factors, religion has come to be recognized as one of the prominent cultural elements that shape people's democratic attitudes and values (Billings and Scott 1994).

Here the larger question to explore is *"does Christianity positively relate with the idea of democracy"?* Historically speaking, modern democracy originated from Western Europe, which many argue was essentially shaped by Western Christianity. Berger (2004) argues that the presence of two vital conditions, essential for democracy to develop, facilitated such historical outcomes in this part of the world. First, the anthropological aspect presumes that every human being must confront God by himself, which eventually became the very basis for *universal human rights*. Second, the sociological aspect that required the separation between the state and the church played its role. The struggle between the Holy Roman Empire and the Papacy, whose result was "pretty much a victory of popes over emperors, laid the groundwork of institutional pluralism and of what later developed into *civil society*" (Berger 2004: 76). On the other hand, Protestantism is positively linked to generating a sort of political culture that fosters individualism, tolerance, and pluralism of ideas. On similar lines, countries that are predominantly Protestant "are more likely to be democratic compared to Catholic and Islamic states" (Tusalem 2009: 883). Protestantism, therefore, seems to have an inherent affinity toward democracy as it demonstrates critical components that act as foundations of democracy. Theological facets such as the emphasis on individual conscience in the light of scriptures, the doctrine of the priesthood of all believers, and more importantly the significance attached to lay education and literacy (Woodberry and Shah 2004: 48–60). Voluntary associations/organizations, through civic engagement, all over the world are emerging as one of the foundations of democracy as they indulge themselves in creating civic values conducive to democracies (Putnam 1991). Civic and democratic attitudes are interconnected in the conceptualization of the idea of democracy and its relationship with religion, in our present context Christianity. To further strengthen our ideas on religion and democracy, engaging ourselves with theory and debates on the idea of democratization at the global political scenario is vital. The following section aims to realize that.

The Idea of Democratization: Theory and Debates

The essence of democratization fructifies only with the transition of a political system from autocracy to that of democracy. After the publication of Samuel Huntington's influential work, *The Third Wave: Democratization in the Late Twentieth Century (1991)*, political scientists and scholars of democracy across the world have arguably come to acknowledge the notion that the spread of democracy comes in waves, followed by reverse waves of authoritarian and undemocratic regimes. These waves could be classified into two categories: *positive waves* that move countries closer to democracy with accountable institutions and *negative waves* that bring countries back to autocracy. For Huntington, a wave is nothing but a group of transitions from nondemocratic to democratic regimes that occurs within a specified period and in which those transitions significantly outnumber transitions in the opposite direction" (Huntington 1991: 15). According to Huntington, there have been three distinct waves of democratization in the world. The *first wave* of democratization uninterruptedly continued from 1826 to 1926 and it left distinct and long-lasting marks on the early 19th century with "male suffrage" as a central criterion for democratization in the United States of America, which came to be identified/recognized as the "*Jacksonian democracy*". Besides the USA, countries such as France, Britain, Canada, Australia, Italy, Argentina, and a couple of other countries have moved to democratic systems. It is observed that 29 countries had become democracies by the end of the first wave (Ibid: 17–18). For Huntington, the first wave is effective with *Jacksonian democracy* based on which he calls the USA "the premier democratic country of the world" (Ibid: 30). Such claims indeed triggered many debates among political scientists across the globe.

Presumably, the end of World War II, which resulted in the victory of the Allied powers over the Axis, provided the impetus for the second short wave of democratization. The *third wave* began with the end of the Portuguese dictatorship in 1974 and spread its "demonstration effect" to other parts of the world, particularly Latin America (Columbia, Costa Rica, and Venezuela), Asia Pacific countries (the Philippines, South Korea, and Taiwan), and Eastern Europe. The third wave had swept across 20 countries moving them toward democratic regimes (Ibid: 26). Many scholars reviewed Huntington's formulation of democracy in waves and questioned the appropriateness of the metaphor "wave" to describe the spread of democracy. His categorization of what is "democratic" and "undemocratic" is often criticized for being too "*electoralist*" in approach as he narrowly focuses on "the extent that most powerful collective decision-makers are selected through fair, honest, and periodic elections in which candidates freely compete for votes" (Ibid: 7).

Taking cues from Dahl (1971), Huntington has defined democracy based on three requirements of *"competition"*, *"inclusiveness"*, and *"civil liberties"*. But in practice, Huntington's analysis ignored the fundamental requirements of "civil liberties and "universal suffrage" as important dimensions of inclusion. Critics have pointed out that Huntington adopted a *"minimum-procedural"* definition of what is democratic and undemocratic, whereby his work has its own set of conceptual flaws and drawbacks.

By ignoring the *suffrage* dimension in the categorization of democratic regimes, it is perhaps possible to consider exclusive regimes as being *"democratic"*. Such an argument, as put forward by Bollen (1980: 373), views voter participation as marginally related to democracy because voter participation can turn out to have a mere symbolic value that is often used/employed in nondemocratic countries too. Bollen (1980) considers a regime with extensive opportunities for liberalization as democratic, even though a small fragment of the population may be allowed to participate in the electoral process. Dahl (1971) terms such regimes as *"inclusive hegemonies"* meaning thereby having an inclusive regime without competition. In a way, inclusiveness and being democratic correlate scarcely, as some regimes view inclusiveness as a symbolic gesture, but not as an instrument of state policy. However, that does not mean we argue against inclusiveness as a characteristic of democracy. Some scholars had raised questions regarding the appropriateness of the *"wave metaphor"* to conceptualize the democratization process. For instance, Doorenspleet (2000: 400) suggests that since reverse waves are not apparent, it may be appropriate to think in terms of *"steps towards democratization"*. Instead of a reverse wave, we may think in terms of *"equilibrium"* wherein a trendless fluctuation is empirically more likely than a reverse wave (Ibid: 401). In other words, a wave of democratization is to be followed not by a reverse wave, as claimed by Huntington, but by an equilibrium that neither increases nor decreases the total number of democracies in the world in a significant way. It is obvious from the above discussion that the relationship between state and religion is not always dichotomous. For a nuanced understanding of religion and state relations, one must go beyond the obvious conflicting interest framework, and such endeavors provide us with a better understanding of democratization. The following section brings forth some of those neglected dimensions.

Religion, State, and Democratization

The role of religion in the project of democratization is better analyzed by turning our attention to the state–religion relationship. The antagonism/tension between state and religion represents only one form of interaction between these two social institutions. More often than not, it is observed that many scholars of social sciences, with reference to modernity and modernization, view the existence of a rigid and stark opposition between the state and religion. Casanova (1994: 6) observes that "what was new and became news was the widespread and simultaneous refusal of religions to be restricted to the private sphere". Significant works by sociologists of religion in a way have refuted the assumption of the weakening of religion in modernization, both in the West and in other parts of the world (Turner 2010; Turner & Salemink 2015). Apparently, the broader idea of placing religion in the private sphere and leaving the public domain for the state is no longer a viable theoretical framework to examine contemporary societies. One needs to go beyond the dichotomy of state and religion to look at diverse forms/modes through which they had long been interacting with each other. These modes of interaction bring together multiple actors, institutions, and agencies from both sides of the spectrum and present us with a different picture altogether. Anthropological research on Islam and democracy, with contextualized historical analysis, clearly negates this sort of assumed narrative of polarization between religion and state (Ahmad 2009; Hefner 2011). In fact, religion is not only seen and depicted as a tool of political opposition but also is increasingly becoming an alternative framework to the failed states. The contested role of religion vis-a-vis democracy is still emerging and hence remain relatively inconclusive in the context of existing social science scholarship across the globe. However, recent studies have explored the unchartered territories by way of looking into how churches played a positive role in East Germany, Poland, and South Africa (Stout 2008; Hong 2009; Fawcett 2000; Woodbury 2012).

A shift from a political approach toward polarized state–religion relationship to that of an institutional approach uniquely facilitates us to examine a complex set of interactions between the two spheres, including aspects of *adaptation, cooperation*, and *competition* (Cesari 2016: 132). It seems that religion can play a positive/negative role in the critical phases of democratic transition. The political competency of religious actors is broadly shaped and reshaped by the history of their interactions with secular/democratic agents at large, and mutual trust developed toward each other. There are concerns about the role of religious actors ranging from helping authoritarian regimes, triggering intercommunal clashes, and to the extent of developing transnational extremist networks. How effective could these religious actors be in society is largely determined by the political culture? In the context of the role of the state and its consequences for democracy, Cesari (2016: 134–154) observes that the state has a crucial role in building *political cultures* – citizens' broader orientation toward politics and their perceptions of political legitimacy – propitious to democracy, particularly in postcolonial societies. Besides the political culture, there are discussions regarding the role of robust and representative institutions coupled with sustained economic growth in determining the democratic outcomes, both successful and unsuccessful. Given the complex, deep, and broader nature of the relationship between religion and state in postcolonial societies like India, it must not be viewed from the dichotomous standpoint, but from a dialectical and interactive stance. The emergence of a democratic state in India both as an institution and practice did not happen suddenly. It is a long-drawn process that took many years involving many actors, interlocutors, and mediating agencies who would challenge the inherited social inequalities and transform the Indian cultural landscape less undemocratic as we learn in the following pages. The demand for the democratization of Indian Christianity is more on behalf of those who have been dealing with multiple categorical inequalities. It is therefore academically meaningful to engage with categorical inequalities in India with reference to Indian Christianities.

Indian Christianities and Categorical Inequalities

There seems to be an overwhelming consensus among scholars of social sciences on the idea that inequality is endowed with a particular potential to threaten democratic values and systems, as democratic politics primarily rests on the principle of equality of participation. Therefore, extreme levels of inequality presumably encourage its beneficiaries to subvert or opt-out of democratic politics for their vested interest. If such inequalities are organized and institutionalized in society, they could be recognized as "categorical inequalities". Even though categorical inequalities are apparently seen as "organized differences" in simplistic terms but they actively indulge in two important social functions. First, it yields net benefits to people/social groups on the one side of the categorical boundary. Second, it constantly indulges itself in the process of reproducing the boundary (Tilly 2003: 37). Human societies have always maintained and sustained such categorical inequalities. Caste, gender, class, and race are categorical inequalities that Indian society is confronting today. Caste and gender, among others, seem to be the two most significant categorical systems of inequalities making their marks on Indian Christianity and its discourse. It is worth examining how caste as a categorical inequality continues to stigmatize people at the receiving end of such unequal systems under the framework of Christian faith, which does not promote such discriminatory ideas as per its religious text.

It is observed that all establishments, including governmental regimes, democratic or otherwise, invariably mediate in the production of inequality in three distinct ways. First, by way of protecting the privileges of their supporters; second, by way of establishing their systems of extraction and allocation of resources; and third, by redistributing public resources among different segments of their population. (Bunce 2001; Przeworski et al. 2000). As every establishment, including a church, makes extensive efforts to maintain boundaries and differences in benefits between its members and others. Such activities naturally involve establishments such as a church, and governmental regimes, in perpetuating some forms of "categorical inequality". On similar lines, one must not shy away from looking at how church and Indian Christianity as an institutional establishment are involved in the production of inequality in terms of their systems of resource allocation and redistribution. Indian Christianities across the subcontinent have often directly engaged in addressing caste and gender discrimination, along with other socially evil practices in society. The following section attempts to throw light on Indian Christianity's engagement with gender, class, and caste inequalities vis-à-vis democratic values.

Indian Christianity's Engagement with Gender and Caste Inequalities

Historically, manners and styles of dress code – among others – remained the most powerful ways of expressing distinctions of social status among caste groups in India. The infamous *breast-cloth case'* in the Travancore province had brought forth the simmering tensions between the newly converted Christians of lower caste background, that is, Shanars and the upper-caste Hindus. This case brings together a particular form of cultural expression through which marginality is attributed to people belonging to the lower caste background, especially women. As per tradition, the Brahmin women were privileged to wear a blouse with short sleeves, usually made of fine cloth, and tied in front with a knot, which is called *mudichi ravakky*. The women of the Nayar caste were allowed to use an upper cloth, which was usually made of cotton. One of the manifestations of caste discrimination against women of the lower castes was expressed by forbidding them to cover the upper part of their bodies (Kooiman 1989: 148). By the year 1812, the larger picture slowly began to change as far as caste-based discrimination over the issues of dress code is concerned. It was particularly so due to the dissenting voices of the newly converted Shanar women who relentlessly articulated their views against such caste practices with the support of the LMS (London Missionary Society) missionaries. Consequently, the "breast-cloth" case became the most prominent issue for the lower caste converts to Christianity in their larger social struggle against civil disabilities imposed upon them at multiple layers of their social world.

Given the complex nature of this social problem, the LMS missionaries were compelled to involve and seek changes in favor of the lower caste women with the help of colonial authorities. In the year 1812, the colonial authorities announced that converted women could cover the upper part of their bodies. Exactly after two years, that is, in 1814, following upon the resistance especially by the Nayar caste groups, these rules were further amended to specify that Christian women were permitted to wear a kuppayam like the Syrian Christian women and the Muslims but not the upper cloth that was usual among the Nayars, just to maintain a certain degree of difference (Kooiman 1989: 149). This decision to amend the previous announcement triggered violent clashes between the Shanars and the Nayars, as the converted Shanars openly opposed the move. This breast-cloth case, though occupied a significant position in the history of Travancore province, was no isolated issue of civil disability confronted by the lower castes. The lower castes of then were facing much larger and comprehensive civil disabilities in the realms of social and religion. As observed by Kooiman (1989: 148), "lower castes were refused entrance into the Hindu temples, courts, and were not permitted to use public roads, and wells, and wear sandals, jewels, golden ornaments, or fine clothes, and carry water-pots on the hips".

Historically, the lower castes of India saw Christianity as an escape route from caste tyranny and discrimination and often viewed as a powerful source to foster new identity and social meanings (Kim: 2003). Eliza Kent (2004) argued that conversion to Christianity was not the function of the imposition from outside and of foreign beliefs and practices, but a dialogical process through the agency of the convert and a series of complex negotiations. In her seminal work, she observed that one of the major attractions of Christianity lay in its ability to raise the level of respectability of their communities in the eyes of their neighbors (Kent 2004: 248). Kent maintains that the acceptance by lower caste women was useful as an expression of resistance to the threat of sexual exploitation by upper-caste men. Such views get further strengthened in the light of "mass movements" to Christianity in the mid-19th and early 20th centuries, wherein the lower castes converted to Christianity in groups (Pickett: 1933). The period of the mass movements to Christianity that roughly spanned between 1840 and 1920 was considered one of the most significant junctures in the history of Indian Christianity as it not only altered the social composition of Indian Christians but also effectively dictated the future course of Indian Christianity. At this juncture, the conversion process was often initiated not by the Christian missionaries but the natives with a hope to escape from the shackles of caste discrimination. The interaction between caste and Indian Christianity projects a contested past and a complex present. Despite intrusions by missionaries from the west and the involvement of many colonial officials who were sympathetic to proselytization, Frykenberg (2003) argues that a large chunk of Indian Christians have continued to maintain their own distinct cultural identities and these cultural identities remained Indian, in a way highlighting the Indianness of Indian Christianity.

Despite overtones, the role of Indian Christianity and Christian missionaries in democratizing the caste and gender spaces, in favor of the oppressed, is indisputable. One could see the contribution of Indian Christianity in terms of promoting ideas for the representation of women both inside and outside the church, education for girl children, the democratization of the medical profession through medical women missionaries, and opening up of religious domains for lower caste women. This argument holds water in the sociopolitical context of many Asian and African societies (Hardiman: 2006; Baru: 1999). The role of Christian missionaries and Indian Christianity in condemning the contested traditional social practices such as "sati" and "child marriages" is well known. On similar lines, Christian missionaries criticized the Indian caste system and saw it as an anti-Christian, antisocial practice and institution that needs to be strongly condemned and discouraged. Hence, many churches in the 19th century promoted events like "intercaste dining" and "intercaste marriages" for their church members. Christian missionary work, directly and indirectly, contributed to the consolidation of caste consciousness among many subaltern social groups, both in pre-independent and post-independent India.

Caste Inequalities, Subaltern Social Movements, and Indian Christianity

Often the term *social movement* is used with different meanings and interpretations roughly concerning issues related to social change. According to Paul Wilkinson (1971:27), a social movement is a deliberate endeavor to promote change in any direction and by any means, not excluding violence, illegality, revolution, or withdrawal into the utopian community. Arguably, the discourse of social movements places a special emphasis on "collective action" either to promote or resist change. TK Oommen (2010) suggests the term "social movement should be used more restrictively in referring only to collective actions". Not every collective action qualifies to be a social movement, but factors such as numerical strength, nature and level of participation, and the time span of collective action and so forth do play a vital role in transforming a collective action into a social movement. TK Oommen (2010) makes a distinction between two types of social movements based on identity: hegemonic and emancipatory. The agenda of the former is "to maintain the status quo and perpetuate the existing patterns of domination" and the latter promotes articulation and constructions of identity to assert justice, equality, dignity, and rights (Oommen 2010: 7).

At the outset, though many socioreligious movements possess characteristics of social movements in general, at the same time they have unique features of their own. A socioreligious movement is one that advocates change in social behavior and justifies such advocacy by one or another form of religious authority. India witnessed a diverse spectrum of socioreligious movements,[1] which in turn compelled the socioreligious fabric of India to undergo substantial changes. Looking at the history of socioreligious movements in modern India, it is pertinent to realize that religion played a dual role; it was the source of legitimization of the status quo as well as the source of authority for the dissent. Kenneth W Jones observes that 19th-century India was a platform for three layers of civilization: the indigenous Hindu–Buddhist civilization; the Perso-Arabic civilization; and the British introduction of Western civilization, which interacted and molded the socioreligious movements of that century (2008:4). He further argues that each socioreligious movement in India had shared its unique pattern of relationships with the spheres of religion, politics, society, and economics that in turn shaped the nature and styles of protest. He asserts that such "religious dissent often attracted dissatisfied and suppressed elements of society" (Jones 2008: 5).

In the context of Christianity and socioreligious movements by the marginalized groups of India, it was the mass conversions to Christianity (1840–1920), a pioneering movement, whose impact the erstwhile Christian establishment neither expected nor were prepared to handle (Pickett 1933). For the first time in the history of modern India, it was the "mass conversions to Christianity"[2] that made the plight of the lower caste, who came to identify themselves as Dalits in modern India, a matter of public concern and outcry in an organized fashion (Webster 1992: 33–76). Keeping the motives or reasons behind such mass conversions to Christianity aside for a moment, the outcome of these movements consistently and convincingly directed the historical course of Indian Christianity in the subsequent decades. These mass conversions to Christianity, particularly in the southern part of the Indian subcontinent, was a direct result of historical subjugation of lower castes and gradual development of caste and religious consciousness, which motivated them to gain their self-respect, human dignity, improvement in social status, equality of treatment, and above all to get freedom from the practice of *untouchability* legitimized by the Indian caste system. The theory of relative deprivation (Gurr 1970) may fail to explain this socioreligious movement in its entirety. As MSA Rao (1979) argues, "relative deprivation is necessary but not a sufficient condition to analyze protest movements" (1979: 207).

Besides religious dissent, the mass movements to Christianity closely interacted with larger socioeconomic and political structures of Indian society. Consequently, attributing relative deprivation as an overwhelming factor behind mass conversions to Christianity would be an attempt toward oversimplification, for it ignores the importance of caste consciousness and ideological aspects in the whole process. One could see these dimensions in the writings of TK Oommen (1977) whose arguments go beyond the framework of relative deprivation to explain social movements and bring forth the importance of consciousness and the ideological aspects of the participants. The predominant role of religious and caste consciousness toward mass movements to Christianity was historically quite evident. In the form of conversions to Christianity, one could see the blend of religious dissent and secular ideas together producing a new ideology of protest. Even though caste has been a subject of controversy among missionaries at one level, scholars did arrive at considerable consensus on matters of underlying motives behind conversion as a search for improved social status, a greater sense of personal dignity, self-respect, and freedom from caste oppression (Oddie 1975; Webster 1992). In the aftermath of mass movements to Christianity, Indian Christianity witnessed substantial changes in order to deal with the emerging challenges of time and space. Sebastian Kim (2008) rightly observes that Asian Christianity needs to be understood as an outcome of dealing with historical challenges in its own cultural context.

Education has long been one of the prominent domains that Christian missions paid their full attention to. Furthermore, but they have also transformed the whole domain of knowledge systems in India to a great extent. More significantly, they drastically altered the literacy demography of India by bringing the marginalized people into the ambit of the educational system. The following section briefly maps the relationship between knowledge inequalities and Indian Christianity, with particular reference to the social institution of education.

Knowledge Inequalities, Christianity, and Democratization of Education in India

Education is an essential public good in a democratic society. The nature and the necessity of the relationship between education and democracy have been conceived down the centuries in different ways by a host of thinkers like Plato, Rousseau, JS Mill, Durkheim, Dewey, Arendt, and Amartya Sen. In recent years, it also has been argued by many such as Lipset (1959, 1960), Barro (1999) (Glaeser, LaPorta, Lopez-de- Silanes, and Shleifer 2004), and Papaioannou and Siourounis (2008) that better education leads to better democratic politics and practices. Education is essential for the realization of democracy in a country like India at least for two reasons. First, since the study of *Sanskrit* and access to education were reserved only for the twice-born men for many millennia, there was a systemic denial of formal education to most people in India. Universal elementary education is an essential value to Indians, for it "erodes one of the crucial bases of social stratification in India, namely the exclusion of disadvantaged classes and castes from the schooling system" (Drèze and Sen 2002: 12) As a result, there was a rampant knowledge inequality in Indian society which froze the egalitarian character of Indian subcontinent. Second, since the hierarchical social ethos of Indian society is deeply ingrained in the collective consciousness of Indians across their caste, class, gender, and linguistic differences, the democratic values of equality, fraternity, and justice are instinctively repugnant to the general Indian populace. Since good education enables a "culture of democracy to develop" (Acemoglu, Johnson, Robinson, and Yared 2005: 44) and cultivates a congenial social ambience by liberating people from prejudices and stereotypes by way of and broadening their mindsets, it contributes to the character of democratic social order.

Education always remains one of the most significant objectives for the subaltern emancipatory project. According to two of its key thinkers, namely, Gramsci and Ambedkar, education is indispensable for the subalterns "to achieve self-awareness and consciousness of their active role in society" (Cosimo Zene 2018: 495). Recognizing its singular importance for the Dalits in India, Ambedkar, the father of Indian constitution, emphasized the need to recast "educational aims for establishing social democracy" (Ibid: 504). His predecessor, Jothirao Phule envisioned education as an agency to build critical thinking among the excluded masses of India as intoned in one of his plays titled *Trutya Ratna* (third jewel) or *Trutiya Netra* (the third eye) and opened the first schools for Dalits in 1848 and for women in 1852 (Ibid: 505). Ambedkar also went further by rightly considering education as an imperative strategic step for the Dalits to be able to occupy "effective positions in the government" (*maaranyachya jaagaa*) and gain political power (*satta*) (Ibid: 505–506). In doing so, Ambedkar acknowledged education as a key emancipatory tool for both social democracy and political democracy in India. In this regard, Christian missionaries' contribution toward education, in general, and mass education, especially in the rural areas, needs to be acknowledged. They did play an important role in this regard, despite the lack of support from the British in many cases, to democratize education in India, which was accessible only to the high-caste social elites for hundreds of years. There is a need to recognize the efforts of missionaries like Bartholomaeus Ziegenbalg, Henry Plutschau, and John Sullivan (Danish Missionaries who started English schools in Tanjore, Madras, Cuddalore, Tinnevelly, and Trichy in the 18th century), William Carrey (a famous Baptist missionary who along with William Ward and Joshua Marshman established the Serampore College in 1818, the second oldest college in British India), Mrs. Day and others (American missionaries who focused on women education, English education, and vernacular schools in the 19th century in Madras presidency in then towns like Nellore, Madurai, and Arcot and the villages around), Rev. Anderson (a Scottish Missionary who founded five girl schools in the 19th Century), Mr. and Mrs. Wyatt (key figures of what is known as "women mission" which was specialized in training women teachers in late 19th century and ran 19 training schools in the then Madras Presidency), Schwartz, and others (the missionaries of Society for the Propagation (SPG) of the Gospel/the S.P.C.K which worked in Tanjore area and administered the Saint Peter's first grade college in Tanjore, eight lower secondary, and 34 primary schools). The host of missionaries from the Basil Mission in the 19th and 20th centuries who contributed to the education of the West Coast of India (which included Hubli, Dharwar, Honovar, Udipi, Mangalore, Kasargod, Cannanore, Tellicherry, Calicut, and Palagat) by managing 150 schools in 23 stations by the end of 19th century and a host of missionaries from the Catholic Church since the Portuguese presence in Goa in the 16th century (Catholic church in India today administers around 46,000 schools up to high-school level, 350 schools for special children, 2,800 boarding schools for the poor, 5,500 Junior colleges, 450 degree colleges, 300 professional colleges, 25 management institutions, and 12 universities/medical institutes) have also been key drivers in the field of education in India. Thus, Christian contribution to primary, technical, professional, higher, and special education since pre-Independent India needs to be acknowledged. That explains why Jawaharlal Nehru, the first Premier of India, extended an open invitation to Cardinal Valerian Gracias of Bombay to "involve the Catholic Church in building up a Modern India, focusing on the areas of health, education and socio-economic development" (Gracias 2012: ix).

Particularly, Christianity imparted education to the Dalit and other oppressed communities, lifted their socioeconomic status noted by Goyal (1981), Ramakrishna (1984), Chintamani (1901), and Ambrose Pinto (2004). To cite a few examples, they provided Western education to Malas and Madigas in the then united Andhra (Ramakrishna 1984), and mostly Pariah's in Tamil Nadu and prepared them and other low-caste communities "for higher professions in life than those castes had assigned to them (Chintamani, 1901:328)" (cited in Pinto 2004: 22). Similarly, Christian missinoaries' educational work among Pulayas and Ezhavas in Kerala, Chuhras in Punjab,

Chamars and Bhangis in Bihar, Uttar Pradesh, and other parts of India, Panos in Odisha, and the Adivasis (like Bhils, Oraons, Mundas, etc.) inhabiting across Gujarat, Madhya Pradesh, Odisha, Chhattisgarh, West Bengal, and so forth went a long way in providing not only knowledge but also new self-confidence, earning them self-respect and human dignity. In this regard, Pinto (2004) writes, "the missionary education made the weaker sections of society more aware of themselves and provided them with a place of dignity and honour" (2004: 25). Education conferred on them a sense of self-worth, and above all presented them with alternative forms of social existence in the newly emerging civil spaces of modern and independent India. Education that these communities received in the last two centuries and the government and private jobs Dalits obtained subsequently secured them not only participation in the governance of the state in varying degrees but also new social visibility and a limited public presence, not available to them before. Dalit and tribal people's engagement with and participation in India's public life, facilitated significantly by Christian education, are some of the important developments of Indian democracy. It is believed that education brings about much-needed changes in communities by breaking the barriers of economic and social inequalities. The following section engages with those issues.

Economic and Social Inequalities and Indian Christian Engagement

Another important mode of Indian Christian engagement is its social service addressing the economic and social inequalities of the poor and the lower castes, which seeks to enhance their capabilities, to borrow the vocabulary from Amartya Sen and promote their wellbeing. In this regard, four key Indian Christian agencies need to be mentioned: Caritas India, an official body of CBCI (Catholic Bishop's Conference of India) for coordinating social works in different catholic dioceses of India; CASA (Church's Auxiliary for social action), the social work wing of NCC (National Council of Churches in India); EFICOR (Evangelical Fellowship of India Commission on Relief) and NEICORD (Northeast India Committee on Relief and Development), the social wings of the EFI (Evangelical fellowship of India). Their work in economic development, community organization, awareness programs, capacity building, and humanitarian services (such as poverty alleviation, relief, and rehabilitation) have been widespread, extensive, and substantive.

Started in 1962, Caritas India has served the poor of India in many significant ways for five decades. It operates through 164 Diocesan (Catholic) Social Service Societies grouped under five zones (South, North, East, West, and North-East) and networks with over 300 partner NGOs. Its counterpart CASA is an outreach arm of 24 Protestant and Orthodox Churches in India, and it operates through three zonal offices in the cities of Mumbai, Kolkata, and Chennai, and 18 sector offices in Guwahati, Imphal, Aizawl, Dimapur, Shillong, Bhubaneshwar, Ranchi, Lucknow, Indore, Raipur, Udaipur, Nagapattinam, Cuddalore, Tirunelveli, Alappuzha, Bapatla, Port Blair, and

Shimla. It monitors its country-wide programs in more than 4,500 villages with around 350 partner organizations. EFICOR, the social work arm of the National Alliance of Evangelical Christians of over 65,000 Churches in India, has a history of 36 years of commendable work in Indian civil society. EFICOR reaches out to the multidimensional poor in the poorest districts of Bihar, Chhattisgarh, Jharkhand, Madhya Pradesh, Orissa, Rajasthan, Uttar Pradesh, Uttaranchal, and West Bengal. Its works involve livelihood and food security, public health, maternal and child health nutrition, disability care, elimination of urban poverty, training and microenterprises, adult literacy, HIV and AIDS awareness, disaster risk reduction, peacebuilding, and climate change adaptation (https://www.eficor.org/). Its new independent subunit, known as NEICORD (Northeast India Committee on Relief and Development) began in 1981 to do more region-specific social service in the Northeast states of India and involves itself in the lives of people of Northeast India, especially during natural disasters, poverty, diseases, famine, and communal clashes, to restore dignity, peace, and tranquility in the region.[3]

Caritas India serves the nation with the vision of "formation of a just and sustaining social order, where the values of love, equality and peace are nurtured and lived". It has spelt out its mission as "Restoration of Human dignity of the poor and the marginalised by partnering with intermediary organizations in extending support and facilitation and advocating for the rights of the people". CASA's primary objective is to strengthen the poor and promote the efforts of marginalized groups of the Indian society toward sustainable development leading to social justice and self-sufficiency. Like Caritas India, CASA's outlook is quite secular, and it seeks to intervene in the lives of the needy and suffering irrespective of religious, ethnic, caste, or political considerations. In a similar vein, EFICOR and its programs too are meant to make India "a responsible and compassionate society" by enabling its church members to offer effective responses "relevant to the prevailing issues of justice and poverty". In fact, the schemes and initiatives of both EFICOR and NEICORD have to be situated within the triple focus areas of EFI itself which are strategic initiatives, capacity building, and forging solidarity. Indian Christianity and its leadership often engage with human rights challenges both at the local level and national scenario. The following section deals with those issues in detail.

Human Rights and Indian Christian Engagement

Another key role that Christianity plays to promote democratic civic and public spaces in India is its advocacy for human rights. The church's involvement in the promotion of human rights has gained greater prominence in the last few years, especially against the backdrop of the growing prominence of political Hindutva and its implementation of political projects. There is a growing consciousness among the Christians to look at "lack of religious freedom" and "communal violence" in India within the broader framework of the "Human Rights" issue. Christian organizations like AICC, Religious Liberty Commission of EFI (https://efionline.org/what-we-do/commissions/religious-liberty-commission/), and institutions like "Prashant" in Gujarat have been strong votaries of this position. Similarly, one of the primary strategies of AICC is to work with civil liberties and human rights organizations at the local and global levels and to involve in international advocacy promoting human rights for Dalits and freedom of faith in South Asia. In the aftermath of religious violence against Dalit Christians in Odisha, there is a paradigm shift in understanding religious violence as a dominant caste Hindu's denial of "fundamental human rights" (which is necessarily constitutive of "religious freedom" as well) to the Dalits and tribes, the most vulnerable social groups in India. AICC and OROSA are great champions of this perspective and represent this issue to various statutory bodies of Human Rights, both national and international. They also network with other minorities, NGOs, and international agencies to muster support for juridical pronouncements, state interventions, and compliance with international laws. They played an active role in developing Joint Stakeholders' Report to the United Nations Human Rights Council for the Universal Periodic Review 2012.

The regional bodies of Caritas India, the catholic charities in Odisha, were also involved in the promotion of human rights among the Dalits and Tribes, especially in the Kandhamal area through their programs such as Human Rights Awareness Campaign, Staff training on Fact-finding and Documentation for Effective Monitoring of Human rights Violations, Formation of District level Human rights Platform, called "kandhamal manavadhikar surakshya manch", Human Rights Day Celebration, a Training program on PESA (Panchayats Extended to Scheduled Area Act 1996), Training Program on Dalit history and Culture and Ambedkar Ideology in the year 2010–2011 (Catholic Charities Odisha Report 2010–11 2012: 21–25). Dalit Human Rights Centre (DHRC) started in 1990 at Chengalpattu in Tamil Nadu by Fr. Yesu Marian SJ, a Dalit advocate, is another center that works for the empowerment of Dalits through legal rights, educationally, culturally, and socially. This center conducts cases in the court of law for the Dalits, offers free legal advice for various target groups, conducts legal awareness training programs for the Dalits and women, provides internship training programs for young lawyers in human rights, and supports the Dalit victims in caste violence. LASS (Legal Action, Advocacy and Services) is another Jesuit-run social service center established in 2004 near Madurai that works for the Human Rights of Women and Children. The Udayani, the Jesuit's social action Forum, in Kolkata played a major role in campaigning and lobbying for and drafting the "Right to food Bill" at the center in Delhi by bringing together social activists, NGOs, and civil society groups to popularize the bill among the common masses and the political parties.

Besides, the people's movements such as *Ulaikkum Makkal Viduthalai Iyyakkam and Kuddankulam Anti-Nuclear Plant movement in Tamil Nadu* and *Fishermen* movement in Kerala to name a few were started and nurtured by Christian leaders spread in small pockets but across India. Ideologically motivated and sustained by "liberation theology", the involvement, dedication, and commitment of Indian Christians in the likes of Jesuit priest Stan Swamy to the struggles of the poor Indians, such as the Adivasis, farmers, and fishermen are no doubt commendable and received well by many like-minded social activists and secular forces but resented at times by the hierarchy, especially in the Catholic Church for the fear of being confronted by the dominant economic and political forces. Besides these, there also have been praiseworthy initiatives by different Christian groups (both at the organizational and individual levels) to reach out to the neglected, marginalized, and innocent people. Christian forum for unorganized workers, the street children program run by the Salesians in different parts of India, antihuman trafficking programs run by different Christian NGOs that also include Caritas India of the Catholic Church and the CASA of NCCI (National Council of Churches in India), and EFICOR and NEICORD embody the Indian Christian dream of making India as a robust civil society wherein all Indian citizens irrespective of class, caste, gender, and religious and ethnic background would have equal access to holistic human wellbeing with dignity and freedom.

In spite of the ongoing efforts of democratization by Indian Christianity described above, we also recoginse that there is a growing demand for the democratization of Indian Christianity in terms of its theology, teaching, responsibilities, resources, and power distribution to further its scope, orientation, social base, and intellectual engagement with Indian society to realize the much envisaged egalitarian society for all Indians. That said, the following section briefly gives us an idea of how this book is organized based on four larger thematic topics.

Chapterization

This volume is divided into four sections. Section I entitled "Indian Christianity, Democratization, and Modernity – Past to Future" consists of chapters by three senior scholars of Indian Christianity who examine the question of democratization of Indian Christianity from various vantage points such as public theology, Church and empire, and church as an organization. Chapter 1 of the volume titled "Indian Catholicism and Democratization" critically analyzes not only the status of the Catholic Church in India as a democratic institution at present but also the potential role it can play in the future to make India a democratic civil society. While unpacking the institutional character of the Catholic church from the viewpoint of democracy, the author, Prof. Wilfred exposes the double hierarchical bind – the inherited hierarchical view of the Church from the missionaries of the Mediterranean western Europe and the caste hierarchy of Indian society – that has entrenched the Indian Catholic church in the mire of discrimination, domination, and inequality. Even while leading the readers through the history of the Catholic church to discuss the question of the relationship of its leadership and lay members to the processes and forces of "democracy" both in India and the world at large, the author also contends that if the Catholic church in India were to become a true follower of its master Jesus and his teachings, it has to necessarily overcome this double bind by cultivating democratic spirit and values within the Church in its life and structures. Crucial to this mission of democratizing Indian church is the centrality of positions that must be accorded to Dalits, tribals, and women in the governance structure and leadership roles of the Church. Only then it can truly become "an agent of democratization in the larger society, infusing the values and ideals it represents in all areas and departments of life".

Viewing Indian Christianity from the emerging field of public theology, the second essay in this section titled "Modernity, Democracy, and Christianity in India" beautifully narrates the story of Indian Christianity's relationship to modernity and democracy. Engaging with Habermas' idea of public sphere and its types and roles in advancing participatory democracy, the author of the chapter provides a comprehensive view of Indian Christianity's contribution to the emergency of public sphere. The latter achieved through various structures of public knowledge construction and communication, such as print-media, modern mass education, and through other initiatives such as advocacy for civil liberties of the subaltern people, and eradication of social evils, made Indian Christianity one of the important agencies in constructing Indian discursive public in modern independent India. Even while deploring that the Church has become a cocooned civil society confined to its own sphere ignoring its larger role for the wider Indian public, the author calls upon the Indian church to become a public body "by imbibing the spirit and practice of democracy, doing away with unmeaning hierarchies" and a civil society "wherein the spirit of participatory democracy among the community of equals can be cultivated". In this context, the chapter presents to the church in India a new roadmap for the future, namely, an active pursuit of public theology, in three arenas, namely: the Church, the academia, and the wider society thereby registering its active public presence in Indian civil society for the wellbeing of democracy in India.

Based on the epistemological difference between the terms – Empire and Ecclesia – the chapter entitled "Democratization of Indian Christianity: Re-claiming Church in the Context of Empire" by Vinayaraj offers a constructive proposal for a democratic ecclesiology which redefines church as a de-imperialized community of all. Building on the ideas and works of Giorgio Agamben and MM Thomas among others, Vinayaraj draws upon scriptural resources of the past and the theological ideas of the present to nullify the forces of domination and marginalization that victimizes the weak and vulnerable in our Indian society. He gives a clarion call to the Church in India to renew its commitment to be a prophetic Church and become a "coming community" that locates itself in a "state of exception" – the site of the marginalized and the excluded. Appropriating MM Thomas' idea of Church as new humanity, the author invites churches in India to consciously dismantle existing epistemes and mental frames of empire and, instead, assume their role of prophetic *diakonia*, wear the mark of crucifixion, and embody an ontology that is in deep solidarity with the victims of the world so that Church can become a democratic community in India.

Section II of the book "Gender and Democratization – Forms of Resistance against Hegemony" endeavors to narrate the contributions of unsung heroes, namely the womenfolk in making Indian church more democratic. Their success story along with the struggles, sufferings, and resistance are highlighted by three case studies. While the first two chapters focus on women from Andhra and Goa, the third one details the life, work, and the limit situations of Catholic nuns in India. To elaborate it more, the first chapter in this section, entitled "The Feminization of Telugu Christianity: An Instance of Democratization of Indian Christianity" is about an understudied topic in Indian Christianity. This book chapter by James Taneti draws our attention to the agency of women in Indian Christianity in that it focuses on the singular role women played in the Telugu region both as Christian missionaries and as recipients and active members of a Christian mission. In particular, the author insightfully narrates the triple role played by the local women as Bible women, medical personnel, and school teachers who spread and nurtured Christianity among the Telugus. In doing so, they indeed democratized Christianity in scope, content, and practice by contextualizing and interpreting Bible and its messages to appeal to and address the real-life issues of common people and including the concerns and strugglers of the poor, weak, and marginalized people especially women among them.

The second chapter in this section is *"Shifting Power Equations for Women in the Catholic Charismatic Renewal"* in which Savio Abreu argues how established churches have traditionally denied space to lower castes and women in their rituals. The predominantly male Church ritual that is under the strict hegemony of the patriarchal Church hierarchy has marginalized communities' privileges in the liturgy of the established churches. This chapter further highlights how the new Christian movements like the Catholic Charismatic Renewal (CCR) have opened new vistas for women and lower castes in Goa. The charismatic movement in Goa began not with priests or bishops or theologians or even men, but with ordinary housewives. Furthermore, this chapter highlights how the Catholic Charismatic Renewal (CCR) has provided the space and the way for women to acquire a certain degree of power, status, and liberation in the patriarchal public religious sphere.

The third chapter in this section "Can Catholic Religious Women Democratize the Indian Church?", by Pushpa Joseph highlights how the catholic nuns function as active and transformative agents in contemporary India. Based on a study done among select catholic nuns, it employs the framework of Christian Social democracy to understand their ministry of empowerment of the marginal communities through education, advocacy for social justice and contribution towards grassroots participation and sustainable practices. While the chapter explores how the works of catholic religious women translates on the ground the principles of Christian Social democracy, it also recognizes that it is essential for Catholic nuns to integrate both the ethos of effectiveness and a sense of critical consciousness. Their practice of ethos of effectiveness bears positive results when they use their resources and positions to transform the lives of the people on the margins, while their critical consciousness interrogates the given and the existing for a more just social order and a sustainable world.

Section III of the book titled "Democratization and the Marginalized – Politics of Accessibility and Hegemony" encompasses a range of opportunities offered and challenges faced by Indian Christianity to make Indian society truly a democratic space both within and outside Christian Churches. The first chapter in this section, "The Christian Churches, Democratic Developments, and People at the Margins: Case Studies from Rajasthan and Odisha", written by Sahoo and James attempts to answer the question: "Is it possible for the deprived sections of the Indian society, the Dalits and tribals, to exercise agency and autonomy, and be part of the larger democratic process?" In trying to answer this question, the authors examine the role played by nonstate actors, especially the Christian Churches and organizations in enabling Dalit and tribal people to overcome the hitherto existing hierarchy and unfreedoms that obstruct their participation in the democratic process. They demonstrate this by narrating two instances of Christian intervention, one in Rajasthan and another in Odisha. The Calvary Covenant Fellowship Mission (CCFM), a local Pentecostal church in Rajasthan, for instance, played a vital role in democratizing the lifeworld of the Bhils in multiple ways; decentralized leadership structure in the church, implemented participatory development activities in local communities; and issued instructions to Pentecostal men to follow a set of strict moral code which includes not only "no alcohol, no smoking, no tobacco" but also the practice of love, respect, and loyalty for one's partner, the latter of which has indirectly undermined patriarchal values and fostered equality and partnership at tribal households. Similarly, in the context of Odisha too, the chapter narrates how Christian social service centers like Jan Vikas have introduced into the lifeworld of the Kandhamal region, the democratic values such as equality, liberty, and human dignity and facilitated the local Dalit Panos to become autonomous subjects through organizational practices of "democratic character" such as people's participation in developmental schemes, women self-help groups, self-governance deliberations, and micro-level partnership programs between the local people and the state government. Even when these community development programs of the Christian organizations brought ruptures in the already existing social fabric of the region, leading to Hindu–Christian communal conflicts during 2007 and 2008, the Catholic Church and its organizations in Kandhamal became a lot more decentralized and democratic in its efforts to rebuild the lives of Dalit Christians in Kandhamal and to restore relationship with non-Christian neighbors.

Introduction 23

The second chapter in this section titled as "Divided Church as a Democratizing Space: Contending Hegemonic Practices in a Village in Northeast India" by Walling argues that divided church in a Naga community be looked at as democratizing space against the established hegemonic norms of the dominant classes in the Northeast. Lived Christianity of a particular village decisively contested the existence of a Church by contenting the choice of site for a church building, eventually leading to division of the church. Studies on NEI have usually tended to concentrate on problems of ethnicity, militancy, identity, and the politics of cultural and religious differences. This chapter acknowledges and builds on such history but goes beyond to explore an ignored and missing perspectives of conflicts arising out of lived–religion (Christianity here), hegemonic customary land-owning practices, usury practices, and similar historical influences within and without.

The third chapter in this section authored by Murugan and Mocherla with a title "Divided Churchyards as Contested Democratic Space in Tamil Christianity: A Sociology of Caste Geography and Social Stigma in Southern India", examines the physically divided churchyards as contested democratic space in Tamil Christianity as they concurrently represent two different narratives of caste domination and contestation of the same. Even though these dividing walls of churchyards are new expressions of caste ideology unknown to caste politics and Indian Christianity to a great extent, but largely aimed at consolidating caste after death and its associated rituals being observed by Tamil Christians. Their chapter argues that these walls of discrimination be viewed as an extension of existing caste geography with both visible and invisible walls of divisions between and among caste groups that we see in rural India. Strangely, this caste geography and stigma have been shared and promoted by people belonging to two different worldviews: caste Hindus and upper-caste Christians. In the context of divided churchyards and competing claims of caste discrimination and justification, this chapter argues for the democratization of Indian Christianity at various levels to put an end to such outright discriminatory practices.

The final section of the book entitled "Everyday Life, Democratization, and Indian Christianity – Unfolding Prospects and Challenges" draws the reader's attention to the potentials of everyday practices and happenings to challenge the structures of domination and to aspire for and experience democratic values and ideals in their everyday lifeworld. The first chapter of Sanal Mohan categorically argues that prayer is an instrument of resistance against the institutionalized forms of caste domination and discrimination in the everyday life of Dalit Christians of Kerala. Through this work, he problematizes the slave castes' everyday life, particularly after joining the missionary churches in the 19th century and afterwards, which he argues underwent considerable changes. Notably, community prayer participated by the Dalit Christians as a group defying the landlords' authority must be seen as one of the most significant forms of public resistance that eventually captured the political imaginations of Dalit Christians to assert their self-respect. Dalit Christians of Kerala, most of them were slave labors, subjected to caste discrimination and stigma not just by upper-caste Hindus, but equally by Syrian Christians. Therefore, the idea of salvation became central to the social and religious imagination of slave caste Christians in Kerala. By recasting slave bodies as sacred ones, prayer in everyday life became an instrument to resist the power of the dominant castes. In doing so, prayer – through the everyday life of Dalit Christians – has democratized both Kerala Christianity and the public sphere in Kerala to a certain degree.

Through the second chapter in this section titled "Via Food ways: Challenging ideas of Christian Equality and Democratization", Miriam Benteler discusses the idea of hierarchy in the cultural context of Latin Catholic Christians of Kerala with reference to food habits and serving practices. She argues that hierarchy must not be seen as the direct impact of caste society but has its roots in Latin Catholic food habits wherein fish and rice constitute a major part. Though food is highly politicized in India, like religion is, the questions of purity and impurity are not directly connected with vegetarianism and meat/fish consumption among the Latin Catholic of Kerala, rather such social hierarchies are observed in serving practices to a great extent. Benteler notes that in the family context, social hierarchies are observed when food is served/consumed and gender and age restrictions particularly become matters of great relevance. While consumption of beef is not considered causing impurity and accordingly vegetarianism is not associated with purity, the ideas of hierarchy and inequality then are derived, not from the doctrine of caste hierarchy, but from hierarchical forms of food-serving practices among the Latin Catholic Christians of Kerala.

The third chapter in this section titled "Naming the Unspoken: Domestic Violence and the Church" by Nuthalapathi argues for the need to reform the church teaching on ideas of hierarchy, family, and gender, in a way to deepen democratic principles of equality. She adopts the feminist historiographical method to narrate the plight of women belonging to different social classes who are "affected". The idea of "affectedness", as argued by Nuthalapati, refers to the victim and object status of oppressed, humiliated, exploited beings who have become the primary target of domestic violence and repression. The idea of "affectedness" goes beyond the physical to engage with psychological humiliation and harassment that women are subjected to in their everyday domestic life. Some of these experiences of psychological humiliations and abuses are truly difficult to verbalize. This chapter further argues that "domestic violence" has become a fundamental threat to women's health in contemporary India. In this captivating context, the attitude of indifference that the Indian church adopted toward this endemic problem makes Indian church not only a corroborator in this enduring violence but also hinders the process of empowering Christian women to realize their intrinsic value and worth as equal beings. Indian church, therefore, through its teachings must confront the patriarchal notions of male superiority and dominance to establish democratic values within the church and Indian Christian community.

Notes

1 These socio-religious movements could broadly be classified into two major categories based on their nature: reformatory and reactionary. They emerged from all corners of religious faiths representing the religious economy of India. These movements took the form of the Bhakti movement, Bhrahmo Samaj, Arya Samaj, Prarthana Samaj, Satyashodak Samaj, Ramakrishna Mission, Theosophical Society, Aligarh movement, Deoband movement, Sikh reform movement, Parsi reform movement, mass conversions to Christianity, and the Self-respect movement.

2 In the history of modern India, Dalits apparently occupy a special place in the tradition of protest, of various forms, against caste system that has long been legitimized and endorsed by the traditional Hindu religious beliefs. The strategy of religious change is most preferred as it not only changes attitudes of individuals and communities but also changes self-images through the forging of new religious identities (Webster 1992: 12–13). Even though the Mahar movement, towards Buddhism, in Maharashtra under the leadership of Ambedkar tends to dominate our thinking about Dalit movement (Zelliot 1969), a sizable number of Dalits converted to Islam, Christianity, and Sikhism across Indian states. It was during these mass conversions that the Dalits of India accepted Christianity as their new faith. The most notable feature of these Mass movements was "group conversions', wherein the decision to change the faith taken not by individuals but by caste elders (Pickett 1933).

3 Please see more details in this weblink: https://www.eficor.org

References

Acemoglu, Daron, Johnson, Simon, Robinson, James A. and Yared, Pierre. 2005. From Education to Democracy?. *The American Economic Review*, 95(2), 44–49.

Ahmad, Irfan. 2009. *Islamism and Democracy in India; The Transformation of Jamaat-e-Islami*. Princeton, NJ: Princeton University Press.

Ahmad, Irfan. 2011. Democracy and Islam. *Philosophy and Social Criticism*, 37(4), 459–470.

Barro, R. 1999. Determinants of Democracy. *Journal of Political Economy*, 107, 158–183.

Bellah, Robert. 1964. Religious Evolution. *American Sociological Review*, 29(3): 358–374.

Berger, P. L. (ed.). 1999. *The Desecularization of the World, Resurgent Religion and World Politics*. Grand Rapids, MI: Eerdmans Publishing.

Beryer, P. L. 2004. The Global Picture. *Journal of Democracy*, 15(2): 76–80.

Beyer, Peter. 1994. *Religion and Globalization*. London, UK; Thousand Oaks, CA: Sage Publications.

Billings, D. and Scott, S. L. 1994. Religion and Political Legitimation. *Annual Review of Sociology*, 20: 173–234.

Bollen, Kenneth A. 1980. Issues in the Comparative Measurement of Political Democracy. *American Sociological Review*, 45 (3): 370–390.

Bruce, Val. 2001. Democratization and Economic Reform. *Annual Review of Political Science*, 4: 43–63.

Caritas Annual Report 2010–11. 2012. New Delhi: Catholic Bishop Conference of India (CBCI).

Casanova, J. 1994. *The Remaking of Religions in the Modern World*. Chicago, IL: Chicago University Press.

Catholic Charities Odisha Annual Report 2010–11. 2012. Bhubaneswar: Catholic Archdiocese of Cuttack-Bhubaneswar.

Cesari, Jocelyne. 2016. Religion and Democratization: When and How It Matters. *Journal of Religious and Political Practice*, 2(2): 131–134.

Chintamani, C. Y. 1901. *Indian Social Reform*, Madras: Thompson & Co.

Dahl, Robert A. 1971. *Polyarchy, Participation and Opposition*. New Haven: Yale University Press.

Doorenspleet, Renske. 2000. Reassessing the Three Waves of Democratization. *World Politics*, 52(3), 384–406.

Drèze, Jean and Sen, Amartya. 2002. Democratic Practice and Social Inequality in India. *Journal of Asian and African Studies*, 37(2), 6–37.

Fawcett, Liz. 2000. *Religion, Ethnicity and Social Change*. New York: St. Martins

Frykenberg, R. E. 2003. *Christians and Missionaries in India. Cross-cultural Communication since 1500*. Cambridge: Eerdmans Publishing.

Frykenberg, Robert Eric. 2008. *Christianity in India: From Beginnings to the Present*. Oxford: Oxford University Press.

Fukuyama, F. 1995. *Trust: The Social Virtues and the Creation of Prosperity*. New York: Free Press.

Fukuyama, F. 2001. The West Has Won: Radical Islam Can't Beat Democracy and Capitalism. *The Guardian* (11 October).

Gibson, J. L. 1995. The Resilience of Mass Support for Democratic Institutions and Processes in the Nascent Russian and Ukrainian Democracies. In: V. Tismaneanu (ed.). *Political Culture and Civil Society in Russia and the New States of Eurasia*. New York: M E Sharpe.

Glaeser, E., LaPorta, R., Lopez-de-Silanes, F., and Shleifer, A. 2004. Do Institutions Cause Growth? *Journal of Economic Growth*, 9, 271–303.

Goyal, B. R., 1981. *Educating Harijans*, New Delhi: Academic Press.

Gracias, Cardinal Oswald. 2012. Forward. In: John Chathanatt and Jeya Peter (eds) *Silent Waves: Contribution of the Catholic Church to Nation Building*, Bangalore: Claretian Publications,

Gurr, T. R. 1970. *Why Men Rebel*. Princeton: Princeton University Press.

Haynes, J. 1998. *Religion in Global Politics*. New York: Longman

Hefner, Robert W. 2011. *Civil Islam: Muslims and Democratization in Indonesia*. Princeton, NJ: Princeton University Press.

Huntington, Samuel P. 1991. *The Third Wave: Democratization in the Late Twentieth Century*. Norman: University of Oklahoma Press.

Inglehart, R. 2000. Culture and Democracy. In: L. E. Harrison and S. Huntington (ed.).*Culture Matters: How Values Shape Human Progress*. New York: Basic Books

Jenkins, P. 2007. *God's Continent: Christianity, Islam and Europe's Religious Crisis*. Oxford: Oxford University Press.

Jones, Kenneth. 2008. *Socio-religious Reform Movements in British India*. Cambridge: Cambridge University Press.

Kent, Eliza. 2004. *Converting Women: Gender and Protestant Christianity in Colonial South India*. New York: Oxford University Press.

Kim, Sebastian. 2003. *In Search of Identity: Debates on Religious Conversion in India*. New Delhi: Oxford University Press.

Kim, Sebastian. 2008. *Christian Theology in Asia*. Cambridge: Cambridge University Press.

Kooiman, Dick. 1989. *Conversion and Social Equality in India. The London Missionary Society in South Travancore in the 19th Century*. New Delhi: Manohar

Lipset, S. M. 1959. Some Social Requisites for Democracy: Economic Development and Political Legitimacy. *American Political Science Review*, 53, 69–105.
Lipset, S. M. 1960. *Political Man: The Social Basis of Modern Politics*. New York: Doubleday.
Lipset, S. M. 1994. The Social Requirements of Democracy Revisited: 1993 Presidential Address. *American Sociological Review*, 59 (1): 1–22.
Lipset, Seymour. 1959. Some Requisites of Democracy: Economic Development and Political Legitimacy. *The American Political Science Review*, 53(1), 59–105.
Moghadam, A. 2003. A Global Resurgence of Religion? In: *Religion in Global Politics*. Cambridge, MA: Harvard University Press, pp. 303–320.
Motzkin, G. and Fischer, Y. 2008. *Religion and Democracy in Contemporary Europe*. London: Alliance Publishing Trust.
Moyser, G. 1991. Politics and Religion in the Modern World: An Overview. In *Politics and Religion in the Modern World*, edited by G. Moyser, London: Routledge, pp. 1–27.
Oddie, G. A. 1975. Christian Conversion in the Telugu Country, 1869–1900: A Case Study of one Protestant movement in the Godavari-Krishna Delta. *Indian Economic and Social History Review* 12: 61–79.
Oommen, T. K. 1977. Sociological Issues in the Analysis of Social Movements in Independent India. *Sociological Bulletin* 26(1): 14–37.
Oommen, T. K. 2010. (ed.). *Social Movements: Issues of Identity*. New Delhi: Oxford University Press.
Papaioannou, E., & Siourounis, G. 2008. Economic and Social Factors Driving the Third Wave of Democratization. *Journal of Comparative Economics*, 36 (3), 365–387.
Pickett, J. W. 1933. *Christian Mass Movements in India: A Study with Recommendations*. New York: Abingdon Press.
Pinto, Ambrose 2004. Education and Democracy in India: Contribution of the Christian Missions. In: Anne Vaugier-Chatterjee (ed.) *Education and Democracy in India*, pp. 15–26, New Delhi: Manohar & Centre De Sciences Humanities.
Przeworski, Adam, Alveraz, Michael, Cheibub, Jose Antonio, and Limongi, Fernando. 1997. What Makes Democracies Endure? In Larry Diamond, Marc Plattner, Yun-han Chu, and Hung-mao Tien (ed.). *Consolidating the Third Wave Democracies*. Baltimore: Johns Hopkins University Press.
Putnam, R. D. 1991. *Making Democracy Work: Civic Traditions in Modern Italy*. Princeton, NJ: Princeton University Press.
Ramakrishna, V. 1984. *Social Reform in Andhra*. New Delhi: Vikas.
Rao, M. S. A. 1979. (ed.). *Social Movements in India*. New Delhi: Manohar
Robinson, Rowena and Clarke, Sathianathan. 2003. *Religious Conversions in India: Modes, Motivations and Meanings*. New Delhi: Oxford University Press.
Stout, Jeffrey. 2008. 2007 Presidential Address: The Folly of Secularism. *Journal of American Academy of Religion*, 76(3): 533–544.
Thomas, S. M. 2005. *The Global Resurgence of Religion and the Transformation of International Relations: The Struggle for the Soul of the Twenty-First Century*. New York: Palgrave Macmillan.
Tilly, Charles. 2003. Inequality, Democratization and De-Democratization. *Sociological Theory*, 21(1): 37–43.
Turner, Bryan S. 2010. *The Blackwell Companion to the Sociology of Religion*. Malden, MA: Wiley-Blackwell.

Turner, Bryan S. and Oscar Salemink. 2015. *Routledge Handbook of Religions in Asia*. Abingdon, UK: Routledge.

Tusalem, R. F. 2009. The Role of Protestantism in Democratic Consolidation among Transitional States. *Comparative Political Studies*, 42(7): 882–915.

Webster, John C. 1992. *The Dalit Christians: A History*. New Delhi: ISPCK

Welzel, Christian. 2006. Democratization as an Emancipative Process: The Neglected Role of Mass Motivations. *European Journal of Political Research*, 45(6), 871–896

Wilkinson, Paul. 1971. *Social Movement*. London: Pall Mall Press. (Key Concepts in Political Science)

Woodberry, R. D. and Shah, T. S. 2004. Christianity in Democracy: The Pioneering Protestants. *Journal of Democracy*, 15(2): 47–61.

Woodbury, Robert D. 2012. The Missionary Roots of Liberal Democracy. *American Political Science Review*, 106(2): 244–245.

Young, Richard F. 2009. *India and Indianess of Christianity: Essays on Understanding – Historical, Theological and Bibliographical – In Honour of Robert Eric Frykenberg*. Grand Rapids, MI: Eerdmans Publishing

Zene, Cosimo. 2018. Justice for the Excluded and Education for Democracy in B. R. Ambedkar and A. Gramsci. *Rethinking Marxism: Journal of Economics, Culture and Society*, 30(4), 494–524.

E Sources

https://www.eficor.org/ (accessed on 15 June, 2021)

https://efionline.org/what-we-do/commissions/religious-liberty-commission/ (accessed on 15 June, 2021).

Section I

Indian Christianity, Democratization, and Modernity – Past to Future

1 Indian Catholicism and Democratization

Felix Wilfred

"Pizza arrives in 30 minutes; the ambulance doesn't", noted an Indian weekly (The Week 2010). Lopsided priorities could destroy the very fabric of democracy. Any Catholic honestly looking at democracy at work in Indian polity today would be the last one to wish a democratic Church. Could Indian Catholicism be anything other than a democracy? However, diminished in practice and downplayed in conception, the issue of democracy remains unavoidable for Catholicism aspiring to integrate itself into modernity and pursue freedom and equality.

It is important right at the beginning of our reflections to take stock of a basic distinction. One thing is democracy as a form of governance with its procedures such as the will of the majority in the decision-making process, formal voting, and election. We could characterize it as *low-intensity democracy*. People who oppose any talk of democracy in the Church, mostly refer to the low-intensity democracy, for example, when they say that the truths of faith and principles of morality cannot be decided by the majority. However, there is another crucial aspect to democracy that we could characterize as *high-intensity democracy*. It represents an egalitarian vision of human society and stands for a set of values, ideals, and ethos. These have not only affinity with faith but are also deeply rooted in the Christian scriptures and tradition. Hence, the absence of democratization in the Catholic Church is more than a failure to keep abreast of political modernity; at bottom, it is a failure to be faithful to the core of the Christian message.

In this chapter, I am not entering into the formal and procedural aspects of democracy but reflect on the vision and core values the ideal democracy stands for. Some of these values are human dignity, equality, freedom, representation, agency, due process, and restraint on power. Those who want to silence any discussion on democracy in the Church, resort to a short-cut and categorical argument: Church is not a democracy. What they mean is that the Church is not an organization governed by elected representatives through a process of party politics. However, the same people fail to say that the Church is not a monarchy. Once democracy is reduced to an electoral system, it is easy to counter it as not applicable to the Church. However, no one can deny that the form of governance in the Church should respect the core values of the

DOI: 10.4324/9781003426035-3

Gospel, which are democratic in nature. Viewed from this perspective, indeed, democratic forms are attuned to respect and defend the dignity and rights of persons created in the image of God than monarchical, feudal, and oligarchic forms of governance. These latter forms, as history shows, infringe upon the dignity and rights of the individuals and their freedom and lead them into a dependent and subservient relationship. The negative attitude to democratic values reminds us of how freedom of conscience was once viewed by the Catholic Church – Pius IX – as "absurd and foolish" (Schillebeeckx 1990: 204; Oftestad 2019).

An investigation into whether and to what extent there is democratization in the Indian Catholic Church will lead us to examine whether discrimination is practiced, whether there is the agency of the people, and whether there is a restraint on power, and participation and inclusion of everyone. All these elements are very much based on faith and the central message of Christianity, as we will see later in this contribution. We shall concentrate on the democratization process within the Indian Catholic Church in the larger framework of contemporary discussion on the Church and democracy (Bokenkotter 1998). We shall conclude with some reflections on democratization as a mission of the Catholic Church in the Indian society and the larger community of the nation. This contextual study of democracy is, indeed, needed and could hopefully contribute to the global discussion. A report on the *State of Democracy in South Asia* has pointed out how the conception of democracy is reworked differently in each context and its practice reshaped by adopting "innovative institutional strategies to handle diversities in society" (A Report by the SDSA Team 2008: 31). This applies as well to the correlation of the Church and democratization in Indian Catholicism.

Convergence of Two Legacies

When discussing about democracy and democratization of the Catholic Church, one mostly tends to see it as an issue of absence of liberal values – freedom of expression, constraint on free thought, absence of election to offices, and so on. The issue of democracy in India does indeed include such a liberal agenda (Douglass and Hollenbach 1994), but the question is much more complex involving the caste structure of the Indian society. As no one could really analyze the Indian democratic process without studying its interplay with caste, the same is true of democracy and democratization in the Catholic Church (Raj 1993; Koilparampil 1982; Ninan Koshy 1968; Mallampalli, 2004). Caste is a hierarchical order of the society based on the principle of purity and pollution, and the major source of inequality, discrimination, and oppression in India. It has been operative in the Catholic Church as much as in the wider society, the most glaring example being the way the Dalits, known once as "the Untouchables" and "outcastes" have been treated in the society and in the Catholic Church.

Historically, the Catholic missionaries hailing from the Mediterranean region, and accustomed to the feudal system, easily accommodated themselves to the caste system and its hierarchy. This is in marked contrast to the Protestant missionaries from the northern parts of Europe who were inspired by the spirit of Reformation and the Enlightenment. Moreover, they mostly hailed from lower ranks of the society and were imbued with a keen sense of justice and equality (Forrester 1979). They were, in general, highly critical of caste against which they protested and brought a greater sense of equality and freedom within the Protestant Churches and in their governance (Frykenberg and Low 2003). As for the Catholic missionaries, besides the feudal cultural background, we need to consider the fact that they came from a Catholic environment of Europe that was resistant to French Revolution and supportive of royalty and nobility. The idea of democracy was viewed as a modern heresy and even thought of as "absurd". Resistance to democracy in the official position of the Church lasted till the middle of the 20th century.[1]

Given this background, the missionaries carried a Catholic culture that emphasized hierarchy, obedience, and loyalty, and was averse to individual freedom of thought and expression. Democracy and democratization were far from their thought and mode of conduct with the local converts. So, then, we have symmetry between the traditional Indian hierarchical system of caste and the Catholic legacy of antidemocratic posture. The present-day Indian Catholicism is the confluence of these two hierarchies and the attitude and values attendant on them. In many respects, the caste system in India found validation in the imported hierarchical thinking of the Catholic Church. Converting to Catholicism while holding onto the shackles of the caste system presented no incongruity to the new Indian Catholic – both clergy and laity. Vatican II and its new vision of the Church as the communion of the people of God, though enthusiastically received in India, has been going through a turbulent process of translation into everyday life.

When Pope John XXIII took the initiative of convoking the Council Vatican II, one of the goals he had in mind was what he called *aggiornamento*, namely updating and renewing the Church vis-à-vis the conditions of contemporary life (O'Malley 2008). *Pacem in terris* was the first encyclical that a pope addressed to "all men of good will", rather than only to Catholics – a paradigm shift from a pope to challenge the Church to think anew and inclusively. More participatory, dialogical, and democratic way in the life and governance of the Church was part of the realization of "aggiornamento". It was followed up by Pope Paul VI, who dwelt in his encyclical *Ecclesiam Suam* on dialogue within the Church and with the world. The democratic openings of Vatican II by understanding the Church primarily as people of God (*Lumen Gentium*), by recognizing Religious Freedom (*Dignitatis Humanae*), and by creating participatory structures set in motion the core values of democracy (Hehir 2016). Greater democratization of the Church does not mean less of the Church but more of it. The Christian communities of the earliest centuries, in fact, bear witness to a way of life that incorporates the best of democratic values – active participation, recognition of a plurality of cultures and ministries, freedom of the Spirit, equitable sharing of goods, and a nonhierarchical model of governance. As historians tell us, in the course of centuries, the Church adopted different forms of governance, of which the monarchical model became the dominant and standard one for a long time.

The Ideological Component

Augustine's theory of two cities introduced a dichotomy and a hierarchy of submission of the City of Man to the City of God. The hierarchical order, inspired by Neoplatonism, was endowed with a mystical aura in that it was claimed that the hierarchy in the Church is the reflection of the divine hierarchy, something which got entrenched in the Christian tradition, thanks to the work of an anonymous early Christian writer – Pseudo-Dionysius, through his work on celestial hierarchy (*De hierarchia divina*). As Jean Leclercq notes, "What is deemed to be the case with the celestial hierarchy is considered to have a counterpart in the structure of the Church" (1987: 31). This kind of hierarchical conception of the Church in the medieval period led to strong centralization and authoritarianism, with little space for fostering the Gospel values the ideal of democracy embodies. In the modern period, a de-historicized conception of truth divorced from any reference to the subjectivity of human beings undergirded the hierarchical and centralized hold of the Church. When the divine right of kings was challenged in Europe and the temporal powers of the Church were threatened through revolutionary movements like the French Revolution and Italian nationalism, a full-blooded antirevolutionary ideology was forged, accompanied by tough disciplining against any liberal and democratic thought.

Drawing from Scriptures and Tradition

Denial of democratization in the Church ignores the spirit and teachings of Christian scriptures and tradition. In the Old Testament, there is a tension between the royal trajectory of accumulation and centralizing power, on the one hand, and the prophets' egalitarian and people-centered trajectory, on the other (Brueggermann 2001). The prophetic message was a check on the unrestrained and irresponsible exercise of power. Absolutist and totalitarian power structures are dehumanizing, and Christianity could never in principle go with any such mode of governance, though we know from history that this was not always the case. There is the need to constantly hark back to the prophetic source to sustain the democratic spirit. Inclusion, especially of the marginalized, is a crucial democratic value that is reflected in the life and teachings of Jesus, the founder of Christianity. Diversity is yet another important component of democracy that could draw inspiration from the Christian conception of God, which is neither monotheistic nor monarchical but Trinitarian – three persons – with equal dignity and in communion with one another. There is individuality of persons and commonality of life. The identity of persons is not at the expense of communion and the common good.

The New Testament times witnessed a "discipleship of equals" in the community of Jesus with different functions according to different charisms as Paul would later elaborate (Küng 1968; Campenhausen 1969). This was counter-cultural in a period and civilization conditioned by a hierarchical approach to the world and human relationships. According to Aristotle, some are born free and others as slaves. This is an extreme and paralyzing determinism with no possibility for change. There is no room for nurturing dreams, developing freedom, and constructing a new self-identity. Equality also means equal opportunity for everyone to express his or her talents in service of the common good. No one is excluded. It means an inclusive community. Equal discipleship and the common priesthood of all the faithful imply fostering of an inclusive community. The birth of monasteries signified a new model of communities whose members decided through mutual consultation everyday matters – spiritual or material. The Christian community was conceived by its founder as a "contrast society", that renounces domination also in its governance (Lohfink 1985: 115–132).

Further, the innovative theological and canonical approach in the medieval period was inspired by democratic spirit. The maxim *quod omnes tangit, ab omnibus tractari et approbari debet* (what concerns all, needs to be deliberated and approved by all) summarizes the spirit that needs to inspire the governance of Christian communities (Congar, 1958). In fact, far from democratic thought flowing from the secular world to the Church, it was the other way round. The medieval canonists provided the theoretical backing for parliamentary and constitutional democracy in their efforts to give a juridical articulation to governance in the Church (Beal 1992).

Democratic values in the Church could be theologically derived also from the reality of baptism, which gives equal dignity and right for every believer and equal opportunity for participation in the life and mission of the Church. "But you are a chosen race, a royal priesthood, a holy nation, God's own people, that you may declare the wonderful deeds of him who called you out of darkness into his marvellous light" (1 Pt 2:9). This truth has been rearticulated in the conception of the Church in Vatican II. Though we spoke of a hierarchical legacy of Indian Catholicism from the colonial mission period, nevertheless, these Biblical and historical data are a challenge to it in today's circumstances.

Democratization and Credibility

Apart from other reasons, I think democratization is a crucial matter touching upon the credibility of the Church. To be able to function as a credible institution today and bear witness to the Gospel, Indian Catholics may not neglect the importance of the democratic ethos to which men and women of our times are attached. The absence of democratic values could lead the Church to a crisis of legitimation (Coleman 1992: 229). When a Church neglects accountability, participation in deliberations for the common good, and fails to enlist the cooperation of all the faithful, how could one expect it to become a credible Church?

As Charles Curran rightly notes, Catholic ecclesiology has a lot to learn from its social teachings (1992). The social teachings directed to the world speak of human dignity, rights, freedom, participation, the principle of subsidiarity, and the democratic form of life. These need to find application within the Church. The Synod on Justice in the world was aware that what the Church preaches to the world needs to be realized within its own domain. It stated,

> while the Church is bound to give witness to justice, she recognizes that anyone who ventures to speak to people about justice must first be just in their eyes. Hence, we must undertake an examination of the modes of acting and of the possessions and lifestyle found within the Church itself.
> (Justice in the World 1971)

The same would also apply to the issue of democracy and democratic practices.

Inherent Difficulties

Vatican II created seven different participatory structures so that the conception of the Church as people of God be translated into practice. These are: Diocesan Synod, Diocesan Finance Council, Presbyteral Council, College of Consultors, Diocesan Pastoral Council, Parish Pastoral Council, and Parish Finance Council. According to Vatican II, these participative bodies are to function, reflecting the collegial and synodal nature of the Church (Andraos et al. *Concilium* 2021/2). The teaching on the collegiality of bishops dismantled a monarchical conception of the papacy and viewed the governance in the Church as being carried out by the college of bishops presided over by the bishop of Rome, the pope. Vatican II effected a shift from the prevalent monarchical approach to an understanding of Church-governance closer to democracy and inspired by democratic vision and values. The new participatory structures introduced by Vatican II are to be understood in the light of the above democratic shift.

In implementing the democratic openings of Vatican II, however, Indian Catholicism experiences some inherent difficulties, some of which are common in other parts of the world too, and others more specific to the Indian situation. The environment for practicing core democratic values stumbles upon a structural and legal problem whose consequence is pervasive in the governance of the Catholic Church anywhere. It is the lack of division of power. For, the legislative, executive, and judiciary functions are vested with the same person of the bishop, resembling a monarchical model of governance, seen from a legal perspective. Further, by and large, the participatory structures proposed by Vatican II are consultative in nature and do not have decision-making powers that are reserved to the clergy (Demel 2016). The new democratic openings of equality and co-responsibility of the entire faithful for the Church and its mission are undermined for want of institutional safeguards and legal provisions.[2]

This inherent weakness in the participatory structures is intensely felt by the Indian laity, who are struggling against clericalism and clerical control of all aspects of the life of the Church. Clerical control and resistance to democratic values are most evident where the Churches have rich material sources of money, assets, large swathes of land and property, institutions, and political clout. In most parts of North India, where Christians are a minuscule minority and widely scattered, and the Church itself has much fewer material means and properties, it has been observed that bishops and priests have a close rapport with the people. They are quite informal in their dealings. This has facilitated the spontaneous practice of all those values of democratic values. There is consultation, dialogue, and interaction among the various segments in the Church – the clergy, the religious, and the laypeople. The same could also be said of North-East Indian Catholicism among the tribal people who are culturally used to an egalitarian way of life, quite different from the fossilized caste structure in the rest of the country.

The South presents a different scenario. In states like Keralam, Tamilnadu, and Andhra Pradesh where there are a relatively high number of Catholics and the Churches are endowed with a lot more material resources and property, there is much less of democratic culture and more of clericalism and monarchical model of governance. But this is not the whole picture. In this latter situation, the laity has tried to use some of the traditional structures to restrain the clerical hold of power. In many parishes of the South, for a long time, there has been a system of what is called parish or village committee composed of lay persons who own and manage the property and material resources of the parish, including the maintenance and salary of the parish priest. The people manage the Church affairs through their committee. It is something akin to the trustee system in the Catholic parishes of 19th-century America, except for the fact that the Indian system bears the mark of caste. Members of upper castes making up the committee exclude other castes and the Dalits. Moreover, the Indian village committee does not allow membership of women. This system has come into clash with the clergy who would like to control by themselves the parish, including its assets. This village committee system has been challenged to some extent by the introduction of parish councils, as per the directives of Vatican II.

Contradictions

Documents and resolutions at all levels have been produced, and sincere efforts were made to introduce the participatory structures. All this notwithstanding, Indian Catholicism, by and large, is far from embodying democratic spirit and values. We could go into a deeper analysis into the contradiction between the proclaimed ideals and actual practice. One important reason is the quality of leadership and the process through which they and the members of the consultative bodies are chosen both in the dioceses as well as in the numerous religious orders. It is the caliber of leadership that will determine whether democratization will happen or not. It has been observed that a leader who is incompetent, not open and ready to listen, and feels insecure, seeks to ensure that in these participatory bodies those espousing his interests and views are elected. As a result, the participatory bodies at the diocesan level becomes the echo-chamber of the bishop who wishes to hear his own views and opinions from the participatory bodies. Similarly, parish participatory bodies simply echo the views and preferences of the parish priest. The body of consultors in religious congregations are so chosen that they simply toe the line of their major superiors (Karambai 2018).

What happens in these participatory and consultative bodies is, so to say, a "gaming" of the system and ultimately a subversion of it. Often there is a lack of honest communication and mutual challenge in these bodies, in contrast to, as for example, what we find in the Council of Jerusalem where there was honest discussion and resolution of issues among Judaizers and those working for the gentiles (Acts 15). It may be recalled here how bishops in early centuries paid serious attention to consult the clergy and the faithful with an open spirit – something that is reflected in the words of St Cyprian.

> I have made it a rule, ever since the beginning of my episcopate, to make no decision merely on the strength of my own personal opinion without consulting you (the priests and the deacons), and without the approbation of the people.
> (as quoted in Congar, 1964: 43)

The current situation undermining the free functioning of participatory bodies requires that the faithful, especially the clergy, be formed with sensitivity to democratic spirit and values and endowed with necessary skills for democratic practice in the daily life and mission of the Church.

Checks and Balances

The trustee system I referred to earlier tried to restrain the clerical power and facilitated the participation of the laity. Understandably, such a trustee system was a source of conflict between the laity and the clergy, the latter claiming ultimate authority and power over the management of the parish. On the other hand, the trustee system also had its weaknesses and limitations. In a society structured around caste, it was common that the trustees hailed from the upper castes and classes, with no power and participation for the lower castes and the Dalits. Though the trustee system may appear democratic, it was, in fact, non-inclusive, elitist and oligarchic in spirit rather than democratic.

As for the Catholic Oriental Churches – the Syro-Malabar and Syro-Malankara – a kind of democratic system, called *Palliyogam*, was in vogue for centuries. Palliyogam or the Church assembly consisted of one member from each family, and this representative body managed the Church affairs. It held in check clericalism. On the other hand, the *Palliyogam* was an assembly of *male* members, and women could not represent the family in the assembly. The introduction of the parish council since Vatican II appeared to remedy the limits of the traditional systems in that this participatory body is expected to be representative across gender, caste, and class.

The various consultative bodies, if they function with an open and inclusive spirit, could become institutions that maintain checks and balances which is very important for practicing democratization in the Church. There is no reason why, what the social teachings of the Church say about the principle of subsidiarity and justice, which reflect the spirit of democracy, cannot be applied to the Church and to its governance.

If a Church leader is threatened by democratic practice, it is not so much because it is against any truth of revelation. Rather because he is afraid that his exercise of power will be checked and restrained. Checks and balances of power in the Church ensure two things: first, that there is no abuse of power; second, power is directed to the achievement of the common good, for which it is meant. As is well-known, the restraint of power on ecclesiastical authorities is a global problem. As I noted earlier, the present Code of Canon Law lets the bishop be the holder of legislative, executive, and judiciary powers all in one. All the three powers are vested with the same person, making it almost impossible to hold a Church authority accountable for wrong decisions and misdeeds. For the Church to be truly democratic, it is in need of correcting this anomaly. An essential component in a democratic form of governance is a legal system that sets limits to the power of governance. This could be achieved through reforms of the present Canon Law so that it becomes really human rights based (Loretan and Wilfred 2018).

Power, Money, and the Lot of Democracy

Philip Berryman, reflecting on the situation of democratization in Latin America, observes that, contrary perhaps to the general expectation, democracy has not been a significant theme in the Church in that continent. The reason he adduces is quite revealing. "The relative lack of personnel, real estate, and money often reduces the distance between the hierarchy and ordinary people" (Berryman 1992: 138). It is the growing power, money, and influence among the leaders of the Church and the clergy which makes democratization an important theme of concern in Indian Catholicism. Hence, addressing the democratization of the Church means at the same time facing the issue of money and power. The material assets and resources keep the people at bay and let the leaders take arbitrary decisions and follow a very authoritarian and undemocratic course. The bishops of South India, Keralam, and Tamilnadu, for example, are among the influential public persons in their states. They command over vast estates and money and enjoy political clout since the Christians represent a sizable population (in Keralam– about 20%), and hence they are sought after by politicians for electoral gains. The power and influence the clergy enjoy in the southern states of the country have made them less sensitive to consultation and participatory governance.

Dalits – Partners in the Making of the Church

The litmus test of democratization in the Church is whether those marginalized and excluded like women and children are included and their voices are listened to. More specific to India would be the case of the Dalits on whose plight I shall confine my reflections, for want of space.

"The lives of the Dalits are historically and contemporarily a saga of denial" (Louis 2020: 388). Besides experiencing negation of human dignity, material resources for survival, education, and employment, they were even denied entry into the Church. It may be recalled here, for example, that the upper-caste Syrian Christians of Keralam were opposed to the conversion of the outcaste Dalits who were retained as slaves. They also stoutly opposed missionary efforts to free the Dalits and provide them education. A recent study has brought out this Syrian–Catholic resistance to any effort toward freedom and empowerment of the Dalits.

> Syrian Christians were major slaveholders and agents of the Portuguese and Dutch in Kerala, and recent studies show how slaves in Cochin were mostly sold by Syrian Christians, as part of their alignment with Dutch East India Company officer.
> (Baby Paul 2021: 53)

Even today, Dalits are mostly viewed as beneficiaries of what the Church doles out. The arrogance of the upper castes and Church leaders expect the Dalits to be grateful and show obeisance. The relationship between the leadership and the Dalits are characterized by paternalism and condescendence, which are bereft of an adult relationship, a presupposition for the democratic spirit to prevail. A recent research in Keralam analyzes the ways upper-caste Syrian Christians discriminate against the Dalits. It notes,

> The public sphere created in the Church is almost like a bourgeoisie public sphere where Dalit Catholics and the marginalized have little chance to be part because the dominant caste Christians monopolize

it... The contribution of the common people, especially the Dalits, is considered trivial and not enriching enough in the administration and organization of the Church and its ministry. The hierarchical setup of the Church tends to consider Dalits who are the last and least as mere clients and recipients of charity and benevolence devoid of dignity and rights of their own. The mood of several Catholics and clergy is imbued with parochialism when sharing the Church's resources with Dalit Catholics is discussed.

(C. J. Mathew 2012: 197)

The point is that Church is not primarily a developmental organization; it is a communion. It is supposed to be a witness to the equality of all sons and daughters of God. The baptismal equality calls for the removal of all walls of separation and renunciation of caste or ethnic discrimination (cf. Gal 3:27–28). The Church happens only when there is the practice of true communion. Where it is, the community grows through dialogue. As it is, the upper castes do not consider the Dalits as equal partners in dialogue within the Church. On the other hand, the Dalits teach the grammar of dialogue and democratization by their fundamental and legitimate claim to be equal partners in the deliberations and decisions that concern everyone in the community. They bring a democratic impulse increasingly within the Church and its management. Acceptance of others as an equal partner is the condition for every genuine dialogue and a democratic mode of governance (Wilfred 2014).

Dalits and the Issue of Inclusion and Representation

India's future will not be decided by the growth in GDP but by the degree of inclusion and affirmation the discriminated community of Dalits are going to experience. Hence, in a way, the future of India as a nation depends on the expansion of freedom, agency, and representation of the Dalits. The Catholic Church would fail to witness the democratic value of inclusion, if in any way in its practice, it does not redress the discrimination against the Dalits within its fold. The ecclesial marginalization compounds the social and political marginalization of the Dalits.

It may be recalled here that the Dalits were politically marginalized while the mainstream was dominated by the high caste people all along. If there is to some extent political participation and agency of the Dalits in the Indian democracy, this is due to the policy of affirmative action or what is called in India the policy of "reservation," for which Dr Ambedkar and other Dalit leaders fought. Thanks to their representation, at least a small section of Dalit people could enter mainstream democracy. Nothing should prevent the Dalits from claiming a similar policy of "reservation" which will ensure their representation and active participation in the life, leadership, and governance of the Catholic Church. The importance of their claim stands out in stark contrast to the number of Dalit Catholics in the country and their inadequate representation in present-day Church leadership. Though Dalit

Catholics are 12 million out of the 19 million Catholics of India, that is about 60% of the Catholic population, as recognized officially by the Catholic Bishops' Conference of India, they have been suppressed by the upper-caste Catholics who garner the leadership position as bishops, major superiors, and heads of large and powerful institutions run by the Catholic Church.

When the missionaries departed, they left, the reins of the Church in the hands of the upper castes, as a result of which there was not a single bishop appointed in India from the Dalit community until the 1980s. Even today, there are a tiny number of bishops and others in a leadership position from the Dalit community, totally disproportionate to the vast number of Dalit faithful. In order to redress the situation, and as a result of the continuous struggles of the Dalit people, the Catholic Bishop's Conference of India (CBCI) came out with a policy document in 2016 (http://www.cbci.in/DownloadMat/dalit-policy.pdf). It wants to ensure Dalit agency and representation in the life of the Church. The good intention behind the document notwithstanding, it remains a pious wish-list for lack of will and absence of a mechanism for implementing the laudable policies declared. There is no auditing and accountability either. Implementing earnestly these policies will bring a greater sense of democracy, inclusion, and participation into the Catholic Church. Experience and history show that the Dalits continue to be excluded in open and subtle ways in the Indian Catholic Church within the existing frame and structures. Their continued struggles for representation and inclusion have not borne any significant result. In such a case, a separate identity affirmation within the communion of the Catholic Church could open up the possibility of attaining the values of democracy such as freedom, equality, inclusion, and agency. In this context, some Dalit Catholic thinkers such as Cosmon Arokiaraj, S. Lourdusamy, Devasagaya Raj, and Antony John Baptist propose creating a "Dalit Rite" (Personal Interview 21 May 2021).

The above proposal needs to be understood against the background of the development of Catholicism since the 1980s. The two Catholic Oriental rites – Syro-Malabar and Syro-Malankara were resentful of the dominance of Latin-rite Goans and the Mangalorians from the Western coast, from among whom bishops were appointed in many dioceses of North and North-East India. The Catholic Orientals, traditionally confined to the state of Keralam, felt that they were discriminated against by the Church leadership dominated by Latin-rite Catholic Bishops. Hence, since the 1980s, they used their rite identity as a strategic means for power-sharing in the governance of the Church by claiming equal right as the Latin rite. They succeeded in expanding their presence far and wide in the whole country, and today they are assured of good representation in all matters of the life and mission of the Catholic Church (Wilfred 2019).

From a theological perspective, Vatican II Council gives due recognition to the various Churches with their own culture, tradition, and history. The difference in culture and context and other circumstances can motivate plurality of Churches within the Catholic communion. The Dalit Catholic thinkers seem to believe that there is enough reason to claim a separate cultural, ritual, and historical identity for a rite of their own within the Catholic communion. It is their hope that such a path will ensure, as it happened with the other two Oriental rites, greater opening for attaining the core values of democracy, which in turn will empower them to be active agents in the world and society.

Democratization as a Mission

The Catholic Church in modern times passed through several stages vis-à-vis democracy – from opposition to reluctant concession and finally support. Samuel Huntington is widely known for his thesis on the "Clash of Civilization". Less known, however, is his observation on how Catholicism has unleashed a "Third Wave" of democratization in the latter part of the 20th century. He notes,

> The third wave of the 1970s and 1980s was overwhelmingly Catholic. Two (Portugal and Spain) of the first three third wave countries to democratize were Catholic ... Overall, roughly three-quarter of the countries that transited to democracy between 1974 and 1989 were Catholic countries.
> (Huntington 1991: 76)

The recent history of several nations of Latin America, the Philippines, and Korea in Asia attest to the role played by institutions and movements inspired by Catholicism to the creation of democratic societies. In this context, it is legitimate to inquire to what extent in history and present times, Indian Catholicism has contributed to the democratization of society and polity.

Catholic Suspicion of Indian Democracy

If the Catholic missionaries, as we saw, were imbued with antidemocratic spirit in the context of the threat experienced by the Church in Europe, this was further reinforced by a certain colonial argument. As Mary John notes after researching into the Catholic literature of the 19th-century and early 20th century, "Most of the Christians and Catholic missionaries supported the British Raj based on the assumption that the British rule was ultimately good for India and that India was not ready for democracy" (John 2011: 42). Such a view is corroborated by the official views of the Vatican on Gandhi and his struggle for freedom and democracy. Gandhi's method of noncooperation and civil disobedience was anathema for the Vatican (Prayer 2009). Not only did Pius XI deny an audience to Gandhi but also the struggle for sovereignty and democracy in India was looked at with suspicion by the Vatican (Mallampalli, 2004). All this notwithstanding, there has been a group of lay Indian Catholics who believed democracy as something important for the future of India (John 2011). This view was entertained and spread by a journal edited by the Catholic laity *The Week* (1927–1932), whereas the antidemocratic missionary view was circulated through the weekly *The Examiner*.

Catholicism and Democratic Challenges of Today

History and experience bear out that the Catholic Church leaders, in general, tend to espouse the view that one should cooperate with civil authorities. We reach a critical point when the civil authority turns out to be totalitarian with antipeople policies and becomes a violator of human rights. The most glaring example is the attitude and practice of bishops during National Socialism in Germany. There are also Church leaders shifting their position when pressure mounts from the people, from the bottom up. A case in point is the democratization of the Philippines, where the Church leaders from the doctrine of cooperation with Marcos' dictatorial regime turned against it galvanizing the swell of democratic forces from the bottom (Bautista 2020). There are examples and similar experiences from the continent of Latin America. Though India is a democratic country, it also experienced a short spell of dictatorship, known as "Emergency" during the prime-ministership of Indira Gandhi when the Constitution was set aside, human rights were trampled upon, and freedom of speech was suppressed. The Catholic Bishops of India, unfortunately, did not speak up for democracy and the rule of law. They were seized by the fear that any challenge to the dictatorial regime would mean jeopardizing the institutions run by the Church, the cancellation of license to receive foreign funds, and missionary work. One of the Catholic bishops, that is, the Archbishop of Bangalore P. Arokiaswamy confessed this failure to uphold democracy at a critical time.

> Personally, I feel very guilty that we bishops did not speak out strongly against the injustice of the Emergency… There was at the time, the difficulty with the government over the appointment of Bishops. Maybe we were afraid to make that problem worse. We have always avoided clashing with the government. The Church is a minority and acts as one. We protested more about the anti-conversion laws that would limit our proselytizing than we did about the jailing, tortures and forced sterilization of our people.
> (As quoted in Roekaerts 1980: 24)

It is said time and again that India is experiencing politically a tempestuous period. When a religious-nationalist party with rugged totalitarian tendencies is in power and Indian democracy is generally perceived to be in deep crisis today, it is legitimate to ask what could be the contribution of Catholicism in these critical times. The context of the Philippines or that of Timor-Leste overwhelmingly with Catholic population is not the situation of India, where Catholics are a minuscule minority. Catholic contribution to democratization cannot but be different in a widely divergent context. The Archbishop of Delhi, Anil Couto, wrote a letter to the Christian faithful on 8 May 2018, before the national elections, referring to the situation of concern in the country. He said, "We are witnessing a turbulent political atmosphere which poses a threat to the democratic principles enshrined in our Constitution and the secular fabric of our nation" (https://www.indiatoday.in/india/story/delhi-archbishop-s-letter-turbulent-political-atmosphere-let-s-pray-for-new-govt-in-2019-1238564-2018-05-22) and exhorted the people to do a prayer campaign for the country. He formulated also a prayer to be said in the churches.

> May the ethos of true democracy envelop our elections with dignity and the flames of honest patriotism enkindle our political leaders. This is our cry, Heavenly Father, in these troubled times as we see the clouds eclipsing the light of truth, justice, and freedom.
>
> (ibid)

This comment on the country's situation and call for prayer was deeply resented by the ruling party. The letter became a matter of public controversy. Despite being a minority, such a stance on the part of even a single bishop regarding public issues affecting the people, their dignity, and rights certainly makes an impact, as could be witnessed from the media coverage and discussion. Afterall, one would find a convergence of the moral foundations of Indian Constitution and the Gospel on human dignity and democratic values (Devasahayam 2007). But, regrettably, the Indian Catholic leadership, by and large, is timid and lacks the courage to speak truth to power. The leaders do not want to rock the boat. Gripped by a siege mentality, the Indian Catholic leadership isolates itself by digging moats all around the citadel of the Church.

Be that as it may, it is at the periphery that priests, religious, and laypeople courageously struggle for democratization of the country in the remotest villages of India in most trying conditions. Priests, men and women religious, and many laypeople and young students were involved since the late 1970s in various human rights movements and have created at the grassroots level consciousness about human dignity and rights, equality, and justice and have promoted the agency of ordinary people and their participation. Joining various grassroots movements and what were known as "action groups", they focused on specific issues – the unorganized laborers, domestic workers, the displaced people, refugees, migrants, victims of human trafficking, etc. Slowly, networks were built by which individual initiatives of groups were mutually strengthened. The Catholic Social Teaching inspired them. At the time of writing, Fr Stan Lourdusamy, a Jesuit priest who spent all his life for democratization of the Indian polity and in defense of the poor and the marginalized and stood for their rights was arrested in his advanced age of 84 and imprisoned allegedly for inciting sedition while he was fighting for the rights of the poor tribals who were exploited by the mining corporate lobby. Precisely, the priests, nuns, and the laity who are in the forefront appear to be the beacon of hope for the future of Catholicism in India, and they are champions of democracy.

The contribution of Indian Catholicism to democratic life in the broader society can take on different forms. It could be in the form of participation by the faithful in democratic and civil society movements focused on specific issues. It could instill democratic spirit through advocacy programs and through media. Most Indian Catholic media are oriented to promote piety and devotion and cover ecclesiastical news about Vatican, bishops, and the religious.[3] Another important way the Catholic Church can nurture democratization is by using the reach and influence it has in education. Do students who attend Catholic schools and colleges acquire a democratic spirit and receive training in democratic values? Have these educational institutions put into practice democratic values? Have the students and staff been trusted to speak their minds without fear and express their views? Another important way the Indian Catholic Church could drive democratization is by including women in leadership positions rather than paying mere lip-service. This would automatically accelerate democratization.

Unlike in the pre-Independent India when there took place, thanks to the active involvement of the laity, discussion among Catholics about public issues, including democracy, today this is almost totally absent (John 2011). However, *Indian Currents*, a weekly journal brought out under the patronage of the Capuchins of North India has been doing a very critical and constructive contribution to the promotion of democracy, justice, peace, and human rights (https://www.indiancurrents.org/). It carries analysis and comments by many intellectuals across religious boundaries bearing upon current social and political events in the country. It is also creating political consciousness among educated Indian Catholics, priests, and bishops.

To trace back history, a Catholic Indian Association was formed in 1889 to bring to the public realm and to the authorities of the state the grievances and demands of the Catholic community.[4] The All India Catholic Union (AIUC) was created in 1919. Among its declared objectives are:

> To spread the influence of Catholic ideals and principles in Indian public life through any medium of communication and promote unity and solidarity among the people of India through Christian endeavour. To be the exponent of Catholic opinion and to make representations to authorities and public bodies in all matters affecting Catholics.
> (www.aiuc.in)

The bishops of the country are so very concerned about their control also of the public realm that even bodies like AIUC cannot function effectively with their freedom curtailed. This shows a certain pattern at work from the early 20th century when "social and political activity could only be allowed to occur under the firm grip of ecclesiastical authority" (Mallampalli 2004: 90). The Indian Catholic Church appears to be immersed, especially in the last couple of decades, in the issue of minority rights and anything connected with their infringement. It has yet to demonstrate its serious engagement with larger political issues like democracy, inclusion, and participation.

To take on the mission of democratization in the broader society, the Indian Catholic Church needs to create an ethos of democracy within its own life. The associational life within the Church could become the nursery for the development of skills that support and sustain democratic life in the society and country. Basic Christian Communities or Basic Ecclesial Communities, wherever they are vibrant have the potential to contribute to culture of equality, dialogue, sharing, and democratic spirit.[5] With all their limitations, they seem to have helped better functioning of the participatory structures introduced by Vatican II.

Conclusion

As for the Indian Catholic community, there may not be the kind of Church exodus as happening in the West due to secularization, Church tax, and so on. In India, the Churches are still full and active to forecast any such scenario anytime in the near future. But what is happening is that within the national polity, the Catholic community has been gradually losing the public influence it wielded and the impact it made, especially through its many educational, charitable, and health-care institutions. Now the corporate sector has succeeded to do and excel in what the Catholic Church has been doing for more than a century and a half. From being viewed as a benefactor in the past, the Catholic Church today is seen as a rival and competitor in many fields in which once it excelled. Ironically, competitive and commercial mindset has infiltrated Indian Catholicism and many Church-run educational institutions have become profit-oriented. The nongovernmental organizations and voluntary groups are doing the kind of charitable work done by the Catholic Church. The revival of Indian Catholicism will depend upon the extent it could be an agent of democratization in the larger society, infusing the values and ideals it represents in all areas and departments of life. This calls for greater political involvement on the part of the Catholic Church.

This larger democratizing mission also requires the cultivation of democratic spirit and values within the Church, in its life, and structures. Fostering democratic values will help the Indian Catholic Church overcome the double hierarchical bind – the inherited hierarchical understanding of the Church from the missionary period and the hierarchical structure of caste, discrimination, and inequality. As is clear, democratization is not simply a liberal agenda, but has more profound implications for the transformation of the Church and the larger society. The test of whether Indian Catholicism is getting democratized will depend upon whether the Dalits, the tribals, and women are included and allowed full and equal participation and leadership in the Church.

The traditional avenues for the Catholic Church to make an impact on society continue to shrink. Against this background, the case of Dalits Catholics offers a bright prospect. Their involvement in the Church and in society will make a difference in terms of justice, equality, inclusion, and representation. These belong to the very core of Christianity. The Dalit Catholics could become the heralds of these values in a hierarchical Church and a caste-ridden society. It is by activating the agency of the Dalit community that the prospects of the future of the Catholic Church could be ensured. For, they know what the absence of value of freedom, participation, and agency mean, and hence could be a formidable force to infuse the spirit and values of democracy into the public life.

Further, a democracy-oriented reform would imply a radical project to uproot the deeply entrenched casteism in the Church – among the people and more importantly among the clergy and the religious congregations. The clergy and religious reflect the reality of caste in the Catholic community and exacerbate it further because of their hold of power. With economic developments, and demographic factors such as increasingly small families among the Catholics, it is likely that in less than two decades there could be a serious crisis in vocation to priestly and religious life. The vocations could drastically drop. The signs are already visible. Hopefully, this would awaken a greater sense of realism and will pave the way to rid off the power-struggle in the structures of the Church. Attention will, then, be directed to most essentials in Christian faith which will foster equality and greater communion in the life of the Church community.

Notes

1 The first indication of the Church's openness to democracy came with the Christmas Message of Pope Pius XII in 1944.
2 What was expected of the Latin Code of Canon Law (1983), namely to reflect the Vatican II understanding of the Church and translate them into legal provisions, unfortunately, did not materialize. The power of governance, for example, is reserved only for the clergy and not the lay faithful. It means that one could exercise the power of governance if only he (no she) is ordained. According to CIC canon 129, the laity do not have any power of governance by themselves, but can only cooperate (*ad normam iuris cooperari possunt*) in the exercise of the clerical power of governance. Cf. Felix Wilfred, "Theology and Canon Law: Journeying Together", in *Concilium* 2016/5, pp. 41–52.
3 The Catholic Church also runs several TV stations. These serve as an extension of Church-activities with almost no public impact. The programmes are designed to cater to the pietism of the Catholics. They transmit mass, rosary recitation, way of the cross during Lent, and such religious activities, and occasionally preaching by Church-leaders and the clergy. See for example: https://catholicmediaindia.blogspot.com/p/catholic-media-india.html.
4 The Indian Catholic Association appears to have been an Indian version of "*Action catholique*" (Catholic Action), which was vigorously promoted in Europe and other parts of the Christian world to safeguard Catholic identity in the public realm and protect Catholics from modern and secular influences.

5 The role of Basic Christian Communities introduced in India in 1980s is ambiguous as to their impact on the larger society and their contribution to democratic values. In many instances, they simply function as an extension of the institutional Church and its management of spiritual goods.

References

A Report by the SDSA Team. 2008. *State of Democracy in South Asia*. Delhi: Oxford University Press.

Andraos, Michel, Thierry-Marie Courau and Carlos Mendoza Álvarez (eds) 2021. "Synodalities." *Concilium* 2. London: SCM Press

Bautista, Julius. 2020. "Catholic Democratizaation: Religious Networks and Political Agency in the Philippines and Timor-Leste." *Sojourn: Journal of Social Issues in Southeast Asia*, 35(2), 310–342.

Beal, John. 1992. "Toward a Democratic Church: The Canonical Heritage." In Eugene C. Bianchi and Rosemary Radford Reuther (eds), *A Democratic Catholic Chuch*, 52–79. New York: Crossroad.

Berryman, Philip. 1992. "Other Experiences, Other Concerns: Latin America and the Democratisation of the Church." In Eugene C. Bianchi and Rosemary Radford Ruether (eds), *A Democratic Catholic Church*, 128–138. New York: Crossroad.

Bokenkotter, Thomas. 1998. *Church and Revolution: Catholics in the Struggle for Democracy and Social Justice*. New York: Image.

Brueggermann, Walter. 2001. *The Prophetic Imagination*. Minneapolis: Fortress Press.

Campenhausen, Hans von. 1969. *Ecclesiastical Authority and Spiritual Power in the Church of the First Three Centuries*. London: Adam & Charles Black.

Coleman, John. 1992. "Not Democracy but Democratisation." In Eugene C. Bianchi and Rosemary Radford Ruether (eds), *A Democratic Catholic Church*, 226–247. New York: Crossroad.

Congar, Yves. 1958. "Quod omnes tangit, ab omnibus tractari et approbari debet." *Revue historique de droit français et étranger* 35, 210–259.

Congar, Yves. 1964. *Power and Poverty in the Church*. London: Geoffrey Chapman.

Curran, Charles. 1992. "What Catholic Ecclesiology Can Learn from Official Catholic Social Teaching." In Eugene C. Bianchi and Rosemary Radford Ruether *A Democratic Catholic Church*, 94–112. New York: Crossroad.

Demel, Sabine. 2016. "From Junior Helpers to Valued Collaborators: Giving the Laity Their Rightful Place in the Clergy-Centred Church." *Concilium* 5, 78–89.

Devasahayam, John Romus. 2007. *Human Diginity in Indian Secularism and in Christianity*. Bangalrore: Claretian Publications.

Douglass, R. Bruce and David R Hollenbach (eds), 1994. *Catholicism and Liberalism. Contributions to American Public Philosophy*. Cambridge: Cambridge University Press.

Forrester, Ducan B. 1979. *Caste and Christianity. Attitudes and Policies on Caste of Anglo-Saxon Protestant Missions in India*. London: University of London.

Frykenberg, Robert Eric and Alaine M. Low. 2003. *Christians and Missionaries in India: Cross-cultural Communication since 1500, with Special Reference to Caste, Conversion, and Colonialism*. Grand Rapids, MI: W.B. Eerdmans Pub.

Hehir, J. Bryan. 2016. "Roman Catholicism and Democracy: The Post Conciliar Era." In George E. Demacapoulos and Aristotle Papanikolau (eds), *Christianity, Democracy, and the Shadow of Constantine*, 232–250. New York: Fordham University Press.

Huntington, Samuel. 1991. *The Third Wave. Democratisation in the Late Twentieth Century* (Norman: Oklahoma University Press.
John, Mary. 2011. *Indian Catholic Christians and Nationalism. A Study Based on the Official Catholic Journals of the Period 1857–1947*. Delhi: ISPCK, p. 42.
Karambai, Sebastian S. 2018. "Consultative Bodies in the Particular Churches Revisited in the Light of Evangelii Gaudium." In Adrian Loretan and Felix Wilfred (eds), *Revision of the Codes. An Indian-European Dialogue*, 283–292. Zürich: LIT Verlag.
Koilparampil, George. 1982. *Caste in the Catholic Community in Kerala: A Study of Caste Elements in the Inter Rite Relationships of Syrians and Latins* Cochin: St Teresa's College.
Koshy, Ninan. 1968. *Caste in the Kerala Churches*. Bangalore: The Christian Institute for the Study of Religion and Society.
Küng, Hans. 1968. *The Church*. London: Search Press.
Leclercq, Jean. 1987. "Introduction." In *Pseudo-Dionysius: The Complete Works*, 25–32. New York: Paulist Press.
Lohfink, Gerhard. 1985. *Jesus and Community. The Social Dimension of Christian Faith*. London: SPCK.
Loretan, Adrian, and Felix Wilfred. 2018. *Revision of the Codes. An Indian-European Dialogue*. Zuerich: LIT Verlag.
Louis, Prakash. 2020. "A Prophetic Evangelization for Dalit Salvation." In Felix Wilfred and John Romus (eds) *Local Churches in South Asia and Evangelization*, 384–401. Kolkata: Morning Star Regional Seminary.
Mallampalli, Chandra. 2004. *Christians and Public Life in Colonial South India, 1863–1937: Contending with Marginality*. London: RoutledgeCurzon.
Mathew, C. J. 2012. *Empowerment and Agency of Dalit Catholics of Kottayam District, Kerala*. Chennai: University of Madras. n.d.
O'Malley, John W. 2008. *What Happened at Vatican II*. Cambridge, MA: Harvard University Press.
Paul, Vinil Baby. 2021. "Onesimus to Philemon: Runaway Slaves and Religious Conversation in Colonial Kerala, India, 1816–1855." *International Journal of Asian Christianity* 4(1), 50–71.
Prayer, Mario. 2009. "The Vatican Church and Gandhi's India 1920–1948." *Social Scientist*, 37(1/2), 39–63.
Raj, Sebasti L. 1993. *Caste Culture in Indian Church: The Response of Church to the Problem of Caste within the Christian Community*. New Delhi: Indian Social Institute.
Roekaerts, M. 1980. *Christians and Emergency in India*. Brussels: Pro Mundi Vita Dossiers, p. 24.
Schillebeeckx, Edward. 1990. *Church. The Human Story of God*. London: SCM Press.
"The Week." 26 December 2010.
Wilfred, Felix. 2014. "Dalit Future: Future of the Nation." *Vidyajyoti Journal of Theological Reflection* 73, 325–336.
Wilfred, Felix. 2019. "Catholics." In Kenneth R. Ross et al. (eds), *Christianity in South and Central Asia*, 211–222. Edinburgh: Edinburgh University Press.

2 Modernity, Democracy, and Christianity in India

Gnana Patrick

Indian Modernity and Its Dialectics

Today postcolonial studies have opened up a vantage point to critically look at the claims of modernity. They have unearthed some of the core contradictions implied in the universal claims of Western modernity – the will to power embedded in them, establishment of empires of knowledge among the once colonized minds, continuance of hegemonic dominance over different others, etc. However, theories have been proposed to look at modernity also in a context-sensitive manner. The proposal of SN Eisenstadt for imagining multiple modernities is a case in point. He argues that "the best way to understand ... the history of modernity is to see it as a story of continual constitution and reconstitution of a multiplicity of cultural programs" (2000: 2). Going by this insight, one might consider an Indian modernity, which unlike the Western variant, created its own modern "cultural program" by retaining a thicker content of beliefs and traditions, while taking in scientific and technological rationalities. Even if one acknowledges Ashis Nandy's highly radical critique of modernity as the very form of violence (Nandy 1999), it is not possible to deny the positive effects of the historical unfolding of modernity in the Indian context. It brought about an opportunity for equality for an average Indian. That a "silent revolution" of emancipation, as in the words of Christophe Jaffrelot (2003), was witnessed to in the Indian society is no less a convincing fact of Indian modernity.

However, that today we are witnessing to some of the dialectics of Indian modernity is a sad reality to be reckoned with. The emergence and sway of ethnocentric cultural nationalism, religious nationalism to be specific, instrumentalizing democracy, is indeed a sad reality. Indian experience of nationalism has a chequered history. As some prominent theorists on nationalism like Ernest Gellner and Benedict Anderson have opined, nationalism, as part of the modern project of constituting nation-states, had its legitimacy in the imperial colonial context (Gandhi 1998). As a manner of achieving one's freedom, the erstwhile colonized countries drew much strength from the spirit of nationalism. That the pioneers of Indian freedom struggle did draw upon Indian nationalism is part of the process of birthing of India as an independent nation-state. However, even at that context, some of the free-minds like that of Rabindranath Tagore doubted the very legitimacy of nationalism and called it a "menace" that corrupted the freedom of consciousness of a citizen. That Gandhi himself wished for closing down the Indian National Congress once freedom was achieved cannot be forgotten. What has unfortunately happened in the postcolonial Indian context is the caricature and manipulation of nationalism to win elections and capture power. As Eric Hobsbawm observed, it has become an atavistic nonprogressive ideology, and even as Edward Said, the famous postcolonial critique himself observed (Said 1993), it has turned out to be a sectarian divisive force in India. The mindless manipulation has generated much hatred between different others, especially between majority and minority others, in addition to reiterating the dominance of the hitherto elites by a hegemonic dynamics of manufacturing consent. That India as a developing nation, emerging out into the global arena, has a certain predicament or a need for constructing its own identity cannot be less appreciated. However, identity construction with the cultural resources of a perceived majority, at the cost of the very substance of democracy and its pillars of citizenship, participation, respect for plurality, and differences, can never be on the right road to democracy. Indian modernity has come to contradict its own wellbeing today.

Liberal Democracy and Beyond

The modern liberal democracy is facing up serious challenges in several parts of the globe as well. As we know, in *The End of History and the Last Man* (1992), Francis Fukuyama argued that with the fall of the Berlin wall (and of the end of the cold war), human political ideological evolution had come to an end and that there was no alternative anymore to liberal democracy in the world. The euphoria of this victorious "proclamation" unfortunately did not last long. Liberal democracy all over the world had to face up to the challenges of terror in the name of religion, religious nationalism, racism, and other sectarian identities which manufactured hatred toward different others; it had to reckon with a burgeoning regime of corrupt practices catering to the greed of individuals and corporate houses, and with "naked" public spheres devoid of values and solidarity. Questions were seriously raised and are being raised today as to whether a liberal democracy which hinges solely on the liberty of the individual subject would take us further.

Against this context, amid attempts to revise and reinterpret the liberal political philosophy to come to terms with the contemporary challenges,[1] there is an attempt also to revisit and revive the ideals of republican democracy in a contextual manner. While republicanism has had a thick historical tradition, which is generally seen as a conservative and elitist political philosophy (Aristotle, Roman *res publica*, Machiavelli, Rousseau, etc.), its revision today as *neorepublicanism* (Hannah Arendt, Charles Taylor, Michael Sandel,

Philip Petit, Iseult Hanon, Cecile Laborde, and others), especially as *civic republicanism*, offers insights which seem to be relevant for us today. Its basic philosophy is that human beings, as political animals, can realize their nature only in self-governing communities, and that the community they constitute is fundamentally political. Unlike the liberalism which begins with the natural rights of individuals, civic republicanism treats rights as basically derived from social living characterized by traditions, but continuously being propounded through a political culture. This derivative right hinges on or becomes effective in shaping up a substantive citizenship, which is built upon the pillars of rule of law, participation, nondomination, and freedom from arbitrary powers. *Participation* means not just involvement, but joining in a political process by cultivating the civic virtue of solidarity with different others to work for common good. It would mean evolving a public political culture from below, recognizing the validity of different others, and dialoguing with different others as the very manner of existence. *Nondomination* stands for "a condition or a possibility" wherein a citizen is not coerced or made to act in a particular way. It differentiates itself from the fundamentals of liberal citizenship like "freedom of self-mastery" and "freedom from interference". The important difference is that neorepublicanism treats the presence of nondomination in the social ambience as indispensable for the ability of an individual to be free. It is not enough to say that no one is visibly interfering in your freedom, but important to consider whether the *condition* created is free. *Freedom from arbitrary powers* stands for freedom from factors which do not become public or do not participate in the public political process, but exert undue unconstitutional authority.

The new civic republican democracy has features which have much relevance to the Indian context today. Its central vision characterized by participatory democracy, absence of dominance, and noninterference from arbitrary powers has much to offer to a context of sequestration of power, rigidly hierarchical and exclusionary social system, and undue dominance of market forces in conjunction with casteist arbitrary powers. A republican vision is not new to India, and it has already been intoned by its constitution. The preamble of Indian constitution presents India as a democratic republic. Bhikku Parekh (1996), an Indian born British parliamentarian, points out that in the original draft the word "republic" alone was used, and in the next, it was replaced with democracy, and in the final version it became "democratic republic".

Discontent to one-sided liberal democracy also has not been new to India. Ambedkar himself, the chief architect of Indian constitution, had to come to terms with the inadequacy of the liberal side of Indian democracy, which ignored the other kindred values of equality and fraternity. He said,

> [P]arliamentary democracy developed a passion for liberty. It never made a nodding acquaintance with equality. It failed to realize the significance of equality and did not even endeavour to strike a balance

between liberty and equality, with the result that liberty swallowed up equality and has made democracy a name and a farce.

(Dreze 2018: 172)

He continues: "Without equality, liberty would produce the supremacy of the few over the many. Equality without liberty would kill individual initiative. Without fraternity, liberty and equality could not become a natural course of things" (Dreze 2018: 171).

Democracy, in Ambedkar's vision, is "a form and a method of government whereby revolutionary changes in the economic and social life of the people are brought about without bloodshed" (Dreze 2018: 170). He said:

> ... political democracy cannot succeed where there is no social and economic democracy... social and economic democracy are the tissues and the fibre of a political democracy. The tougher the tissue and the fibre are, the greater the strength of the body.
>
> (Dreze 2018: 170)

He cautioned also against the "divine right" of the majorities. He said,

> [U]nfortunately ... Indian nationalism has developed a new doctrine which may be called the Divine Right of the Majority to rule the minorities to the wishes of majority. Any claim for the sharing of power by the minority is called communalism while the monopolizing of the whole power by the majority is called nationalism.
>
> (Thorat 2018: xvii)

Sukhdeo Thorat, a known educationist, says:

> [I]n Dr Ambedkar's view, a democracy is not confined just to a form of government and state apparatus; rather it is more than a system of political governance – it embraces social governance... (it) is primarily a mode of associated living with an attitude of respect and reverence towards fellowmen. Therefore, the roots of political democracy are located in social relationship among the people in a society.
>
> (Thorat 2018: vii)

Jean Dreze, the well-known economist, is of the opinion that Ambedkar had a visionary conception of democracy which needs be rediscovered today. In his words: "The future of Indian democracy depends a great deal on the revival of Ambedkar's visionary conception of democracy. This vision, I believe, also needs to be enlarged and updated in the light of recent experience" (Dreze 2018: 170).

To reconstruct Indian democracy along the line of Ambedkar's more integrated emancipatory vision, I think one could draw upon the features of the new civic republicanism to transform Indian "liberal" democracy into an emancipating participatory democracy.

Participatory Democracy and Public Spheres

Public spheres, indeed, are the primary spaces of participatory democracy. Jurgen Habermas, with whom theorizing on modern public sphere is generally associated, understood public spheres to be spaces wherein debates took place to form public opinion which weighed upon decisions for public life. He thought of three types of public spheres: 1) public spheres in the political domain (a domain which is proximate and yet different from the state, preparing individuals for statecraft), 2) public spheres in the "world of letters" (discussion and debates in the domain of literatures, academia, press, clubs, etc.), and 3) public spheres in the "town" in coffee houses, salons, etc. Jose Casanova, a scholar of public religion, thought of different public spheres operative at various levels of civil society, political society, and the state; civil society in its voluntary organizations/initiatives, political society in legislatures and political parties, and state in its bureaucracy. Thus, there are different identifications and categorizations of public spheres. The commonality among them is that they are discursive fora, contributing to the formation of public opinion and the general will of the people. Discussion (lexis), according to Habermas, embodies the *public reason*, whose characteristic elements are neutralization of status, inclusiveness, and debates on matters of public concern. "Neutralization of status" means a certain "disregard" for status-positions of the discussants involved in discussion, and inclusiveness meant a seamless intersubjective universality. These features make the public debates effective carriers of public opinions, which participate in decision-making on matters concerning public policies, common good, and public life in general. Creating appropriate fora for such public discussions, learning the skills of public debates or discussions, and actively participating in public spheres need to get priority in constructing a civic republican participatory democracy today.

There has been much debate as to whether any normative argument of ethical or religious nature could participate in public reasoning. The concern of liberal democracy has been whether such normative arguments could be universal enough to represent the voice of the general humanity or those concerns of the general public. It used to be argued that normativity would base itself on particular traditions which would not be intelligible to outside others or on particular sources of authority which would come into conflict with the universality and the neutrality of public reason. However, there have also been questions as to whether public reason, devoid of normative ethical or faith-dimensions, could be historically factual and effective to inspire actions for common good. Liberal theorists like John Rawls tried answering the questions first of all by acknowledging the value of ethics and religion for public life and then by suggesting the method of "translation", that is, translating the message of ethical or religious doctrines into "secular" language so that it could be intelligible to all. The contemporary "post-liberal world" has cast serious doubts upon the relevance of Rawls' suggestions, and has come up with other methods like "conversations" between different incommensurable ethical or religious comprehensive doctrines for common good.

The contemporary postliberal political philosophy, by and large, accepts the need of bringing in ethical or religious doctrines into the public sphere for the cultivation of virtues of solidarity, sacrifice, respect, reverence to different persons, etc. Similarly, it is positive toward the role of religion in the public sphere. Such a positive openness is born upon multiple realizations: first, religion as an influential category is already present in the public sphere, controlling the political behavior of individuals and collectives involved in the political process; secondly, the attempt to be neutral under the garb of being secular has not been a successful endeavor, because secularity per se is not a neutrality, but a position against religion or a bias against religion; thirdly, there is a growing realization that the so-called secular liberal public spheres have not succeeded in achieving universally egalitarian politics, but, on the other hand, have impoverished the political morality, ethics, and experiences of transcendence. It would therefore be necessary to acknowledge the publicness of religion, treat it as any other language or perspective, and integrate it in public conversations. Religions, indeed, have been active components in public spheres or political decision-making across space and time. The Indian experience would vouchsafe for it. Religion, religious sentiments, visions, doctrines, and beliefs are indeed present in the modern Indian political processes. However, there has been a hesitation to articulate them in public spheres. In such situations, what passes for is a taken-for-grantedness of the legitimacy of the religious presence or influence of the dominant or the numerical majority, while those of different others, especially of minority others, get vilified or antagonized. It would therefore be a matter of fairness that religious presence in the Indian public sphere is acknowledged and articulated in public conversations or dialogues. It is in this context that one would think of the role of Indian Christianity for nurturing a participatory democracy.

Christianity and the Indian Discursive Public Sphere

Christianity's relationship with the Indian discursive public – a prototype of the civil sphere, has indeed been complex, characterized by processes of involvement, contestation, differentiation, and distinction. Though we do not have many studies focusing on the way Indian Christian community related with the native public during the first 15 centuries of the Common Era, what emerges as a concerted opinion among the scholars today is that it was a multidimensional relationship, interacting with native cultures and religions even while maintaining its distinctiveness. The anecdotal statement made by Pacid J Podipara that Indian Christianity of the time was "Hindu in culture, Christian in religion and Oriental in worship" conveys the sense of the relationship. Being a trading community that had established commercial relations with others and had struck marital ties with the natives, Indian Christians of the time had been to a large extent socioculturally integrated, but continued to be religiously distinct. As AM Mundadan would put it, "[T]he life St. Thomas Christians had been leading till the arrival of the Portuguese spanned two worlds: the geographical, political and social world of Malabar or Kerala (India), and the ecclesiastical world of East-Syrian or the Persian Church…" (2001: 145). Though spanning the two worlds, the Syrian Christians (St. Thomas Christians) lived their lives more as natives than outsiders, and as Susan Bayly would put it, were "honoured and rewarded" by native rulers on account of their being "warriors, traders and Church notables" (Bayly 1989: 243–44). The native rulers seemed to have constructed Church buildings and donated lands, finance, etc. to the Syrian Christians. Such a benefaction, as Bayly would narrate, points to a considerable level of integration of the Syrians with the native community. Moreover, they shared a rich content of religious beliefs and cultural practices with the natives, including their purity–pollution laws (Bayly 1989: 243–44; Viswanathan 1993). Thus, a specific manner of native existence, though sharing in different sociocultural and political worlds, characterized the life-world of Syrian Christians of India from earlier times.

Christianity's relationship with the Indian discursive field became more pronounced during the modern era. Aided by the availability of the inchoate print media, Christian missionaries began to interact with the wider public from the 16th century onwards. Catholic missionaries in the southern Tamil region – starting with Henrique Henriques (1520–1600), who introduced the printed Christian literature, to Robert de Nobili (1577–1656) and Joseph Constantine Beschi (1680–1747) who produced varieties of rich literatures, prose, and poetry, had embarked upon public conversations and disputations on religious and philosophical matters. Disputations on religious themes went hand in hand with adaptations of Indic language, symbols, and traditions to express and shape up a native Christian tradition. Literary creations like epics, tales, commentaries, dictionaries, and translations of Indian classics into European languages created a base for early public discursive practices emergent during the 16th to 18th centuries. This is not to deny the existence of discursive fora prior to their introduction by Christian missionaries; the vibrant debating fora of the last Tamil Sangam (circa 400 BCE–200 BCE), the interreligious dialogical forum run by Akbar as recent as mid-16th century CE, and the "intensifying religious interactions" during the Mughal period (Dalmia and Faruqui 2014) are good examples of their earlier existence. However, while the latter debating spheres existed more among rulers and experts, the former began to include wider sections of people.

The Protestant missionary presence, beginning with the first Protestant missionary Bartholomew Ziegenbalg who had installed a printing press at

Tranquebar, and the Serampore trio, who had established a printing "industry" at Serampore during the 18th century, contributed to the emergence of a printed-literature-based discursive field in the Indian public. The subsequent eventful missionary activities of the classical missionary societies and of the Anglican churches during the 19th century contributed multidimensionally to the relative strengthening of the discursive public. Translations of Bible into native languages and printing them, and undertaking the "mission" of imparting modern education to wider sections of Indian population, along with making efforts to do away with discriminatory and oppressive practices in the Indian sociocultural systems, went a long way in enhancing the Indian discursive public, which, along with the rule of law and the relatively more rationalized administration of the British India, began to grow steadily. Founding of various institutions by "orientalists" for study of native literatures and printing the Indological classics to circulate them among the public markedly changed the demography of readership in the Indian subcontinent. A process of democratization of Indian classics, along with the spread of modern mass education, contributed significantly to the emergence of the channels of public communication. It is no less significant a fact that Indian Christianity was a singular contributor to this process.

However, it needs be noted that there were also elements which kept isolating Indian Christians from the wider public. For example, the exclusivist discourse of "no salvation outside the church", embedded in both the Catholic ecclesiology and the Protestant evangelical proclamation, kept other religiously knowledgeable persons at a distance and vice a versa; the manners, customs, food habits, and other cultural markers of the colonizers with whom Indian Christians were identified with was yet another source of isolation; and, as Chandra Mallampalli has shown, the British rule effectively shifted the Indian Christians to the margins of the Indian public, when it came to the application of laws related to inheritance, property holding, etc. (Mallampalli 2004). And, finally, the emerging Indian nationalist discourse, though secular in character, made the Indian Christians self-conscious about their identity as a minority amid a majority.

The postcolonial era has brought forth a different scenario as regards the presence of Christianity in the Indian discursive public. A phase of post-independent national integration, combined with the project of Five-Year plans for development, saw Indian Christians involved enthusiastically in welfare schemes, programs of poverty alleviation, literacy programs, disaster management, sanitation, health, and primary/higher/professional education of the Indian population. The spread of modern education to further layers of Indian population set in a "silent revolution" as observed by Christophe Jaffrelot (2003) and Indian Christians came to consider modernization as an ingredient of humanization, which in turn, was an instance of Indian Renaissance. Advocacy for civil liberties of the subaltern people, involvement in movements for various social goals, voluntary initiatives for amelioration and eradication of social evils, etc., became important sites of Christian presence. In terms of relationship with other religions, they undertook interreligious dialogues, study centers, and ashrams for interreligious experiences.

All these were done in an ambience of relative spontaneity and freedom! The scenario changed with the political ascendance of the far-right, with its religio-cultural nationalism. As studies show, violence against Christians (Sahoo 2018) has rapidly increased, and conversion has become a thorny issue between those who affirm their Constitutional right for conversion and others who oppose it not merely in debates but also through acts of violence. Majoritarianism in politics has given a hegemonic power to the religious majority in the domains of culture, knowledge, education, and even civil rights, and it has been adversely instrumentalized by a small section that has self-assumed the religious leadership of the majority, by collating an ideology with religion, and this religion with patriotism. Indian Christians, as a result, seem to develop tendencies to "in-grow", to become self-conscious, etc., rather than actively participate in the public life of the nation. The religio-cultural nationalism of the self-assumed leadership goes to the extent of implicating the Indian Christian identity to be culturally conflictive and politically divisive, with an implied accusation of preventing the Indian nation from emerging into the global world as a united political power; it is as if the patriotism of Indian Christians, along with that of other religious minorities, needed to be proved on a day-to-day basis. One could think of the isolation of Indian Christians also as one suffered by a subaltern identity in a ritual framework of purity and pollution characteristic of the Indian caste system.

Indian Democracy and Christian Public Theology

Transforming the democratic state into a substantive one, with participatory discursive public and civil spheres, obtains priority for political and public Christian theologies in India today. A substantively participatory democracy is of great value because of peoples' hopes and aspirations attendant upon such a political vision for India. When a constitutional democracy was born in India, the hopes especially of the subaltern people of India were raised; they began to imagine a political community which would ensure economic equity, social equality, civil liberties, human rights, and dignity to all sections of people. Dr. Ambedkar, the chief architect of the constitution, sought to integrate these transforming hopes in the democratic instrument. The constitution opened up an agenda for social justice (the affirmative action), embodying the ardent wish for retributive justice. The focus was on *opening the public* to everyone, beyond ascriptive exclusions. That the constitution provided for the right of the state to intervene and open up the temples for the subalterns is a case in point. An Indian Christian public theology would then premise itself upon this hope of "opening the public", opening up the spaces of freedom and opportunities to the excluded.

David Tracy speaks of three publics wherein public theology can be meaningfully practiced: Church, Academy, and Society (Tracy 1981).[2] I find these three domains relevant, *mutatis mutandis*, also for the Indian context. I am aware of the differences between the Western and Indian contexts. One major difference would be the very confidence of Tracy to place the Church as one of the publics. In India, one will have to think of "religious/multi-religious publics" in the place of the Church. However, since this particular reflection here is undertaken from the Indian Christian perspective, I find it meaningful to speak of the Church as a public.

(1) Church is the home of faith for Christians. They draw resources of faith from the faith-community, that is, the Church. As a voluntary community based on faith, the Church is an active player in the civil society, and this opens not only a wider site but also a dynamic possibility for the practice of faith. It can network with other voluntary organizations, and help create an interactive sphere, whereby spiritual energies, ethical sensitivity, and theological visions can be transmitted for transforming the wider society. It can help create an interactive sphere between the multiple religious traditions operative in a particular vicinity and contribute to the creation of "community of communities" (Kim 2011), consisting of various religious communities. It may even help create an interactive sphere between the so-called social groupings (communities in the Indian societal sense) and help them get liberated from inward looking ethnic closures and become open communities to participate in the wider public in a healthy manner to build up the democratic polity.

In so far as it is part of the civil society, the Church itself functions as a civil society within its own sphere. As is known, the primary trait of a civil society is the democratic public sphere within itself. The Indian Church needs to establish this democratic public sphere within itself. First of all, every individual church needs to make itself people-based and democratic. It is the power of the people that is going to give every church the power to negotiate the wider democratic society and bring meaning and vitality to itself. We need to therefore empower the people with theological education and various pastoral/institutional roles. Second, Indian Christians need to establish a communicative sphere between the various individual churches, including the denominational and independent churches. It needs to urgently forge this solidarity, taking into account the fact that all the churches together constitute the Indian Church and together they share a common identity in the public sphere. And, therefore, establishing and shaping up the inner-church communicative sphere is a manner of becoming an effective player in the wider civil society.

To that end, Church in India needs to become a *public body* today. It needs to become public not so much to project itself and its activities as to bear witness to its faith in a transcendent God, whose revelation the community called the Church experienced in the words, deeds, death, and resurrection of Jesus Christ, the incarnate God. It was in Jesus Christ this community began to experience the encounter of history and mystery of transcendence in a transforming manner. A call for transformation of relationships, embodying mutuality, creativity, and peace, was the core of this encounter. This transforming experience needs to continue through history and Church, as a community, needs to be a catalyst in this. In so doing, the Church finds the democratic institutions of the state and civil society, however fragile and failing though, the most solicitous, and brings itself in participatory solidarity with these institutions to mediate the experience of transforming relationships.

Inasmuch as these institutions are public, the Church body itself is a public. It cultivates the character of publicness within its own body as much as in the wider society. It makes itself a public body, by imbibing the spirit and practice of democracy, doing away with unmeaning hierarchies; it makes itself a public sphere, wherein a "public reasoning" can take place among the believers; and it makes itself a civil society wherein the spirit of participatory democracy among the community of equals can be cultivated. It should become public also in the sense of becoming more interactive in the wider public. There are several ways in which it can become publicly interactive. A very unassuming but firmly witnessing way is to bear witness to the Christian values whenever or wherever one holds public offices. Christian subjects, in their embodied personhood, can be the best witness to the transforming values. Another way of becoming public is interacting in "conversational publics" with the Christian vision of events and issues. Needless to point out to the fact that the Christian voice does not emerge significantly in media publics, at least not proportionate to the education that it has received. Yet another important way, challenging though, is becoming accountable to the wider public in matters public. Churches have the highest level of human resources, individually and collectively; but, what is its output to the wider society? Can there be an auditing of human resources in the Churches? Similarly, can mechanisms for social auditing be operative in the Churches? These are questions only to see that the Indian Church becomes truly public, effectively interacting in the public, without burying its head in deep furrows of self-pity and defeatism.

Similar to such "Public Christianity", there can also emerge "Public Islam", "Public Hinduism", and the like. In his article titled, "Religion in Politics and the Politics of Hinduism", written as an introduction to his edited volume on *Political Hinduism – The Religious Imagination in Public Spheres* (Lal 2009), Vinay Lal ends the article with a query whether a political Hinduism – a Hinduism that is sensitive to the political goals of establishing justice, citizenship rights, human rights, community rights, development, and peace is not possible. He calls it a political Hinduism, which away from the Hindutva variety of political ideologies, but one that represents the religious aspirations of the majority of Hindus to construct a polity which is deeply democratic and egalitarian. Such Hinduism, according to him, can be shaped up, not so much from the Brahminical religious traditions, but from the religious traditions of the subaltern or marginal people of India. One would be intoned by this to think of the socioreligious movements which arose during the modern era, constructing emancipatory identities for the subaltern people. Can such religious traditions be found today? If yes, they can become the participants of public theological conversations in India.

Indian Christianity needs to be involved in an educational praxis, both formal and informal, for participation in public spheres. Similar to the informal education or literacy campaign in which different civil society organs, including the churches, are involved in, Churches need now to be involved in "education for public reasoning", which would focus on political participation, citizenship, dialogue of cultures, religions, and ideologies, social justice, equality, solidarity for common good, decentralized power for statecraft, etc., along with fine skills of argumentation, disputation, and conversation. Education, in its multiple variants, has been at the root of transformations, and education aimed at public reasoning would transform an individual to be a citizen, a particular will to be the general will, individual aspirations to be ideals of the state, and individual frustrations to public acts of resistance. It will bring the particularities of culture, religion, ethics, and aesthetic preferences into dialogue with one another, and synergize a vibrant public resource. In an important way, it will also help learn to live intersubjectively with different religious others, without fear and hatred.

(2) Academia is yet another public proposed by David Tracy (2000) for doing public theology. It is unfortunate that the contemporary academia seemingly serves the interests of the dominant forces – political or economic. As a domain of knowledge and wisdom, it must function in an independent autonomous sphere of the civil society. While the freedom of the civil society is meaningfully furthered by the academia, the latter's creativity draws its wisdom and commitment from the power of the civil society.

Indian Church is a major player in academia, starting with the formal school education to the higher education and to the vast arena of nonformal education. With its centuries-old commitment in the field of modern education, the Indian Church had imparted the knowledge to a people, who had empowered themselves with this education; they became aware of their rights and dignity, and by demanding their civil liberties, civilized the public sphere of India to a large extent. To the extent it involved in this process of "humanisation", the Indian Church was doing indirect public theology, mediating Faith, and contributing to the unfolding of salvation (as MM Thomas would have it). However, the involvement in education has become rather dubious during the present times: whether the Christian involvement is contributing to mediation of Faith that gives us an experience of transcendence or to a more technological professionalization (of a certain section which self-perpetuates its own comfort) that inhibits and impairs the human ability for transcendence is a critical question Indian Church has to ask itself. Its open-minded participation in the civil society will invite such questions from the wider society and clarify its goals in the light of wider criticisms. This ability to interact with the civil society as regards its involvement in education is one of the ways in which Indian Church would do a very basic public theology today.

It has also its own sites of academia like theological colleges, research institutes, departments of theologies or religious studies, wherein it can effectively do public theology and mediate faith. Tracy would propose systematic theologies to be pursued in Christian academia as a way of doing public theology. Systematic theology is one by which Christians formulate their faith-claims and pursue their meaningfulness in wider publics shared by different denominational and religious others. In our contemporary context, where there are increasing numbers of denominational Churches along with their own theologies and many religious traditions establishing their study centers or departments in the academia, it is the duty of the Indian Church to systematically pursue public conversations with them in order to be able to mediate the vitality of faith in these circles.

(3) Society at large is the wider public, Tracy suggests, a public theology should engage itself with. Wider public includes those spheres where we pursue social, cultural, economic, and political interests with the goal of common good. The wider public in India today is threatened by multiple closures! The most visible one is, as mentioned above, majoritarianism in politics, backed by religious nationalism and sectarian communalism. Not merely a case of travesty of democracy, this closure threatens to revive the forces of social and cultural hegemonies, with a will to dominate over the public sphere. It means loss of freedom not merely to the religious minorities, but to social minorities as well. The less visible, but, more substantive form of closure is the one caused by the market forces today. As if "there is no development outside the market", the contemporary world is getting organized by the neoliberal invisible hand that threatens the life-world of the people, with commercial urges entering even into the moral, ethical, esthetic, and cultural veins of the people. The general humanity seems to lose the power to transcend the closures caused by these commercial impulses. Along with these two forms of closures, age-old oppressive and discriminatory systems like caste and patriarchy, with the combination of residual feudalism (mainstay feudalism in many rural areas), get expressed in such uncivil acts like honor killing, rape, moral policing, and so on. These oppressive systems are further compounded by the increasing cleavage between the rich and the poor. These realities, sustaining a serious imbalance in socioeconomic and political systems, present a fertile soil for the production of fatalism, deterministic thinking, reductionism, fundamentalism, and violent reactionary forces. In this context, religion, otherwise a fountainhead for the experience of transcendence, turns into irreligion. Public theologies, pursued from different religious traditions, will go a long way in nurturing the experience of transcendence in public spaces.

Religions need to play appropriate roles in the civil sphere to help humanity nurture a sense of autonomous self along with the spirit of transpersonal relationships characterized by sacrifice, dedication, and mutuality, which are abiding values of democracy. Civil society is the sphere where different religions can come together in an ambience of freedom to work for common good. A participatory democratic state provides the space where people as citizens can be related to one another even on a transcendental basis, journeying toward ever-greater realizations of common good.

Conclusion

This chapter has sought to present an argument for pursuing public theologies, Indian Christian public theology in this case, to cultivate the virtues of participatory democracy in India. It begins by observing that Indian modernity, in spite of contributing to emancipatory transformations, has met with its dialectics. The most perceptible field of such dialectics is that of democratic politics, wherein antidemocratic elements like majoritarianism, religious communalism, hegemonic caste identities, and those of neoliberal market have come to instrumentalize the democratic system for their own ends. This happens in an ambience of a global retreat of liberal democracy which had been centering round the rights of individuals. It is time democracy, as a form of political behavior, took note of the role of communities and traditions, and lend itself for participatory practice of democracy. Participation in democracy can well be nurtured by conversations in public spheres. In such a context, religious communities, in this context, Indian Christianity, which has hitherto been an significant contributor to public spheres, would do well to pursue public theology, in the three arenas of the Church, academia, and the wider society for the wellbeing of democracy in India.

Notes

1 John Rawls, for example, makes a sustained effort to reinterpret it for our times.
2 Sebastian Kim, another important proponent of public theology in the contemporary context, thinks of six areas of the public sphere as sites for doing public theology: state, market, civil society, academies, media, and religious communities. These sites are more differentiated than Tracy's scheme. However, I use Tracy's scheme here for its brevity and pastoral effectiveness.

References

Bayly, Susan. *Saints, Goddesses and Kings – Muslims and Christians in South Indian Society 1700–1900* New York: Cambridge University Press, 1989.
Dalmia, Vashua and Munis D. Faruqui, eds. *Religious Interactions in Mughal India.* New Delhi: Oxford University Press, 2014.
Dreze, Jean. 2018. "Dr. Ambedkar and the Future of Indian Democracy," in Suraj Yengde and Anand Teltumbde, eds. *The Radical in Ambedkar – Critical Reflections.* USA: Penguin Allen Lane.
Eisenstadt, S. N. 2000. "Multiple Modernities," *Daedalus*, 129 (1).
Gandhi, Leela. 1998. *Postcolonial Theory.* NSW, Australia: Allen & Unwin.
Jaffrelot, Christophe. 2003. *India's Silent Revolution – The Rise of the Low Castes in North Indian Politics.* New Delhi: Permanent Black.
Kim, Sebastian. 2011. *Theology in the Public Sphere – Public Theology as a Catalyst for Open Debate.* UK: SCM Press.
Lal, Vinay ed. 2009. *Political Hinduism – Religious Imagination in Public Spheres.* New Delhi: Oxford University Press.
Mallampalli, Chandra. 2004. *Christians and Public Life in Colonial South India 1863–1937 – Contending with Marginality.* London: Routledge Curzon.

Mundadan, A. M. 2001. *History of Christianity in India – Vol. 1: From the Beginning up to the Middle of the Sixteenth Century*. Bangalore: Church History Association of India.
Nandy, Ashis. 1999. "The Politics of Secularism and the Recovery of Religious Tolerance," in *Secularism and its Critics*, ed. Rajeev Bhargava, 321–344. New Delhi: Oxford University Press.
Parekh, Bhikhu. 1996. "Minority Practices and Principles of Toleration," *The International Migration Review*, 30 (1), 251–284.
Sahoo, Sarbeswar. 2018. *Pentecostalism and Politics of Conversion in India*. Cambridge: Cambridge University Press.
Said, Edward W. 1993. *Culture and Imperialism*. New York: Vintage Books.
Thorat, Sukhadeo. 2018. "Foreword," in Christophe Jaffrelot and Narender Kumar, eds. *Dr. Ambedkar and Democracy*. New Delhi: Indian Institute of Dalit Studies & OUP.
Tracy, David. 2000. "Public Theology, Hope, and the Mass Media – Can the Muses Still Inspire?" in Max L. Stackhouse with Peter J. Paris, eds. *Religion and the Powers of the Common Life*. Pennsylvania: Trinity Press International.
Tracy, David. 1992. "Theology, Critical Social Theory, and the Public Realm," in Don S. Browning and Francis Schussler Fiorenza, eds. *Habermas, Modernity, and Public Theology*, 19–42. New York: The Crossword Publishing Company.
Tracy, David. 1981. *Analogical Imagination – Christian Theology and the Culture of Pluralism*. London: SCM Press.
Viswanathan, Susan. 1993. *The Christians of Kerala*. New Delhi: Oxford University Press.

3 Democratization of Indian Christianity
Reclaiming Church in the Context of Empire

Y. T. Vinayaraj

Introduction

Reclaiming church in India today is not an easy task. There are several reasons for that. The very first reason is that India is becoming a totalitarian state under the control of the undemocratic and authoritarian forces. The neocapitalist corporates control the whole commonwealth of our nation. The farmers' protest at the capital city of our country exemplifies it. The exclusion of the ingenious sections and their fatal protest against the exploitation of their livelihood by the corporates have come to the crucial stage of human right violations, which is exemplified in the judicial custody death of Fr. Stan Swamy. Another important reason is the problem of the emergence of religious fundamentalism in terms of Hindutva politics and cultural nationalism and the failure of religions to become sources of social democracy and open secularism that have always been the focus of our religious communities in this land of religious coexistence. Among these, the most significant issue is the "credibility-loss" of the church and Christianity at large to be a progressive movement of radical change and social transformation in the emerging context of neoliberal economy, culture, and spirituality. We have had the stories of Christian participation in the nation-building processes in post-independent India and the secular engagements for justice, peace, and fraternity in this country. Today, Christian communities have become conformist in their theology and lethargic in their social responsibility. In the crucial Indian context of political marginalization, economic destitution, and cultural hatred, how can be the church in India a community of solidarity in favor of the victims and the excluded? How does church in India reclaim it as a democratic community in terms of its theology, liturgy, and administration?

Rethinking Church as a democratic and egalitarian community needs to be theologized with caution in the very particular context of empire. Empire as a political and social system of power reinstates a global liberal community of market. As it manipulates peoples' minds, bodies, and their territories in favor of liberal culture and economy, empire fosters a civil society in terms of economic destitution and political hierarchy (Negri & Hardt 2000).

Democracy in the age of empire is a liberal democracy that demands the freedom of the liberal individual while accepting the sovereign power of the state or the political rule. Italian philosopher Giorgio Agamben calls this political dilemma of the liberal democracy "the state of exception" in order to expose the inherent problem of the biopolitics of the sovereign state and the people.[1] Thus, the quest for a just and democratic church in the context of empire demands a radical ecclesiology of radical democracy that exists in favor of the excluded and the unqualified by the biopolitics of the state. Giorgio Agamben has exposed the pitfalls of defining democracy within the notion of sovereign state. According to Agamben, unless and until we de-sovereignize the nation and redefine our democracy by addressing the issues of the excluded and the marginalized, we will not be able to envision a democratic state in our land. This inadequacy of the modern state and democracy has been exposed in India by Ambedkar in the post-Independent India; however, it hasn't been engaged with the due seriousness and attention. Hence, in order to embark on a social democracy that includes everyone without any discrimination, church in India has to look into the Ambedkarite visions that still locates itself in the progressive track initiated by Marx, Gill Deleuze, and Agamben.

Another important issue in the case of the democratization of church in India is about the question of the de-imperialization of the church within it. Being the structure of patriarchy and hierarchy, many a time in history, church has claimed its authority and power in terms of administration and liturgical theology over its people. Though the clericalism and the Papacy have been challenged at the time of reformation in the medieval times, church has had its legitimate relationship with the empires of the times. As Giorgio Agamben opines, the church has become yet another empire in terms of hierarchical administration and liturgical exclusion (Agamben 2012: 26). Looking at the liturgical legitimization of the secular–sacred divide, ordained–laity separation, and the gender–transgender discrimination at the pews, Fr. Kappen and S. Vattamattam (1988: 34) once called church as the necropolitical system (political system of the dead bodies). The continuing existence of caste, gender-divide, and exclusion of unordained people from the administration of the church still necessitate reformation in the theology and the administration of the church in India. Legitimizing hierarchy, patriarchy, and clericalism in and through liturgy, theology, and biblical hermeneutics demands a thorough deconstruction and reconstruction of the church in India. It is here, we realize the imperative to differentiate the logic of empire and ecclesia as they differ in their logic of inclusivity and openness. Keeping this ambience as setting, this chapter tries to delineate the epistemological difference between the terms – Empire and Ecclesia and thereby offer a constructive proposal for a democratic ecclesiology which redefines church as a de-imperialized community of all. Christianity is reimagined here as a "religion without religion" or a de-imperialized religion.

Church and Empire: Deconstructing the History of an Illegitimate Alliance

Joerg Rieger, while analyzing the relationship between Church and Empire, offers two different responses (Rieger, 2007: 9). On one side, he argues that early Christianity was a critique of the Roman Empire which constituted the context of early Christianity. The Jesus' movement and the apostolic traditions envisaged counter-imperial communities that denied the imperial practices of exclusion and marginalization. At the same time, Rieger points out that Christianity after the Constantine era assumed a hierarchical/ imperial structure. The early ecumenical councils convened by the emperors signify the involvement of the imperial forces in the formulation of Christian doctrines and dogmatics. It is really exciting to read Giorgio Agamben, when he investigates the context of the emergence of the theology of *oikoumene* (economic trinity) in the patristic period over against the totalitarianism of the Constantine political power (Agamben, 2011: 50). Thus, the relationship between the empire and church has always been apprehensive and cryptic. This is true as we go through the historical periods of crusades and the modern mission strategies of the Western Church colluded with the European colonialism.

Exposing the trajectory of the conviviality between church and empire, Elizabeth Schussler Fiorenza (2007) offers a theological treatise on the anti-imperial ecclesiology in her incredible work – *The Power of the Word: Scripture and the Rhetoric of Empire*. In this book, Fiorenza speaks about Church as a political space – "the radial democracy of equals" (Fiorenza, 2007). The radical democracy of Fiorenza is the *ekklesia of wo/men* which offers the language and space for the imagination to develop a public religious discourse, "wherein justice, participation, difference, freedom, equality and solidarity set the ethical conditions" (Hernandez, 1997: 31). Fiorenza, in contradiction to the Kyriarchal model of the empire, defines church as a radical political space where the logic of domination and subordination is denied, and equality and justice for all is affirmed. Fiorenza articulates Christian community church as the radical democratic assembly of all, the *cosmopolis* of God's very different peoples (Fiorenza, 2001: 56).

Alluding to Paul, Alain Badiou signifies the Pauline theology of Christ-Event as the "counter-community of resistance" to envisage a radical ecclesiology in the emerging context of Empire (Badiou, 2003). Richard Horsley's *Paul and Empire* and *Paul and Politics*, offers a convincing case of defining church as an anti-imperial imagination (Horsley, 1997). In his *Insurrection of the Crucified*, Theodore W. Jennings, Jr., provides another hermeneutical approach for envisaging church as an anti-imperial community (Jennings, 2003). Engaging with Michel Hardt and Antonio Negri, Joerg Rieger and Kwok Pui-lan embark an "Ecclesia of the Multitude", in their well-read book *Occupy Religion: Theology of the Multitude*. According to them, the church of the multitude is the "gathering of diverse people, and it orients them toward service in the world, particularly toward the least among us" (Rieger &

Pui-lan, 2010). Here empire is envisaged as the hegemonic logic of neoliberal capitalism which legitimizes the ideology of exclusion, the politics of refugization, and the economy of destitution. For them, church as an anti-imperial imagination which deconstructs its hierarchical ontology and other-centered diakonia, envisages a radical democratic community of justice and equality for all. The task before the church in the context of empire is to be the church of the multitude. The church of the multitude envisages church as "a radical assembly of equals" without hierarchy and patriarchy. It is a community where the tortured and the crucified of this world become the agents of salvation, and thus the diakonia (public ministry of the church) will become a reverse practice, that is, the poor and the weak become the subjects of churches' ministry, not the objects.

Church as Coming Community: Giorgio Agamben

It is Giorgio Agamben, the Italian philosopher/ theologian, who rightly analyzes and exposes the imperial inheritance of the church in the post-Constantine period (Agamben, 2011: 104). Alluding to Paul, Agamben contends that by claiming itself as the kingdom of God or the divinely legitimized empire, the church denied its call (*klesis*) to be *paroikousa* (sojourner) and ended up as *katoikein* (to dwell like an empire). When the church becomes a sovereign power of rule and its liturgies become the celebration of the sovereign God, the calling of the church is nullified and reversed. Engaging with the Pauline corpus, Giorgio Agamben offers an extended discussion on the "calling" (*kletos*) of the church. It is a calling that calls back or revokes every other vocation. According to Agamben, the calling of the church is a call for a messianic vocation that revokes all other vocations in the context of the reign of the emperor. For him, the church is a "messianic community" that lives in messianic time (Agamben, 1993: 1–2). Messianic time, as it is well explained in the Pauline corpus, is the time that remains – the time in-between the ascension and *parousia*. It is the time that remains in-between church and kingdom of God – the time the *ekklesia* takes to come to its end. End time, thus is not a futuristic time; rather, it is a qualitative "now" – the time of redemption within the present time (Agamben, 2005a: 6–7). Agamben defines church as a "coming community" that locates itself in a "state of exception" – the site of the marginalized and the excluded and thereby envisages political ontology of the crucified.

By "coming community" or "the community that comes", Agamben means a community of those who have no community. It is a community of people who are being "excluded in" or "included out" in the sovereign political paradigm. It is a community that cannot be co-opted by totalitarian forces. Or it is a community where the sovereign law is being inactivated. It is the community of the de-imperialized subjectivities. Agamben finds this sense of inoperability of the logic of empire in the kenotic act of Christ on the cross. First and foremost, the cross signifies the inoperability of the biopolitics of sovereignty and offers a radical politics of community by replacing himself on the cross in the place of a political victim in the Roman imperial context. In his reading on Paul, Agamben comments that the calling of the church is to "enslave" itself to this Messiah who becomes weak for the most wretched of the earth (Agamben, 2012: 13–14). For Agamben, church is called to be the ontology of the marginalized, the tortured – the multitude.

The Church as a "coming community" embodies the messianic politics through which it takes a turn from liturgy to politics. It is through messianic politics that the church becomes part of the democratic process that challenges the contemporary sociopolitical and economic sovereign powers. It is through messianic politics that the church reinvents its ontology in relation to "social ontology". Defining politics as a "social ontology", Chantal Mouffe says that

> the political cannot be restricted to a certain type of institution, or envisioned as constituting a specific sphere or level of society. It must be conceived as a dimension that is inherent to every human society and that determines our very ontological condition.
>
> (2005:3)

Church as a "coming community" envisages a "social ontology" that challenges the exclusionary practices of the sovereign power and embodies the agonistic politics of the excluded and exempted in our democratic process. It is the *messianic politics* that signifies church in the contemporary socioeconomic and political context of empire. It is the messianic politics that makes redemption happen in the everyday life of the people. The messianic politics invokes Indian church today to follow the footsteps of human rights activists like Fr. Stan Swamy to stand in solidarity with the weak and the vulnerable and to offer a radical political witness rather than reclaiming its minority status and FCRA status and thereby maintain its "necro-political" liturgical life.

Church as New Humanity: MM Thomas

Among the Indian Christian theologians, it was MM Thomas who proposed an authentic political ecclesiology in Indian context. Responding to the state of emergency declared at the midnight of June 25–26, 1975, Thomas said: "It is nothing but the onslaught on democracy and a betrayal of the nation". Thomas contended that the effort to quell people's revolts for the sake of internal peace, economic progress, and self-reliance through a state of emergency was nothing but the repudiation of all human rights envisaged by a welfare state and its democracy. Thomas envisages a participatory democracy where the sovereign power of the state is nullified and the rights of the marginalized are celebrated. Redefining church as the sign of the secular Koinonia and New Humanity, Thomas envisions radical ecclesiology as it destabilizes the logic of empire within (Vinayaraj, 2017: 119).

Thomas' theology of state and democracy is founded on his theology of the cross. According to Thomas, Jesus' cross is a protest against the sovereignty of the Roman Empire and the act of crucifixion was to nullify its logic of domination and marginalization. Replacing a political victim on the cross, Jesus exemplified his political solidarity and identification. Jesus' cross signifies the end of the totalitarian power and the beginning of a new community – kingdom community – a universal community where there are no dichotomies. In the new community, "there is no longer any distinction between gentiles and Jews, circumcised and uncircumcised, barbarians, savages, slaves and free; but Christ is all and in all" (Col.3:11). The new human community is constituted as a single body – the body of the crucified God in history. The crucified body of Christ is not a new thing; rather it is the body of the slain lamb from the creation of the world and it continues to be slain till the end of the world fighting against the totalitarian forces of powers. The mark of crucifixion continues to be the sign of the suffering struggle of God against the principalities and powers till the end of the world. The mission of the church today is to embody this mark of crucifixion and to reconstitute its ontology in solidarity with the victims of the world.

According to Thomas, the church is entrusted with a prophetic *diakonia* to discharge its duty based on the servant hood exemplified by the crucified God. Thomas writes:

> The church in India is called to proclaim the gospel of the crucified and risen Christ as the source of redemption of all spiritualities underlying religion as well as ideologies, and to demonstrate the Koinonia in Christ around the Eucharist as the nucleus of a movement of the larger Koinonia in Christ uniting peoples of diverse religions, ideologies and cultures—as well as the cosmos with its bio-diversity.
>
> (1995: 15)

Based on his theology of cross, MM Thomas explains the features of the mission of the church in India: (1) the calling of the church is to resist the idolatry of power and wealth and other gods of death in India's collective life, (2) to be in solidarity with the poor and the oppressed in their struggle for justice, and (3) to give up communal self-interest and self-identity for the sake of creating in India a secular national community in the midst of India's religious and ideological pluralism through manifesting a fellowship in Christ, transcending class, caste, ethnic, and religious communal divisions (Thomas, 1990:11).

Thomas's theology of humanization through which he upholds an anti-imperial ecclesiology and missiology makes him so significant and relevant. Thomas finds the foundation for his eschatological anthropology in the theology of Spirit who raised Jesus from the dead, as the first fruits of the New Creation. Thomas's hope in the future of humanity is incorporated in his understanding of the Risen Christ and His coming. He cites Paul: "We await a Saviour, the Lord Jesus Christ who will change our lowly body to be like his glorious body, by the power which enables him even to subject all to himself" (Phil.3:20–21). Becoming the tortured body of Christ, the church is being composed and constituted as an open community of all to resist the logic of empire theologically, liturgically, and hermeneutically. According to Thomas, it is this call and the composition of the church to be and becoming a messianic community only signifies its relevance in the contemporary context of empire.

Making Church a Democratic Community in India Today

Generally speaking, empire in India today takes many forms of hegemony in terms of cultural, economic, political, and religious realms. The logic of empire intrudes into the everyday aspect of human life. It denies our rights to food, clothing, study, and belief. Passing of anticonversion laws in the BJP ruling states, discourses on uniform civil code, issues regarding Citizen Amendment Act (CAA), hate speeches against Muslim women, and the political otherization of the minorities are some of the visible examples of the political and cultural imperialism of the dominant. Social security and safety of Dalits, women, and sexual minorities in the public space have been challenged and even denied. Religions are being manipulated politically to be enslaved in the track of cultural nationalism and, thus, become communal and fundamentalist. Today, the economy of the empire is nothing but the "economy of suicide" that demands the farmers to sacrifice their life for development. The 2020–2021 protest of farmers in the capital city of the country was the protest of the whole country against the corporatization of our economy and agriculture. The cultural, religious, and linguistic minorities are in anxiety and fear. Dalits are termed "anti-nationals". The people who stand for human rights are being either killed or jailed.

Responding to the custodial death of Fr. Stan Swamy, Arundhati Roy said it is "a microcosm of the not-so slow-murder" of the Indian democracy. Intolerance constitutes the public life. On the other hand, the national elites, the multinational corporations, and the international nuclear regimes find home in India. The notions of state, democracy, and the public are being manipulated in favor of the corporate capitalism. Arundhati Roy expresses the situation more clearly:

> [Neo-liberal capitalists] have mastered the technique of infiltrating the instruments of democracy—the "independent judiciary, the "free" press, the parliament—and molding them to their purpose. The project of corporate globalization has cracked the core. Free elections, a free press, and an independent judiciary mean little when the free market has reduced them to commodities available to the highest bidder.
> (2004: 3)

The church in India finds difficulty to respond to this scenario. The silence of the churches is regarded as the conspiracy for the empire.

Let me add some painful stories here from my own place. Recently, a nun abused case was raised against a bishop. Some nuns connected with the abused sisters were in hunger strike demanding the arrest of the accused bishop. However, the church that the Bishop belonged to and the other established churches observed either silence or were very reluctant to address the issue at hand. The public in India was of the opinion that the illegitimate alliance of the church with the ruling government helped to disrupt the police enquiry and save the accused. It is a clear example that the established churches in alliance with the power-centers deny justice to the victim particularly a victim who belongs to the body of church. This is one among the many cases as we see the illegitimate alliance between the church and empire through which it excludes the poor and the vulnerable. Another incident is that when the Christian bishops met the Prime minister of India during the time of the farmer's struggle, they never raised the concerns of the poor and the marginalized; rather, they submitted the political needs of the church. When the media asked them whether they had raised at least the case of struggling farmers, they said they never went there for political bargaining!

Conclusion

The challenge before the church in India today is not just to preach about its inherited salvation to the world around; rather, it is to envisage a democratic community within it and express it solidarity with the weak and the vulnerable. The challenge before the church is to be the church of the crucified people. As Agamben opines, it is an act of retreat for the church to "inoperate" its inherent juridical structure and to become a democratic community, a "coming community" – a community which is a community of those who have no community. By becoming the messianic community of the weak, it engages critically with the exploitative systems of our society to make it just and egalitarian. It is here the desire for a democratic church becomes the desire for a democratic society. Radical ecclesiology is a call within the call of the church (*klesis*) to become the "weak church" of the Crucified God by becoming the body of the crucified people "now" (Robbins, 2011: 24). Envisaging it as a body of the crucified Christ, church becomes the potential community to be a vanguard movement for the democratic society in the contemporary age of empire. Church as a democratic community in India is to be reimagined as a "coming community" where there is no caste, class, and gender discriminations and no power hierarchies for the sake of liturgical-theological doctrines and dogmas. Church in India needs to be de-doctrinated and de-dogmatized in favor of the weak and the vulnerable in this country (Vinayaraj, 2020: 6). Agamben exhorts that the task of the church today is to find its eschatological moment – the moment when it becomes the open church of all – even to the people those who have no communities at all (Agamben, 2012:13). Living in this time, experiencing this time, is thus not something that the Church can choose, or choose not, to do. It is only in this time that there is a Church at all.

Note

1 Biopolitics is the term coined by Michel Foucault to expose the discursive formation of our bodies. For Foucault, our biological and social bodies are formulated in certain discourses of power. Michel Foucault, *The History of Sexuality, Vol.1: An Introduction* (London: Allen Lane, 1973), 143.

References

Agamben, Giorgio 2011. *The Kingdom and Glory: For a Theological Genealogy of Economy and Government*. Stanford: Stanford University Press.
Agamben, Giorgio 2005a.*The Coming Community*. Minneapolis: University of Minnesota Press.
Agamben, Giorgio 2005b. *The Time That Remains: A Commentary on the Letter to the Romans*. Stanford, CA: Stanford University Press.
Agamben, Giorgio 2012.*The Church and the Kingdom*. London, New York, Calcutta: Seagull Books.
Badiou, Alain 2003. *Saint Paul: The Foundation of Universalism*. Stanford: Stanford University Press.
Hernandez, Adriana 1997.*Pedagogy, Democracy, and Feminism: Rethinking the Public Sphere*. New York: State University of New York Press.
Rieger, Joerg & Pui-Lan, Kwok 2010. *Occupy Religion: Theology of the Multitude*. New York & UK: Rowan & Littlefield Publishers.
Jennings, Theodore W. 2003.*The Insurrection of the Crucified: The "Gospel of Mark" as Theological Manifesto*. Chicago, IL: Exploration Press.
Kappen, Sebastian & Vattamattam, S. 1988. *Paristhithi Samskrithi* (Malayalam). Changanassery: Maanusham Publications.
Mouffe, Chantal 2005. *The Return of the Political*. New York: Verso.
Horsley, Richard, ed. 1997. *Paul and Empire: Religion and Power in Roman Imperial Society*, Harrisburg, PA: Trinity Press.
Robbins, W. Robbins 2011. *Radical Democracy and Political Theology*. New York: Columbia University Press.
Roy, Arundhati. 2004. *An Ordinary Person's Guide to Empire*. Cambridge: South End.
Schussler Fiorenza, Elizabeth 2007. *The Power of the Word: Scripture and the Rhetoric of Empire*. Minneapolis: Fortress Press.
Thomas, M.M. 1995. *A Diaconal Approach to Indian Ecclesiology*. Rome & Tiruvalla: CIIS & CSS.
Thomas, M.M. 1990. "The Church in India—Witness to the Meaning of the Cross Today," in *Future of the Church in India*, ed. Aruna Gnanadason. Nagpur: NCCI.
Vinayaraj, Y.T. 2017. *Theology after Hardt & Negri: Empire, Church and Multitude*. Delhi: ISPCK.
Vinayaraj, Y.T. 2020. *Faith in the Age of Empire: Christian Doctrines in a Postcolonial Sensibility*. New Delhi: ISPCK/CWM.

Section II

Gender and Democratization – Forms of Resistance against Hegemony

4 The Feminization of Telugu Christianity
An Instance of Democratization of Indian Christianity

James Elisha Taneti

Introduction

Despite the residues of patriarchy within the ecclesiastical structures, any casual observer who happened to pass by a gathered group of Telugu Christians would perceive Telugu Christianity to be a movement of women because women outnumber men during the worship services. Neighbors and critics would consider the community and her rendering of the gospel to be feminine. The Jesus that the Telugu Christians introduce cares for women and children. The local women shaped the Christian beliefs and practices in significant ways. The avenues of leadership they inherited and appropriated indicate the democratization of a religion transplanted from the Atlantic world. Even while not white-washing the dominance of men in the ecclesiastical structures, one needs to analyze the historical sources of the feminization of Telugu Christianity both in the pre-Christian cultures of the Dalit communities who converted to Christianity *en masse* and also women's role in the appropriation of Christianity in the Telugu states – Andhra Pradesh and Telangana. I refer to the process in which women appropriate a given worldview or culture to assert themselves. I draw extensively from Ann Douglas's *The Feminization of American Culture* (1998). Although it would be equally profitable to study the contributions of women to all Christian communities – Catholic, Protestant, and post-liturgical, I will, in this chapter, focus on the impact of Telugu women in the evolution of Protestant Christianity in the region.

In an earlier study, I have attempted to study the theologies and history of Telugu Biblewomen, women preachers of Lutheran and Baptist backgrounds in the coastal districts of Andhra Pradesh (James Elisha Taneti, *Telugu Christians*, 2013). I have demonstrated how the Telugu women, especially the Biblewomen, took advantage of the opportunities available in Protestant Christianity and the colonial context to shape Telugu Christianity. In the very process of transmitting Protestant Christianity, Telugu women subverted it. Through their leadership, they defined the new faith and modeled its piety. Reading further the missionary sources, I realize that Telugu female schoolteachers and nurses have also been equally accessible to the communities and influential in teaching the Bible, interpreting the tradition, and modeling Christian piety. Women remained in constant contact with their non-Christian neighbors daily, lived out their faith, and impacted the perceptions of neighbors about Christianity. Women's claim on Christianity should not surprise us. In their pre-Christian worldviews, Telugu women have led their families and communities in matters of faith. Evangelical Christianity with its foci on scriptures, literacy, and health opened additional opportunities. The missionary movement they allied with was itself feminine. Drawing from the roots and resources, women have transformed and shaped the texture of Telugu Christianity, contributing to its democratization as narrated in the sections that follow.

Women in Local Cultures

As mentioned earlier, Telugu culture was heterogeneous with multiple communities, each with its subculture. The place of women in each social group varied, as did their roles in transmitting and safeguarding the worldviews. For example, Dalit women traditionally held relatively better ritual power than their counterparts in caste communities. It may not have always and necessarily translated into the social sphere (Wilber Theodor Elmore, 1915, 29–31). With some exceptions, women's place within the caste communities was slightly different. The higher the ranking of a social group claimed, the more oppressive it was to its women. The land-owning communities saw the control of women's bodies and their relationships to be a credible means of preserving the purity norms, status quo, and thereby the economic order. In rural settings, where agriculture was the primary source of income, Dalit women labored along with men to make ends meet. Their labor did not guarantee them an equal share in the family's decision-making, but the ability to move beyond home and be a part of the family economy. Their contribution to the family income provided them a relatively better status compared to their counterparts in caste communities at least before their conversion to Christianity and/or subsequent Sanskritization.

At the symbolic level, goddesses dominate the Dalit pantheon. Dalits worship goddesses, such as Maramma, Poleramma, Poshamma, Gonthi, Ellamma, Kaamma, Morasamma, Matangi (Mathamma), Somalamma, and Moosamma (T. Elmore, 1915, 19–28). Dalits looked up to these deities in seasons of need and calamity. In addition to paying their obeisance, Dalits subtly goaded the landlords to offer a libation to the goddesses at the times of sowing and harvest. With an implicit conviction that the land belongs to the local goddess and that anyone tilling the land needed the divine sanction, their non-Dalit neighbors regardless of their caste, placated the presiding (Dalit) deity during the times of threshing corn, building new houses, or opening newly dug wells. This belief subtly drew the land-owning communities to join Dalits in the worship of their goddesses. The popular belief that the land belongs to the native goddesses and that the Dalit priestess represents the deity may have caused this unlikely alliance between the Dalit communities and the land-owning castes.

At the ritual level, Dalit woman priests, by and large, led their male counterparts (Henry Whitehead, 1916, 63). Through oracles, they represented the deity. Matangi, a Madiga priestess named after the goddess, represented the latter. While men priests inherit their office, a Madiga woman becomes a Matangi through possession and after a series of tests by the community. There are exceptions though. Woman priestess in the cult of Nukalamma inherited the office from her mother (Edgar Thurston, 1909, 295–305). In either case, priestesses presided at the purificatory ceremonies to prepare for the village feasts and festivals. Male priests, by and large, assisted their female counterparts. During appointed seasons of a year, Matangi led ritual processions. She visited every street in the village, which otherwise were closed to her. She entered caste houses at her will. The high-caste residents grudgingly tolerated her freedom. During her march, she abused the landlords and spat on them, a gesture considered to be purifying (Elmore, 1915, 25).

Dalit priestesses uttered divine oracles, often prescribing remedies for the epidemics or famines that plagued villages. John Carman, a historian of religion and son of a medical missionary, described a ritual during which a Kolpula woman transmitted the oracles from the cholera goddess (Luke & Carman, 1968, 57). The male priests invoked the goddess through drums and butchered sacrificial animals. A woman, on the other hand, typically was an intermediary between the deity and her village. Thus, the religious systems that Dalit groups had evolved and promoted among the socially dominant provided more space for women.

The status of women among the caste communities is much more complex and ambivalent. Again, it would be highly problematic to characterize their status, as there were numerous subgroups among Hindus. Caste women may have been active in farm and household leadership, but were not allowed to venture out beyond to minimize their possible interactions with men of other communities. The gold they inherited from their mothers and maternal ancestors was their primary bargaining tool. Dowry and other assets brides brought at the time of the wedding became the property of the husband. By and large, men inherited the family properties and the "purity of the caste" was safeguarded through arranged marriages.

In the Shaivite tradition, both men and women undertook pilgrimages, offered pujas at the temple, and observed ritual baths and weekly fasts. Given their proximity to children, women ordinarily transmitted and translated the tradition to the next generation. In the bhakti tradition, an outgrowth of Vaishnavism, goddesses were subservient to gods in its epics. Women had space to interpret the tradition both in public and family spheres. The Dalit goddesses, such as Gonthelamma, are negative reflections of their counterparts in Hindu mythology. The Hindu epics demonized Kunthi's assertion, but Dalits deified her. The interpretive lens and agenda of the community play a critical part in every time an epic is retold in or by a community. While rerendering epics, such as Ramayana, Telugu Dalits mitigated the status between gods and goddesses.

These interpretative processes of the tradition mirror the places women occupied in each community. As custodians of the tradition, Dalit women retained Sanskritic goddesses, but as catalysts of change. In doing so, women claimed a certain amount of agency in the cultural change and carried these roles into Christianity.

Telugu Women and Western Missionaries

The missionary movement the Telugu women encountered was a women's movement. With the establishment of female seminaries, women in the north-Atlantic world found missionary careers abroad attractive. They considered marrying an outgoing male missionary to be a helpful strategy to accomplish their missionary calling. For example, Mount Holyoke Female Seminary in the United States of America trained women to accompany male missionaries as wives (Johnson, 1904, 146). Seminary administrators collaborated with mission societies to connect their students with men destined to go abroad as missionaries.

With the opportunities to engage in roles traditionally beyond theirs during the Civil War and lessons learned from the experience, American women were ready to make an impact beyond their households, and some beyond their national boundaries. While some historians interpret this interest as a willingness to be "useful" in God's household, others find social aspirations in women's eagerness to make the world their household (Robert, 1984, 417; Hill, 1985, 36–40). During the American Civil War, a considerable number of women acquired the skills needed for public engagement. While men were away engaged in combat, women had to lead their families and communities. After the war, American women looked for opportunities to continue their leadership in public life. Foreign missions provided an ideal opportunity to do that. As a result, in the decade following the Civil War, five Presbyterian, four Baptist, three Congregational, and two Methodist women's mission boards emerged (Hill, 1985, 13). From across the border, Canadian women joined their American counterparts abroad, feminizing the missionary workforce in the Indian subcontinent.

With this interest in missionary work and perhaps due to the dearth of eligible men or out of a desire to remain autonomous, many women joined the missionary force as single-woman missionaries. They substantially increased the number of women at mission stations. Lavinia Peabody, an American Baptist missionary and Mount Holyoke alumna, was the first single-woman missionary to arrive in Telugu country. She reached Nellore in 1871. Emma Rauschenbusch-Clough, an alum of Rochester Female Seminary, followed three years later. Meanwhile, Kate Boggs was the first Lutheran single-woman missionary. She arrived in 1881 followed by Anna S. Kugler two years later. Due to illness, Boggs returned the same year. Agnes I. Schade joined the Lutheran missionaries in Andhra in 1890 and Amy S. Sadtler two years later. The arrival of single-woman missionaries altered the female–male ratio in mission compounds. For instance, there was one single-woman missionary in 1882 among Canadian Baptist missionaries while there were 13 by 1906 (Craig, 1908, 217). Among Lutheran missionaries, there were two female single missionaries in 1890 compared to four missionary families, that is, the ratio of 6 women to 4 men. By the end of the 19th century, the number of single-woman missionaries increased to 7 while the number of missionary families was nine, that is, 16 women and 9 male missionaries (Drach & Kuder, 1914, 265–280). While male missionaries travelled along with native preachers, women missionaries invested their skills and energies in hospitals, schools, and the work among women.

The local conditions and cultures have forced the missionaries to periodically reevaluate their goals and strategies. Protestant missionaries needed local allies. What precipitated the alliance between women missionaries and their local counterparts? First, access to local women was one of the primary challenges Western missionaries faced. The cultural taboos restricted access to native women for any men other than their immediate family members. No man – local or foreign – would ordinarily be trusted or welcomed to enter a house unless they are related to the host family. Given their social location as foreigners and, therefore with their perceived ability to defile the host families, women missionaries were not welcomed either. When compared to their missionary counterparts, local women had easier access to the local women. Second, missionaries had undergone language learning but the limited knowledge of the vernacular hampered their ability to communicate the Christian message with the natives. Their local allies were better equipped to translate the gospel in the Telugu cultural idioms. Third, missionaries were not accustomed to the local temperature which was intolerably hot most of the year. Many missionaries contracted illnesses and some even have died with their inability to cope with the climate (Hugald Grafe, 2010, 13). Confined to their bungalows due to the scorching heat, missionaries depended on their local allies to travel and transmit the Christian message. Fourth, the institutions that missionaries established and the programs they launched needed more personnel than missionaries had. The local interlocutors were willing to collaborate with their missionary allies. The local conditions demanded native collaborators. In their encounters with Christianity, Telugu women – Dalit and Sudhra – saw not only a movement of the women but also opportunities to shape the nascent church.

Bible Women: With Bible in Hand

Recognizing their limitations as well as the gifts and interest of the local women, Protestant missionaries transported the office of Biblewoman in the region. This profession has its origins in the east end of London when the British Bible and Foreign Society appointed Marion Bower, a working-class woman of Irish descent, as Biblewoman in 1857 (LNR [Ellen Ranyard],

1860, 25). Reporting to Ellen Ranyard, the founder of London Bible and Domestic Female Mission, Bowers traversed the streets in the east end and taught Bible, hygiene, and self-help skills to the women there. Appropriating this lay ministerial office of Biblewoman to their needs, local Telugu women allied with women missionaries to introduce Christianity to their neighbors, teach the faith to native Christians, and model Christian piety.

At work by 1869, Lydia, whose full name we do not know, may have been the earliest appointee (*Baptist Missionary Magazine*, 1869, 258). A native of Visakhapatnam, Lydia was an active member of the London Missionary Society parish there. She eventually moved south to Nellore and served as Biblewoman. Lydia might have worked with Martha Porter, an LMS missionary and a British and Foreign Bible Society ally, in Visakhapatnam. After moving to Kadapa, Porter herself recruited three more Biblewomen in the region, starting with the appointments of Mary Wesley and Martha Rueben in 1871, and of Bethsheba a year later (Porter, 1871, 125). Mary Wesley worked with her son Samuel, a native medical missionary. Together they served in Proddutur (Porter, 1872, 51). They were probably related to Peter Wesley, a local evangelist. Mary used her house as a dispensary and served the visiting patients. She also visited women in the town and introduced Christianity (Porter, 1871, 276). Appointed in the same year was Martha. Employed along with her catechist husband "Edward", Martha Rueben served in Kadapa. The naming of her husband "Edward" after the resident LMS missionary Edward Porter indicates the level of their nexus with the missionary family (Porter, 1871, 125). Recruited a year later, Bethsheba was the third on the payroll. She served in Nandyala.

Missionary reports do not mention either the family name or the caste identity of Lydia. However, the manner of her visits to the LMS congregation and the resistance of the family to her conversion hint at her non-Dalit background. Hailing from Visakhapatnam, she heard of Christianity through a group of native Christian women assembled in a house church (David Downie, 1924, 51). After visiting them four times, she decided to embrace Christianity and was baptized in the local LMS chapel in the early 1860s. She had eventually moved to Nellore and allied with American Baptist missionaries. Lydia preferred to live in mission compounds rather than with her non-Christian family, lest her association with Christianity stigmatize the family or her family interferes with her Christian practice (David Downie, 1924, 53). Celebrated by American Baptist missionaries for her "sweetest and most stirring language", Lydia worked with them for more than 30 years from the early 1860s in various positions (*Baptist Missionary Magazine*, 1872, 178). When the office of Biblewoman was imported to the region, women missionaries did not have to look far to find someone more eligible than Lydia.

As the abovementioned appointments indicate and other recruitment patterns attest, the majority of the Biblewomen were of "high" caste origins, at least until the mid-1920s. The tides of massive Dalit conversions were only beginning when the office of Biblewoman was imported and therefore not many Dalit women would have been considered eligible for the office. Literacy and the ability to visit all neighborhoods – caste and outcaste – were key to doing the job, two things initially inaccessible to Dalits. With increased access to education and the founding of Bible Training schools for women, Dalit women increasingly joined the profession in the 20th century and diversified the office.

Bible has been at the center of Biblewomen's work. In their interactions with women, Biblewomen narrated tales from the Bible. Their songs related the gospel story in streets and on verandas. Narrating and singing faith was not novel to Telugu women. Reading and reciting scriptures was. Equipped to read the scriptures, a skill denied to them earlier often because of their gender and their social location as Dalits, Biblewomen memorized and recited scriptural texts. In doing so, they challenged the scholars in other religious communities who often were male and Brahmin. For example, Mariamma's previous work experience also helped her candidature. Having been a Dalit (Madiga) priestess, Mariamma acquired the skills and confidence to engage in "wordy fights" with Brahmin priests (Orville Daniel, 1973, 47).

The work of Telugu Biblewomen was not confined to preaching. Drawing from their Evangelical faith, Biblewomen occasionally served in clinics. They visited patients at dispensaries and introduced Christianity. As mentioned earlier, Mary Wesley of Proddutur hosted a medicine dispensary and served as Biblewoman-Nurse along with her doctor-son. Abishekamma, a chief nurse and Biblewoman at Medak Hospital, is another example. At the hospital founded by the Wesleyan Methodist missionaries in 1896, Abishekamma repeatedly related this story to the outpatients (Munson, 1913, 43).

In addition to preaching, Biblewomen carried medication and vaccines to villages during plagues and distributed them. Reminiscing the life of Charles W. Posnett, a British Wesleyan missionary in Medak, Frank Colyer Sackett recorded that the villagers during a plague requested the medical missionary to send medicine with a Dalit Biblewoman (Sackett, 1951, 125). According to him, the local community admired the Biblewoman for her adventurous spirit. Biblewomen's familiarity with basic hygiene and the Bible prepared them to care for patients and preach the gospel in hospitals.

Given their basic education, Biblewomen also taught children in schools and occasionally other women at their homes. Biblewomen, by and large, have attended teacher training classes (*Among the Telugus*, 1924, 51). For example, upon his arrival in Samarlakota, Americus V. Timpany, a Canadian Baptist missionary, started a school there in 1880. Ellen, an Anglo-Indian Biblewoman, was its founding teacher. Occasionally, Biblewomen played all the roles that a school needed. Neela, a Biblewoman in Bobbili, was a chef, teacher, and matron of the boarding school. Her colleague and sister-in-law, Sayamma, was a schoolteacher and Biblewoman (Churchill, 1916, 283).

With Bibles in hands, Biblewomen traversed within and beyond their neighborhoods. This practice took Biblewomen to houses of Dalit, Muslim, and

Hindu women, some of which ordinarily were closed to them. By becoming female preachers and traversing in other caste neighborhoods, Biblewomen boldly transgressed the social boundaries of the day. The office of zenana workers paralleled that of Biblewomen. There were differences in goals and strategies, but these were negligible. With a few exceptions, zenana workers visited the homes of Muslim and Hindu women and taught reading skills as well as Bible lessons regularly. Because of their need to visit to the homes of the "high" caste and Muslim women, zenana workers mostly were women of "high" caste backgrounds. On the other hand, Biblewomen visited women of all backgrounds and focused on teaching the Bible (Chamberlain, 1925, 57). Occasionally, the same women served both roles.

Health Workers: Agents of Healing

Caring for health needs had been integral to evangelical piety. The professions of nursing and that of Biblewoman were construed as two arms. While one cared for the body, the other attended to the soul (LNR [Ellen Ranyard], 1875, vii). Both the body and the soul ought to be cared for, as "human souls live in bodies" (LNR [Ellen Ranyard], 1875, 291). As evangelicals, Protestant missionaries with their evangelical faith recognized the need to care for both. As a result, some of them were trained physicians and nurses. Of course, their commitment to Jesus known for his healings may have spurred this interest. After their arrival, Protestant missionaries established general hospitals as well as specialized hospitals. In the Northern Circars, John Davis, a Canadian Baptist missionary, founded a leprosy hospital in Ramachandrapuram in 1893 (John E. Davis, 1918, 170). In the State of Hyderabad, Isabel Kerr, a British Wesleyan medical missionary, founded a leprosy hospital in Dichpally in 1911 (Protchard, 2014, 95–96). In the southern region, Thomas V. Campbell, an LMS missionary and an alumnus of the University of Edinburgh, established hospitals in Jammalamadugu and Chikkaballapuram as well as the Arogyavaram Tuberculosis Sanatorium in 1915. In the northern end of coastal Andhra, Canadian Baptist missionaries Ben Gullison and Mary Evelyn Gullison founded an eye hospital in Sompeta in 1935 (Dekar, 1993, 152).

With more than half of the missionary personnel being women and some of them trained as doctors and nurses, there was an augmented focus on women's health, especially on maternity care. American Reformed missionaries in Rayalaseema started a hospital in Madanapalli in 1863 to care for women's health. Between 1863 and 1906, Protestant missionaries founded at least 13 clinics among the Telugus. This data collected from six missionary societies illustrates the missionary enthusiasm to work for the health of the local women. With their emphasis on health, Roman Catholic missionaries were equally active in medical missions. As part of equipping the local agency, Christian missionaries started Nursing Schools and Medical Colleges to train native women. The Vellore Christian Medical College founded by Ida Scudder, an Indian-born American Reformed missionary, was the most reputed of such in the south. Started as a one-bed hospital for women and children at the turn of the 20th century, it had eventually become the Missionary Medical School for Women in 1914. An ecumenical venture in its inception, the Medical School for Women trained numerous female doctors for mission hospitals in the southern and central provinces. Many of its alumni served in the Telugu regions.

Chegudi Dhanamma Joshua from Guntur was one of the earliest graduates to matriculate with a Licentiate Medical Practitioner diploma from the Medical School for Women at Vellore. Upon her graduation in 1922, Dhanamma had joined the Mission Hospital in Guntur founded by Ann Kugler. Dhanamma succeeded a Malayalee doctor Paru. Before proceeding to study at the Medical School for Women, Dhanamma had earlier studied at a mission college in Chennai in 1917 (Kugler, 1928, 38). She was raised by Christian parents (*Lutheran Women's Work*, 1923, 425). Her sister Victoria was a schoolteacher at the local Stall Girls' High School where both sisters studied (Kugler, 1928, 38). After serving at Kugler Women's Hospital for 10 years, Dhanamma moved to Repalle and opened a private clinic there, using her medical skills beyond the mission settings (*The Annual Report of the Foreign Missions of the United Lutheran Church in America*, 1932, 17). According to Anna Kugler, the American Lutherans invested in her education and likely with an understanding that she would work for a designated period in one of the mission hospitals (Kugler, 1928, 38).

Karra Mary Moses was another notable doctor. Matriculating from the Vellore Medical College in 1928, Mary Moses, a Licentiate Medical Practitioner, joined the Lutheran Mission Hospital in Rajahmundry (Dolbeer, Augustus, & Swavely, 1955, 130). After serving there at the Women's Hospital for two years, she moved to and supervised the Augustana Hospital in Bhimavaram founded in 1931 (Swavely, 1942, 283). She returned to Rajahmundry Mission Hospital in 1935. The missionary chroniclers do not mention the caste identity of Mary Moses, but her family name suggests she was a Dalit, and likely may have been a Madiga. As a second-generation Christian parented by Shanthamma and Moses, Mary may have had access to education in mission schools (Martin Dolbeer et al., 1955, 130). Looking at the family names, one can surmise that both Dhanamma Joshua and Mary Moses were Dalits. In an age when educational opportunities were sparse to girls, and, if available, were limited to girls of "high caste" background. As cultural centers of the Telugu societies, Guntur and Rajahmundry had women's schools. Dalit Christian women took advantage of the educational opportunities offered in and by the missionary establishment to pursue their basic and professional education.

To support the medical services offered in their hospitals, Christian missionaries established numerous nursing schools long before the establishment of Medical School for Women in Vellore. American Lutheran missionaries started Nursing schools in Guntur (1899), Rajahmundry (1918), Rentichintala (1921), and Chirala (1924) (Swavely, 1942, 287–289). Of the data available,

American Lutheran missionaries trained more than 308 nurses by 1941, that is, seven or eight women every year (Swavely, 1942, 287–289). Most of their alumni sought and found employment in mission hospitals. Given the stigma attached to the profession, Telugu women initially did not show interest in the field, but gradually found this to be an attractive employment option (Swavely, 1942, 287). The profession required touching bodies and there might have been resistance and fears from caste and Dalit women to this critical sector. Declaring a new day in the region, FP Manly, an American Lutheran missionary, observed that working in hospitals provided women, most of who were of Dalits, avenues to enter the lives of "aristocratic Hindu homes" (Manly, 1923, 598).

Schoolteachers: Empowering Literacy

By the end of the 19th century, women gained access to literacy. The colonial administration of the Madras Presidency, local Maharajas, Hindu reformers, and Christian missionaries together facilitated this access (Leonard, 1991, 26). It needs to be located in the contemporaneous cultural reforms in terms of the marriage age of girls and widow marriage. Telugu women engineered and perpetuated the reforms as students and teachers. In the 1870s, there was a sudden and dramatic upsurge of interest both to start and attend girls' schools. The number of schools designated for girls attests to this. According to John Leonard, a social historian, there were 136 schools for girls in 1870 in the Madras Presidency and the number of girls' schools increased fourfold in the next 10 years, that is, 546 schools by 1880 (Leonard, 1991, 26). 98 more schools were added in 1881. It may not have been the sole catalyst, but the 1867 visit of Mary Carpenter, a British social activist, played a role in this women's education in the subcontinent (Ramakrishna, 1983, 93). Influenced by the ideology of Brahmo Samaj and Western liberal thought, local princes started numerous schools for girls. For example, in 1868, the Maharajah of Pithapuram founded a girls' school in Kakinada with monthly and annual grants for its maintenance (Ramakrishna, 1983, 93). In the same year, the Maharajah of Vizianagaram founded one for Brahmin and Kshatriya girls in his capital.

Brahmin dissenters, such as Kandukuri Viresalingam and Gurajada Venkata Apparao, architects of the Telugu Renaissance, on their part, initiated social reforms within the caste Hindu communities (Vakulabharanam Rajagopal, 2005), 45–77. Influenced by the Brahmo ideology, they advocated widow marriages and boldly solemnized some. They also denounced the early marriage of girls. It was not until 1929 the colonial government with its Sarada (Sharda) Act intervened and legislated a minimum age for marriage to be 14, and that too after intense lobbying by the All India Women's Conference (Adami, 2020, 70). Even while retaining their Hindu identity, Telugu "social reformers" reinterpreted the Hindu scriptures to improve women's social status. They used the girls' schools that the local princes founded to disseminate their ideas. For example, in 1879, Viresalingam lectured at Vizianagaram Girls' School, founded by the Maharajah, on the practice of widow marriage (Leonard, 1991, 85). The reforming programs of the Brahmin dissenters and Kshatriyas focused only on the social status of caste women, especially those of Brahmin origins (Malik, 1982, 316). According to V. Ramakrishna, a social historian, these reform movements offered an alternative to Christianity which by then was drawing conversions from Dalit communities and was making inroads into the caste communities (Ramakrishna, 1983, 186).

Recognizing the need for women's education and the opportunity to introduce literacy and Christianity, Christian missionaries established schools, some of which were for girls. At the resistance from the "high" caste parents to send their children to study with Dalits, some missionaries occasionally made concerted efforts to enlist caste girls by establishing "caste schools". The new generation of literate women these schools had produced eventually became teachers and championed literacy among the women. The curricula in the mission schools aimed at teaching what they called three "R"s. The skills they wanted to impart were: i. Reading; ii. Writing; and iii. Arithmetic. They added a subtle fourth "R", a less pronounced but consistent program to teach their Christian faith (Drach & Kuder, 1914, 235). As an ancient civilization, Telugus were not new to letters and numbers, but the knowledge of the latter was denied to Dalits. Missionaries had an agenda in introducing the first three. With their version of literacy and calculations, missionaries ushered Telugus into the Western Enlightenment values of liberty, equality, and comradery, an ethos that would potentially undermine the traditional Telugu learning. As people of the book, missionaries wanted the natives to read and grasp the Bible, hoping that the very reading of the text would transform the latter's worldview. After all, building up leadership for the society and church and thereby influencing the Telugu society was their agenda.

The dearth of personnel in the mission schools and the need for local agency warranted the missionaries to recruit Telugu schoolteachers – both women and men. There were not many equipped to perform the given tasks and hence the need for teaching training. John Clay, an SPG missionary, started a Teacher Training School in Mutyalapadu, near Kadapa, as early as 1860 (Hibbert-Ware, 1912, 62). With a heightened accent on the education of girls, missionaries encouraged the Telugu Christian women to become schoolteachers. As a result, almost all denominations started teaching training schools and enrolled women. American Lutheran missionaries started one in Tarlapudi, Reformed missionaries in Chittoor, and their Canadian Baptist counterparts in Kakinada, to name a few.

Writing as late as 1912, after almost three decades of educating women, George Hibbert-Ware named the need for women teachers as their "greatest" (Hibbert-Ware, 1912, 170). Given the agenda of imparting religious education, most of those employed were Christian. The schoolteachers did have opportunities to subtly or openly introduce their evangelical faith and influence children in their classrooms in their formative ages.

Conclusion

What have these women done to the Christian community? With the opportunities these professions offered, women impacted the evolution of Telugu Christianity. While men dominated the appropriation of the faith through their sermons and hymns, women created spaces for themselves to influence it. As mentioned earlier, Biblewomen visited homes and introduced the Christian faith. New converts and nascent congregations looked up to them for instructions in seasons of life when religion mattered. Biblewomen offered advice in matters of faith and practice. Meanwhile, doctors and nurses demonstrated Christian values and lifestyles and occasionally introduced their faith to patients and families when opportunities arose. Meetings with patients invariably opened up conversations about beliefs. Schoolteachers, on the other hand, modeled and occasionally taught evangelical lifestyles. Through their lives and work, these women transmitted and translated the Christian message.

How have these women represented the Christian message? Of course, the context of interpretation determined their rendering of the text. Most of the available topics point to women's fascination with the gospel stories. According to an antecedent reported by Arley Munson, Abishekamma, a chief nurse and Biblewoman at Medak Hospital, repeatedly retold the story of Elizabeth's conception, one of the Lucan infancy narratives (Arley Munson, 1913, 43). The story would certainly have appealed to this audience and heightened their hopes for a child, as most of them were childless and were visiting the hospital with a hope for a child (Arley Munson, 1913, 43). Women presented Jesus as someone who cares for women and children as much as he cares for men. They highlighted the texts in the gospels where Jesus interacted with women and children. The importance afforded to children and women by God would have drawn women towards their message. Jesus was not merely a teacher or preacher, according to them. He was a healer, one who cares for their health needs.

The political dynamics under the colonial context and the missionaries' presence, no doubt, influenced the reception and articulation of the Christian faith by the local Christians. So did their social aspirations, political interests, and willingness to accommodate each other. The confluence between Hindu traditions, Christian beliefs, and Dalit worldviews continued in the postcolonial context, but in a new environment and with heightened confidence among the Telugu Christians. The God they preached cared for the immediate needs of the people. The opportunities women availed to preach, care, and teach influenced substantially the trajectory and texture of Telugu Christianity and transformed it into a democratic and inclusive organization in that they facilitated the participation and involvement of women including Dalit women in new capacities and in new places.

References

Adami, Rebecca. *Women and the Universal Declaration of Human Rights*. New York: Routledge, 2020.

Among the Telugus: Canadian Baptist Foreign Missions Annual Report, 1924, 51.

Chamberlain, Mary Eleanor Anable. *Fifty Years in Foreign Fields: A History of Five Decades of the Women's Board of Foreign Missions, Reformed Church in America*. New York: Board of Foreign Missions of the Reformed Church in America, 1925.

Churchill, Matilda. *Letters from My Home in India*. Edited by Grace McLeod Rogers. Toronto: McClelland, Goodchild & Stewart, 1916.

Craig, John. *Forty Years among the Telugus: A History of the Mission of the Baptists of Ontario and Quebec, Canada, to the Telugus, South India, 1867–1907*. Toronto: Canadian Baptist Foreign Mission Board, 1908.

Daniel, Orville E. *Moving with the Times: The Story of Outreach from Canada into Asia, South America, and Africa*. Toronto: Canadian Baptist Foreign Mission Board, 1973.

Davis, John E. *The Life Story of a Leper: Autobiography of John E. Davis*. Toronto: Canadian Baptist Foreign Mission Board, 1918.

Dekar, Paul. *For the Healing of the Nations: Baptist Peace Makers*. Macon: Smyth & Helwys Publishing Co., 1993.

Dolbeer, Martin Luther, R.D. Augustus & Clarence H. Swavely. *Biographical Record of the Pastors, Missionaries and Prominent Laymen of the United Lutheran Church Mission and the Andhra Evangelical Lutheran Church*. Rajahmundry: Silver Jubilee Committee of the Andhra Evangelical Lutheran Church, 1955.

Douglas, Ann. *The Feminization of American Culture*. New York: Farrar, Straus and Giroux, 1998.

Downie, David. *The Lone Star: A History of the Telugu Mission of the American Baptist Foreign Mission Society*. Philadelphia: Judson Press, 1924.

Drach, George & Calvin F. Kuder. *The Telugu Mission of the General Council of the Evangelical Lutheran Church in North America*. Philadelphia: General Council Publication House, 1914.

Elmore, Wilber Theodore. *Dravidian Gods in Modern Hinduism: A Study of the Local and Village Deities of Southern India*. Hamilton, NY: privately published by the author, 1915.

Grafe, Hugald. *The History of the Work of the Hermannsburg Mission and Evangelical Lutheran Mission (ELM) for the South Andhra Lutheran Church (SALC)*. Chennai: Inter-Church Service Association Books, 2010.

Hibbert-Ware, George. *Christian Missions in the Telugu Country*. London: The Society for the Propagation of the Gospel, 1912.

Hill, Patricia. *The World Their Household: The American Woman's Foreign Mission Movement and Cultural Transformation, 1870–1920*. Ann Arbor: The University of Michigan Press, 1985.

Johnson, Clifton. *Old-Time and School-Books*. New York: MacMillan & Co., 1904.

Leonard, John Greenfield. *Kandukuri Viresalingam (1848–1919): A Biography of an Indian Social Reformer*. Hyderabad: Telugu University, 1991.

Luke, P.Y. and John B. Carman. *Village Christians and Hindu Culture*. London: Lutterworth Press, 1968.

LNR [Ellen Ranyard]. *The Missing Link, or Bible-women in the Homes of the London Poor*. New York: Robert Carter & Brothers, 1860.

———, *Nurses for the Needy or Bible-women Nurses in the Homes of the London Poor*. London: James Nisbet & Company, 1875.

Kugler, Anna S. *Guntur Mission Hospital, Guntur, India*. Philadelphia: Women's Missionary Society of the United Lutheran Church in America, 1928.

Malik, Yogendra K. *South Asian Intellectuals and Social Change: A Study of the Role of Vernacular-Speaking Intelligentsia*. New Delhi: Heritage Publishers, 1982.

Manly, F.P. "The New Day in India" in *Missions: American Baptist International Magazine*, November, 1923, 598.

Munson, Arley. *Jungle Days: Being the Experiences of an American Woman Doctor in India*. New York: Appleton & Co., 1913.

Protchard, John. *Methodists and their Missionary Society, 1900–1996*. New York: Ashgate, 2014.

Rajagopal, Vakulabharanam. "Fashioning Modernity in Telugu: Viresalingam and His Interventionist Strategy," *Studies in History* 21:1 (2005): 45–77.

Ramakrishna, V. *Social Reform in Andhra: 1848–1919*. New Delhi: Vikas Publishing House, 1983.

Robert, Dana. *American Women in Mission: A Social History of Their Theory and Practice*. Macon, GA: Mercer University Press, 1984.

Sackett, Frank Colyer. *Posnett of Medak*. London: Cargate Press, 1951.

Swavely, Clarence Hess, ed. *One Hundred Years in the Andhra Country: A History of the India Mission of the United Lutheran Church in America*. Madras: The Diocesan Press, 1942.

Taneti, James Elisha. *Caste, Gender and Christianity in Colonial India: Telugu Women in Mission*. New York: Palgrave MacMillan, 2013.

Taneti, James Elisha. *Telugu Christians: A History*. Minneapolis, MN: Fortress Press, 2022.

Thurston, Edgar. *Castes and Tribes of Southern India*. Vol. 4. Madras: Government Press, 1909.

Whitehead, Henry. *Village Gods of South India*. New York: Oxford University Press, 1916.

5 Shifting Power Equations for Women in the Catholic Charismatic Renewal

Savio Abreu S. J.

Introduction

Many of the works on Indian Christianity are written more from the perspective of "theoretical" religion involving creed, doctrines and dogmas, and theology rather than from the perspective of "practical" religion that focuses on the concrete ways and means by which religion is lived by the masses in their everyday lives. As a result, many studies on Indian Christianity are textual and theoretical in nature and written from a theological perspective that tends to overlook the deep divisions and fissures and the intra-church conflicts that have beset Indian Christianity for centuries. My article on the changing power equations and ideas of democratization for women in the Indian church explores among other themes dichotomy between "believed religion" and "lived religion" in the context of the Pentecostal-Charismatic movement that has emerged and grown in global Christianity, which is the theme I have explored in my last book.[1] In this chapter, I look at the new possibilities for power and spaces of liberation that the Pentecostal-Charismatic movement has opened up in the male-dominated church for traditionally marginalized communities like women, while acknowledging the gender paradox that exists in the movement. The Pentecostal-Charismatic movement is often viewed by the lower sections of society as a means of asserting themselves and gaining power and social privileges. According to Bayly (1989), conversion in the lower castes was not so much an attempt to avoid caste-based disabilities as it was to create a ritual arena, which allowed them to improve their social status within the region's wider caste hierarchy of ritual purity and pollution by adopting a Christian caste life-style. Thus, apart from analyzing the Pentecostal-Charismatic movement as a protest movement in the Church that contested and challenged the traditional historical denominations, we shall also study how they are viewed by the disadvantaged sections of society as a means of upward social mobility and increasing democratization of Indian Christianity.

While the literature on Pentecostalism is constantly on the rise, they mostly focus on Western societies and are predominantly from a theological perspective. There is a dearth of well-researched studies that critically analyze the phenomenon of Pentecostal-Charismatic Christianity in India. The mainline historic Churches with their long history and well-documented written traditions are amenable to theological studies from the perspective of "theoretical" religion, unlike the new Christian groups like those belonging to Pentecostal-Charismatic Christianity, which stress on oral tradition and experience and neither have a long history nor keep proper written records. Also, given the secretive nature of most of these groups who are constantly jostling in a limited religious market space, they are rather cautious about sharing information with outsiders. In such a scenario, an anthropological study of religion from the perspective of "lived" religion that focuses on the concrete ways and means by which beliefs and doctrines are lived out by the adherents in their day to day lives is preferred over merely a theological understanding of religion. For example, my study of the rite of baptism among neo-Pentecostals through participant observation and interviews with the newly baptized members brought out several notions and symbolisms of baptism that add to the theological interpretation of baptism.[2]

My study in trying to understand Pentecostal-Charismatic Christianity in Goa as a rapidly expanding and overtly evangelistic movement within the pluralistic Goan society focuses on division and conflict in the religious space in Goa and thus explores the link between religion and violence in social, religious, and physical spaces. This conflict is not just between the Pentecostal-Charismatic groups that are at the periphery of the religious space in Goa and other religious communities that occupy the mainstream of religion in Goa, but are often found within the church itself between the conservatives and the liberals, the erstwhile elites, and the marginalized groups, often due to the unfulfilled project of transforming the church into a democratic institution that provides equal status and dignity to all without any discrimination whatsoever.

The mainline churches that are patriarchal and hierarchal in nature have traditionally denied space to lower castes, women, and other disadvantaged communities in their rituals. In Goa, after conversion the village Church has replaced village temples as the focus of the socio-religious life of the community and has become the center of the relations of power and hierarchy within the Catholic community (Robinson 1998). Bayly, quoting from David Mosse, identifies ways in which Christianity has become embedded in the indigenous social and religious order of the locality of a Hindu-Christian village in South India (1992: 5,6). Thus, the Church articulates, maintains, and redefines these relations based on caste status, gender roles, and ownership of land or control within the local panchayat. The conflict among the Catholics of Cuncolim over *Confraria* membership and the roles of the members of different castes is an example of how the Church redefined caste relations in Cuncolim (Newman 2001: 141–142). The Church, acting in a tough manner through the Archbishop of Goa, closed the Cuncolim Church and forced the Catholic *Gauncars*[3] to relinquish their exclusive control over the *Confraria*, in the process opening the membership to Church associations and organizations to all Catholics irrespective of caste, sex, or age.

The Catholic Church makes a distinction between the universal priesthood of all the faithful and the ministerial priesthood which is exclusively meant for males.[4] That is why when Pope Francis washed and kissed the feet of two young women at the Casal del Marmo, a juvenile detention facility in Rome during the Holy Thursday liturgy on 28 March 2013, it sparked a furious debate among some conservatives and liturgical purists, who lamented that the pope had set a questionable example. No pope has ever washed the feet of a woman before, and Pope Francis' gesture was a dramatic departure from church rules that restrict the Holy Thursday ritual to men. All the previous popes have carried out the Holy Thursday liturgy in Rome's grand St. John Lateran basilica, choosing 12 priests to represent the 12 apostles whose feet Christ washed during the Last Supper before his crucifixion. So, Pope Francis' gesture of including women in his inaugural Holy Thursday Mass as pope was remarkable and very unconventional, given that current liturgical rules exclude women from this important ritual of the Catholic Church.

History of the Catholic Charismatic Renewal in Goa

The history of any religious movement generally reflects the perspective and the bias of the dominant group of that movement. In the case of Pentecostal history writing and Pentecostal historiography, voices from around the world have been ignored by earlier Pentecostal historians originating mainly from the US, who were biased in favor of the West, the US, and white males. Women and indigenous people who carried the message and transformed it into something indigenous to various cultures have been overlooked, marginalized, or forgotten altogether. It is only in recent years that these voices, which have not been heard previously, are increasingly involved in the worldwide discussions on the origin and history of Pentecostalism and have challenged and, in some cases, even set aside the findings of earlier historians.[5]

Pentecostalism began as an interracial movement, attracting people from all over the nation, regardless of race and boasting of a much higher proportion of women than any other form of Christianity at the time, white bishops and black workers, Asians and Mexicans, white professors and black laundry women mixed equally, while white Church leaders were ready to have hands laid on them in a community led by Blacks (Hollenweger 1986: 5). When the Assemblies of God, the largest Pentecostal denomination in the world today, was formed in 1914, a third of its ministers and two-thirds of its missionaries were women (Anderson 2004: 274). But social pressure soon prompted the emerging Pentecostal Churches to get segregated into black and white organizations just as most of the other Churches had done and the promotion of the ministry of women practically disappeared in the later Pentecostal movement.

The global Pentecostal-Charismatic movement which began with the classical Pentecostal movement from the late 19thcentury onward has seen many waves and shifts and the emergence of various groups. One of the later waves in this movement led to the entry of Pentecostalism in the 1960s in the mainline Protestant churches and also within the Catholic church, and this wave was rechristened as the Charismatic Renewal. Pentecostalism within the Catholic church, which came to be known as the Catholic Charismatic Renewal (henceforth CCR), first came to India through Minoo Engineer, a Parsi civil engineer who had converted to Christianity, and his Puerto Rican wife Luz Maria, the Pentecostalized couple who returned from USA to Bombay in February 1972 (Abreu 2020: 49). Individuals and teams from the Charismatic groups in Bombay were invited to other dioceses for retreats and so the CCR began spreading rapidly throughout the country.

Like the classical Pentecostal movement, the CCR in Goa began not with clerics or theologians, but with Mrs. Teresa Muniz, a housewife from the village of Aldona in north Goa, who had gone to East Africa and had an experience of the Charismatic Renewal there. She came back with stories of people being touched by the Holy Spirit. One of her neighbors, Fr. James D'Souza, who was actively involved in the Charismatic movement in Bombay, had come down for holidays and suggested to Teresa that they could have a prayer meeting in her house. She contacted a few friends and the first Charismatic prayer meeting in Goa was held in Aldona in 1974. In the same week, another prayer meeting was held in her friend Mrs. Phyllis Dias' house in the town of Mapusa, around 8 km from Aldona. While the Aldona prayer group discontinued after some years, the Mapusa group has continued to function vibrantly and is the oldest existing prayer group of the CCR in Goa. Initially all the members of the Mapusa group were women, mainly housewives. While the first meeting was conducted by Fr. James D'Souza, very often the prayer meetings were managed by the lay people themselves. They would conduct the praise and worship and some among them even gave talks on different spiritual topics. In many ways Phyllis, the founding leader of the group, can be regarded as the mother of the Charismatic movement in Goa. Phyllis and some others from Goa attended the first National Charismatic Convention held at St. Mary's School grounds, Bombay in December, 1974. She played a crucial role in the forming of the Goa Service Team (henceforth GST), the regional body that oversees all Catholic Charismatic phenomena in the state of Goa, and became its first chairperson from 1978 to 1981.

Most of the early Charismatics were from urban, English-educated middle-class backgrounds and so all the early Charismatic prayer groups were urban, English-speaking groups. The diversity and de facto pluralism of religious traditions in cities, the density of populations, and the patterns of first-generation immigration to cities have made American urban locations places of religious vitality, creative adaptation and cultural synthesis according to a study by Rhys Williams (2005). His analysis shows that changes across space (geographic mobility) and the changes over time (adaptation, pluralism, and assimilation) produce new religious forms and this explains why the Catholic Charismatic movement, whether in USA or India or Goa, all originated in cities. While the history of the CCR in Goa reflects an increased role and special prominence for women in the movement, it appears to be mainly for urban, English-speaking, middle-class women. But that is not the case as the Charismatic movement in Goa spread to rural areas and the first Konkani prayer group was started in the village of Merces[6] in 1982, by a teacher from Panjim, Ms. Alzira Antao. Alzira had entered the Renewal in 1978 and was attending the prayer meetings of the Aldona prayer group which was started by Teresa Muniz. She felt God telling her repeatedly, "Alzira, look after my sheep".[7] So, she collected all the Catholic housewives in Merces and thus the Merces prayer group began.

But over the years the numbers of the Merces group declined, apparently due to lack of leadership in the group and lack of support from the parish priest. Then in 1992, Flora Rodrigues, a housewife from Merces, was chosen as the leader of the group. She already had experience of the Charismatic Renewal before marriage and with the support of the parish priest and another female Charismatic she was able to revive the prayer group. Though Flora was only a housewife with education up to SSC, her charismatic personality combined with a natural gift of teaching and preaching helped her to lead the group successfully for nearly eight years during which the group increased substantially. The CCR over the years has spread to most of the parishes in the archdiocese of Goa and Daman and nearly 95% of the groups in Goa are parish-based and Konkani-speaking, while more than 75% of the groups are rural based.[8] The history of the Pentecostal-Charismatic movement, whether it is classical Pentecostalism from the late 19thcentury onward or the emergence of the Charismatic Renewal in the mainline churches in the 1960s or the CCR in Goa from 1974 reflects an increased role for women in the religious sphere. The spread of the CCR to rural parts of Goa and the prominence of rural women in this spread highlight how the Charismatic movement has thrust rural women out from the kitchen into the male-dominated public domain.

Demography of the Catholic Charismatic Renewal in Goa: Gendered Perspectives

The demographic data that is presented here is taken from my field work, where a questionnaire was administered to 362 respondents chosen by random sampling and representing all the four zones and from 13 different sectors of the CCR (Abreu 2020: 61). Thus, the findings of the questionnaire present a representative socioeconomic profile of the CCR in Goa, which includes all the members of the prayer groups registered under the GST, the prayer groups and independent ministries which do not come under the GST and the large number of Catholics who are not attached to any prayer group, but who consider themselves as Charismatics. Among the 362 respondents, 319 were women (86.5%) while 49 were men (13.5%), but this numerical dominance is not reflected in the decision-making and governing bodies of the CCR. The GST is the center, the spider of the web-like organization of the CCR in Goa. It coordinates and regulates all the activities of the CCR in Goa. In the GST, which was elected in September 2006, there were only two women out of the 11 members. In 2007, out of the 23 sector leaders, only nine were women. In the 35-year old history of the CCR in Goa only two women have been elected chairperson of the GST. All the remaining 11 chairpersons have been men.[9] The names of the various chairpersons of the GST over the years given below reflect the miniscule presence of women in the decision-making structures of the CCR:

1978–1981	Mrs. Phyllis Dias
1981–1983	Mr. Anthony Correia
1983–1984	Captain Louis Mendonca
1984–1986	Bro. Mulligan
1986–1989	Bro. Mulligan
1989–1991	Mr. Francis Menezes
1991–1993	Dr. Noemia Mascarenhas
1993–1995	Mr. Jorim Mendonca
1995–1997	Mr. Francisco Dias
1997–2000	Mr. Jorim Mendonca
2000–2003	Mr. Savio Mascarenhas
2003–2006	Mr. Savio Mascarenhas
2006	Mr. Eric Correia

The preponderance of women in the CCR is in keeping with the demographic trend of Christians in Goa, whose sex ratio of 1129 women per 1000 men is much higher than the Hindus (929) and Muslims (905) (Census of India 1991). The feminine character of the CCR is also found in other parts of India. While conducting research in Pune on Pentecostals, Chad Bauman attended a prayer meeting of the CCR and found the group to be very feminine with women in the group asking more questions than men and many of them were clearly recognized as leaders (Bauman 2015: 72–3). The feminine nature of the CCR has also led to teenagers and youth keeping away from the movement. Table 5.1 shows that only 7% of the Catholic Charismatics in Goa are 30 years and below, while Table 5.2 shows that the overwhelming majority of the respondents are married, around 82%. One reason for the low percentage of youth is that the CCR in Goa right from the beginning, deliberately or inadvertently projected an image of being a family-oriented, pious religious movement and so appears to have mainly attracted "pious" married women. According to Mrs. Phyllis, the founding leader of the Mapusa prayer group, all the members of the Mapusa group initially were women and mainly housewives. As the present data shows, the CCR has a preponderance of married women and so predominantly caters to issues related to piety, religiosity, family and marriage. This type of a profile has kept teenagers, youth and singles away from the movement.

Table 5.1 Age-wise Distribution of Catholic Charismatics in Goa

Age	Frequency	Percentage
Blank	4	(1.1%)
Up to 20 years	7	(1.9%)
21–30 years	18	(5%)
31–40 years	37	(10.2%)
41–50 years	86	(23.8%)
51–60 years	123	(34%)
61 and above	87	(24%)
Total	362	100%

Source: Abreu 2020: 62.

Table 5.2 Marital Status of Catholic Charismatics in Goa

Marital Status	Frequency	Percentage
Married	298	82.3
Single	40	11.0
Divorced	1	0.3
Widowed	23	6.4
Total	362	100.0

Source: Abreu 2020: 62.

Table 5.3 reveals that more than 71 % of the respondents are homemakers, assuming the 42 female blank entries most likely indicate household work. And if we take into consideration those involved in domestic work and those retired, then three-fourths of the members are located in the domestic sphere. A comparison of the work participation rate (the percentage of total workers to total population) of the Catholic Charismatics with that of the general population of Goa reveals some interesting gender variations, which could explain the paucity of women in the decision-making bodies of the CCR. While the male and female work participation rates for the state of Goa are 54.6% and 22.4% respectively in the 2001 census, the respective figures for the Charismatics are 67.3% and 13.5% (Abreu 2020: 64). Thus, Charismatic men are five times more involved in economically productive work than the women, the majority of whom are homemakers. The preponderance of women in the domestic sphere coupled with the high working rate of men in the public sphere could provide an explanation as to why so few leaders in the CCR are women.

CCR: Redefining Power Equations and Opening up Spaces of Liberation for Women

Though the CCR in Goa is dominated by women with 86.5% of the Catholic Charismatics in Goa being female, this numerical dominance is not reflected

Table 5.3 Gender-wise Occupation of Catholic Charismatics in Goa

Occupation of respondent	Male		Female	
	Frequency	Percentage	Frequency	Percentage
Blank, N.A.	5	1.4	42	11.6
Homemakers	1	0.3	215	59.4
Tailor	0	0	2	0.6
Agriculture	0	0	2	0.6
Service (Doctor, banker, engineer, teacher, etc.)	22	6.1	24	6.6
Domestic work	0	0	5	1.4
Business	6	1.7	3	0.8
Retired	8	2.2	7	1.9
Student	2	0.6	6	1.7
Artist (musician)	1	0.3	2	0.6
Full-time Evangelist	1	0.3	1	0.3
Social worker	2	0.6	4	1.1
Cook	1	0.3	0	0

Source: Abreu 2020: 63.

in the decision-making and governing bodies of the CCR. While the power relations in the CCR is skewed in favor of men, with few women involved in decision-making structures, it is also true that the Charismatic movement has brought rural women out from the domestic sphere to the public domain. The CCR has provided liberation for its female members from the sense of exclusion that they have experienced in the predominantly male Church ritual. It has provided the space and the door for women to enter into the mainstream of Catholicism. The following two case studies from my field work among the Catholic Charismatics in Goa provide examples of women who through participation in the CCR have acquired a certain degree of power, status, recognition and liberation in the patriarchal public religious sphere.

Case 1. Ms. Alzira Antao, the Mother of the Konkani Charismatic Renewal in Goa

She is 74 years old and an unmarried, retired school teacher. She has been a teacher all her life and has taught in different government schools. One of the schools she taught in was the government primary school in Merces and that is where she started the Merces Charismatic prayer group, the first Konkani prayer group in Goa. She has been involved with the Renewal since 1978 and can be rightly called the mother of the Konkani Charismatic Renewal in Goa. Alzira was born and brought up in Panjim, though her parents were from Benaulim, Salcete.

As an ordinary school teacher involved in the Charismatic Renewal, she had no ambitions to take up leadership, but she felt God telling her repeatedly "to open a group and teach my people". So she collected all the women in Merces who were willing and interested to experience Jesus and to know about the Holy Spirit. Her Konkani was not very good and she would tell the people that hers was Portuguese Konkani. Around the same time, a woman named Olga opened a Charismatic group in the neighboring Santa Cruz village and requested Alzira to help her. Alzira was already busy since she was teaching in an English medium school though her education was in Portuguese. Thus, besides the effort of learning English and teaching it to the students, she got the additional work of studying the Konkani Bible and teaching the Santa Cruz and Merces prayer groups. At around the same time, she attended a Bible course conducted by a Jesuit scripture scholar. She got completely confused by the different quotations and found it difficult to grasp the Bible, but that course gave her the necessary confidence and she started learning the scriptures by reading and memorizing. She also began attending many other Bible courses.

The news about the Charismatic movement spread rapidly and soon there was lot of demand for Konkani retreats. So, Alzira got together some other Charismatic members and started the Konkani retreats in different places in Goa. Since many of the people to whom she gave these Life-in-the-Spirit retreats belonged to the Gauda and Kunbi communities (tribal communities) and did not know to read or write, she would write the Bible quotations on the board. She also prepared a lot of material in the form of charts, pictures, paintings, and other visuals to teach these Gaudas. She walked miles and miles to different villages in Goa to give Charismatic Konkani retreats to the people. In the 1980s it was unheard of for a woman, especially a lay person, to be actively involved in the public domain of religion, teaching Christian doctrine to villagers, both men and women. The fact that she spoke Portuguese well and was from the city of Panjim gave her an exalted status among the simple village folk and they addressed her as "sister".

She also got the status of being a "holy woman" due to the following incidents: she used to go to Neura Church every day for proclamation of gospel during the novenas. Before the novena she would spend time praying in the Church before the Blessed Sacrament. She was praying for a miracle for the people. She asked for the Holy Spirit and suddenly water fell on the altar like a fountain gushing down. Another time she laid her hands on a child who was sick and the child became all right. Due to such miracles people began to come to her and ask her to pray over them. Through such powerful signs she was able to exercise Foucault's pastoral power by convincing the people who came to her that she was able to perform miracles in their lives and thus lead them on the path of eternal salvation.[10] While analyzing the political and cultural meaning of a miracle that occurred in Velim, Goa, Newman (2001: 147–163) interprets miracles and visions as a powerful tool that can mobilize people and focus their aspirations, especially those long powerless and long exploited. Stirrat (1992) related demonic possession to gender roles saying that possession is not just a manifestation of the subordinate role of women, but it is also a means through which such subordination is produced. Alzira, a lay woman, by performing miracles and healing people who were sick or possessed by evil spirits challenged the subordinate role of women in the religious sphere and made a case for superior identity and higher status.

Besides starting new prayer groups, Alzira also occupied several positions in the Charismatic Renewal. Due to her long and active involvement in the Renewal she came into contact with several well-known Charismatic evangelists and got a chance to go to Rome in 1988 and meet the pope. An ordinary school teacher with elementary Portuguese education, who taught in government schools all her life, through her involvement in the Charismatic movement was able to appropriate Foucault's pastoral power and thus influence the lives of many village folk in Goa. She is therefore highly regarded as "Sister", "Holy woman", and the mother of the Konkani Charismatic movement. This case study illustrates how the CCR has facilitated the movement of women from the domestic sphere to the public sphere and has provided them with certain amount of power, autonomy and liberation in the patriarchal church. This shift in the power equations of women in the CCR leading to increased democratization and more say in the decision-making processes of the Catholic Church in Goa is further illustrated by the following case study.

Case 2. Ms. Flory Rodrigues: From Housewife to Leader of a Charismatic Prayer Group

Flory, a married, 41-year-old housewife, with two daughters, has been in the Charismatic Renewal for the last 17 years and was also a leader of the Merces Prayer group. Before her marriage, she was part of a Charismatic group led by the well-known Charismatic preacher Fr. Savio Gama. He had at that time prophesized that Flory would start a Charismatic prayer group. When Flory joined the Merces prayer group, it was going through tough times and hardly anyone was coming for the prayer meetings. With the support of the parish priest and another woman, Flory was able to revive the prayer group and the membership gradually increased. In 1992, when they had elections, she was chosen as the leader and remained as the leader till 2000, when she was advised bed-rest due to the delivery of her daughter. This housewife, with only secondary schooling and despite her household duties and family responsibilities, learnt how to study the bible and comprehend the word of God. She was guided and counselled in learning the Bible by the Merces parish priest, who taught her how to change her life.

Initially, as the leader of the prayer group, all the group work used to fall on her. As the leader she had to arrange for people to go for different Charismatic meetings and programmes. People were reluctant to go and often she had to go alone for these meetings and programmes. Only because her in-laws and husband supported her involvement in the CCR by looking after the children when she was out, she was able to take part in these activities. Through the Life-in-the-Spirit seminars and other Charismatic programmes Flory learnt a lot and was able to persuade many people to join the prayer group. She also has a natural flair for preaching and teaching and is able to convince people using persuasive arguments and formulating reasonable and plausible explanations. For example, initially many of the Catholic women would not come to the Charismatic prayer meetings because they were offended by the clapping and dancing. Flory explained this practice in the following innovative manner: "If a minister comes here will you not clap? Then what about Jesus, who is the biggest minister, the king of kings? Why should we feel shy about clapping and dancing to him in our prayer meetings?" Besides her responsibility as group leader, the parish priest also made her a Eucharistic minister (one who assists the priest during liturgical services by distributing communion) and she was also elected to the Parish Pastoral Council of Merces. According to Foucault, power is multidirectional operating from top-down and also from bottom-top and this is seen in the case of Flory, who despite being only a housewife was able to influence and impact many people in her prayer group, her parish and the wider Charismatic movement in Goa.

Despite being only a housewife she was able to exercise power in the family by inculcating the Charismatic dispositions in her family members through various practices like reading and explaining the Bible, teaching Charismatic ideas and making them all do "praise and worship", the Pentecostal style of prayer. Often her husband would get frustrated in his work and complain that God is not answering their prayers and is sending evil on them, but she would correct him by telling him that God does not send evil on them. She taught him that it is due to their sins that pain and suffering comes on them. Also, in her natal family all her three brothers were unemployed. She taught them the Bible and all three began reading the Bible regularly and subsequently all of them got employed. Thus, this housewife Flory got power and recognition through the CCR as a lay religious leader in the public religious sphere. She was entrusted with important responsibilities in the Charismatic movement and in the parish Church and has been able to realize and develop her natural gifts of preaching, teaching and leadership, which she would not have been able to do so in the liturgical rituals of the Catholic Church.

While the above two case studies illustrate how the CCR has facilitated the movement of women from the domestic sphere to the public domain and provided them with certain amount of power and liberation in the male-dominated church, we notice the "gender paradox" that exists in the Pentecostal-Charismatic movement and which has been analyzed by many researchers of Pentecostalism (Martin 2002: 169). Though both the CCR and the neo-Pentecostal groups reveal a high prevalence of female members, the construction of social and ritual life on biblical precedent implies that the office of the pastorate and other leadership roles are predominantly male-controlled and women are excluded from them. Early Pentecostalism taught that the same Spirit who anointed men also empowered women. The use of women with charismatic gifts was widespread throughout the Pentecostal world. This resulted in a much higher proportion of women in Pentecostal ministry than in the historic Churches which barred women from entering the ministry (Anderson 2004: 273).

However, the early emphasis on the ministry of women reduced later in Classical Pentecostal missions and the importance of the experience of Spirit baptism in the lives of female ministers had to take second place to the general patriarchal structure of Church and society (Ibid: 275). This patriarchal bias is seen in the Indian Pentecostal Church of God (IPC), wherein there are no women pastors due to cultural reasons. The faithful at the grass root level do not accept a woman as a pastor. Similarly, there are no women pastors in New Frontiers International[11] (NFI) and in my field work I never came across any female neo-Pentecostal pastor in Goa. Neo-Pentecostal women help out in various ministries related to charity, couples, or children, and the significant women in the Church are normally the pastors' wives. Most of the wives of pastors are actively involved in ministry work but in the NFI Church women are not allowed to preach or become part of the group of elders. According to Hollenweger (1972: 487), the pastor's wife often has greater intellectual gifts than her husband, but is the gentle, tender, brave but submissive helpmate of her husband. The pastor of the NFI Church, Panjim, while preaching about the qualities that elders of the church should possess, said

> I love women and have no quarrel with them, but the Bible is so very clear that leadership role in the church is for men alone. In today's world there is a fight for equality between man and woman, but there is an order in the church of God which does not change because of the culture today.
>
> (Abreu 2020: 195)

Since the written word of God is equivocal, the neo-Pentecostal groups selectively choose certain biblical passages, especially from the letters of St. Paul that define the role of women as belonging to the domestic sphere and not in Church leadership, while ignoring passages that have revolutionary potential in their interpretation of gender roles.

Women can lead Praise and Worship, make announcements, give testimonies, make intercessions, help in organizing the hall, teach in Sunday Catechism school, prepare, and serve coffee and snacks at the end of the Sunday service, but the NFI believes that biblical evidence[12] points to God ordaining men to lead and so women cannot become pastors. While the official position of the NFI Church is clear-cut and categorical, the views of the members of the NFI Church, whom I interviewed, are divided. The majority view is that God made men to lead and so women cannot become pastors. The minority view holds that the choice of a woman pastor is a grey area.

They agree that according to the word of God a woman cannot be a pastor, but times are changing and if God decides, he can raise up a woman to become a pastor. On the other hand, the process of imbibing patriarchal values enshrined in their New Testament model is noticed in all the women I interviewed who readily agreed with the majority view that women cannot become pastors. One woman said, "If women lead prayer cells with men in it, then men have to submit to the authority of women, which is not biblically correct" (Abreu 2020: 196). The Charismatic *habitus* embodies biblical text into social practices, resulting in the dispositions and biases of the society of the New Testament shaping the neo-Pentecostal discourse on patriarchy more than the gender sensitization of contemporary society.

Conclusion

In this chapter, I have analyzed the new vistas for power and democratic spaces of liberation that the Pentecostal-Charismatic movement has opened up in the male-dominated church for traditionally marginalized communities like women, while acknowledging the gender paradox that exists in the movement. The history of the Pentecostal-Charismatic movement, especially the spread of the CCR to rural parts of Goa, highlights how the Charismatic movement has thrust rural women out from the kitchen into the male-dominated religious sphere. The two cases of Catholic Charismatic women highlight the liberating space, though rather limited and still regulated, provided by the CCR for women to enter into the predominantly male Church ritual. One woman, an ordinary Government school teacher with no religious or theological training, through her involvement in the Charismatic Renewal was able to reach out to so many village folk in Goa through the Life-in-the-Spirit retreats and is regarded as the mother of the Konkani Charismatic movement in Goa. The other woman, a housewife with only high school education was able to develop her natural gifts of preaching, teaching and leadership without any formal theological training. She was also entrusted with important responsibilities in the parish and in the Charismatic movement. Like the above two cases, other women in the Pentecostal-Charismatic movement have experienced a partial realignment of gender/hierarchy relations reflected in the opening up of new vistas for power and spaces of liberation in the Church. But we also find a gender paradox in the Pentecostal-Charismatic movement, which on the one hand has a high concentration of female members, but on the other hand, the construction of social and ritual lives on biblical precedent leads to women being excluded from the office of the pastorate and other leadership roles and being assigned the gendered role of housewives assisting the man who is the head of the family. Thus, the attempt of the Pentecostal-Charismatic movement to reform and critique the patriarchal hierarchy of mainstream Catholicism and expand the democratization of Christianity in India has had limited success.

Notes

1 Savio Abreu, *Heaven's Gates and Hell's Flames: A Sociological Study of New Christian Movements in Contemporary Goa*, New Delhi: Oxford University Press, 2020.
2 Several notions of baptism that it is a funeral service, a bridge-burning act, similar to circumcision of the OT, it leads to empowerment of the self, it is different from spirit baptism, etc. are discussed in Abreu 2020: 177–185.
3 Founder member of village community.
4 For a brief description of the Catholic idea of priesthood, see Rahner & Vorgrimler 1983, 411–412.
5 For more details on Pentecostal history writing and Pentecostal historiography, see the works of W. B. Godbey's *Commentary on the New Testament* (1896), Alma White's *Demons and Tongues* (1949), H. J. Stolee's *Speaking in Tongues* (1963), Walter Hollenweger's *The Pentecostals* (1972), Vinson Synan's *The Holiness-Pentecostal Tradition: Charismatic Movements in the Twentieth Century* (1997), and Allan Anderson's *Spreading Fires: The Missionary Nature of Early Pentecostalism* (2007).
6 Merces, just 5 km from the capital city of Panaji, is regarded not as a village but rather an outgrowth of Panaji by the 2001 census, according to which Merces has a population of 11,012, of which Catholics are the majority (Census of India 1991: 12–13).
7 Taken from my interview with Ms. Alzira Antao on 27 August 2008.
8 Taken from *Shalom*, the newsletter of the National Catholic Charismatic Renewal Services, Goa Branch.
9 All this data about the CCR is taken from various issues of *Shalom*.
10 Foucault's understanding of pastoral power, an old power technique which originated in Christian institutions, is that it is salvation-oriented, as opposed to political power; it is oblative (offered to a god) as opposed to the principle of sovereignty; it is individualizing as opposed to legal power; it is coextensive and continuous with life; it is linked with production of truth – the truth of the individual himself. For more details on Foucault's pastoral power, see Abreu 2020: 209.
11 New Frontiers International founded by Terry Virgo is part of the 'New Churches' movement, which is the fastest growing and largest Pentecostal-Charismatic Church group in the UK with over 400,000 affiliates (Anderson 2004: 157).
12 Texts like 1Timothy 2: 11–15; 3:1–13 are quoted to justify their patriarchal system.

References

Abreu, Savio. 2020. *Heaven's Gates and Hell's Flames: A Sociological Study of New Christian Movements in Contemporary Goa*. New Delhi: Oxford University Press.

Anderson, Allan. 2004. *An Introduction to Pentecostalism: Global Charismatic Christianity*. Cambridge: Cambridge University Press.

Bauman, Chad. 2015. *Pentecostals, Proselytisation, and Anti-Christian Violence in Contemporary India*. New York: Oxford University Press.

Bayly, Susan. 1989. *Saints, Goddesses and Kings: Muslims and Christians in South Indian Society 1700–1900*. Cambridge: Cambridge University Press.

Census of India. 1991. *District Census Hand Book-North Goa, Part XII-A & B*. Goa: Directorate of Census Operations.

Hollenweger, Walter. 1972. *The Pentecostals*. London: SCM Press Ltd.

Hollenweger, Walter. 1986. 'After Twenty Years' Research on Pentecostalism,' *International Review of Mission* 75(297): 3–13.

Martin, David. 2002. *Pentecostalism: The World Their Parish*. Oxford: Blackwell Publishers.

Newman, R. S.2001. *Of Umbrellas, Goddesses & Dreams: Essays on Goan Culture and Society*. Mapusa, Goa: Other India Press.

'Pope Francis Washes Women's Feet in Break with Church Law,' 2013. *Deccan Herald Newspaper*, March 29, https://www.deccanherald.com/content/322414/pope-francis-washes-womens-feet.html, accessed on April 5, 2021.

Rahner, Karl and Herbert Vorgrimler. 1983. *Concise Theological Dictionary*. 2nd Edition. London: Burns & Oates.

Robinson, Rowena. 1998. *Conversion, Continuity and Change: Lived Christianity in Southern Goa*. New Delhi: Sage Publications.

Stirrat, R. L. 1992. *Power and Religiosity in a Post-Colonial Setting: Sinhala Catholics in Contemporary Sri Lanka*. Cambridge: Cambridge University Press.

Williams, Rhys H.2005. 'Introduction to a Forum on Religion and Place,' *Journal for the Scientific Study of Religion* 44(3): 239–242.

6 Can Catholic Religious Women Democratize the Indian Church?

Pushpa Joseph

Do catholic nuns in India contribute to the democratization process of the Indian church and society? Are they transformative and autonomous agents or are they merely victims of patriarchal inscriptions? Catholic nuns in India confront numerous challenges that stem from gendered socialization, patriarchal inscriptions, societal expectations, ecclesial norms, and theological concepts. These factors significantly impact their lives and limit their autonomy within the Church and religious life. Recent studies have shed light on the extent of these challenges and their implications for the growth and empowerment of women religious in India. However, this does not mean that they are merely victims. Through their endeavors in various areas, Catholic nuns in India emerge as transformative agents within the Church and society. They actively promote empowerment through education, empowering individuals and communities through their dedicated initiatives. Additionally, they advocate for social justice, amplifying the voices of marginalized communities and working toward building a more equitable society. By fostering grassroots participation, and sustainable practices, they ensure that marginalized perspectives are included in decision-making processes. While our contemporary sense of democracy has been heavily influenced by notions of success and efficiency prevalent in today's productivity-driven culture, a Christian Social democracy necessitates a broader perspective. It entails embodying an ethos where effectiveness becomes an all-encompassing way of life, prioritizing the dignity and wellbeing of every individual, especially those who have been marginalized. This chapter argues that the profound efforts of Catholic nuns in India exemplify this ethos, serving as a testament to the transformative power of a Christian Social democracy rooted in sustainability. Recognizing and accepting the autonomy and leadership potential of women religious is crucial for harnessing their transformative power to benefit the Church and society at large.

This chapter builds upon existing literature and incorporates the insights of 16 women religious who were interviewed using a check listed questionnaire. These interviews represent a diverse group of women[1] from four religious congregations, including formators, social workers, rural health workers, and teachers/principals. The respondents were selected through

DOI: 10.4324/9781003426035-9

random sampling and covered a range of age groups. The findings from these interviews provide valuable firsthand accounts of the challenges faced by women religious in India and offer insights into their experiences within the context of their specific roles. The study aims to capture a broader understanding of the issues at hand and contribute to a more comprehensive perspective on the lived realities of women religious in India. The chapter commences by providing a brief overview of religious congregations in India, with a particular focus on women religious. It proceeds to examine the various challenges and paradoxes encountered by women religious in India. The subsequent section introduces the theoretical framework utilized in the chapter, followed by an exploration of the contributions made by Catholic nuns to the democratization of the Indian church.

Catholic Women Religious in India – A Short Profile

Catholic religious life has a history of more than nine centuries in India. The first religious order which sent its members to the Southern State of Kerala in the mid-13th century was an Italian Franciscan Order of men religious. Though, this first group did not see continuity due to various reasons, a strong presence of religious men and women in the Indian soil was evident by the early 16th century after the arrival of major congregations like the Franciscans and the Dominicans[2] (Kalapura, 2019). By the end of the 16th century, Jesuits, Augustinians, and others established religious houses in different parts of India. In the year 1680, the Oratorians, the first indigenous congregation was founded in Goa. From the middle of the 19th century, the number of international congregations and some indigenous congregations of men and women religious started increasing in the Indian soil. Today, there are more than 400 congregations of religious in different parts of India of which nearly 50% are of Indian origin. The total number of members in all these religious congregations together is more than 1,40,000, and the largest share of the Church's ministerial work is being carried out by religious men and women[3] (Vallipalam 2001).

Women religious form the backbone of the Church in India. Despite the increasing challenges, they continue to be a manifestation of the vitality of the Church in different parts of our country.[4] According to statistical data, the number of women religious in the country are approximately 1,22,000 belonging to around 350 congregations.[5] The 2011 census (the last census held) states that Christianity in India has 29 million followers, constituting 2.3% of India's population. Women religious form approximately 0.1 million of the Christian population. As stated in *Redemptoris Missio*,[6] they become a sign of God's love in the Indian society through their works of building unity, reconciliation, forging bonds of solidarity among the least, and their healing care for the rural poor[7] (Vallipalam 2001). Throughout the history of the global Church, women religious have often played a vital role as agents of internal critique, challenging the Church and society when they veer toward compromising with worldly ways. This holds true for women religious in India as well, as highlighted by Raj (2019).[8] The immense contributions of Indian nuns to the nation's development cannot be overstated. However, there is a prevailing sentiment among them, expressed by Sr. Nirmalini Nazareth AC, the president of the Conference of Women Religious, India,[9] that while they have the power to transform others, they are not fully aware of their own power. In light of this realization, there is a growing recognition of the need to empower sisters to become more assertive and maintain their dignity while playing creative and influential roles within the Church.[10]

Challenges before the Catholic Religious Women in India

In a groundbreaking study commissioned by the Conference of Religious India (CRI) Women, Dr. Hazel D'Lima, Cletus Zuzarte, and Pallavi Xalxo[11] shed light on the challenges faced by Catholic nuns within the Indian church. The study highlights the absence of respect, prevalence of clericalism, and mistreatment experienced by women religious. Issues such as property disputes, unequal wages, harassment, negative criticism, and denial of sacraments underscore the violations of human rights they face. Sr. Noella D'Souza, MCJ, an organizer of the study, attributes the low status of religious women to the patriarchal and hierarchical system within the Church. The study also exposes bullying, spiritual blackmail, and the eroding of dignity and agency suffered by nuns. These experiences align with Pope Francis' call to confront clericalism and emphasize the importance of mutual respect between clergy and women religious.[12]

Another finding of the study indicates that women in religious communities have assimilated patriarchal beliefs, which hinder their capacity to advocate for themselves and perpetuate gender disparities.[13] Overcoming these beliefs is crucial for women religious to embrace their strength and assertiveness. The limited voice and representation of women religious in Church policies and governance structures further constrain their roles.[14]

The interviews conducted with 16 religious women as part of this study provide supporting evidence for the internalization of patriarchy among women religious. Only three respondents raised concerns about patriarchy and gendered rules. This suggests a potential lack of awareness or critical engagement with these issues within the larger religious community. In India, the influence of religion strongly shapes the mindset of its adherents, particularly women who are socialized in a gendered manner. Indian women religious, being devout followers of their faith, tend to internalize these norms and values to a greater extent than other segments of the Christian community. Although all 16 respondents had advanced education and held leadership positions in their congregations, they, in general, did not feel the need to critically engage with or question the restrictive interpretation of vows and the exercise of power. Despite their education and leadership roles, 82% of the responses indicated that topics such as democratization, centralization of power, and autonomy were not discussed within their communities. While the respondents expressed dedication to their religious calling and work, their responses suggested that fostering dialogue on structural change and navigating power dynamics may not be a significant concern for the majority of them.

Gayatri Spivak's essay "Can the Subaltern Speak?"[15] raises concerns about marginalized and oppressed groups, referred to as the subaltern, and their ability to voice their experiences within dominant discourse. Their voices are often overshadowed by narratives of the dominant groups, limiting their representation and agency. Spivak critiques the assumption that subaltern groups can easily articulate their struggles within existing linguistic structures shaped by colonial and dominant ideologies. The language used to express subaltern experiences is marginalized or dismissed. Efforts to study and understand subaltern experiences can unintentionally reinforce power dynamics, appropriating their voices without leading to tangible change. These dynamics are reflected in the responses of the study's participants.[16] Within the prevailing neocolonial framework, it is important to examine whether their responses and conversations, as well as the conditions of the religious congregations they belong to, reinforce, and perpetuate neocolonial imperatives of religious dominance. According to Indian feminist theologian Kochurani Abraham[17] (2023), understanding the experiences of women religious within the patriarchal structure of the Indian church requires us to consider the significance of consciousness. It is not an overstatement to say that the majority of these women operate from a conflicting consciousness. Consequently, they face difficulties in challenging the dominance of those who wield religious authority over them. As a result, their behavior adheres to prescribed guidelines set by the dominant group. It is only by transcending these prescribed behaviors that they can truly experience their own unique identity. This requires the application of critical thinking.

Fostering critical thinking is crucial for a healthy democracy and empowering individuals. Paulo Friere[18] (1970) emphasized the role of dialogue in cultivating critical thinking, enabling individuals to recognize the need for change and work toward overcoming oppression. In the training of women religious, there is often a gap in developing critical thinking skills. Emphasis on obedience and conformity may hinder independent thought and critical engagement with the world. By equipping women religious with critical thinking skills, they can better address the complexities of the modern world, contribute to social transformation, and navigate the dynamics of authority within their religious institutions. A holistic approach that integrates intellectual and spiritual formation is needed to enhance the training of women religious and promote their critical thinking abilities. Feminist theologians in Asia and India have critiqued the issue of authority in the formation of women for religious life. Cucci[19] (2020) explores the differences in power dynamics between men and women in religious communities. Male religious often have more openness and autonomy due to their access to orders and pastoral possibilities. This raises questions about power imbalances and structures within women's religious communities. It is important to reevaluate how authority is exercised and distributed, promoting dialogue, participation, and agency for women in decision-making processes.[20] By challenging traditional structures and embracing inclusivity, women's religious communities can create empowering environments that support the growth and flourishing of their members.

One respondent who was interviewed expressed her views regarding authority as it is practiced.[21] She notes:

> Though we speak about decentralization of power and democracy in religious circles in actual practices a vivid pyramidical structure still exists. Actually, in the name of democracy we have some practices but major decisions are imposed and controlled by the authority (centralized). For example, in the local level when we feel the need for something, we study the situation, reflect, discern and plan but the last word is with the centralized authority. Then where is democracy and what is the value for lived experience.[22]

The publication "New Wine in New Wineskins: The Consecrated Life and its Ongoing Challenges since Vatican II",[23] a collection of Vatican documents addressing various aspects of consecrated life, acknowledges the need for community models that align with the feminine identity of consecrated women. It emphasizes the importance of preventing subjection and disparities among women religious. Another respondent in the study, a young woman religious from Central India who recently made her final profession and is currently involved in formation work, explains,

> As a formator many a time I have felt that my autonomy was not respected due to the influence of the experienced formators who were with me in the team. As a result, I had to give up many of my plans and ideas.[24]

In India, despite the commitment of women religious to live out their vocations in line with democratic values, the presence of authoritarian structures hinders their growth. Addressing this gap is crucial to promote the democratization and flourishing of women religious, allowing them to contribute their unique gifts to the Church and society. Despite these challenges, many women religious in India actively work toward making the Indian church and society more democratic. They reject the notion that power and decision-making should be monopolized by a select few and instead advocate for inclusive and participatory structures within the Church and Religious life. Through their commitment to social justice, they challenge existing hierarchies and promote the empowerment of marginalized communities, especially women. These efforts by women religious in India align with the principles of Christian

Social Democracy,[25] which accentuates the significance of inclusive and participatory structures in both the Church and society.

Christian Social Democracy

Christian Social Democracy is a public theology rooted in the fundamental principles of creation, seeking to establish a social order that reflects God's design for human flourishing.[26] It embraces the fundamental principle of equality and prosperity as seen in the *Basileia*[27] vision of Jesus in the gospels employing divine principles to guide social and even political realms. Recognizing the inherent dignity of all individuals as children of God, it seeks to prioritize their holistic wellbeing. Public engagement in Christian Social Democracy is based on the understanding of interconnectedness among individuals, promoting solidarity and rejecting self-interests in isolation. Christian Social Democracy advocates for policies that promote social justice and equality, aiming to create an inclusive and just society. Responsible stewardship of resources, including environmental practices and equitable distribution, is a key aspect of Christian Social Democracy. It values the sanctity of human life at all stages and supports healthcare, education, and social welfare programs and sustainable practices that uplift individuals and communities. Social activism, according to Christian Social Democracy, serves as a means to manifest solidarity and work toward the common good. It calls for an engagement that upholds social justice, alleviates suffering, and promotes human dignity. The commitment to solidarity extends beyond religious communities, influencing decision-making processes to strive for a just and inclusive society for all.

In this framework, the contributions made by Catholic nuns in India serve as a tangible example of the ethos that underpins a Christian Social democracy where effectiveness permeates every aspect of life, including social relationships, economic systems, and the overall wellbeing of individuals and communities. It places value not only on measurable outcomes but also on the inherent dignity and worth of every individual, particularly those who are marginalized. Through their multifaceted roles in education, social work, advocacy, and sustainable practices, they contribute to various dimensions of societal wellbeing. Their efforts aim not only to address immediate challenges but also to foster long-term sustainable change. Beyond their tangible contributions, Catholic nuns in India actively participate in the democratic process and advocate for the rights of the marginalized. Their involvement in such endeavors is deeply rooted in spirituality, which serves as a potent force for personal and collective transformation.[28]

Promoting Education and Empowerment

From the standpoint of Christian Social Democracy, education plays a crucial role in enhancing equality of opportunity with its power to empower individuals, broaden horizons, deepen values, and facilitate meaningful conversations between faith and culture. In the past, when access to education was limited, especially for girls who were often married off at a young age, Catholic nuns played a vital role in bringing education and empowerment to millions of children, women, and immigrants. Their focus was particularly on teaching those on the fringes of society and providing English education, which was often inaccessible to women. One of the key aspects emphasized by women religious in their educational endeavors is value-based education. They believe that educational institutions have a responsibility to cultivate socially responsible and critically literate democratic citizens.[29] In a society where moral decadence is a concern, parents often choose Catholic schools for their daughters because they are dissatisfied with the moral standards in public schools and are concerned about their children's moral development and future public life.[30]

Additionally, women religious in India play a crucial role in empowering marginalized individuals by running special schools for children with disabilities. They recognize the importance of education in achieving social justice and strive to equip these children with the necessary skills to enable them to have a meaningful place in society, thereby fostering equality. These special schools cater to the unique needs of vulnerable children who might have been overlooked by mainstream educational programs.[31] The efforts made by Catholic sisters in admitting sexually exploited children from the slums, many of whom are victims of incest, are particularly significant. Testimonies from alumni of these special schools reveal stories of transformation and empowerment, as these individuals become independent and courageous despite their challenging pasts.[32] "Education for Women's Empowerment" is a central focus shared by numerous congregations of women religious in India. The education provided by women religious instills values of compassion, justice, and social responsibility. Students who have been influenced by the sisters develop a strong sense of empathy and a commitment to making a positive difference in society. They are equipped not only with academic knowledge but also with an ethical compass that guides their actions and inspires them to champion causes of equality and social justice. One of the interlocutors is a woman religious in her late 60s who has dedicated over three decades to education, serving as a principal in three schools within the congregation. She notes:

> Empowerment of women and children, especially the girl child, has been very close to my heart. I accepted to pursue a profession in education when my superiors asked me because I always knew that education is the best tool that can empower especially Indian women. Through various programmes and lectures I have tried consciously to instil in my students a sense of justice and concern for the marginalized. Ensuring that every woman lives in dignity and self-respect is a passion that kept me alive with a sense of mission through my long years of vocation as an educator.[33]

Convent education in India has been subject to both criticism and positive reviews. While some scholars argue that it can reinforce gender stereotypes and perpetuate societal ideologies that subjugate women, other studies highlight the courageous resistance of nuns against patriarchal attitudes within the Catholic Church. One research study titled "Identity Issues of Girls from Single-Sex Convent Schools in India", raises concerns about the hidden curriculum in convent education that may uphold gender norms and restrict women's ability to challenge societal customs[34] (Pandey 2020). This critique suggests that the empowering potential of convent education to challenge and transform social beliefs in Indian society may be limited.

However, there are also studies that shed light on the transformative work of nuns in India. The article "The Indian Mission of the Institute of Blessed Virgin Mary (IBVM) Nuns: Convents, Curriculum, and Indian Women," by Nilanjana Paul (2022) examines the profound impact of Loretto nuns, showcasing their efforts to prepare women for traditional roles while simultaneously empowering them to challenge societal norms and achieve economic independence.[35] This research critically assesses the contributions of the IBVM nuns, highlighting their confrontations with Christian patriarchs and their unwavering dedication in advocating for women's rights. Through a comprehensive analysis, the study illuminates the complex nature of the nuns' endeavors and their role as catalysts for change within a diverse social landscape. Their commitment to justice and empowerment serves as a testament to their efforts in challenging established norms and promoting the advancement of marginalized women in India.

Advocating Social Justice and Human Rights

The ultimate freedom attained through a democratic order lies in safeguarding the freedom of others. Catholic women religious in India play a vital role in empowering women groups that have experienced extreme violations and devaluation due to their work. An examination of the structural discrimination prevalent in domestic work reveals its diminution in terms of social status, inadequate compensation, confinement to the private sphere, and its association with "feminine" roles that are often considered less valuable. This situation is further exacerbated for migrant domestic workers, who may lack the same legal and social protections as others. The exploitation of domestic workers is a political act that perpetuates and reproduces patriarchal hegemony. It is against this backdrop that we must appreciate the work of Catholic nuns in the empowerment of domestic workers. By challenging the existing structural discrimination and striving for equitable treatment, they contribute to the vision of a society where all individuals, regardless of their work or gender, are afforded equal opportunities and dignity.[36]

The efforts of women religious in combating human trafficking resonates strongly with the principles of Christian Social democracy.[37] They actively engage in raising awareness about human trafficking, both within local communities and at national and international levels, and educate individuals about the risks, signs, and consequences of trafficking, empowering them to protect themselves and others. By disseminating information and organizing campaigns, they contribute to the broader goal of preventing human trafficking and challenging the societal conditions that enable it.[38] Their efforts not only contribute to the individual empowerment of survivors but also challenge the systemic factors that perpetuate human trafficking, such as poverty, lack of education, and gender inequality. By addressing these root causes, they contribute to the larger goal of building a society that upholds the principles of Christian Social democracy, where all individuals are valued, protected, and empowered. Their engagement in various social spheres stems from their progressive exploration of personal rights and their commitment to transformative change.

Sr Leela, one of the respondents notes:

> In the beginning, I was a person overwhelmed by fear, unsure of how to face the challenges that lay before me. However, as the years went by I underwent a transformative journey. By standing up against societal injustices, I aimed to create a world where every woman could reclaim her voice, find solace, and experience the respect and equality she deserved. And so, fueled by this profound purpose, I dedicated myself to the pursuit of justice and empowerment for all those affected by oppression. Through this ongoing journey, I have come to understand the immense power that lies within the collective efforts of individuals united by a shared cause. Together with my fellow advocates, I strive to create lasting change, fostering a society that cherishes the rights and dignity of every human being.[39]

Democratizing Theology

Women religious in India have been at the forefront of efforts to democratize theology, advocating for a gender-sensitive Church and society.[40] They emphasize the importance of gender equity and recognize that achieving true equality requires the active involvement and support of men as well.[41] Through organizations like the Indian Women Theologians' Forum, they strive to create equal opportunities for women to express their intellectual and spiritual capabilities.[42] Collaborating with feminist theologians worldwide, they promote a feminist consciousness that affirms women's full humanity and confronts all forms of gender-based violence.[43] In particular, feminist theologians, many of whom are women religious, have made significant contributions to the development of a liberative feminist theology that challenges and complements mainstream theological perspectives.[44] They critically examine and question male-centered theologies that limit the divine to male forms or propose that only men can mediate between humans and the divine.[45] Through their writings, they challenge the legitimization of women's subordination within religious structures and advocate for a redefined Christian theology that embraces inclusivity, egalitarianism, and liberation in all aspects of Christian life and knowledge.[46] These women religious also advocate for the declericalization of the Church and the establishment of new structures of participation. They argue that the current hierarchical structure, based on priestly ordination, contradicts the spirit of the Gospel and the model of Christian leadership. They envision a transformed Church that embraces democratic principles, with worship and decision-making led by individuals, regardless of gender identity, who are prepared and guided by the Spirit.[47] They challenge the Church to transcend caste, class, and gender politics, enabling power-sharing in a spirit of mutuality, in order to embody the reign of God. Moreover, they challenge complacent service ministries, such as the permanent diaconate, which often perpetuate gender norms and limited roles for women. They highlight that service should not be viewed as solely a woman's duty but as an essential aspect of Christian spirituality for all believers.[48] They emphasize the need for the Church to embrace a holistic understanding of service (diakonia), rooted in love and contributing to the transformation of society. By challenging age-old norms and upholding democratic values within the Church, women religious are actively working toward a fair, inclusive, and open way of life. Their advocacy for gender equity, declericalization, and new structures of participation demonstrates their commitment to democratizing theology and fostering a more just and egalitarian Church and society.

The involvement of women religious in teaching roles within seminaries has witnessed a notable increase. Their contributions have expanded beyond traditional roles, with more women now writing articles that focus on feminist perspectives in prominent theological magazines and journals. Additionally, they utilize vernacular newspapers, tabloids, and magazines as platforms to voice their concerns, thereby challenging patriarchal norms and structures. The presence of women religious in seminaries as educators brings diverse perspectives and insights to the formation of future clergy.[49] Their inclusion enriches the learning environment, promoting a more holistic understanding of theology and spirituality. By voicing their concerns and advocating for justice, women religious play a crucial role in shaping a more progressive and egalitarian future for the Church.[50]

Internal Critique and Prophetic Voice in the Church and Society

The practice of internal criticism is a necessary condition for the process of democratization. Critical appraisal, alternative perspectives, and even dissent play a crucial role in maintaining the vitality and integrity of democracy.[51] (Peters 1974). Women religious have become an influential voice that calls for accountability within the Church. Particularly in recent times, they have openly challenged the Church and its leadership to take responsibility for the growing sex scandals and abuses against women, including women religious.[52]

While this has shaken the established structures of the Church and its leadership, numerous lay organizations and movements see it as a wake-up call for the Church to become truly democratic and ensure the safety of its members. In India, women religious play a pivotal role in upholding the ethical standards of the Church. They actively urge the Church to renew its dedication to serving the people and advocate for accountability in addressing social challenges. By doing so, they serve as a moral compass for the Church, ensuring that it remains committed to its mission and actively responds to the needs and concerns of society. The Church, existing in God's name, has a responsibility toward the ordinary people. Through their ongoing mission to serve the poorest of the poor and adapt to the changing needs of the times, women religious play a crucial role in reminding the Church of its original purpose.

We have seen how the work of Catholic Religious Women in India extends far beyond providing assistance to the poor. It involves uplifting marginalized communities and empowering them with a renewed sense of dignity through multifaceted efforts. Despite facing their own vulnerabilities and navigating imbalanced power structures, including patriarchal dynamics, these women remain steadfast and unwavering in their endeavors. Their resilience and selflessness serve as a powerful testament to the transformative potential of compassion and commitment to both the Church and society. In their dedication, Catholic nuns in India become not only agents of change but also critical voices calling for accountability within the Church and society. By actively engaging in the promotion of democratic principles and advocating for inclusive governance, they emphasize the importance of sustaining democracy and promoting sustainable practices.

Sustainability serves as a crucial pillar of Christian Social Democracy, emphasizing the responsible stewardship of resources and the preservation of the environment for future generations. It entails recognizing the interconnectedness of social, economic, and environmental wellbeing. Nurturing sustainability within this framework requires a holistic approach that promotes sustainable development, environmental conservation, and ethical practices. Catholic nuns in India play an essential role in nurturing sustainability as part of Christian social democracy.[53] They actively engage in sustainable initiatives by promoting ecofriendly practices, conservation efforts, and sustainable livelihoods within their communities.[54] Through education and awareness campaigns, they empower individuals to adopt sustainable lifestyles, emphasizing the importance of environmental stewardship and the protection of natural resources.[55] Additionally, their work often extends to sustainable agricultural practices and environmental advocacy, fostering a sense of ecological responsibility and sustainable development.[56] They effectively integrate Christian values with the broader goal of creating a just and sustainable society, showcasing the profound impact that faith-driven action can have in bringing about meaningful change. Their efforts serve as a powerful testament to the effectiveness of their approach, inspiring others to embrace sustainability as a vital component of their own faith-based endeavors.

The Ethos of Effectiveness

Italian philosopher Giorgio Agamben's notion of effectiveness[57] emphasizes the transformative power that individuals possess when they align themselves with a higher purpose or calling. In this context, effectiveness transcends mere efficiency or achieving predetermined goals; it involves embracing a spiritual dimension and recognizing oneself as an active vessel through which the divine can manifest.[58] Agamben's notion suggests that individuals who embrace their role as animate instruments of the divine not only fulfill their individual potentials but also contribute to a broader collective transformation by embodying principles of compassion, justice, and love.[59] The ethos of effectiveness, as elucidated by philosopher Giorgio Agamben, positions Catholic nuns as active and transformative agents of divine presence in the Indian church and society. Their commitment to sustainable projects and empowerment initiatives exemplifies their role in fostering positive change within communities. However, despite their significant contributions, Catholic nuns often grapple with a contradictory consciousness. On one hand, they possess the capacity to bring about positive transformations, while on the other hand, they may find themselves constrained by institutional structures and dogmas that limit their ability to critically question and challenge the status quo. To move forward, it is essential for Catholic nuns to integrate both the ethos of effectiveness and critical consciousness. By embracing critical consciousness, they can analyze and question the existing systems and structures, identifying areas for improvement and pushing for necessary changes. Simultaneously, the ethos of effectiveness empowers them to leverage their position and resources to implement tangible solutions and make a real difference in their own lives and in the lives of those they serve. The combination of these two approaches will enable Catholic nuns to navigate the complexities of their roles, address contradictions, and continue their invaluable work toward creating a more just and sustainable world.

Conclusion

This study sheds light on the impact of Catholic Religious Women in India as they navigate through intricate paradoxes and emerge as catalysts in the ongoing process of democratization within the church and society as a whole. Some critics argue that the influence of Catholic Religious Women may be limited within the hierarchical structures of the church and the broader society. They contend that despite the efforts of these women, the entrenched patriarchal systems often impede substantial progress. Additionally, these dissenting voices highlight the challenges faced by Catholic nuns in balancing their religious commitments with their desire for societal change, raising concerns about the potential dilution of their impact. However, it is essential to recognize the transformative power these women possess despite these dissenting views. While they may face obstacles and limitations, Catholic

Religious Women in India continue to push boundaries and challenge the status quo. Their efforts not only have the potential to reshape the church but also contribute to a more meaningful and inclusive democratic system that effectively addresses the needs of all individuals, particularly marginalized communities. Through their commitment to justice, dignity, and empowerment, Catholic Religious women introduce a distinct and invaluable dimension to the concept of democracy, enriching it and fostering its sustainability. By harmonizing their faith, Christian social democracy, and a critical and impactful consciousness, Catholic nuns in India exemplify how individuals can wield transformative power, molding democracy into a more meaningful and inclusive system that effectively addresses the needs of all.

Acknowledgments

I am deeply appreciative of the two reviewers who provided constructive feedback during the revision stage. I am indebted to Dr. George Thadathil, SDB, for his unwavering support and encouragement. His meticulous reading of my drafts and the valuable suggestions he provided contributed significantly to the completion of this chapter.

Notes

1 The group of women religious interviewed consists of 16 individuals hailing from five distinct Indian states, each with their unique cultural backgrounds. Among them, two are aged above 70, three are between 60 and 70, five are between 50 and 60, three are between 40 and 50, two are between 30 and 40, and one is below 30 years old. Their ages encompass a wide range, contributing to the diversity within the group. Moreover, their experiences further emphasize their diversity. Three of them have served on missions abroad, expanding their exposure to different cultures and perspectives. Additionally, three have worked outside their congregations and provinces, gaining valuable experience in various organizations and institutions. Furthermore, two of these women have dedicated their efforts specifically to women's empowerment, collaborating with other organizations toward this cause. Additionally, two have been actively involved in grassroots movements, advocating for change at the local level. Their commitment to empowering women and their involvement in grassroots initiatives highlight their dedication to social progress. In summary, this group of 16 women religious not only represents the diversity of five different Indian states and their respective cultures, but also showcases a range of ages and a breadth of experiences.
2 Jose Kalapura SJ, "Catholic Religious Life in India: A Historical Perspective," *Goethals News: The Goethals Indian Library and Research Society* XXII, no. 1 March (2019): 2–3.
3 Mathew M Vallipalam, "The impact of Consecrated Life on Indian Society," in Social Compass, 48/2, (June 2001): 263–277.
4 See, Jo Ann Kay McNamara's book, *Sisters in Arms: Catholic Nuns through two Millennia*, London: Harvard University Press, 1996. It presents a compelling exploration of the role and contributions of Catholic nuns over the past two thousand years. With meticulous research and insightful analysis, the author argues that these women religious have played a crucial and often overlooked part in shaping the history of the Catholic Church and broader society. For

studies on Catholic Religious Women from the Indian context, see Shalini Mulackal, "Women Religious as Vanguard of Women's Participation: A Critical Study of the Role of Women Religious in the Church and Society," in Pruller-Jagenteufel/Bong/Perintfalvi (eds), *Towards Just Gender Relations: Rethinking the Role of Women in Church and Society*, Vienna University Press, 2019, pp. 71–80; Pearl Drago, *Indian Feminist Theology and Women's Concerns: Reviews, Resources and Remembrance, in Birthing a New Vision: The Empowerment of Women Religious in India*, Vol 21, Pune, Streevani Publication, December 2013; Fr. Thomas Edamattathu, and Sr. Ida Rodrigues, "Contribution of the Religious Sisters to the Church in Northeast India," *Indian Missiological Review*, Vol 12, December 1990, 123–139; Shalini Mulackal, "Sr. Valsa: The Prophet-Martyr of Pachuwara," in *People's Valsa: In the Foot Steps of Her Master*, edited by Mary Scaria SCJM and Helen Saldanha SSPS, Delhi: Media House, 2013, 53–67; Hazel D' Lima, Keynote Address "Women Religious Journeying Solidarity: Discovering our Communion with God's Creation" (CRI Meeting 1999), as quoted by Daniela, "The Role of Women Religious in the Transformation of the Social Order," *The Living Word*, Vol. 107, No. 6 (November–December 2001): 358–373.

5 At the Synod of Consecrated Life in 1994, it was recognized that women comprise 75% of religious personnel in the Church. In India, religious women comprise 82% of the religious in the country.

6 Pope John Paul II, *Redemptoris Missio: On the Permanent Validity of the Church's Missionary Mandate*, Encyclical, Vatican 7 December 1990, pp. 39–45.

7 Mathew M Vallipalam, "The Impact of Consecrated Life on Indian Society," in *Social compass*, (June 2001): 263–277.

8 Felix J. Raj, "Consecrated Life, A Sign of the Church's Vitality," *Goethals News: The Goethals Indian Library and Research Society*, Vol XXII, no 1 January–March (2019): 1–2.

9 The President of the CRI is chosen through election during the General Assembly which happens once in three years.

10 Thomas Scaria, "Indian Nuns Transform Others, But don't Know Their Power," in Matters India: India's Complete Socio-economic & Religious News, 3 March 2022. This article contains Sr. Nirmalini Nazareth's first interview after being voted upon as the President of CRI.

11 Dr Hazel D'Lima, Cletus Zuzarte, Pallavi Xalxo, *It's High Time: Women Religious Speak Up On Gender Justice in the Indian Church*, Conference of Religious India (Women), Delhi, 2018.

12 For an analysis of Clericalism, See Eamonn Conway (Limmerick), "A Church Beyond Clericalism," in Pruller-Jagenteufel/Bong/Perintfalvi (eds), *Towards Just Gender Relations: Rethinking the Role of Women in Church and Society*, Vienna, University Press, 2019, pp. 121–136.

13 Virginia Saldanha, "Women's Rights in the Church– In the Context of Sex Abuse," *Asian Horizons*, March 2019, pp. 75–85. In another article, she notes that women have internalized patriarchal Christianity. They are comfortable with just a little space that is given to them. See Virginia Saldanha, "The Power of Religion over Women in India," in *Global Sisters Report*, GSR: A Project of National Catholic Reporter, November 2016.

14 Ryan P. Murphy, *Wait, She's One of Us: American Catholic Nuns, Gender, and Sexuality*. SocArXiv, (Open archive of the social sciences), July 2019. doi: 10.31235/osf.io/fcx4b. Ryan P. Murphy in this study on Catholic nuns argues that religious sisters occupy a liminal space in the Church which is a hierarchical organization that has marginalized them through reinscription of structures of gender inequality, while simultaneously requiring their unfailing obedience to carry out the Church's ministry. She affirms that women religious are outsiders within the Catholic Church.

15 Gayatri Chakravorthy Spivak, "Can the Subaltern Speak?" in Cary Nelson and Lawrence Grossberg (eds). *Marxism and the Interpretation of Culture*, London: Macmillan, 1988. pp. 24–28.
16 Two of the participants did not respond to two sets of questions – one, on the link between autonomy and the vow of obedience and two, on Democratization and Religious life. When asked the reason, they said that women outside are struggling with greater problems. When we work for their empowerment we experience contentment and empowerment.
17 Kochurani Abraham, "Can Indian Women Religious Speak? The 'Rights' Question," A Paper Presented at the Conference on 'Christianity and Human Rights' organized by the Department of Christian Studies in the University of Madras on 24 February 2023. (Awaiting Publication).
18 Paolo Friere, *The Pedagogy of the Oppressed*, New York: Seabury Press, 1970, 23.
19 Giovanni Cucci, "Authority and Abuse Issues Among Women Religious," in *La Civilta Cattolica*, 1 August 2020. DOI: La Civiltà Cattolica, En. Ed. Vol. 4, no. 08 art. 7, 0620. DOI:10.32009/22072446.0820.7
20 Shalini Mulackal, "Women Religious as Vanguard of Women's Participation: A Critical Study of the Role of Women Religious in the Church and Society," in Pruller-Jagenteufel/Bong/Perintfalvi (eds), *Towards Just Gender Relations: Rethinking the Role of Women in Church and Society*, Vienna University Press, 2019, pp. 71–80. According to Shalini Mulackal, there has been a shift toward more democratic decision-making processes in some congregations. She gives the example of her congregation the Presentation Sisters of the Blessed Virgin Mary. This shift has led to the emergence of new structures within these religious communities.
21 This response is from a woman religious of an international congregation. Her response regarding how authority is practiced clearly reveals the perpetuation of neocolonial imperatives of religious dominance. Shalini Mulackal argues that many Religious Orders, particularly those with international membership, have experienced significant renewal in areas such as self-understanding, lifestyle, mission, charism, and governance. She supports this by highlighting changes in terminology, such as renaming the "General Chapter" to "Congregational Gathering" and adopting new leadership titles. Mulackal asserts that language change is essential to transform reality, as language reflects and shapes our consciousness. However, it should be acknowledged that oppressive language still persists in certain congregations and as indicated by these survey responses the manner in which authority is practiced is reminiscent of neocolonial religious dominance as feminist theologian Kochurani Abraham points out.
22 Interviewed on 27 January 2021.
23 Congregation for Institutes of Consecrated Life and Societies of Apostolic Life, *New Wine in New Wineskins: The Consecrated Life and Its Ongoing Challenges Since Vatican II*, Rome, Catholic Truth Society, 2017, 40–42.
24 Interviewed on 03 February 2021.
25 Christian Social Democracy as envisioned in this paper draws from the catholic social teachings, the Basiliea vision of Jesus and the social theology of Abraham Kuyper, the Dutch Theologian. See Matthew J. Tuininga, "Abraham Kuyper and the Social Order: Principles for Christian Liberalism," in *Seminary Faculty Publications*, 32. https://digitalcommons.calvin.edu/seminary_facultypubs/32, 2020, pp. 337–361.
26 Matthew J. Tuininga, "Abraham Kuyper and the Social Order: Principles for Christian Liberalism," in *Seminary Faculty Publications*, 32. https://digitalcommons.calvin.edu/seminary_facultypubs/32, 2020, pp. 338–339.
27 In Elisabeth Schussler Fiorenza's work *Discipleship of Equals* (1993), she highlights the *Basileia* vision of Jesus and its emphasis on wellbeing and inclusivity as central themes in the Gospels. She asserts that within the Jesus movement, a profound democratic vision emerges. This vision revolves around the *Basileia*, an

alternative society envisioned by God, characterized by freedom from oppression and the absence of exclusion. See Elisabeth Schussler Fiorenza, *Discipleship of Equals*, New York: Crossroad, 1993, p. 14.

28 This resonates with the spiritual activism espoused by Gloria Anzaldua, bridging the connection between the personal and the collective, two distinct yet interconnected realms of social change. Gloria Anzaldúa's spiritual activism encompassed the belief in interconnectedness, the reclamation of indigenous wisdom, and the transformative power of spirituality. She emphasized the importance of personal and collective healing, the exploration of liminal spaces, and the fusion of spirituality and social justice. Anzaldúa's spiritual activism called for the integration of art and creativity as tools for resistance, inviting individuals and communities to bridge the realms of spirituality and activism in pursuit of a more just and inclusive world. Cf. AnaLouise Keating and Gloria Anzaldúa (eds.), *This Bridge We Call Home: Radical Visions for Transformation*, New York, Routledge, September 2002.

29 See Susan Verducci, "Education, Democracy and the Moral Life," in Michael Katz, Susan Verducci and Gert Biesta (eds), *Education, Democracy and the Moral Life*, New York, Springer, 2008. Pp. 9–30.

30 Santosh Digal, "Catholic Schools, a bulwark against society's moral crisis," in *AsiaNews*, 14 December 2004. INDIA Catholic schools, a bulwark against society's moral crisis (https://asianews.it).

31 See the arguments in Rose Rotuno-Johnson, "Democracy and Special Education Inclusion," The College of Mt. St. Joseph. https://nnerpartnerships.org/wp-content/uploads/Article-10-2010-NNNER-Democracy-and-Special-Education-Inclusion.pdf (https://nnerpartnerships.org)

32 Thomas Scaria, "Apostolic Carmel nuns complete 150 years as pioneers of women's education in India," in *globalsistersreport.org.*, 18 May 2021.

33 Interviewed on 28 January 2021.

34 Sneha Pandey, *Identity Issues of Girls from Single-Sex Convent Schools in India*. Education and Society, McGill University, Canada, ProQuest Dissertations Publishing, 2020.

35 Nilanjana Paul, "The Indian Mission of the Institute of Blessed Virgin Mary (IBVM) Nuns: Convents, Curriculum, and Indian Women," *Journal of International Women's Studies*: Vol. 24: Issue 2, Article 2 (2022) Available at: https://vc.bridgew.edu/jiws/vol24/iss2/2

36 The National Domestic Workers Movement (NDWM), founded by Sr. Jeanne Devos and operating in 18 Indian states, works to empower domestic workers, protect their human and child rights, provide legal aid, and raise awareness about trafficking. Inspired by Sr. Devos, other nuns, such as Sr. Sophia Arockia Mary of the Holy Spirit Sisters, collaborate with domestic workers to advocate for fair wages, improved working conditions, and welfare measures. These sisters draw inspiration from diverse sources and unite marginalized communities through collective action, negotiations, and rights advocacy.

37 Cf. Annie Jesus, "*Mary's fight against sexual slavery is her 'crusade',*"*Agenzia Fides, Information Service of the Pontifical Mission Societies since 1927*, Asia/India, 11 January 2021; Reporter, "The Commitment of Talitha Kumi Nuns against human trafficking during the pandemic", in *Agenzia Fides, Information Service of the Pontifical Mission Societies since 1927*, Asia/India, 17 July 2020. Over 1000 women religious in India actively combat human trafficking. This extensive network forms a substantial movement. Catholic nuns in India participate in diverse initiatives to empower marginalized communities, but I have chosen to focus on these two movements due to their vastness and far-reaching impact.

38 Catholic Religious women in India have made significant contributions across various domains and in various movements, serving as lawyers, advocates for human rights, and even sacrificing their lives as martyrs for the marginalized. Their profound influence has reverberated widely, leaving an indelible mark on

society. See Shalini Mulackal, "Sr. Valsa: The Prophet-Martyr of Pachuwara", in *People's Valsa: In the Foot Steps of Her Master*, edited by Mary Scaria SCJM and Helen Saldanha SSPs (Delhi: Media House, 2013), 53–67; Daniela, "The Role of Women Religious in the Transformation of the Social Order", The Living Word, Vol. 107, No. 6 (November–December 2001): 358–373.
39 Interview of 15 February 2021
40 See Evelyn Monteiro, *Church and Culture: Communion in Pluralism*, Delhi: ISPCK, 2004; Rekha M. Chennattu, *Biblical women as Agents of Justice and Peace*, pp. 124–58 in *Word of God: Source of Justice and Peace*, A Peter Abir, (Ed.) Tindivanam: CBF, 2008.
41 Sr Vimala Chenginimattam, the first moral theologian from the women religious in India says, "Gender equity can be reached only when men think that gender inequality is their crisis too. See James F Keenan, "Theologians Meet to reflect on India's Moral Issues," *National Catholic Reporter*, 4 September 2012. Also, Pushpa Joseph, "Women's Perspectives in Bioethics: A Case Study from Tribal India," in Linda Hogan (ed.), *Applied Ethics in a World Church: The Padua Conference*, (Mary knoll, New York: Orbis Books, 2008), 98–108.
42 Reporter, "Indian women theologians seek new ways of being Church," *Matters India*, May, 2016.
43 Metti Amirtham, S.C.C., Women in India: Negotiating Body, Reclaiming Agency, Delhi: ISPCK, 2011.
44 Rekha M. Chennattu, *Johannine Relationship as a Covenant Relationship*, (Peabody: Hendrickson Publishers, 2006).
45 See the articles in S.C. Evelyn Monteiro & M.M. Antionette Gutzler, eds., *Ecclesia of Women in Asia: Gathering the Voice of the Silenced*, Delhi, ISPCK, 2005.
46 Pushpa Joseph, "The Myth of Ideal Womanhood in Modern India: A Post Colonial Feminist Critique", in Kiyoshi Seko (eds) *Inquiring Post Colonial Asia*, (Tokyo: Asian Christian Review, 2012) 36–58.
47 See the essays in Agnes M. Brazal and Andrea Lizares Si (eds.), *Body and Sexuality: Theological-Pastoral Perspectives of Women in Asia* (Manila: Ateneo De Manila University Press, 2007).
48 My own work has focused on feminist heremeneutics in Biblical Interpretation. See Pushpa Joseph, "Feminist Hermeneutics", in Mathew Elanjikal (ed.), *Hermeneutics: Multicultural Perspectives* (Chennai: Satya Nilyam Publications, 2009) 226–246. See my own work in the area of Indian Feminist Hermeneutics. Pushpa Joseph, *Feminist Hermeneutics: A Contextual Reconstruction* (Darjeeling: Salesian College Publications, 2010).
49 See Shalini Mulackal, "On being the first woman to lead Indian theologians", *Global Sisters Report*, 5 April 2016, accessed 5 June 2020.
50 See Pearl Drago, *Indian Feminist Theology and Women's Concerns: Reviews, Resources and Remembrance, in Birthing a New Vision: The Empowerment of Women Religious in India*, Vol 21, Pune, Streevani Publication, December 2013 for a detailed analysis of the contribution of Women Religious in India to theology and the Church.
51 R. S. Peters, *Psychology and Ethical Development*. London: George Allen and Unwin, 1974.
52 Virginia Saldanha, "Women's Rights in the Church – In the Context of Sex Abuse," in *Asian Horizons*, March 2019, pp. 75–85.
53 See Pushpa Joseph, "Indigenous Knowledge for Survival: A Descriptive Enquiry", in Felix Wilfred (ed.), *Knowledge Ethics for Our Times: Jeevadhara Journal for Socio-Religious Research* (Vol. XXXIX No. 229, January 2009) 74–77.
54 See Thomas Scaria, "Farming Nuns promote eco-centric spirituality, organic farming", in *Matters India: India's Complete Socioeconomic and Religious news*,

28 April 2023; Saji Thomas, "Sisters Change Lives for Waste pickers of Central India," in *Global Sisters Report: A Project of National Catholic Reporter*, 27 June 2016; Thomas Scaria, "Catholic nuns support fisherpeople protesting new international seaport in India," in *Matters India: India's Complete Socioeconomic and Religious news*, 4 October 2022.

55 See Pushpa Joseph, "Eco-Feminism and Faith: Reclaiming a Subverted Global Wisdom" in *Sanyasa: Journal of Consecrated Life*, Vol. VIII, No.2, July–December 2013.

56 NISARGA, an NGO operated by the Franciscan Missionaries of Mary (FMM), is dedicated to empowering farmers and landless laborers in India. With a mission focused on the wellbeing of farmers, NISARGA implements various initiatives such as water shed programs, organic farming, and the adoption of organic agricultural and irrigation practices. For more information, visit the official website of Nisarga-FMM Sisters at https://nisargafmm.in

57 For a clear understanding Cf. Klaus C Yoder, "Instruments of Immolation: Giorgio Agamben and the Eucharistic reformations of the sixteenth century," in *Critical Research On Religion*, Vol. 9(1), 2021, 48–64.

58 Emily M. Lauletta, "Renegotiating Liminal Spaces: Catholic Nuns as Spiritual and Feminist Activists," *Undergraduate Honors Theses*, Hollins University, 47, 2022.

59 Klaus C Yoder, "Instruments of immolation: Giorgio Agamben and the Eucharistic Reformations of the Sixteenth Century," in *Critical Research on Religion*, Vol. 9(1) Sage, New York, 2021, 49–50.

Bibliography

Abraham, Kochurani. 2023. "Can Indian Women Religious Speak? The 'Rights' Question," A Paper Presented at the Conference on 'Christianity and Human Rights' organized by the Department of Christian Studies in the University of Madras on 24th February 2023. (Awaiting Publication).

Amirtham, Metti. 2011. *Women in India: Negotiating Body, Reclaiming Agency*, Delhi: ISPCK.

Brazal, Agnes and Andrea Lizares Si (eds.). 2007. *Body and Sexuality: Theological-Pastoral Perspectives of Women in Asia*, Manila: Ateneo De Manila University Press.

Chennattu, Rekha M. 2006. *Johannine Relationship as a Covenant Relationship*, Peabody: Hendrickson Publishers.

Chennattu, Rekha M. 2008. Biblical Women as Agents of Justice and Peace, in *Word of God: Source of Justice and Peace*, A. Peter Abir (ed.) Tindivanam: CBF, pp. 124–158.

CICLSAL. 2017. *Catholic Church, New Wine in New Wineskins: The Consecrated Life and Its Ongoing Challenges Since Vatican II*, Rome: Catholic Truth Society.

Cucci, Giovanni. August 2020. *Authority and Abuse Issues among Women Religious*. La Civilta Cattolica.

D'Lima, Hazel, Cletus Zuzarte, Pallavi Xalxo. 2018. *It's High Time: Women Religious Speak Up on Gender Justice in the Indian Church*, Delhi: Conference of Religious India (Women).

Drago, Pearl. December 2013. *Indian Feminist Theology and Women's Concerns: Reviews, Resources and Remembrance, Birthing a New Vision: The Empowerment of Women Religious in India*, Vol 21, Pune: Streevani Publication.

Emily, Lauletta M. 2022. *Renegotiating Liminal Spaces: Catholic Nuns as Spiritual and Feminist Activists*, Undergraduate Honors Theses, Hollins University. 47.

Friere, Paolo. 1970. *The Pedagogy of the Oppressed*, New York: Seabury Press.

Hogan, Linda (ed.). 2008. *Applied Ethics in a World Church: The Padua Conference*, Mary Knoll, New York: Orbis Books.

Jagenteufel, Pruller, Sharon Bong, Rita Perintfalvi (eds). 2019. *Towards Just Gender Relations: Rethinking the Role of Women in Church and Society*, Vienna: Vienna University Press.

Jesus, Annie. January 2019. *Mary's fight against sexual slavery is her 'crusade'*. http://www.asianews.it/news-en. Fides, Agenzia. August 2021. The Commitment of "Talitha Kum" nuns against human trafficking during the Pandemic Asia/India.

Joseph, Pushpa. 2009a. "Feminist Hermeneutics," in Mathew Elanjikal (ed.), *Hermeneutics: Multicultural Perspectives*, Chennai: Satya Nilyam Publications, 226–246.

Joseph, Pushpa. January 2009b. "Indigenous Knowledge for Survival: A Descriptive Enquiry," in Felix Wilfred (ed.), *Knowledge Ethics for Our Times: Jeevadhara Journal for Socio-Religious Research*, Vol. XXXIX, No. 229, 74–80.

Joseph, Pushpa. 2010. *Feminist Hermeneutics: A Contextual Reconstruction*, Darjeeling: Salesian College Publications.

Joseph, Pushpa. 2012. "The Myth of Ideal Womanhood in Modern India: A Post Colonial Feminist Critique," in Kiyoshi Seko (eds) *Inquiring Post Colonial Asia*, Tokyo: Asian Christian Review,36–58.

Joseph, Pushpa. 2013. "Eco-Feminism and Faith: Reclaiming a Subverted Global Wisdom," *Sanyasa: Journal of Consecrated Life*, Vol. VIII, No.2.

Kalapura, Jose. March, 2019. "Catholic Religious Life in India: A Historical Perspective." *Goethals News: The Goethals Indian Library and Research Society* XXII: 1.

Keating, AnaLousie and Gloria Anzaldúa (eds.). 2002. *This Bridge We Call Home: Radical Visions for Transformation*, New York, Routledge.

Keenan, James F. 2012. "Theologians meet to reflect on India's Moral Issues." *National Catholic Reporter*.

Klaus, Yoder C. 2021. "Instruments of immolation: Giorgio Agamben and the Eucharistic Reformations of the Sixteenth Century," in *Critical Research on Religion*, Vol. 9(1) New York: Sage, pp. 48–64

McNamara, Jo Ann Kay. 1996. *Sisters in Arms: Catholic Nuns through two Millennia*, London: Harvard University Press.

Monteiro, Evelyn. 2004. *Church and Culture: Communion in Pluralism*, Delhi: ISPCK, 2004;

Monteiro, Evelyn & M.M. Antionette Gutzler. eds., 2005. *Ecclesia of Women in Asia: Gathering the Voice of the Silenced*, Delhi, ISPCK.

Mulackal, Shalini. April 2016. "On being the first woman to lead Indian theologians," *Global Sisters Report*, April 5, 2016 On being the first woman to lead Indian theologians|Global Sisters Report, accessed 5 June 2020

Mundadan, A Mathias. 2003. *Indian Christians: search for identity and struggle for autonomy*. Bangalore: Dharmaram Publications.

Murphy, Ryan P. 2019. *Wait, She's One of Us: American Catholic Nuns, Gender, and Sexuality*. SocArXiv, open archive of the social sciences, July 19. doi: 10.31235/osf.io/fcx4b

Pandey, Sneha. 2020. *Identity Issues of Girls from Single-Sex Convent Schools in India*. Education and Society. McGill University, Canada, ProQuest Dissertations Publishing.

Paul, Nilanjana. "The Indian Mission of the Institute of Blessed Virgin Mary (IBVM) Nuns: Convents, Curriculum, and Indian Women," *Journal of International Women's Studies* 24 (2): 1–14. Article 2 (2022).

Peters, R. S. 1974. *Psychology and Ethical Development*. London: George Allen and Unwin.

Raj, J. Felix. 2019. "Consecrated Life, A Sign of the Church's Vitality." *Goethals News: The Goethals Indian Library and Research Society* 1–2

Reporter. May 2016. "Indian women theologians seek new ways of being Church," Matters India.

Rozario, Rock Ronald. 2021. *A Passionate Mother of Transgender People*. UCANEWS.

Saldanha, Virginia. November 2016 "The Power of Religion over Women in India," in *Global Sisters Report*, GSR: A Project of National Catholic Reporter.

Saldanha, Virginia. March 2019. "Women's Rights in the Church – In the Context of Sex Abuse." *Asian Horizons*, 48 (2): 75–85.

Sarwar, Firoj High. 2012. "Christian Missionaries and Female Education in Bengal during East India Company's Rule: a Discourse between Christianized Colonial Domination versus Women Emancipation." *Journal of Humanities and Social Science* 4 (1): 37–47.

Spivak, Gayatri Chakravorthy. 1988. "Can the Subaltern Speak?" in Cary Nelson and Lawrence Grossberg (eds). *Marxism and the Interpretation of Culture*. London: Macmillan. 24–28.

Tuininga, Matthew J. 2020. "Abraham Kuyper and the Social Order: Principles for Christian Liberalism." Seminary Faculty Publications. 32. https://digitalcommons.calvin.edu/seminary_facultypubs/32

Vallipalam, Mathew M. June 2001. "The Impact of Consecrated Life on Indian Society." In *Social Compass*, pp. 263–277.

Section III
Democratization and the Marginalized – Politics of Accessibility and Hegemony

7 The Christian Churches, Democratic Developments, and People at the Margins

Case Studies from Rajasthan and Odisha

Sarbeswar Sahoo and James Ponniah

While India has been a democracy for more than 70 years, a large section of its population is deprived of basic social welfare and citizenship rights. Given this failure of the Indian state to ensure equal rights for all citizens, several scholars have argued that India is only a formal democracy, not a substantive one (Jayal, 2013, Roy, 2016; Sahoo and Chaney, 2021). In a substantive democracy, all citizens are equal; they are able to freely exercise their agency, autonomy, and citizenship rights. This is, however, not the case when it comes to the marginalized population, especially Dalits and tribals who live at the margins of the state. In the last 70 years, the postcolonial Indian state has not done enough to reach out to these communities effectively, bring them out of poverty, and provide them basic social welfare facilities, such as education and healthcare. As a consequence, a large majority of the Dalits and tribals still live in poverty and are deprived of exercising their fundamental democratic rights. In this context, the question is: how could the Dalits and tribals exercise their agency and autonomy, and be a part of the larger democratic process? Given the failure of the Indian state, some non-state actors, especially the Christian churches, have come forward to work with Dalits and tribals and enable them to overcome the hitherto existing hierarchy and unfreedoms that obstruct their participation in the democratic process.

In this chapter, we examine the role of Christian churches among the tribals and Dalits of Rajasthan and Odisha and show how these churches have transformed the socioeconomic and political lifeworld of marginal groups over the past few decades. We argue that the marginal people's participation in the democratic process does not occur automatically; it is a long-drawn process and the Christian churches have played a vital role in converting the tribals and Dalits into "autonomous (political) subjects". This process of autonomous subject formation began with the intervention of the Christian churches, which have worked with the tribal and Dalit communities through their various developmental programs. Specifically, in the context of Rajasthan, the Calvary Covenant Fellowship Mission (CCFM), a local Pentecostal church, has played a vital role in empowering the Bhils through its various "active social ministries" (Miller and Yamamori, 2007: 1). Contrary to other churches, which maintain a strict hierarchy and authority

DOI: 10.4324/9781003426035-11

structure, the CCFM is very democratic and people oriented. It has decentralized its leadership structure and encouraged active participation of the community in development activities. Particularly, the CCFM has taken up activities that were the responsibilities of the state, such as providing education and healthcare. Most importantly, the church requires Pentecostal men to follow a set of strict moral code – no alcohol, no smoking, no tobacco, and love, respect, and loyalty for one's partner – which has not only improved the economic condition of the family but indirectly undermined patriarchal values and given rise to equality and partnership in democratic decision-making at the household level.

Similarly, in the context of Odisha, the Christian churches through their educational institutions and social service centers have introduced into the lifeworld of the Kandhamal region, democratic values such as equality, liberty, and human dignity and facilitated the locals, mostly the Dalit Panos and, to some extent, tribal Kandhos, to become autonomous subjects through organizational practices with "democratic character" such as people's participation in developmental schemes, women self-help groups (SHGs), self-governance deliberations, and micro-level partnership programs between the local people and the state government. These initiatives and community development programs of the Christian organizations brought also ruptures and fissures in the already existing social fabric of the region. It produced anger and jealousy between caste/tribal Hindus and Dalit Christians in Kandhamal, consequently leading to several Hindu–Christian communal conflicts between 2007 and 2008. In its efforts to rebuild the lives of Dalit Christians in Kandhamal and to restore peace and harmony in the locality, the Catholic Church and its organizations in Kandhamal became a lot more decentralized and democratic. Its social works organization Jan Vikas in Nuagaon expanded its network base recruiting part-time lay volunteers and entrusting them with the responsibility to not only reconstruct people's lives but also to restore relationship with non-Christian neighbors. Based on these two cases, this chapter discusses how the Pentecostal and Catholic churches have played a vital role in transforming the everyday lifeworld more democratic by injecting new values and energies into the social relationship between men and women, caste and tribes, and Christians and non-Christians in Rajasthan and Odisha. It also shows how these churches have transformed the so-called marginalized populations into autonomous subjects through their multifarious programs and schemes.

A Note on Methodology and Rationale for Comparison

This chapter is a part of both of our broader interest on Christianity among the marginalized communities of India. We have conducted fieldwork among the marginal communities of Rajasthan and Odisha over several years. Particularly, the first author has conducted a major part of his extensive fieldwork with CCFM between 2011 and 2018. Specifically, he examined the role

Christian Churches, Democratic Developments, People at Margins 131

of CCFM among the Bhils and how it transforms their everyday socioeconomic and political lifeworld. As a part of his fieldwork, the first author travelled to several villages, attended various prayer meetings, participated in Christmas fairs and New Year events, witnessed healing sessions, visited welfare project sites, and conducted in-depth interviews with numerous Pentecostal pastors and the ordinary believers in the region. Similarly, the second author had undertaken a fieldwork in Kandhamal in 2012. He made several visits to the institutions, schools, churches, homes, and villages, conducted focus group discussions with villagers and cooperative society members, undertook in-depth interviews with church leaders, activists, village heads, NGOs, retired Christian bureaucrats, social work personnel, attended village or organizational-level development programs, participated in SHG meetings, and visited new neighborhood settlements built by Christian organizations to accommodate the victims of communal violence.

Thus, the insights discussed in this chapter draw on from both of our interactions and critical engagements with tribal and Dalit Christians and missionaries in these two regions. While the rationale of comparing these two states may not be obvious to people, we argue that both Rajasthan and Odisha provide a fitting context for comparison for several reasons: (1) both states have a significant tribal and Dalit population who have experienced marginalization for long; (2) both states suffer from extreme poverty and the institution of state in these states have failed to provide basic welfare services to the tribal population; (3) both historical marginalization and state failure have provided the context for mission work since the colonial times; although Christian missionaries first came to the tribal areas as a part of the colonial civilizing mission, most recently, the idea of (holistic) development has guided their work, which could be described as a modern incarnation of the civilizing mission; (4) both states have also experienced increasing incidences of violence against Christian minorities – while Odisha has witnessed large-scale violence against Christians (e.g., Kandhamal violence and killing of Pastor Graham Staines), in case of Rajasthan such violence has remained small-scale but occurring more frequently; (5) both states are dominated by a upper caste Hindu culture – while Odisha has the dominance of the Hindu Jagannath cult, Rajasthan has the dominance of Hindu Rajput ideology; this has vital implications for Christian social life in these two states. Given these diversities of context, we argue that a comparison of Christian social life in Rajasthan and Odisha will highlight the important aspects of the complex and dynamic relationship between the church and people at the margins and its implications for the larger processes of democratic development in India.

Part I: State Failure and Marginalization of the Bhil in Rajasthan

The Bhil, one of the largest indigenous communities of India, are classified by the state as the "Scheduled Tribes" (STs). The name Bhil is derived from words *Billu* or *Villu*, which means bow – thus popularly known as the "bowmen" of Rajasthan. The Bhil are an ethnic group who speak various local dialects of Indo-Aryan languages such as Bhilli and Vagri. In Rajasthan, tribes constitute 13.48% of the population of the State. Some of the tribal groups are: Meena, Bhil, Garasia, Sahria, Damor, and Kathodi. Almost 95% of the tribal population live in rural areas, especially in the mountains, plateaus, and forest areas. The Bhil are the second largest tribal community in the State and are heavily concentrated in the southern part of the state. They constitute almost 40% of the population and in some blocks like Kotra, the concentration of Bhils is as high as 90%. Kotra is commonly known as the *kalapani* – extremely remote and inaccessible – where the government officials are sent on "punishment posting" (Sahoo, 2013).

Although men and women are considered equal, the Bhil family and social structure is predominantly patriarchal and patrilineal in nature. Their religious system is dominated by Hindu gods and goddesses. They worship Ganesh Ji, Ram Ji, Bheru Ji, and Durga Ji. In particular, the Bhil worship Lord Shiva and goddess Gowri or Parvati. Gavri is thus a major festival of the Bhil. Every year, many Bhils also visit Beneshwar Mahadev and take a holy dip on the confluence of river Mahi, Som, and Jakham on the day of Magh Poornima. Besides Hindu gods and goddesses, the Bhil also worship several local deities and spirits. While the village shaman, known as *Bhopa*, acts as the mediator with the spirit world, the village priest, *Bhagat*, performs other religious duties for the Bhil.

Economically, the Bhils are very poor. The primary sources of their livelihood are shifting cultivation, hunting, collection of forest produce, animal husbandry, and wage work. Since the Bhils live in the mountains, they do farming in the hill slopes. Women and children collect fruits, tuber, gum, ber, honey, and wood from the forest and sell them in the local market to meet their everyday needs. Collection of *mahua* flower is also very important, as the Bhils use it for making alcohol. However, with the arrival of the British, the Bhils were classified as a violent "criminal tribe"[1] and their rights to use the forest became heavily restricted. In the postcolonial period, the Government of Rajasthan implemented several community development, poverty reduction, and employment generation programs. However, due to the hierarchical structure of public administration, alarming bureaucratic corruption, and huge network of patron–client relationship, the postcolonial state has failed to uplift the economic status of the Bhils and provide them basic educational and health facilities (Sahoo, 2013). As a result, the Bhils have suffered from abject poverty and "backwardness".[2]

Although the percentage of people living below the poverty line has recently declined in Rajasthan, almost half of its population lived below the poverty line a few years ago, the majority of them tribals. This abject poverty and lack of employment has forced the Bhils to leave their home and migrate to nearby cities in Gujarat in search of work. The tribals also perform miserably in many of the socioeconomic and human development indicators. According to the 2011 Census, only 66.11% people are literate; female literacy is very low in the state – almost 50% of female of are still illiterate. When it comes to the tribals, female literacy is as low as 30.52%. While fertility rate among the tribals is extremely high (TFR 2.86), their life expectancy is very low. Furthermore, tribal maternal and infant mortality rates are very high. According to data, during 2011–2013, the maternal mortality rate in the state was 244 (per 100,000 live births).[3] While the overall infant mortality (IMR) rate in Rajasthan is 47 (per 1000 live births), among the tribal population it is as high as 100.[4] The major reasons of IMR among tribes are acute respiratory infections, diarrhea, and anemia (Nagda, 2004: 4). A majority of tribal women had low body mass index, indicating higher nutritional deficiency among them (Nagda, 2004: 1). The state has failed to intervene and address these developmental deficits of the tribal society. Besides state failure, alarming health conditions, extreme poverty, and lack of employment among the Bhils have resulted in their economic marginalization and political powerlessness.

Given this, Christian missionaries and numerous other non-state actors[5] have come to work with the Bhils. The first missionary who worked with the Bhils was James Shepherd of the Scottish Presbyterian Church. He came to Udaipur in 1877 when cholera broke out in the tribal-dominated hill areas (Sahoo, 2018). While medical mission was a vital aspect, the colonial project of "civilising mission" and social reform were integrally included with it in the evangelization of the Bhils. As Shyamlal has pointed out,

> in Rajasthan, the tribals attracted the attention of missionaries owing to their horrific practice of human sacrifice, deplorable socio-religious and economic conditions, and their exploitation by the higher caste Hindus or moneylenders, Rajas, petty police officials, and traders in the tribal areas.
>
> (1989: 193)

Although the Christian missionary work has significantly increased among the Bhils since then, the major growth occurred during the early years of the postcolonial period with the work of south Indian Pentecostal missionaries. The Pentecostals have used "active social ministries" not only to spread the Gospel but also to empower the Bhils. As a consequence, Pentecostalism has emerged as "tribal religious movement" in south Rajasthan (Lukose, 2009; Sahoo, 2018).

Growth of Pentecostalism among the Bhils

Although Christianity first came to south Rajasthan in 1877, its major growth occurred with the arrival of Indian Pentecostal Church missionary Thomas Mathews. According to Abraham (2011: 128), between 1920 and 1960, "the general spiritual climate of denominational churches [in north India] was in decline". Pentecostalism began to spread its roots and experienced generous growth in north India in the next 40 years with the arrival of south Indian missionaries (Abraham, 2011: 129). In South Rajasthan, Thomas Mathews arrived in 1963. He was miraculously saved by God from drowning in 1962 and after this accident, he dedicated his life to serving the Lord in "the hardest mission field" (FBC, 2017: 4). After his arrival in Udaipur, Mathews worked with the Bhils; he cycled to the remotest tribal villages and read the Gospel to the people. However, since religion is a sensitive issue, it was difficult for an "outsider" like Mathews to gain the trust of the people and spread Lord's message.

In the beginning when Mathews entered the Christian service, he was an advocate of "cross-cultural mission"; however, his experience among the Bhils made him realize that he needs to transform himself and instead focus on "contextual mission" (Lukose, 2009: 119). Mathews made necessary changes to his life and mission. He worked hard, encultured himself with the local culture and lifestyle of people, gave up his rice-eating habits and ate *chapati* with the Bhils, and learnt the local language (Sahoo, 2018: 33).[6] Most importantly, Mathews "recognized the importance of equipping the natives rather than focusing on cross-cultural missionaries. He found that native missionaries are more effective, fruitful and acceptable in north India" (Lukose, 2009: 120). Considering this, Mathews established the Native Missionary Movement in 1964, which initiated several local revivals and accelerated the church growth process in Rajasthan. To provide theological training to native missionaries, Mathews founded the Filadelfia Bible College in 1982. By 2017, the FBC had trained more than 1600 students who are planting churches and spreading the Gospel in different parts of the country (FBC, 2017: 6). As a consequence, hundreds of churches have been established under the banner of Filadelfia Fellowship Churches of India. During his 42 years of ministry, Thomas Mathews established more than a thousand churches in 13 states of north India; this meant at least two new churches were established every month (Lukose, 2009: 119–120; see also Sahoo, 2018: 33).

The Filadelfia Fellowship Churches of India, which Mathews established along with his wife Mary, took the lead and opened a space for other Pentecostal groups in Rajasthan (Sahoo, 2018: 34). The Rajasthan Pentecostal Church, which is a major Pentecostal church in Rajasthan, is also affiliated to the Filadelfia Mission. Some of the other major Pentecostal organizations are the Calvary Covenant Fellowship Mission (CCFM), Covenant Ministries, the Agape Fellowship Church, and Bethel Fellowship (Sahoo, 2018: 34). According to Lukose (2009: 132), there are at least 12 Pentecostal groups that are working in Rajasthan, apart from many independent congregations in various places.

Broadly, in Rajasthan today, there are two major Pentecostal groups that are actively working among the Bhils – (a) the so-called "Kerala missionaries" and (b) the indigenous Bhil missionaries. The former are the dominant agents, led largely by the Filadelfia group. These are the first generation of Pentecostal missionaries who came from Kerala and Tamil Nadu after

Independence and played a vital role in the spread of the Gospel in Rajasthan. Institutions like the Filadelfia Fellowship Mission, Filadelfia Bible College, Rajasthan Pentecostal Church, Native Missionary Movement, and several others are associated with it. They also have strong connection with other Pentecostal missions in India and abroad. By contrast, the second group includes missionaries who belong to indigenous Bhil communities, and they have largely remained independent. Such indigenous and independent groups are referred in the literature as neo-Pentecostal churches (Grim, 2009: 486; Sahoo, 2018: 7). One such major neo-Pentecostal church with which one of the authors has conducted his ethnographic fieldwork is the Calvary Covenant Fellowship Mission (CCFM); the CCFM was established in 1991 by Pastor Manohar Kala, a third-generation Pentecostal pastor. Over the last three decades, the CCFM has not only addressed some of the developmental deficits of the tribal society but has worked constantly to empower the tribals by encouraging their participation in democratic and development process.

The CCFM and Democratic Development

The CCFM is a neo-Pentecostal Mission organization that was founded by Pastor Manohar Kala in 1991 under the Rajasthan Societies Registration Act of 1958. Some of its major objectives are evangelism, church planting, leadership training, and social development. Due to the faith-based nature, the CCFM's idea of "development" is very different from that of the state or other development organizations. To "convert people to a morally inspired existence" (van der Veer, 1999: 23) is its priority, and "reforming" the behavior of the tribals is considered the necessary first step. According to leaders of the CCFM, tribals are superstitious and have several bad habits (*buri prabrutiyan*) such as belief in evil spirits, child marriage, stealing, consumption of alcohol and *tambakhu*, and excessive expenditure on expensive marriage ceremonies and communal feasts, which need to be reformed to overcome poverty and marginalization. Thus, in order to reform the behavior of the tribals, the CCFM has employed its members in the villages. Some of these members have gone through the Bible training and taken the leadership role.

Decentralizing Leadership

In order to carry out the reform activities and preaching of the Gospel among the Bhils, the CCFM has followed a decentralized leadership structure. Particularly, the church operates at three levels: (a) the higher-level church is known as the umbrella church, which operates from the city, (b) the community church that works with a cluster of villages, and (c) the house fellowships, which are evening prayer groups in the villages.

The umbrella church is located in the city of Udaipur; it has the responsibility to look after all other churches and make overall planning for the development of the church, the members, and the community. While the umbrella church is a registered organization, the community churches and the house fellowships are not registered; they come under the administration of the umbrella church. Through Bible training, the umbrella church develops Christian leadership who work with the community-level churches, which works with a cluster of villages outside the city. Particularly, the CCFM provides religious training and develops the capabilities of local tribal youths as local Christian leaders who are not only able to preach but also do social work. The CCFM has 12,000 members and prepared 140 local tribal religious leaders from the Bhil, Garasia, and other tribal communities. These leaders have received Bible training for one to three years. The CCFM also provides training to Sunday school teachers and house-church leaders. The major objective of this Christian leadership training is to facilitate evangelism and to plant churches. The CCFM has already planted 60 community churches that are run by these leaders who decentralize the church vision of CCFM. Although these churches are affiliated to CCFM, they enjoy a sense of autonomy as well. They are run by gifts and donations from members and support from Christian organizations in India.

Finally, the house fellowships operate at a very small level within a village. The CCFM has followed the "friendship evangelism" approach (Miller and Yamamori, 2007: 197), where the evangelists/pastors constantly visit people in the villages, establish a relationship with them and gain their trust, discuss their needs and problems, and heal the sick and pray for their wellbeing. They then start evening Bible studies and devotional gatherings wherein the Bhils articulate their individuality in terms of life-challenges they face and god-experiences they have undergone, eventually leading to the formation of a fellowship or congregation of believers. Initially, this congregation is organized as a "house fellowship" (meeting at a member's house for prayer), which is a basic form of fellowship. When the house fellowship continues for three to five years and is able to attract more people from the community, the CCFM decides to plant a "community church". It should, however, be noted that the establishment of a community church is largely dependent upon the interests/commitments of the believers and local Bhil Christian leaders, and local political configurations such as the support of the village councillor (*sarpanch*) and others.

Rationalizing/Modernizing Religion

The tribal worldview and belief system makes a distinction between the "evil" spirits and the "good" spirits. The Bhil believe that the evil spirits cause not just diseases but also all other problems in their lives; it is a sign that the gods are angry. In order to make the spirits and gods happy, the tribals visit the traditional spirit medium or shaman/exorcist, locally referred to as *Bhopa*. The *Bhopa* organizes elaborate religious and tantric rituals that require not only the offering of coconuts, fruits, milk, and incense sticks but also blood sacrifice in the form of chickens and goats. As the Bhils are economically very poor and marginalized, to organize such rituals, they often borrow money from the local Hindu upper caste and Muslim moneylenders with high rate of interest. Despite all these rituals and sacrifices, the patients are often not cured, which made them question the efficacy of their own traditional faith system. So, they seek the help of modern medicine. However, since the state has failed to open primary healthcare centers in the villages, the tribals go to hospitals in the city. Here, they find the doctors inaccessible, as they lack what were popularly perceived to be modern, "civilized" social interaction skills. Moreover, when the doctors examine the patient, they prescribe expensive tests and medicines, which often do not cure the patient.

In such contexts, the CCFM members and other Pentecostal believers in the village advise the family members to visit the church and pray the wellbeing of the patient. The Bhil took a "leap of faith" and visited the church as a last resort (Sahoo, 2018). At the church, the pastors explain them the ongoing "spiritual warfare" (Robbins, 2004: 128) between the evil spirit and the good spirit and carefully link the "good spirit" with the "Holy spirit". In particular, the pastors advocate that the Bhil do not any more need to "appease a whole pantheon of spirits through magic means, but one spirit, the Holy spirit" (Miller and Yamamori, 2007: 25) who is all powerful and capable of doing miracles and wonders. Moreover, for them, the Christian God (Jesus) is more powerful than the Hindu gods and goddesses, which many tribals have found very attractive. When a patient comes to the church, the pastors give him/her some modern medicine (*daba*) but also mention that that medicine alone will not work; s/he needs the blessings of Christ (*dua*) because Christ is all powerful; he is the miracle master. The pastors prayed for the wellbeing of the patients and the combination of *daba* and *dua* created miracles and cured many patients. As my respondents pointed out, over the years, many illnesses have been cured and peace has returned to families, which has strengthened not only their faith in the church but also in Christian modernity and monotheism.

Empowering Bhil Women: Equality and Dignity

Although the Bhil women enjoy a lot of freedom, they have a weaker position, as patriarchal structures are widespread in the tribal society. According to Mosse (2005: 57), in a Bhil society, "women are rather than have property". While being treated as property, Bhil women are also tortured and abused by their drunken husbands. The CCFM members point out that such behaviors of men were due to "the handiwork of the Satan" (*saitan usko ulti buddhi deta*) and to control such behavior, the CCFM follows a set of very "strict and rigid rules" about alcohol, tobacco consumption, polygamy, extramarital sexuality, and violence. Such strict codes of conduct have attracted the tribal women to church. As Aaron (2009: 109), in his study of the Dangs, has noted, "deliverance from alcohol addiction ranks next to healing as a cause for allegiance to Christianity, particularly among women, who readily accept Christ after their husbands give up drinking".

Hefner (2013: 10) has argued that "some of the most subjectively demanding prohibitions take aim at men. Their pre-conversion privileges are represented as sins and misdeeds indulged at the expense of their female partner and children". The man is "morally disciplined" and is required to "maintain a state of inner purity necessary to receive empowerment from the Holy Spirit" (Hefner, 2013: 9). Particularly, the CCFM has played a vital role in counseling partners to respect and treat each other equally. During prayer meetings, pastors and church leaders discuss the issue of gender discrimination and violence in the country and emphasize that both men and women are equal. Discussing the Delhi gang rape case at one of the New Year prayer meetings in 2013, a pastor emphasized that if all men begin respecting women and treat them equally, violence against women will be completely eliminated from our country (*agar hum* [we, men] *mahilaon ko izzat dena shuru kar dein, unka sammaan karein, aur unko barabari se dekhein, toh yeh sab samasyaein humare desh se puri tarah khatm ho jayengi*). Thus, as a result of constant counseling by the CCFM, "physical torture, beatings and verbal abuse by drunkenness have been eliminated to a large extent. The relationship between husband and wife has improved significantly at home. The male converts seem more concerned about and responsible for their families" (Sahoo, 2018: 109). Furthermore, the CCFM has spread the values of love, trust, respect, dignity, and equality among the Bhil men and women and prepared them to become "good" Christian citizens.

Promoting Partnership in Community Development

With the failure of the state to provide basic welfare programs, the CCFM has actively engaged with the developmental problems of the tribal society. Through their various "active social ministries" (Miller and Yamamori, 2007: 1), such as education, counseling, health and medical assistance, agriculture and economic development, and relief work, they have actively intervened in tribal society (Sahoo, 2018: 38). Interviews with the leaders reveal that the CCFM runs several adult education (*proudha shiksha*) centers, which are run in the village in the evening by church members. The CCFM provides slates, chalks, and gaslight to the center and a nominal 700 rupees to the teacher as remuneration. Besides this, the CCFM runs several child education centers and an orphanage (*anathashram*).

With regard to health, the tribals suffer from various diseases due to poverty, lack of sanitation, and poor hygiene. Superstition and ignorance also make them believe that evil spirits cause diseases. In such contexts, CCFM generates awareness among believers and teaches them about hygiene and cleanliness. Further, it organizes health camps, provides free medicines, and installs handpumps in the tribal villages; most of these projects, which aim to bring "holistic development", are supported by Christian organizations such as Gospel for Asia, Operation Agape, World Vision, Seva Bharat, and Christian Broadcasting Network. These development ministries have helped tribals in the villages and show that the CCFM has been able to offer basic services that the government has failed to supply.

Through its preaching and prayer meetings, the CCFM continuously encourages believers to inculcate "good" habits. For example, on 1 January 2013, a New Year prayer meet was organized at a church near Udaipur. The meeting started with prayers and devotional songs. The participants performed *bhajan mandalis*. Following this, the pastor preached the gospel and linked it with everyday problems of the tribals. Bergunder (2008: 19) is right to note that "Pentecostal teaching and spirituality are strongly related to experience and praxis". The pastor then read the newspaper, discussed the Delhi gang rape case, which was then making the headlines, and emphasized the need to respect women and treat them equally. Quoting a local proverb, he noted that there is an urgent need to give importance to the upbringing and care of the girl child because they have long been discriminated against. He further noted that one does not need to worry much about a boy child because "if you have a good son he will find his way to earn and if you have a bad son he will spend everything that you have" (*put suput hai to kamalega; put kuput hai to udalega*). Furthermore, the pastor discussed issues such as afforestation, agriculture and irrigation facilities, healthcare, children's education, and various government policies for tribal development. Toward the end, the pastor discussed bureaucratic and political corruption in the country and urged people to make 13 promises for 2013, such as give up bad habits, do good work, not to cheat others, to help people, to come nearer to God, to believe in God and pray, to be grateful to God, and not to deviate from faith. The pastor then read 13 messages from the Bible and prayed for the socioeconomic wellbeing and transformation of tribal society. Interviews with the converts showed that the presence of the CCFM has had significant positive effects on the community.

Broadly, the above discussion shows that the CCFM has effectively used the gospel and development ministries not just to spread the Pentecostal faith but also to bring social, cultural, and political transformations among the tribals of Rajasthan.

Part II: Christianity in Odisha – The Kondha–Pano Dynamics

Kandhamal, one of the 30 districts of Odisha, has a substantial population of two marginal communities in India, namely, Scheduled Castes (SCs) who constitute 15.76% of the population and Scheduled Tribes (STs), 53.58%. Among the latter, 93% of them belong to Kondh tribe, while 88% of the SCs in this district hail from the Pano caste. The socioeconomic situation in Kandhamal is characterized by low employment and lack of income-generating opportunities in the area. A large percentage of the population here lives below the poverty line (BPL). According to UNDP Odisha Human Development Report 2005, 75% of the total population in the district live under the BPL while 87% of the SCs and 92% of the STs in the district live under the BPL. It is so primarily because the tribal and the local people whose primary occupation has been traditionally agriculture (69 out of 100 people being agricultural workers in the district) have been disenfranchised over a period of time. Before the British, community owned all the land. But the British land laws recognized only individual land ownership, not the community ownership which turned all community owned land into state property. With that, the tribal people became encroachers on the land which was their ancestral habitat for centuries. Besides, though the forests of the district have a considerable NTFP (Non-Timber Forest Products) potential, the local people do not profit by it. For instance, while Kandhamal produces lots of turmeric, the major portion of profit out of it has been taken by middlemen as there is no organized system in place to market the final product.

As per religion, 79.16% of the population in Kandhamal are Hindus, 20.31% are Christians, and 0.29% are others. While both Hinduism and Christianity are spread among both among SC Panos and ST Kondhs in the district, Panos outnumber Kondhs in Christianity while Kondhs outnumber Panos in Hinduism. Hence in public perception, Dalit Panos are generally associated with Christianity and ST Kondhs with Hinduism. Historically speaking, the relationship between the Kondhs and Panos was often unequal as the Panos were employed also by the Kondh landlords for servile occupations.[7] One of the key responsibilities of the Panos in the past was to supply *Meriah* (offering of humans for sacrifice to God) to the Kondhs. The relationship between Kondhs and Panos got strained over a period of time, caused by multiple factors and players. It was when the Kondh district came under regular civil and police authority of the British in 19th century that the latter caused the very first recorded instance of conflict between the two by abolishing the gruesome Meriah practice in 1861 with the help of missionaries (Swaro, 1990) While trying to abolish the Meriah sacrifice, the British not only made themselves a political enemy to the Kondh, they also brought animosity between the Kondhs and Panos. After the Meriah custom was outlawed, the Panos, having lost their livelihood, were forced to win the favor of the British. This made the Panos come close to the Christian missionaries and they began to get converted into Christianity. "The Kandhas (sic) started hating the Christian Panas (sic) blaming them as traitors to their old religion and the society as well" (Mohanty 2017: 179). Describing this situation, Mohanty (2017) notes that "This was the major reason of caste conflict because the Kandhas (sic) had been seeing the total landscape on their own and they had given some land to the Panas (sic) to live and supply Meriah as per requirement" (Ibid.). As per Kondhs' religious worldview, their failure to perform Meriah sacrifice would bring God's wrath upon them and their land with the failure of rain. Subsequently, when chickenpox broke out in 1866 causing many deaths, they were not only convinced that the British and their new faith could not save the land and its people (which made a group of Christian Kondhs to return to their original religion) but also their anger and hostility was further intensified toward the Panos who discontinued their duty of supplying Meriah and become Christians, choosing an alien God and siding with their enemy, the British.

Another source of rivalry between the Kondhs and Panos was the widening disparity between the Christian Panos and Hindu Kondhs in terms of economy, education, and development. With education, developmental opportunities, finical aid, and logistical support during calamities offered by Christian organizations, the Panos progressed economically faster than the Hindu Kondh neighbors in the region. In the absence of such support and opportunities, the Hindu Kondhs grew jealous of the Panos and it resulted in social tension between the two (Mohanty 2017: 183). The third source of conflict between the two is the role played by big traders, the migrants from hinterland, for instance, the Kumuti community in Raikia, who tried to fracture the relationship between the poor Hindus and the Dalit Christians (Mohanty 2017: 178). With the introduction of new income-generation schemes, the locals, especially the Dalit Christians, not only stopped borrowing money from the Oriya money lenders like the Kumuti people but also started their own shops. Finding themselves at these loosing ends, the outside traders joined hands with the Sangh Parivar in accusing the Christian Panos of being cheaters and grabbers of caste, land, and jobs from the Hindu Kondhs and set the Adivasi Hindus against the Dalit Christians (Ponniah 2017).

Christianity, Panos, and Development

In our view, Dalit Panos seem to have embraced Christianity for five substantive reasons related to development. First, Panos' relationship to Christianity in 19th century had to do with protection of their land against the local little kings who attempted to disenfranchise them. To cite an example, in 1883 the Panos of Kattinga village invited Fr. J. M. Dupont to settle the land dispute with a local king and the Panos became Christians as a way of acknowledging the missionary's intervention in their struggle for better living (Bishoyi 2018: 75). Second, there is a relationship between their search for new sources of income and their relationship to Christianity. Panos embraced Christianity in the process of finding alternative livelihood when they lost their traditional job of supplying meriahs to Kondhs. At that point, while they took up more jobs in agricultural sector, they also began to pick up government-sponsored work as daily laborers as a way to supplement their farm work and earn extra money. "This proved to be economically successful for them, and situated them in British favor over the Kandhas (sic) because of their willingness to adhere to colonial policy, learn the language, and eventually convert to Christianity" (PUCL and Kashipur Solidarity Group 2009: 29). To put it differently, since Christianity, in public perception, was seen as part of alternative form of livelihood and survival offered by the British, the Panos embraced the new religion of Christianity. Thirdly, Panos took to Christianity as it offered an alternative path and a new way forward promising them liberation from their existing social conditions, local customs, and religious obligations, all of which kept them low in social status. Fourth, Panos embraced Christianity because the new faith provided them education and health services that improved their quality of life. Fifth, they opted for Christianity also because Christian organizations not only offered developmental and occupational schemes to improve their lives and livelihoods but also made it possible for them to access such schemes offered by state and non-state agencies. With the new world of possibilities unfolding before them mediated through Christianity, the Panos could hope for self-dignity and new social visibility hitherto unavailable to them.

Christianity and Social Transformation in Kandhamal, Odisha

Christianity which took roots in Kandhamal in the second half of 19th century did bring about considerable social change in the region over a period of time. It is through the tireless work of Baptist missionaries like John Goadby, William Hill, Abiathar Wilkinson (known for his translation of the Gospel of Mark into Kui language in 1893), Arthur Long, Tom Wood, and John Biswas and Catholic MSFS missionaries, Fr. Jean-Marie Dupont and Fr. Philippe Richard that Christianity was able to impact the social and cultural milieu of Kandhamal in multiple ways. Significant among them was the establishment of educational institutions and healthcare facilities by the missionaries. "These missionaries were the pioneers in setting up modern centres of education and health in Kandhamal. Any achievement that the district has today in these fields is because of the efforts of the missionaries" (PUCL and Kashipur Solidarity Group 2009: 31). To cite some examples, Fr. J. M. Dupont established a primary school at Katingia in the late 19th century and the first Middle English school in the whole of Boudh-Khondmals came into being in 1914 at G. Udaygiri (Gudripari). Subsequently, two Upper Primary schools in Malikapodi and Konbagiri and two high schools, O. J. Milman High English School and Hubback High English School, were also established in G. Udaygiri by the Baptists. The Roman Catholics also established Primary, Middle English, and High Schools in the Raikia area. According to The District Gazetteer (1983). "These schools went a long way in providing education not only to Christians, but also to non-Christians" (as cited in PUCL and Kashipur Solidarity Group 2009: 31). In this context, we also need to make a mention about the establishment of orphanages in Surada of Ganjam district in Odisha during the great famine (1866–1887) which caused the death of nearly half a million people in Odisha alone. During this time, the missionaries not only helped the poor children overcome starvation deaths but also provided primary education to all the orphans and destitute children. As discussed in the introduction of this book, education is a game changer for the people especially for the ones on the periphery as it not only produces new consciousness and a sense of confidence, and provides accesses to new opportunities of employment but also aims to impact the social ambience with the democratic values of equality, human dignity, individual liberty etc. Further, Christianity had also introduced medical facilities in region. Fr. J. M. Dupont had created a healthcare center at Katingia already in 1880s, while the Baptists went on to set up the Moorshead Memorial Christian Hospital in 1939. Such facilities furthered the quality of life for the poor and the wellbeing of society at Kandhamal region. It is not only through education and healthcare but also through other substantiative forms of development, participatory programs, rights-based schemes, and ameliorative initiatives that Christianity altered the social milieu of Kandhamal. In the following sections, we will focus on the Christian organization Jan Vikas and its offshoot ORSSA and look at their functions and contributions that seek to make Kandhamal lifeworld more democratic.

Jan Vikas and Strategies for Inclusive and Holistic Development

Christianity's transformative mission in this region was carried out by Christian organizations and non-state agencies such as Jana Vikas, Catholic Church's social service wing, exclusively established for the people of Kandhamal in 1988. Jan Vikas today works in 1596 villages under 67 GPs of 12 blocks in the Kandhamal District of Odisha with the goal of achieving self-sustainable development for the poor and marginalized social groups such as Dalits, Adivasis, and Other Backward Communities in Kandhamal district. While initially its focus was on providing basic amenities to the locals, it shifted to nonformal education and elimination of common diseases in 1992. The organization took to leadership trainings and facilitating Panchayat Raj Institutions in 1995 and it kickstarted cooperative movement with the creation of SHGs in Kandhamal district in 1996. SHGs mobilized women from marginal and poor communities to start Mahila Vikas cooperative in 1999 and Jana Vikas gave seeds worth of Rs 3000 to the SHGs for cultivating turmeric. While SHGs created jobs and contributed to economic growth of the society, it also played a vital role in protecting people from the exploitation of the local money lenders and business traders as SHGs were involved in the sales of turmeric and transferred the benefits directly to women themselves. Over the years, two more cooperatives were registered such as, Vikas Jyoti Multipurpose Cooperative Ltd and Jeeban Vikas Multipurpose Cooperative Ltd. Jana Vikas facilitates these cooperatives for regular meetings, for business planning, and for getting loan for investment in various income-generation activities (IGA).

In 2000, Jana Vikas adopted a social analysis approach which enabled local communities to identify their own issues and problems. This led to creating awareness, starting with campaign against *bidis* (hand rolled smoking tobacco) and bad roads etc. Positively, this approach gave birth to joint programs by Government and Jana Vikas such as ICDS (Integrated Child Development Service) Centre, evening schools, and low-cost housing for tribal people. Taking cognizance of Orissa Human Development report (2004) that pointed to the increase in Kandhamal's poverty index from 71%

in 1975 to 75% in 1993, Jana Vikas carried out its first strategic planning programs in 2005, which included improvement of livelihoods and governance, strengthening of people's movements, promoting effective functioning of SHGs, creating awareness of rights and responsibilities among the marginal people, enhancing human rights, launching watershed project with people's participation, and creating micro enterprise models. As SHGs became a threat to local traders, cooperatives were attacked by traders between 2007 and 2010. During the communal violence between Hindu rights groups and Christians in 2008, Jana Vikas' office was burnt, its staffs were attacked, and its properties and infrastructural facilities were extensively damaged. As a result, the cooperatives' activities remained suspended for almost a year and the members were very reluctant to come forward for work.

However, Jana Vikas' leadership and administrative team demonstrated courage, resilience, and determination to carry out relief operations, to look at human rights violations, and to handle legal issues. Training on trauma counseling by NIMHANS, Bangalore was also organized for the staff and for the voluntary workers of the organization. In the post-violence period, Jana Vikas had courageously and thoughtfully launched various programs that took care of not only the immediate needs of the riot-affected people such as trauma counseling, legal aid, resettlement and rehabilitation of the displaced but also the general needs of local communities such as health, livelihood, and education of children. Another important contribution of Jana Vikas during this period was its peace building project. This included peace in action activities like sports activities, street plays, and cultural programs which brought together the locals, the Hindu Kandhos, and Christian Panos as one village community.

> Under this project Jana Vikas established Peace Committees to disseminate peace messages among the communities, promoted village task force to identify and resolve various issues in the villages, organized trainings on advocacy and lobbying for staff etc., to create harmony and bring development in the region.
> (Kusters et al. 2015: 15)

While such post-violence peace programs showed new areas and methods by which Christian organization can decentralize its sphere of operation by involving people and ensuring their participation for the envisaged outcomes, it also "realised that understanding human and social capital is essential for development" (Ibid.).

In 2013, Jana Vikas developed a new strategic plan for 2014–2018 and worked out a specific strategy to engage with the government departments and participate in the government funded projects and programs, which brought about a new optics for Jana Vikas, namely, that it is a Christian organization that works for the holistic development of all people beyond any religious affiliations. To do so, it has to sever its ties with the Catholic

Charity[8] and became an independent unit. Its new strategic plan embarked up a new vision of "a holistic and sustainable society where people live in unity amidst diversity based on social and human values of justice and equity"(Ibid.) and a mission

> to sensitise, organise, enable, empower and develop the poor and the marginalized, especially the Adivasi, Dalit and OBCs, to respond to their issues, needs, problems, vulnerabilities and bring forth changes for common goal and interest by using their existing potential, strength and resources, through collective reflection, decision and action.
> (Ibid.)

To achieve its vision and mission, it has chalked out its strategies with a focus on five key programs such as (a) Livelihood Development, (b) Education, (c) Governance and Rights, (d) Women empowerment and tackling violence against women, and (e) Peace building. For paucity of space, let us discuss only two of the above five programs, namely, "Governance and Rights" and women empowerment.

Governance and Rights

The programs in the strategic area of "Governance and Rights" include awareness building of community on different schemes, programs, and their rights and entitlements, capacity building of staff on good governance and entitlements of different target communities, facilitating communities and CBOs (Community-based organizations) to participate in Palli Sabha and Gram Sabha, imparting and improving capacities of community to conduct social audit, making people active members of different committees at different levels and bring forth issues of governance and rights to the notice of officials and influencing them to act upon the issues, facilitating people representatives known as "barefoot communicators" to identify and document issues of misgovernance and nonfulfillment of rights and entitlements, and linking up the barefoot communicators with media to take up local issues and highlight them.

Empowerment of Women

The programs in the strategic area of "Women empowerment and Violence against Women" include awareness building of women and men on the issues affecting women, sensitization of youth on sexual harassment and abuse, linking the victim with available legal and justice delivery bodies and systems, building alliances with organizations working on women issues to influence policies and their implementation, capacity building of women PRI (Panchayat Raj institution) members on their roles and responsibilities, rights, powers, and duties as a PRI, strengthening women capacities for active participation in Palli Sabha, Gram Sabha, and in the decision-making bodies at gram panchayat, panchayat samiti, and zila parishad (district council). When one of us visited Kandhamal in 2013 and conducted a FGD (focus group discussion) in Nugaon with the women from the villages, they informed us that Jana Vikas organized women SHGs in 1300 villages in four blocks, promoted micro finance among them so that women make their own business investments and not depend on local traders. To facilitate SHGs and monitor their schemes, Jan Vikas had employed around 100 staff and volunteers to work in these villages. Majority of them are based in the field, rent houses, and stay with the people. One such program initiated then was a project called "Sustainable Livelihood enhancement". The goal of the project is to create sustainable livelihood for the poor and the marginalized families by strengthening SHGs among women to ensure the wellbeing of the community. The impression that we got in the FGD was that Jan Vikas had enabled people's participation in community development through SHGs. Mohanty also notes that after Kandhamal violence, another Christian agency, Evangelical Fellowship of India Commission on Relief (EFICOR), to help people rebuild their lives and livelihoods routed their programs through women's SHGs and women volunteers on the ground. A close study of EFICOR annual reports indicates that the organization has adopted more sustained and decentralized approach in implementing projects such as Sahyog Sustainable Development, Peace Building programs etc.

When we analyze the abovementioned activities and the programs of Christian organizations like Jana Vikas, it seems to be doing quite a lot to involve the local people, the Dalits, and Adivasis in implementing its programs. It has taken adequate steps to decentralize its activities, empower people, and entrust them with responsibilities to plan and execute their economic life. All its efforts, initiatives, and its comprehensive strategic plan 2014–2018 are founded on an ambitious vision of making Kandhamal villages a democratic society with decentralized structures of administering its economic and social life. But the extent to which the vision and dream of Jana Vikas has been actualized on the ground needs to be explored further and, perhaps, to be investigated by an evaluative study.

Christian Organizations and Minority Rights

Christian organizations and its leaders in Odisha, of late, have proactively involved, both personally and organizationally, in articulating their concerns against issues related to a range of rights, such as human rights, women rights, child rights, SC and ST rights, minority rights etc. Fr. Manoj, the then director of Jan Vikas, articulated his concerns as follows:

> We are working for the Dalit rights, raising voice against government when it fails to protect them and their rights and freedoms. By raising voice against government we are trying to help the people to speak for

Christian Churches, Democratic Developments, People at Margins 147

their rights. We are with the people by providing legal support to them. Jana Vikas is not against government but holds the state accountable when the human rights of the Dalits and women are violated.[9]

Another key Christian organization that does advocacy for human rights is ORSSA (The Orissa (Odisha) forum for Social Action), founded by Fr. Richard Vas and revisioned by Fr. Ajay Singh. It is the social action center of Catholic Church in Odisha, whose primary goal is to develop perspectives according to Ajay Singh. He detailed the center's prolife as follows.[10]

> This centre's role is to coordinate the efforts of social works of the Catholic Church in odisha, The centre is mandated to develop perspectives within the Catholic church in Odisha for its programmes related to social action, peace and justice. Even though the Church in the state has already institutions that engage in such programmes, we are trying to understand how best they can be carried out more effectively for real social transformation. Secondly, the centre's role is advocacy and lobbying from these perspectives in support of rights for Dalits, tribals and women. As the director, I have planned to address four major areas: 1. Abuse against tribal and Dalit women by some upper caste and business people; 2. Policy changes at the state level. Since 40% of the state population are Dalits and tribal, they need proportional allocation of funds and resources for their development. Unfortunately, even the allotted budget is not utilized properly. Hence the centre's work is advocacy and lobbying with the MLA's and policy makers and to make the government and the bureaucracy more accountable; 3. Atrocity reduction against SC's and STs: There is SC & ST atrocity act but it does not function. The centre is linked to the network of national campaign on Dalit human rights. As a local unit, we monitor the Dalit human rights violation at the district and state levels; 4. Communal Violence: In communal violence, the Dalit and tribal people are worst affected both in Kandhamal and in the state. We are trying to see how the corporate, communal and caste forces work in collusion. This is also new area of interface between church and non-church agencies. In pursuance of this area of focus, we are involved in religious freedom issues and the coordination of 'relief and rehabilitation measures' with justice and human rights perspectives.

While the above interview conducted in 2013 highlights the vision of the center, a cursory survey of the center's programs in subsequent years illustrate how it has gone about implementing its perspective building mission. The center's programs primarily involve workshops, seminars, and awareness camps that aim at imparting knowledge, providing motivations, and alternative perspectives to the leaders, both ecclesiastical and civil, grass-root level local representatives and institutional heads. Major topics of such programs[11] include "Challenges before secularism and Democracy", "Building a just and harmonious society", "Trafficking and Forest Right Act", "A two day people's Tribunal" with 750 participants who presented their case before the Juries, workshop on "Human Rights" "Child Protection Policy and Sexual abuse at work place", "Child protection Policy and Anti-trafficking Rule" Child Rights Convention focusing on rights of Minority Children of Odisha; CMDRR training for community leaders and NGO leaders; Workshop on the Research Findings of the Study Report "Discrimination during Disasters"; Dalit-Adivasi Budget Analysis 2017–2018; and workshop on "Building Strategies for Policy Reforms Preventing caste Discrimination during Disasters", "Reservation for Minority communities in the Panchayat Raj body elections as found in Sachar Committee Recommendation", etc. ORSSA also organizes various events that illustrate multiple strategies this Christian organization employs to empower people and make Odisha and Kandhamal more people-centric and participatory social space. To cite some examples, it organized the submission of memorandum to the Governor of the state on 25 August 2013 by the Dalit and tribal community leaders regarding issues such as low conviction rate and inadequate compensation to victim survivors of Kandhamal violence. It facilitated the interaction of Prof. Hiener Bielefelt (special Rapporteur for freedom of religion and belief, UN) with the local people on right to freedom of religion.

Conclusion

The above discussion presented two case studies of Christian organizations in Rajasthan and Odisha and the role they have played in transforming the socioeconomic and political lifeworld of the tribal and Dalit populations living at the margins of the state. Particularly, we argued that in a context where the state has failed to reach out to the poor and marginalized sections of society, in such contexts, non-state faith-based organizations like the Calvary Covenant Fellowship Mission and the Jan Vikas have played a vital role in addressing the developmental deficits that tribals and Dalits have experienced. Most importantly, both organizations have not only initiated different developmental and social welfare programs to address the educational and health deficits of the people but also specifically worked for the empowerment of the women and so on. In doing so, they have made available to the marginal people different "capabilities" (such as education, good health, economic independence, and social mobility), increased their substantive freedoms, and enhanced their wellbeing, to borrow Amartya Sen's ideas (1993). The instrumental and mutually constituting nature of all these multiple freedoms (such as economic, social, and political) not only produced their development but also facilitated the exercise the human agency (i.e., freedom to act toward new ways of being, which is also instrumental for collective action and democratic participation (Sen 1999)) of marginal people who in turn could enter and register their presence in the emerging democratic spaces of Independent India.

Christian Churches, Democratic Developments, People at Margins 149

In the context of Rajasthan, the CCFM has combined active development ministries with the preaching of the Gospel to bring "holistic" community development in the Bhil society. As a part of its community development programs, the CCFM has established several adult education centers and organized health camps, which are carried out by its leaders. By giving responsibility to the native Bhil youth to spread the Gospel and to bring awareness in the community, the CCFM has not only decentralized its leadership but also strengthened the agency and autonomy of the Bhil Pentecostals. These native leaders have also played a vital role in counseling the male members to give up alcohol and tobacco and treat their partners with respect and dignity. As a result of constant counseling from the leaders, it is observed that the relationship between husband and wife has improved in the family; the male members have become more loving, caring, and responsible toward their family; they also no longer make unnecessary expenses which has in fact improved the economic conditions of the family. In a sense, the Pentecostal ethics of the CCFM has reduced what Elizabeth Brusco (1995) calls "machismo" or patriarchal values and made both husband and wife equal partners in the family. Thus, by decentralizing leadership, by addressing the absence of the state through active development ministries, and by reducing machismo, the CCFM has not only improved the socioeconomic conditions of the Bhil Pentecostals but also democratized the development process at the grassroots.

Similarly, in the context of Odisha, Christianity has improved the quality of life in Kandhamal by imparting education and healthcare to the locals, especially to the marginalized communities in the region. By introducing modern medicine in 19th century at Kandhamal area and providing healthcare to all people, regardless of their background, Christian agencies have democratized the then-existing medical system. By imparting education to the poor and the marginal people, Christian institutions not only democratized the channels of knowledge acquisition accessed only by the male twice born in the subcontinent for millennia. Education as indicated in the introduction also made social actors to receive democratic values and participate in democratic processes that slowly began to unfold in the lifeworld of the common people in Kandhamal as elsewhere in India. Further, as we have seen, Christian organizations like the Jan Vikas had also taken concrete steps, however less or more successful they were, to democratize the Kandhamal social milieu by enabling women and SC/ST people to overcome categorical inequalities. They were able to achieve this by accessing various people-centered occupational programs, pro-poor economic activities, women-specific schemes, and community monitored development plans offered by Jan Vikas and participating in the ORSSA-sponsored events and programs that covered a range of issues such as violation of human rights and religious freedom for the Dalits, failure of state machinery to provide educational opportunities and related benefits to SC/ST children, atrocities against poor women, etc. Thus the marginal people of Kandhamal could sign themselves in the social register of Kandhamal as autonomous democratic subjects thanks to their active engagement with the local governance issues and the wider policy matters of the democratic nation state.

Notes

1 The Criminal Tribes Act of 1871, modified in 1897 and 1911, categorized some groups of people as born criminals. It noted that (1) "all persons born in a particular group, or caste are criminal by birth", and (2) "once a criminal always a criminal" (Kapadia 1952, p. 99). Thus, the act required all people of the group to register themselves with authorities and inform them of their movement. This particularly gave authorities the power to restrict the movement of the people and harass them.
2 This "backwardness" is a generic term used by non-tribals and the postcolonial state to refer to not just the economic marginalization and powerlessness of the Bhils but also their social and cultural backwardness expressed in their dress and deportment, lifestyle, and aspirations (Baviskar 2005: 5105).
3 https://www.hindustantimes.com/jaipur/maternal-mortality-rate-in-rajasthan-declines-by-45-points-srs-data/story-M92IhFA5UfGP4v7Oe4P7tK.html (accessed on 12 October 2020).
4 https://www.indianpediatrics.net/dec2016/dec-1117.htm (accessed on 12 October 2020).
5 Prior to 1950, the number of established NGOs in Rajasthan was only eight, but since then the number has increased significantly. The NGO registration office in Udaipur reports that 3163 organizations of different kind have been registered in Udaipur between 1988 and 13 February 2007 under the Rajasthan Societies Registration Act 1958. As a result of the increasing number of NGOs, Udaipur has been derisively described not by its traditional name, the "city of lakes", but as the "city of NGOs" (Sahoo 2013, p.10).
6 Later, "*chaval aur* Malayalam *chodo, chappathi aur* Hindi *apnavo*" (give up rice and Malyalam, accept *chappathi* and Hindi instead) became Mathews' slogan (Lukose, 2009: 119).
7 LSS O' Malley, Bengal District Gazetteers, Balasore (Calcutta: Bengal Secretariat Book Depot, 1907), 18.
8 Catholic charity is one of the units of Catholic Church's social service organization known as "Caritas". Jana Vikas is the sub-unit of Catholic charity.
9 Interview with Fr. Manoj, the director of Jana Vikas in Nuagaon on 29 May 2013 (11.30 a.m. to 12.30 p.m.).
10 Interview with Ajay Sing in Bhubaneswar on 28 May 2013 (11.30 a.m.–1.00 p.m.).
11 The data collated and presented in this section is obtained from https://www.facebook.com/governanceforodisha/?ref=page_internal (last visited 15 March 2021) and https://www.facebook.com/orosa.bhubaneswar (last visited 16 March 2021)

References

Aaron, S.J. (2009). Emulating Azariah: Evangelicals and Social Change in the Dangs. In D.H. Lumsdaine, ed., *Evangelical Christianity and Democracy in Asia*. New York: Oxford University Press, pp. 87–130.

Abraham, S. (2011). Ordinary Indian Pentecostal Christology. PhD Thesis, University of Birmingham.

Baviskar, A. (2005). Adivasi Encounters with Hindu Nationalism in MP. *Economic and Political Weekly* 40(48), pp. 5105–5113.
Bergunder, M. (2008). *The South Indian Pentecostal Movement in the Twentieth Century.* Grand Rapids: Eerdemans.
Bishoyi, U. (2018). *Flames of Faith in Kandhamal.* Bhubaneswar: Shades Publications.
Brusco, E.E. (1995). *The Transformation of Machismo: Evangelical Conversion and Gender in Colombia.* Austin: University of Texas Press.
Filadelphia Bible College (2017). *Student Handbook of Filadelphia Bible College.* Udaipur: Filadelphia Bible College.
Grim, B.J. (2009). Pentecostalism's Growth in Religiously Restricted Environments. *Society* 46(6), pp. 484–495.
Hefner, R.W. (2013). Introduction: The Unexpected Modern – Gender, Piety and Politics in the Global Pentecostal Surge. In R.W. Hefner, ed., *Global Pentecostalism in the Twenty-First Century.* Bloomington: Indian University Press, pp. 1–26.
Jayal, N.G. (2013). *Citizenship and its Discontents: An Indian History.* Cambridge, MA: Harvard University Press.
Kapadia, K.M. (1952), The Criminal Tribes of India. *Sociological Bulletin* 1(2), pp. 99–125.
Kusters, C., Mohapatra, B.P., Sethi, S., Buizer, N.N., Das, A., Bhatra, R.W. and Sen, P. (2015). *Endline report – India, Jana Vikas. MFS II Country Evaluations; Capacity of Southern Partner Organisations (5C) Component.* Wageningen: Centre for Development Innovation, Wageningen University.
Lukose, W. (2009). A Contextual Missiology of the Spirit: A Study of Pentecostalism in Rajasthan, India. PhD Thesis, University of Birmingham.
Miller, D.E. and T. Yamamori. (2007). *Global Pentecostalism: The New Face of Christian Social Engagement.* Berkeley: University of California Press.
Mohanty, R.K. (2017). The Extant of Conflict among Marginalised Communities: A Study in Kandhamal District of Odisha. *Sociological Bulletin* 66(2), pp. 174–190.
Mosse, D. (2005). *Cultivating Development: An Ethnography of Aid Policy and Practice.* London: Pluto Press.
Nagda, B.L. (2004). Tribal Population and Health in Rajasthan. *Studies of Tribes and Tribals* 2(1), pp. 1–8.
Ponniah, J. (2017). Communal Violence in India: Exploring Strategies of its Nurture and Negation in Contemporary Times. *Journal of Religion and Violence* 5(1), pp. 79–101.
PUCL and Kashipur Solidarity Group. (2009). *Crossed and Crucified: Parivar's War Against Minorities in Orissa.* Delhi: Kashipur Solidarity Group.
Robbins, J. (2004). The Globalisation of Pentecostal and Charismatic Christianity. *Annual Review of Anthropology* 33, pp. 117–143.
Roy, A. (2016). *Citizenship in India.* New Delhi: Oxford University Press.
Sahoo, S. (2013) *Civil Society and Democratisation in India: Institutions, Ideologies and Interests.* London: Routledge.
Sahoo, S. (2018) *Pentecostalism and Politics of Conversion in India.* New Delhi: Cambridge University Press.
Sahoo, S. and Chaney, P., eds., (2021) *Civil Society and Citizenship in India and Bangladesh.* New Delhi: Bloomsbury.
Sen, A. (1993). Capability and Well-Being. In Nussbaum and Sen eds., *The Quality of Life.* Oxford: Oxford University Press, pp. 30–53.
Sen, A. (1999). *Development as Freedom.* Oxford: Oxford University Press.

Shyamlal. (1989). Planting a Mission among the Bhils of South Rajasthan. In M.K. Raha, ed., *Tribal India*, Vol. II. New Delhi: Gyan Publishing House, pp. 192–212.

Swaro, D. (1990). *The Christian Missionaries in Orissa*. Calcutta: Punthi Pustak.

Van der Veer, P. (1999). The Moral State: Religion, Nation, and Empire in Victorian Britain and British India. In P. van der Veer and H. Lehmann, eds., *Nation and Religion*. Princeton: Princeton University Press, pp. 15–43.

8 Divided Church as a Democratizing Space

Contending Hegemonic Practices in a Village in Northeast India

Wati Walling

Introduction[1]

Hegemony rather conveniently seems to find its way home in many aspects of human functionalities, from the most mundane to the sacred element, such as religion. The hegemony of dominant ideology makes certain groups more powerful and culturally significant. It is the authority, dominance, and influence of one group or society over another, typically through cultural, economic, or political means. Hegemony appears as the "common sense" that guides our everyday, mundane understanding of the world. It is a view of the world that is "inherited from the past and uncritically absorbed" and which tends to reproduce a sort of social homeostasis or "moral and political passivity" (Gramsci, 1971).

American Baptist missionary at Sibsagar (Assam) made his first journey into the Naga Hills in December 1872 (Thomas, 2007), which brought about significant transformations, empowering the people of Nagaland. Christianity, since its inception in the 19th century (Clark, 1907) in Northeast India (NEI), began its influence not only within the parameters of churches but in all aspects of Naga tribal lives, namely in the field of education, healthcare, culture, politics, and economic development. However, a substantive and deeper analysis of this heritage suggests that customary hegemonic practices of the pre-Christian times have also been reproduced and propagated over the years. Such practices have led to contention within a sacred space like the church. A divide between what religion teaches and how the followers live out (especially in contrast) is worth pursuing. Here, the concept of lived Christianity becomes meaningful,

> because religion-as-lived is based more on such religious practices (lived) than on religious ideas or beliefs, it is not logically coherent. Rather, it requires a practical coherence: It needs to make sense in one's everyday life, and it needs to be effective, to 'work', in the sense of accomplishing some desired end...
>
> (McGuire, 2008)

DOI: 10.4324/9781003426035-12

Contrary to "believed Christianity", "Lived Christianity" has long been a powerful tool to advance hegemonic influence inside the church administration. Hence, this chapter proposes to examine the vantage point of the conflict arising from religion and customary land ownership practices. Therefore, critical events such as the historical practice of usury in *Yimti village*,[2] which led to landlessness among many villagers, and the division of the church into two different groups of the same Christian denomination are explored to analyze the condition of lived Christianity. In a burgeoning conflict-ridden region,[3] this phenomenon deserves closer attention to realize the belief system's myriad influence upon the indigenous tribal societies and vice versa in the NEI and beyond.

The question of the "church" with respect to a village I call "Yimti" is used in terms of an institutionalized physical building rather than looking at it as an individual (soul) as the Christian biblical interpretation. Another dimension to the study of villages in NEI is the exclusive tribal population, unlike the rest of mainland India. This work also allows one to look at the lacunae and limitations of the earlier village studies of the region, juxtaposing the dynamics of religion with existing and emerging patterns of hegemonic ideologies.

A Northeast India Village Context

There exists a rich literature on village study in Indian society. For instance, land ownership, caste, and lineage provided the basis for a faction in Srinivas' work (1976). SC Dube's *Indian Village* (1955), a case study of Shamirpet brought out many specific aspects of rural life into sharper focus shift from tribe to the village and from studies of "isolated" groups toward writings on contemporary communities in the sociology of the subcontinent. Beteille's (1966) study of Sripuram village in Tamil Nadu studied power and considered caste and class for analysis. Between Marx (Material – economy) and Weber (Protestant Ethics), Beteille provided a different perspective on intensive field studies.

However, the variation in the structure, composition, and function of tribal villages in India, which is overwhelmingly diverse, deserves more nuancing. The Indian village communities were little republics, as Gandhi envisioned as a village Swaraj,[4] having nearly everything they wanted themselves and almost independent of neighbors' relations. It was India whose essence was to be found in the village. Moreover, in that respect, each village was an inner world, a traditional community, self-sufficient in its economy, and patriarchal in its governance; Yimti village, in many aspects, fits into such history. "However, the idea of 'inequality' and not that of 'community' characterized India" (Jodhka, 1998). While status could come from one's community identity, power was almost always a function of the land. Land ownership was the best-understood road to personal and familial prestige, and ownership meant and still is not only wealth and status but power over people. The traditional Naga society held that land is a gift from God to human beings to support and sustain their lives (Xaxa, 1999). Hence, this idea of village identity and the perspective of land ownership should be delineated from the rest, as we shall see the consequence of the loss of land in the context of NEI.

In the context of the NEI, perhaps the nomenclature of "villagers" can be interchangeable with "tribes" since it is only in the rarest case that a non-tribal inhabits a village setup. Only cities and major towns find people from outside indigenous tribes. In Nagaland, for instance, the Scheduled Tribe (ST) population is 89.1%,[5] out of which more than 87% of Naga tribes live in villages. In this respect, the observations on village and village-based policies inevitably need more attention. However, "tribe" has never been studied in the right spirit in India but is described as having become a caste society, peasant society, or a socially differentiated society (Xaxa, 1999).

On the other hand, although mainly carried out in the framework of caste, village studies did point to the crucial role of land ownership patterns in village social life (Jodhka, 1998). Hence, the commonalities of village study in the Indian subcontinent do remain. However, the bourgeoning loss of land, the use of usury, and the conflict contributing to contention even in the most sacred spaces are peculiar to Yimti village.

Villagers – two-thirds of the Indian population – do not shape the land through their labor. They also shape their own and others' political, social, and cultural worlds. "In many ways, 'the village' is an integral aspect of this world-shaping activity" (Mines & Yazgi, 2010).

> For them, the village itself was not a functional microcosm of the Indian whole, but merely a territorial convenience, a unit of residence that could be at least considered a secondary social fact, not a primary one for explaining Indian social structure.
>
> (Mines & Yazgi, 2010)

People, Place, and Field Setting

Nagaland, India's 16th state and home of the Nagas, borders the NEI. Nagaland is one of the eight states comprising the country's Northeast frontier. NEI also forms South Asia's northeastern borderland and South East Asia's north western borderland. The region has much more geographical contact and proximity to other nations than the Indian mainland. It is connected to mainland India by a meagre 21-km-long landmass, often described as the "chicken's neck", which is less than 2% of the 5000-km combined perimeter formed by the eight Northeastern states, while the remainder borders China, Myanmar, Bhutan, Bangladesh, and Nepal.[6] The Northeastern states have a comparatively smaller electorate (3.8% of India's total population) and hence, allotted just 25 out of 543 seats in the Lok Sabha.

The study employed a case study and stratified purposive sampling method. Altogether, 128 respondents were selected based on Slovin's formula. In-depth interviews were conducted with 15 individuals representing different clans, different church members, and the dissenting groups' leaders and members. This chapter also relied on responses through questionnaires, personal diaries, and semi-structured interviews. Secondary sources were also used, both published and unpublished books, documents, souvenirs, letters, correspondence, etc. Akin to most villages in NEI and Nagaland today, Yimti is not a pristine village. Its socioeconomics, politics, and religion have been impacted much by modernization and the coming of Christianity, out-migrations, political fragmentation,[7] and the militarized influence of the sociopolitical scene in the Nagaland state. Among several other critical events in Yimti village, the one that stands out is the division of the sole church of the same denomination in 1993. This event is taken as the midpoint of the analysis of this chapter to understand the history of the village Church on the one hand and the merger of the church after the odd 23 years on the other hand.

Many discussions on political processes in village studies cantered on factions' politics.

> Division of a village into two or more mutually opposed factions was a permanent feature of rural social structure. Faction, although it was not completely autonomous. They intermingled with other structures in rural society. Landownership, caste, and lineage provided the basis for faction.
>
> (Srinivas, 1976)

The leader of a faction was invariably one of the big landowners of the village, who also belonged to the "dominant caste". Lewis identified the following factors in order of preference that determined who could become a leader: wealth, family reputation, age and genealogical position, personality traits, state of retirement, education, connections and influence with outsiders, and finally, the numerical strength of the family and lineage (Jodhka, 1998). Wealth was a primary criterion for leadership. Factions were undoubtedly a manifestation of inegalitarianism, but they forged strong bonds between unequal partners and provided another countervailing force to the horizontal ties of caste and class (Srinivas, 1976). In place of factions, Beteille conceptualized village politics in terms of power blocks

> …most of the Harijans I got to know tended to describe their relations with higher caste people in terms of power both economic (in terms of who employed whom or their dependence on the land of employment) and political (in terms of authority and the ability to punish)
>
> (Jodhka, 1998)

Clan, Land Ownership, and Church Affiliations

Besides other influencing factors that weave the social fabric of the Yimti village, it is observed that loyalty toward one's clan, land ownership dynamics, and church affiliation stand out. Therefore, this discussion endeavors to locate one of the chief contending commodities – land and interrelate it with clans and church affiliation. To a Yimti villager, a clan is where a person is born and cannot be changed. Hence, the clan's name becomes part of one's identity by having it as a part of one's name. "Clan is one thing a person takes pride and so women folks chose to retain their clan name (in the form of surname/last name) even after marriage".[8] It is recorded that certain clans are known for their bravery. For example, even today, the Ozuku clan is regarded as "nokzenketer", which can be interpreted as a "brave-warrior-with-a-charm". Likewise, women folks of the Linger clan are considered intelligent, assertive, and outspoken. However, a term like "nokzenketer" is found across clans and not just confined to a particular clan. Hence, clan identity is at the core of all social relations in a village like the Yimti village.

NEI has a unique land ownership pattern, with private and community owning the major portion of land, leaving just a meagre portion owned by the state (Marchang, 2018). For example, 88.32% of forest land in Nagaland is owned by the private and a meagre 11.68% is owned by the state.[9] "Until today, there is no accurate account of the land owned by the State in Yimti village. However, it is just countable (meaning the number of plots owned by the state government)".[10] Analysis of the land ownership shows that, out of the 11 clans, nine are taken for this analysis as the remaining two[11] are in Yimti village only for a specific time and purpose thus, do not possess any land or have any extended families. Therefore, the two clans, Chari (one household) and Longkumer (two households), are not a part of this analysis. Only three clans in Yimti own a large quantity of land that extends more than ten acres. They are Aierer, Ozuku, and Tzudo. The Tzudo clan is not only more in population but also owns about half of the total village land (both inhabitable and cultivable). The Tzudo clan also has the highest number of landless households. It is found that a significant portion of cultivable land is owned by the Tzudo and Ozuku clans put together. The Ozuku clan is the second largest population and land ownership in Yimti village. The Aierer clan, about 7% population, has a family with a large area of land. The Aierer clan also has a substantial percentage (36.36) of landless households compared to other clans. Out of the nine clans, there are only two clans, namely, Pongen and Lemtors, who do not have landless households (Table 8.1).

Identifying a household (read as clan) according to church affiliation is rather indispensable since there are social gatherings, festivities, and celebrations in which one ought to assert its membership in one way or the other. In Yimti, an occasion like Christmas is marked by having the entire village attend church and participate in the festivity. No household on this occasion

Table 8.1 Table showing clan, population, and land ownership correlation

Sl. No	Clan Name	Landless / owning <1 acre land	Owning 2–4 acre land	Owning 5–7 acre land	Owning > 8 acre land	No. of House holds	Population In %
1	Lemtors	-	5	1	-	6	4
2	Sempo	2	5	-	-	7	4
3	Longcha	3	3	2	-	8	5
4	Pogen	-	9	1	-	10	6
5	Aierer	4	6	-	1	11	7
6	Linger	1	9	1	-	11	7
7	Mir	1	18	1	-	20	13
8	Ozuku	4	23	8	2	37	24
9	Tzudo	6	32	6	4	48	30
Total		21	110	20	7	158	100

Table 8.2 Table showing clans and church affiliation pattern

Sl. No	Clan Name	Plain-Side Church	Hill-Side Church	No. of Households
1	Lemtors	-	6	6
2	Sempo	4	3	7
3	Longcha	4	4	8
4	Pogen	1	9	10
5	Aierer	2	9	11
6	Linger	5	6	11
7	Mir	2	18	20
8	Ozuku	14	23	37
9	Tzudo	14	34	48
Total		47	114	158

dares to go to another church where he/she is not a member. It is so because of the feasting and the embarrassment of being identified as an uninvited guest. Households or individuals who never attend church gatherings throughout the year are also expected to attend the church to which their family or he/she is affiliated (Table 8.2).

Out of the nine clans, there is only one clan – Lemtors, whose entire clan is a member of the church situated on the hillside. Other clans like Pogen, Aierer, Mir, Ozuku, and Tzudo also show most of their households endorsing the hill-side church. On the other hand, there is a clan – Sempo, whose majority of households belong to the plain-side church. Clans like Longcha and Linger have more or less equal membership of the households in the two churches. Clan-based settlement in the village or clan-based affiliation to the church is insignificant from the abovementioned observation. However, the core members of the contending group[12] ironically belonged to the Tzudo,

Ozuku, and Aierer clans. This observation leads us to examine the shift in landownership pattern and the factors that influence its skewness.

Churches in Nagaland – From Darkness to Light

Nagaland has 1649 churches[13] (Baptist denomination) and hundred more other denominational and nondenominational churches across the state. Baptist Church in Nagaland has an association, which then is headed by the Nagaland Baptist Churches Council (NBCC). NBCC is affiliated with the Council of Baptist Churches in Northeast India (CBCNEI) and the Baptist World Alliance (BWA). Nagaland also has the distinction of having the largest Church in Asia,[14] with a seating capacity of 8,500. The year 1997 marked the 125th anniversary celebration of the coming of Christianity with the theme – "From Darkness to Light".[15] True to its motto, NBCC professes to "fellowship, proclaim and serve" with all churches and their members. The Church in Yimti village was established in 1896, and with that, changes in education, healthcare, and sociocultural took place perpetually. According to Samanir,[16]

> Church was undisputedly viewed as sacred, honourable and beneficial for welfare and wellbeing of the entire village. However, a certain element of dominance by the landed, rich, and powerful people always existed inside the church. Since they were the putu,[17] they had a stronger opinion despite not holding much leadership position in the church.

Putu, the governing body of the village council, is perhaps robust by traditionally adhering to equal quota representation of the clans to the council. Hence, no clan can have more representation than the allotted member. An older man commented that this system may have held the village together from further bifurcation of the village council even when the church was divided.

Land Ownership as a Source of the Church Fragmentation?

Outwardly, the reasons for the church division seemingly trace back to a dispute over the choice of the Church-building construction site. The analysis of clan, land ownership pattern, and Church affiliation additionally does not show worthy significance to cause contention and division in the church. However, a little history of landownership suggests that there have been ongoing and active changes over the past years. The more pertinent question is what led few households to landlessness in their own village? This question is imperative since villages in Nagaland are traditionally well known to be founded on equal land distribution among its founding members, followed by clan-owned and community (village)-owned land, etc.

Among other phenomena, one remarkable and consistent narrative is the emerging issue of landlessness and its relation to the customary practice of usury. Over the years, customary practices concerning land ownership have been in the hands of the powerful, influential households and the rich, enabling few sections within clans to possess more land. In this process, landless villagers eventually either migrate out of the village or remain mere laborers. In the absence of state policy on land, multilayered dimensions of land use and ownership need closer attention. Issues such as this may elude both the Center and the State government due to the lack of the State ownership of land in the village and lack of historical understanding of the place and the people to appropriate policies to suit regions like NEI and the Yimti village at hand. Therefore, in the absence of a robust state judiciary and community biasedness toward the landed section of the community, contending within a sacred space was perhaps the only option left to register resistance and foster the democratization of religion in its true sense.

The Divided Church and Lived Christianity

Yimti figures among late comers to Christianity (1896) compared to the other and immediate neighboring Ao[18] tribal villages in Nagaland. It took more than two decades for Yimti village to accept Christianity after her immediate neighbor did. This reason is attested as one critical pointer by many educated Yimti villagers (both living within the village today and many permanently residing in different towns in Nagaland) to be the reason for firmly adhering to many customary cultural practices until today. The villagers understood then that accepting a new faith would mean a custom shift. Like any other society, the church is considered a divine institution. However, the uniqueness of Yimti was once having two churches within a span of about 150 meters (1993 to 2016), which is an unusual practice within a single Christian denomination. Furthermore, this raises vital questions about creating a different identity formation within a small and close-knit community like Yimti.

The history of Yimti village from 1896 (acceptance of Christianity) until 1993, when the division of the church occurred, had witnessed a significant out-migration and skewed distribution of wealth (mostly land). One of the factors for the emergence of the skewed distribution of land is examined in light of the practice of usury in the following section. However, it is noted that the conflicts revolved around land ownership and not just the contention for a newer church location as it manifested. The conflict leading to divisions also needs to be seen from the perspective of how the two churches got polarized until its unification in January 2016. At one point, even horse trading was happening in Yimti to retain more members in their respective churches. Temsu,[19] an elderly man, noted that "there were instances in the village where a family changed its church membership in order to avail credit facility from a particular shop". A credit amounting to Rs. 29,080 was recorded for a particular household.[20] This indicates the solidarity the wealthier church members extend to the less privileged and the strategy employed to gain or retain more significant members of their respective church.

Another instance is the case of a youth who was seeking employment with a church. However, a condition was laid that the entire family members ought to register with the employing church. Situations such as this have brought about conflicts within institutions and within family members and clans who were compelled to switch church membership. This difference in membership is upheld on many occasions, including social gatherings and other Church-based activities. Limited social contact existed, which was invariably restricted because of the division. Temsu lamented that

> curbing criminals in the village has become quite a task with law and order being let loose due to lack of cooperation and conflict between the two contending churches. There was a clear impact in the governance and village administration due to the division in the church.

The social fabric of Yimti village indeed hit rock bottom with dwindling natural resources, lack of basic health amenities and infrastructure, deteriorated government-owned middle schools, etc. Such was the lived Christianity within the confines of the divided church.

"Tzuktem" as a Customary Practice of Usury

An unusual practice of usury was observed in the customary paddy-lending practice known as *tzuktem*.[21] It was a form of usury practiced in Yimti village, which deserves deliberation. Almost all households in Yimti village practice Jhum cultivation on one's land or clan-owned land. However, land ownership tipped down in the 1950s–1960s when land ownership by certain individuals rose astronomically, leaving some significant households without land. The most exploitative system of land alienation, as for Meren,[22] is the standard customary practice of lending paddy in Yimti. In the past, there were famine and epidemics in and around Yimti village. Along with such tragedy, there were households whose harvest would not suffice for a whole calendar year. Many households had no option but to borrow paddy for their square meals during such instances.

While bowering paddy from a rich man, as per a customary practice, an agreement of mortgaging the land from the borrower with a deadline, usually for one year, was done verbally. According to customary practice, paddy, once borrowed (anytime between a month to a year from the time of borrowing), a tin of paddy (12 kgs) while returning, has to be a tin and a half (18 kgs). Half a paddy tin (known as pua) accounted for an interest. The modern-day measure amounts to 50% interest (*tzuktem*). The deal gets settled if the debtor pays back the right measure of grain on time. However, if the debtor cannot settle the full measure on time (within a calendar year), then the amount of the grain becomes double the current debt, that is, by the end of the second year, the person has to return three tins of grain (18 + 18 = 36 kgs which is three times the amount borrowed two years back[23]). If he fails to repay this measure, the debtor is forced to relinquish his property without a further chance to redeem his mortgaged property (mostly land). Debt repayment was always difficult as the villagers solely depended on one harvest in a calendar year. This *tzuktem* has been the tool for the rich in the name of customary practices to capture and accumulate numerous plots and cultivable land for themselves. Until today, agriculture is the only source of sustenance for many villagers of Yimti without surplus for most households. It is an accepted phenomenon that almost every year, some households in the village would harvest insufficiently due to the diminishing return from agriculture and virtually no produce from the wild lately. This is how the loss of land in the Yimti village began. As rightly pointed out in the work of Jodhka (1998), "Village was close to people, their life, livelihood and culture" and they were "a focal point of reference for individual prestige and identification". The loss of land inadvertently led to the crisis of one's pride and identity in the village, which finds root in the division of the Church at Yimti village.

How Divided Church Become a Democratizing Space?

Colonial ethnographers and anthropologists have considered Naga society as an egalitarian society.

> However, contrary to this notion, many facets of inequalities have existed then and are more conspicuous now. There are grey areas of inequality and the emergence of class formation in Naga society, which contradicts the representation of tribal equality in various forms of media and publications
>
> (Kuchle, 2019)

In the study by Andre Beteille, sources of inequality are not merely measured by technical devices but are visible to the naked eye (Gupta, 2005). Similarly, the case of Yimti's lived Christianity evoked rather contrasting virtues such as social inequality, the practice of usury, land grabbing, hegemonic cultural practices, leading desecration of the church, etc. It is noted that the steady flow of population from the rural to the urban areas started in 1963, the attainment of Nagaland's statehood being one of the reasons. This phenomenon awaited an impending contestation of the long hegemonic practices of the wealthy landed villagers. Households who moved from the village to town were exposed to better education, health, and employment. Hence, they consolidated well to make their voice heard for decision-making processes in Yimti village eventually.

> The early 1990s saw the emergence of a few strong families who left Yimti village during the 1960s. Their educated sons and daughters, who are now profitably employed in the government service or

prestigious private firms, were an asset to the otherwise voiceless villager. It was then that the construction of a new church building came to the public debate, echoed Achila[24]

Invariably, dissenting voice to build a new church in a different location came mainly from the family and kith and kin with strong socioeconomic and political support from Yimti villagers but families who are now settled outside the village. The year 1993 saw significant conflict with the commencement of the church construction on a new site – a hilltop that was considered creditable to be affiliated to the council of churches in Nagaland (NBCC). Most dominant landowners, who are also influencers of the church, wanted the status quo and retained the existing church site. The other group, backed by the few yet powerful families settled in towns, endorsed the new site for the church construction.

The existence of a church in Nagaland is meaningful and powerful depending upon two aspects namely, its affiliation to the Council of Churches and the number of its members. Nagaland's predominantly Baptist Christian denomination mandates local churches affiliate with its parent tribal apex association. It is so because this apex association is the sole licenser of ministerial activities such as baptizing its members,[25] officiating Holy Communion,[26] solemnizing weddings, conducting funerals, etc. No clergy is authorized for the aforementioned practices without the license. An elderly woman[27] recounted that

> in case a person needs a recommendation certificate[28] from the church, he/she first needs to approach the elders of the church (which is headed by a Pastor). Here, an unwritten norm applies that the entire family of the applicant should be a member of that certifying church.

Such hegemonic practice was followed by the newly constructed church situated on the hilltop, which has been recognized by Mungdang.[29] On the other hand, the other church, which is a few yards away (the older church situated toward the plain) was not recognized by Mungdang. The reason is that two churches of the same denomination are not permissible within a village.

> Besides many clichéd reasons quoted by the churchgoers for the affiliation which was made possible for the church on the hilltop, one reason was clearly the strong lobby of the educated class of the Yimti villagers who are now settled outside the village and wanted to object to the extension of hegemonic practices inside the church. However, what they were least concerned about was that the church also was being hegemonic in the pursuit of lobbying to get the church affiliation[30].

This could be one of the reasons why the number of church members of the latter dwindled, whereas the hilltop Church gained memberships. According to a respondent[31] from the plain side, several privileges were forfeited for her church members, namely, besides not being able to partake of any symbolically sacred and meaningful religious practices, no marriage ceremonies (highly esteemed and prescribed Christian marriage for all members of the church) were entertained since the church is not affiliated to the central governing Mungdang. This entailed many consequences to the households in the plain-side church since marriage outside the church is considered taboo. Children and youth suffered a more significant loss since the church could not afford to continue their Sunday schools[32] and youth services.[33] "Finally, you have lands; I have the church" murmured Achila.[34] "Predicaments such as these were inflicted upon the church on the plain side, where majority of the olden day massive land owners gathered to worship".[35]

Concluding Remarks: United Church Democratizing the Village

Returning to the assertion of the topic, did the divided church serve as a democratizing space? Lived Christianity indeed seamlessly endorses unbiblical cultural practices without many critical evaluations. This layered analysis of lived Christianity depicts that a relatively long history of latent conflict village had passed on customary hegemonic practices (such as *tzuktem*; which has caused landlessness), despite the coming of Christianity and the biblical teaching thereof, to love one's neighbors as one love themselves.[36] Imbalanced land ownership as the result of *tzuktem* as the use of usury found its interlinkages in that it polarized the landed and the landless households. Outmigration, both family-wise and as individual, also finds its role in the way the dissension came about in the run for the bifurcation of the Church at Yimti village. Despite much criticism from churches and the council of churches in Nagaland, Yimti's Church became a highly contested space.

On the one hand, it was the manifestation of one's power, prestige, and status quo, and on the other, the democratization and the expression of agency amid the conflict. The words of Purnungsang,[37] in a way, sum up the idea of being divided or staying united in Yimti village

> ... the village (village-council here) had to remain undivided (despite the church's division) all these while because there was a threat to revoke the state's recognition of the village which would result in forgoing all government aides and privileges of the village.

Then again, it is perhaps imperative to enquire about the idea of democratization of Christianity vis-à-vis the contested space such as the church. To go beyond the contested space is perhaps where we would find the agency whose defeated selves are resolute in fighting the hegemonic agendas and practices even in the sacred of all places – the church. Perhaps, the fundamental role of religion (Christian belief here) is not tantamount to how Yimti villagers perceived lived Christianity. Therefore, even the dysfunctional role of the church to withhold privileges to the members of the other church members, the

Divided Church as a Democratizing Space 165

villagers' contention on the church (as a space) is critical in advocating democratization. The year 2016 saw the church unified. However, there are reports of a few contending group leaders who are yet to come to terms with each other. Ajungla[38] comments that.

> Handful of families not associating (attending) the church is nothing in comparison to the divided church (village)! My family (especially my children) and I feel delighted that the church is alive again and their Sunday schools and youth services have reopened to all now.

Conflict in one form or the other exists and goes on today. However, the division of the church in Yimti (1993–2016) did create an opportunity to challenge the customary hegemonic practices within the lived Christianity in the Yimti village. Another element that emerges in the shift of attention beyond religious institutions and ideologies is the theme of individualization and agency (Doggett & Arat, 2018). Perhaps, democratization over customary hegemonic practices and their contestations within the most sacred spaces – the church – is perhaps worthy, should the unified church evolve and add an agency to transcend lived Christianity. So then, how does the unified church at Yimti village keep the democratizing temperament and agency in good check?

Notes

1 According to the census of India 2011 https://www.census2011.co.in/data/religion/3-christianity.html
2 Yimti is located among the hills and forests in the district of Mokokchung – Nagaland of NEI. About 290 km away from the state capital Kohima. It is exclusively inhabited by the indigenous Ao-Naga tribe. Yimti is about 30 km away from the nearest town. The village has 161 households and a population of 810 persons – 403 females and 407 males (from fieldwork note), including all males, females, young (1 year and above), and old. Economically, Yimti village has not produced any economic surplus of the harvest nor have any active engagement of labor to date. Yimti does not add any revenue generation to the state in any sense.
3 The *Naga insurgency movement* is considered as one of *India's and Asia's oldest* conflicts spanning 103 years (The first sign of Naga resistance was seen in the formation of the Naga Club in 1918) https://indianexpress.com/article/india/india-others/everything-you-need-to-know-about-nagaland-insurgency-and-the-efforts-to-solve/
4 https://www.mkgandhi.org/indiadreams/chap24.htm browsed on 26 July 2021.
5 https://censusindia.gov.in/Tables_Published/SCST/dh_st_nagaland.pdf
6 Robert Thongkholal Haokip in http://www.freewebs.com/indiaslookeastpolicy/lepandnortheastindia.htm Pommaret, F. *Ancient Trade Partners: Bhutan, Cooch Bihar, and Assam (17th–19th Centuries), Journal Asiatique.* 287: 285–303. Retrieved on 4 February 2020 http://www.bhutanstudies.org.bt/journal/vol2no1/v2n/ancienttrade.pdf
7 This apparent fragmentation is due to electoral delimitation. Yimti village, along with another neighboring village, has been categorized into another cluster constituency which is considered a huge impediment for small villages like Yimti and its surrounding villages.

8 Wapangla is a 48-year-old woman interviewed on 28 March 2019 at Yimti village.
9 As stated in Directorate of Economics and Statistics, Government of Nagaland, Kohima: Statistical Handbook of Nagaland, 2007, p. 407.
10 Excerpt from an interview with Mr. Temsu, a 74-year-old man interviewed on 9 April 2018 in Yimti village.
11 They are one Chari household and two Longkumer households, who came to the village on government posting. Their families are settled in different towns where the children pursue their education. Therefore, only 158 out of the 161 households are analyzed for this study.
12 Two groups carried on to create two separate churches. The contention was based on a mere choice of location for the new church building. The two churches remained separated for 23 odd years.
13 https://www.nbcc-nagaland.org/statistics/ retrieved on 24 August 2021
14 https://economictimes.indiatimes.com/news/et-tv/nagaland-builds-asias-largest-church-at-zunheboto-town/videoshow/58348486.cms?from=mdr
15 https://www.nbcc-nagaland.org/statistics/ retrieved on 24 August 2021.
16 Excerpt from an interview with Samanir, 76-year-old man interviewed on 9 October 2019 in Yimti village.
17 Putu is the name of the office as well as the office bearers of the village council in Yimti village.
18 One among the other 16 tribes officially recognized by the Nagaland State government.
19 Temsu is a 74-year-old man interviewed on 9 April 2018 in Yimti village.
20 This amount is almost equivalent to a medium family's standard two years' food expenses in the village. Moreover, no interest is levied, which is very much in contrast to the village's earlier customary practices of usury.
21 A measure of a tin of paddy is usually borrowed for a calendar year. A tin measured up to approximately 12 kg. There are other lesser/more measures, but this is considered for accuracy and convenience. The literal word "tzuktem" means an interest. Usually, an interest in terms of borrowing paddy, which was the commonest and the standard exchange commodity.
22 Meren is a 60-year-old man interviewed on 1 April 2019 at Yimti village.
23 This amount is only for illustration. In reality, the paddy borrowed used to be in a much more significant number, depending on the size of the family, which used to be usually big.
24 Excerpt from an interview with Achila, a 78-year-old woman interviewed on 10 October 2019 in Yimti village.
25 One of the chief tenets of the Baptist denomination of protestant Christians is to undergo whole-body water baptism. Water baptism is an act of merging one's entire body inside water. This is a symbolic act of washing away one's past life (sin) and accepting a new life with Jesus as the Master.
26 Symbol practice of remembering Jesus' last supper with his disciples, where he served bread and wine, signifying his imminent broken body and blood shed on the cross. Also known as Eucharist or the Lord's supper among Christians.
27 Excerpt from an interview with Tantsu, a 68-year-old woman interviewed on 6 April 2019 in Yimti village.
28 Usually happens when a student wants to seek admission to a theological seminary for studies
29 A centrally governing body of all churches in the Ao tribal region known by the name of Mungdang (Council of churches)
30 Excerpt from an interview with Tantsu, a 68-year-old woman interviewed on 6 April 2019 in Yimti village.
31 Sakula is a 67-year-old widow interviewed on 15 November 2015 at Yimti village.

32 A form of schooling especially designed in almost all Christian churches (only on Sundays) for children from kindergarten to Class 12. Typically, teachers are involved from within the church voluntarily or some remunerated. Most churches have a designated head of this Sunday Schools, the Christian Education Director or Leader – Children ministry. This school's objective may be seen as manifold, but the core is educating children with biblical teachings and allowing parents to attend church without interruption. In an urban setting, Sunday school is perceived as a place to learn their respective vernacular language.
33 Youth Service is similar to Sunday schools for children taken care of by a church. Appropriately seem like a continuation of the Sunday schools with the same modus operandi with the church youths, typically college-going students.
34 Excerpt from an interview with Achila, a 78-year-old woman interviewed on 11 October 2019 in Yimti village.
35 Ibid.
36 https://www.biblegateway.com/passage/?search=Mark+12%3A31&version=NIV
37 Excerpt from an interview with Purnungsang, a 63-year-old man, interviewed on 3 April 2019 at Yimti village.
38 Excerpt from an interview with Ajungla, a 53-year-old mother of four children, interviewed on 5 April 2019 at Yimti village.

References

Beteille, Andre. (1966). *Caste, class, and power: changing patterns of stratification in a Tanjore village*. Bombay: Oxford University Press.
Clark, M.M. (1907). *A Corner in India*. Philadelphia: American Baptist Publication Society. 5 p.
Doggett, Luke & Arat, Alp (Ed). (2018). *Foundations and Futures in the Sociology of Religion*. London: Routledge.
Dube, S.C. (1955). *Indian Village*. London: Routledge and K Paul.
Gramsci, Antonio. (1971). *Selections from the Prison Notebooks of Antonio Gramsci*. Translated by Q. Hoare and G. N. Smith. New York: International Publishers.
Gupta, Dipankar (ed). (2005). *Anti–utopia: essential writings of Andre Beteille*. New Delhi: Oxford. 282 p.
Jodhka, S.S. (1998). From "Book View" to "Field View": Social Anthropological Constructions of the Indian Village. *Oxford Development Studies* 26(3): 311–331.
Kuchle, Andreas. (2019). *Class formation, social inequality and the Nagas in North East India*. New York: Routledge, p. 1.
Marchang, R. (2018). Land, Agriculture, and Livelihood of Scheduled Tribes in North-East India. *Journal of Land and Rural Studies*, 6(1): 67–84.
McGuire, M.B. (2008). *Lived Christianity: Faith and Practice in Everyday Life*. New York: Oxford University Press, 15 p.
Mines, Diane P. & Yazgi, Nicolas (eds). (2010). *Village Matters: Relocating Villages in the Contemporary Anthropology of India*. New Delhi: Oxford University Press, 2–3 p.
Srinivas, M.N. (1976). *The Remembered village*. Delhi: Oxford University Press, p. 221.
Thomas, J. (2007). *Missionaries, Colonialism and the Writing of History among the Nagas*. New Delhi: Routledge, 21 p.
Xaxa, V. (1999). Transformation of Tribes in India: Terms of Discourse. *Economic and Political Weekly*, 34(24): 1519–1524.

9 Divided Churchyards as Contested Democratic Space in Tamil Christianity

A Sociology of Caste Geography and Social Stigma in Southern India

M. R. Premram and Ashok Kumar Mocherla

Introduction

Indian Christianity has long been confronting multiple challenges, both external and internal in origin, to evolve itself as a democratic and public social space to articulate the interests of diverse social groups in its religious fold. The promise of equal and democratic space for all its members, especially for the lower castes and marginalized groups on whose behalf the demand for true democratic space is needed, remains a much-desired yet unaccomplished dream of Indian Christianity as of today. Since the advent of Christianity in the Indian subcontinent, it is evident through scholarly writings, caste with its varied expressions remains one of the most formidable challenges that Indian Christianity has been confronting with (Oddie 1995; Forrester 1980; Mosse 2012; Robinson 2010; Webster 2009). There seems to be a certain degree of consensus among scholars over the nature of caste among Indian Christians; clearly, there is no room for the caste system in its entirety among Indian Christians but caste ideology as an influencing factor is certainly present in their *lived religion*. As Dumont rightly argues, caste exists among non-Hindu groups in the "absence of ritual justification" (1970). However, Indian Christian institutions are not homogenous in their approach toward caste equations both among Indian Christians and other religious communities. Consequently, both historically and today, the religious and political outlooks of various denominations of Indian Christianity toward caste was not homogenous. Their views toward caste hierarchy and caste ideology remain thoroughly contextual and hence produced conflicting perspectives as to how to deal with caste among Indian Christians. To continue in this line of inquiry, it further argues that Foucauldian analysis of a notion "pastoral counter-conducts"[1] would provide a methodological tool to look at the dynamics of caste dissent in Indian Christianity.

To be precise, one has to contextualize and analyze the idea of pastoral counter-conducts in the social climate wherein Christian religious text does not legitimize the caste hierarchy or caste-based discrimination but caste practices would continue to be one of the most visible determining factors in their lived religion. Lived religion of many Indian Christians shares a fundamentally paradoxical relationship with their professed religion (Mosse 2012). There exist scholarly gaps in terms of both identifying and understanding alternative sources of legitimacy that Indian Christians claim or draw from in order to justify caste and non-Christian practices in the domain of lived religion. Through this chapter, we attempt to fill some academic gaps by addressing the following questions: how the production of social stigma, parallel to Hindu religious practices, strengthens the idea of "caste discrimination" among Indian Christians to contribute their bit for existing systems of social order and power relations, and also how such an exercise could challenge the Indian Christians in return; how the production of social/caste stigma, both material and symbolic, and the idea of "caste geography" effectively make Indian Christians resistant to social change and imperceptibly ensure caste reproduction both inside and outside the church; how manifestations of caste geography and reproduction of caste/social stigma must not be delinked from established and emerging forms of power relations and larger systems of social order in Indian Christianity for a nuanced understanding; how and where do we must locate "social stigma" and analyze the processes of "production and reproduction of social stigma" with a special reference to caste stigma and Dalit Christians; and how does such a line of analysis could potentially break new ground in the discourse of caste and Indian Christian religiosity in relation to the idea of democratization of Indian Christianity?

The above-mentioned ideas are examined in the light of empirical data collected from Nagaravoyil and Midtown[2] of Tamil Nadu. In the recent past, few scholars have brought the question of caste differences, discrimination, stigma, and conflict into the study of religion and religiosity (Viswanathan 2014; Nathaniel Robert 2016; Mocherla 2017). This scholarship creatively traces the material relationship of caste, Christianity, and postcolonial scholarship beyond the conventional gaze on conversion and religious identity. In other words, they attempt to argue that the framework of religion itself emanates from a reminiscence of historiography. Dalit questions broadly linked to labor, capital, and how Dalits critique the edifice of polity, economy, and society are demonstrated in their work. Moreover, Nathaniel foregrounds his work on the domain of anthropological discourse, morality/ethics, and conversion in Chennai slums. These narratives do not fall into the trap of apologetic or sympathetic language. Also, the notion of secular views is conceived through the contours of caste materiality than the received notion of the meta-religious frame of otherworldly spirituality. Indeed, scholarly literature on Christianity in India or South Asia often mentions the lacunae in understanding the distinctive aspects of Dalits who practice Christianity. Moreover, it encourages research sources that attempt to highlight the variations in life chances of various social groups affiliated with Christian institutions of belief and faith (Robinson 2010).

The notion of "public" seems to be understood always in contrast to dimensions of private in the popular vocabularies. It is assumed that popular vocabularies may not attune to the nuance perspectives of Dalit articulations.

Hence, this chapter foregrounds the egalitarian ethos of Dalit articulation and their resistance toward "power" embedded in Christian religiosity. However, this resistance never boils down to the notion of empty self (subjectivity) rather describes a life of pain, sarcasm, labor values, and lessons to take up the struggle for denied opportunity/equality and claim for the inclusive social process. It is observed that if the language of secularism mimics the apparatus of state or regimes of ruling ethos, then it denies the possibility of expressing diverse world views and tend to be caught up in the political rationalities of governmentality than foregrounding the promises of enlightenment and its critical reasons.

In the light of institutionalized discriminatory practices in Indian Christianity, the claim toward inclusive religious practices by the marginalized communities takes the form of protest and demands the agency of State to intervene in resolving the issue of contested space such as separate churches and divided cemetery[3] in Christian institutions. These are, perhaps, deepening the process of democratic claims by Dalit Christians. It is well established through ground realities that material resources such as land, property, and access to resources/opportunities are under the control of dominant communities of caste structure. The same pattern seems to be reflecting in Christian institutions as well. For example, the tendency of equating the church properties with caste properties of dominant groups seem to be manifesting itself time and again, on many occasions, in many denominations across Tamil Nadu. Such an attitude is leaving the Dalit Christians further marginalized within the Christian community. Fr. Unmeipesum Athigaram, one of our field respondents, expressed his views as below:

> There is no adequate representation of Dalits in the decision making body of Christian institutions. Dalits have been strategically denied the opportunity to hold any responsible positions such as superior general, proctor, rector, and seminarians. Christian institutions are considered to be parallel to government institutions. Caste prejudices of authority in the Christian institutions made a deliberate attempt to fail Dalit candidates in the interviews, magnifying the weakness of Dalit candidates. Christian leadership tends to take disciplinary action against Dalit Christians quickly, but such issues would be simplified/compromised when uppercases involved in in same kind of violations. Dalit students are not getting proper training and face strategic ploys (trap) made by the dominant caste which eventually led to exclusion from regular training practices. When Dalit students are opting for the courses like mathematics, physics, and other demanding subjects for their graduate and postgraduate courses, they were discouraged from opting for such desired courses. The fourth and third-grade positions were advertised widely among Dalit candidates and likely to be recruited for those posts. However, positions with power and higher social status were strategically denied to Dalit Christians. In case Dalit Christian students

demonstrate their academic excellence, they would still be admitted to academic programmes under the reserved category just to fulfil the conditions of reservation policy. Such strategic efforts of dominant castes groups/authorities in denying the opportunity of other Dalit students to enter into educational premises constitute everyday narratives of Dalit Christian students in Christian institutions.

Based on the abovementioned narrative, we argue that caste prejudice explicitly operates, both overtly and covertly, in the daily-life of Church-operated institutions and their modes of day-to-day interactions. Further, he emphasized,

> In recent decades, the number of Dalit candidates joining the religious vocation has been on the rise. The calculated attitude of indifference towards Dalit students causes severe problems like teenage and post-adolescence crisis. These crises have to be dealt with on their own and institutional support is often not extended to Dalit Christian students. For examples, Dalits students are forced to leave the religious vocation and it led to the loss of their life. This kind of death count to be a natural death and no authority takes the responsibility for this kind of death. One could observe three stages where Dalits face various hindrances in the process of a religious vocation. In the initial stage, Dalits were completely screened. In the intermediate stage, Dalits were identified as deviant and abnormal and in the final stage they were completely demoralized by authorities, unclosing the methods of character assassination. Academic evaluations of the growth of the candidates during the process of a religious vocation are, in reality, not as objective as they are claimed to be. There are two kinds of scripts that exist; one is a public script that is silent about caste nuances and the next private script that is full of caste acts of vengeance. Christian authorities are caste biased and antipathy towards Dalits. These stages of hindrances are viewed by some as psychological warfare. Hence it is suggested that Indian church authorities and power structures need to be democratized to shield the Dalit Christians from caste bias and privileged lobbying groups within the church-operated institutions.

These narratives fit into the frame of pastoral counter-conducts that Foucault observes from 1978 onward. Its emphasizes on the dynamics of internal resistance toward the genealogy of Christianity in the Western societies – how pastoral power tied with the notion of obedience, confession, discipline, knowledge, and responsibility (Chrulew2014). The same notion can be exegetically used in this chapter to analyze the operations of pastoral power and its resistance in the Indian context to trace the residual factors of caste excess (surplus) of pastoral power in perpetuating the caste statusquo of church authorities and Dalit resistance and claim to democratize church authorities.

There are several Dalit organizations and associations organizing themselves to demand for inclusive policies and democratize the religious domain for all practical and political purposes. The "Dalit Christian Liberation movement"[4] is one such organization whose primary agenda is to demand for an affirmative policy for Dalit Christians both within and outside the church.

Sociology of Caste Stigma and Geography in India

It is extremely interesting, in many ways, to examine the logic behind the spatial arrangement pattern of rural India. Caste geography is one of the unceasing notions and most blatantly manifested spatial patterns, arguably drawing its legitimacy from the Hindu religious faith and associated caste-based stereotypes. As a direct result of such caste-based stereotypes and religious beliefs, based on the doctrine of purity and impurity, the internal spatial arrangement of Indian villages is true to its caste ideology and caste geography; each caste community lives in a designated space with symbolic and invisible boundaries demarcating residential settlements of one caste community from the other. On similar lines, one can further argue that each Indian village has both "village-core" and "village-periphery". Villagecore consists of prominent Hindu temples, village public infrastructure such as panchayat office, hospital, library, postoffice, bank, if any, and residential areas of both the twice-born and the dominant caste groups. The village periphery consists mainly of residential localities of Dalits and Tribes.

It is the backward castes that occupy the transitional or intermediary zones, which are considered to be neither core nor periphery. Despite active social interactions across the core and peripheral zones, the prejudice of caste geography and caste-based social stigma unceasingly manifests itself across time and space. Therefore, the ever-increasing social interaction across caste groups in rural India should not be mistaken as a sign of the waning of caste ideology and its manifestations, as no amount of social interaction can truly challenge the spatial organization of caste groups and how the framework of caste geography functions and reproduces its boundaries. This caste geography is one of the fundamental manifestations of caste ideology driven by the doctrine of "purity and impurity". Any deviance, be it on part of an individual or a group, from the established norms of caste geography of a village will be dealt with seriousness and hence follows stark social ramifications, including ex-communication from their community as well as from the village. In some cases, such deviant behavior may invite or trigger caste disputes depending upon the magnitude of the issue under scrutiny. Prejudices of caste geography breed the seeds of the status quo, which to a great extent serves the interest of the privileged castes in India (Subramanian 2019).

Academic scholarship on the rural sociology of India demands a nuanced explanation of the changing dynamics of caste values. The growing caste conflicts/tensions revolve around the struggle over access to material resources and challenging the caste-based ritual hierarchy (Desai 1956). Since

Divided Churchyards as Contested Democratic Space 173

Independence, the relationship between agrarian structure and caste dynamics is been undergoing rapid changes due to urbanization, migration, rural unemployment, and so forth. It is also an unending debate to look at these social changes through multiple theoretical frames (Dipankar Gupta 2005).

The prevalence of caste differences and caste discrimination among the Christians suggests not only its occurrence but also a rather insidious character of caste among the Christians. This is most emblematically reflected in the construction of walls dividing the cemeteries along caste lines in Midtown. But before we come to discuss this extreme form of caste segregation, we would discuss the caste-based discriminations that we found to be prevalent in two villages of Tamil Nadu where we carried out our fieldwork. The villages Agaram and Thenpennai are located in the Nagaravoyil in Northern Tamil Nādu. In the following discussion, we briefly state the caste-wise division of the village as taken for this study.

Field-Setting and Empirical Context

There are three upper castes mostly Telugu-speaking communities residing at Agaram village – Naidu, Reddy, and Mudhaliar Catholic Christians – and the lower caste consists of Paraiyar Christians. Naidu, Reddy, and Mudhaliar constitutes 150 households, and Pariayar Christian amounts to 250 households. The total population of this village is predominantly the Catholic Christian community. Similarly, four communities reside at Thenpennai village: Naidu Christians, Paraiyar Christians, Paraiyar Hindu, and Arundhathiyar Christians constituting 560 households, 75 households, 60 households, and 55 households, respectively.

In Agaram, agriculture remains a major source of livelihood with *paddy-*being the most cultivated crop of this village. This land is very fertile due to the proximity of river banks such as *Madurantakam lake*. The houses of upper castes look more modern and built with brick and cement. Some of the Dalit households still reside under a thatched roof. Most of the Dalits depend on cows and buffalos for their livelihood. In Thenpennai, mostly Naidu Christians own a considerable degree of agricultural land. Paraiyar and Arundhathiyar Christians work as agricultural labor in the lands of Naidu Christians. Like any other village in India, the source of livelihood for Dalits is largely determined by the prevailing caste relations. Some of the Arundhathiyar caste own leather shops near the small town of this village. As well, some of the Paraiyar castes own cows for selling milk and their domestic purpose. The main public facilities like electricity transformer, water pumps, kids school (*palvadi*), and higher secondary school are located nearby the upper-caste residential areas, that is the villagecore.

Though this chapter analyzes the questions of Christian religious practices that are discriminatory toward Dalits, it also argues that these discriminatory practices are materially grounded in the structural organization of Indian society. The first detail of importance in this regard is that both these villages exhibit empirical and spatial divisions among caste groups that inhabit these villages. Dalits being the most marginalized segment of the village population carry and experience this marginalization physically and spatially. One of the main reasons behind the marginalization of Dalits directly corresponds to the fact of their dependence on the upper castes for subsistence. The Dalits are landless labors and their livelihood is directly related to agricultural fields owned by the upper castes. The material marginalities of the Dalits feed into their religious marginality as well. The fact that public infrastructure and common resources like schools, electricity transformers, main water pumps, library, hospital, and so forth are situated in the upper-caste neighborhoods not only shows the upper-caste domination over the village political economy but also shows the complicity of state agencies in maintaining the statusquo and upper-caste domination. Upper-caste domination over religious as well as civic life/spaces in the village flows directly from their control over material resources. The abovementioned aspect of geographical segregations and caste discrimination in those spaces make us think about the question of space and production of caste in the religious domain.

Production of Social Stigma in Religious Domains

As Jaspal (2011) emphasizes that

> Identity process theory recognizes two processes involved in identity construction, namely (1) the assimilation – accommodation process, whereby new information (for example, social representations, events) are absorbed into accommodated within the identical structure and (2) the evaluation process, which continuously confers meaning and value upon the content of identity. These processes are universal across all human beings.
>
> (2011)

This suggests that how Dalits get stigmatized through the process of marginalization, and denying access to resources perpetuates and maintains the status quo in and with the help of existing social structure. In this context, it is pertinent to understand how stigmatizing and the essentializing processes have been unfolding themselves in the domain of Indian Christian religiosity.

Since 1980s, Dalit Christians of this region have been contesting the discriminatory religious practices in this South Indian church. Besides analyzing caste normativity and marginalization of Dalits in South India at large, there is a compelling need to engage with questions of how Dalit's resist these forms of caste normativity which are materially embedded in social fabrics. In this context, it is significant to invoke the notion of Foucault's pastoral counter-conducts to analyze the forms of caste discrimination within church institutions. Based on empirical insights collected from Tamil Nadu, one could argue that embedded forms of caste norms percolate into the edifice of church authorities that demands Dalits' confession and obedience to the modality of caste norms than the theological discourse. In contrast to this, Dalit agencies act as "counter conducts to pastoral power" for claiming their inalienable rights that are historically rooted. These acts can be interpreted as resistance movements within the genealogy of Indian Christianity itself in an attempt to democratize Indian Christian church. The extracted narratives from respondents clearly show various forms of resistance toward caste discrimination and how it was practiced earlier and is challenged in the recent decades. In the Thenpennai village, for example, the church leadership in the past directly promoted caste discrimination. One of our field respondents mentioned as below:

> lower caste were instructed to sit in the corner of the church. High caste (Reddy, Naidu, and Mudaliar) people used to sit in the front rows of the church. The spatial difference allowed the upper caste to discriminate the lower castes. The religious rituals too were not insulated from the discriminatory caste practices. For instance, the priest used to give priority to the upper caste while conducting the mass. The Dalit Christians were never allowed to read verses from the bible in the church and were not permitted to join the church choir. At the end of the mass ceremony, priests tend to go directly to the sitting place of the upper caste to bless them. Lower caste Christians had to wait till the end to receive blessings from the priest.

On the eve of the Church festival, respondents informed that the wooden-chariot car has to be pulled around the villages and finally it reaches the church. However, though not surprisingly the chariot would not enter into the Dalit neighborhood. Even the posters and pamphlets announcing the programs of the festival carry only various subcastes (*Manchisety, Rayapa, Varigilan, Nelapati, Kundibili*) of Naidu, not Dalits, as organizers and coordinators on behalf of the church. In the most shocking manner, the voluntary contributions to organize/conduct the church festival are collected only from the upper-caste Christians, while the Dalit Christians are excluded from the process. As one of our respondents, Uzhiyan[5] mentions:

> In the year 1998, Dalits started demanding access to the chariot and seeking changes in the route map of the church festival procession so that the chariot could pass through their neighbourhood too. These issues had been a subject of discussion at various Catholic forums locally. Dalit Christians had given representation to the local parish priest. However, the parish priest could not respond to it positively. Though a priest is supposed to be treating everyone equally he is clearly under the pressure to favour a social group, as he could not go against the views of dominant castes. Sometimes the caste identity of the priest himself makes a huge difference in reinstating such caste prejudices between lower caste and upper caste Christians in Tamil Christianity.

For Dalit Christians of this region, the idea of social existence itself turns into a mode of existence of power and subordination. However, these forms of socio-historical practices are not left unchallenged. Dalit Christian activists in the recent past have strongly been challenging the caste prejudice within the Christian institutions and carved out a path to approach state agencies for justice and many had to sacrifice their normal life to face the court cases. Hence state becomes a pertinent precursor to formulate Dalit Christian activist strategies to seek justice from the lived Christianity, which is discriminatory toward Dalits Christians, and had to provide creative artifacts and artillery for Dalit Movements in Tamil Nadu to deconstruct elitist arguments of "naturalizing caste".[6]

Walls of Discrimination and Divided Churchyards in Tamil Nadu

The idea of space is an important social category to understand the everyday dynamics of caste and its practices. The criticism of the Indian village social system by Ambedkar and many others shows the centrality of space in understanding the question of caste. The spatial arrangement of the Indian village is religiously conceptualized and sanctioned. Therefore, it becomes extremely difficult for the people to have a shared social space across caste boundaries, especially beyond caste terms. This spatial distribution of population in the village also reflects the distribution of material resources, which is based on caste, and more precisely on the victimization and marginalization of Dalits. These views tend to subscribe to the idea that urban spaces as much-desired pockets of liberation and empowerment, in a relative sense. At the same time, it is not to argue that urban spaces are free from caste and religious prejudices. However, as Gopal Guru and others have argued that the urban spaces are not devoid of institutional discriminatory practices of caste and foreground their views for the historically embedded space (Guru and Sarukkai 2012: 71–106). In the recent scholarship on space, rights, and democracy, Subramanian (2009) largely draws her analysis of space from the academic scholarship of anthropology, geography, and history and departs her scholarship from existing South Asian scholarships and their frame of universal contours of derivative concepts. In contrast, she foregrounds her work to look at the dialectic relationship between "regional histories of claim-making and transnational histories of circulation" to understand the process of democracy and rights discourse with reference to caste (2009: 6).

Having laid out the theme of space which foregrounds the question of caste beyond the setting of the village provides a lens to delineate the aspects of the divided cemetery in "midtown' as a complex and nuanced understanding of the nexus between caste, polity, and Christian religiosity. The cemetery of Catholic church is located in the heart of the midtown nearby a warehouse. The history of Christianity in midtown is as old as the Travancore province and its social history of Indian Christianity. These divided churchyards in this region have registered four decades of infamous history of caste dissent, with diverse forms of local dynamics, in the church. Dalit and other liberal groups had done a lot of protest demonstrations to break the wall. Ethnographic narratives related to these divided churchyards have been constructed from the sources based on in-depth interviews from the field. Earlier, Hindus of various castes used to bury/burn their dead bodies right on the bank of the *Kaveri* river. Midtown is located near the banks of the Kaveri river. The long history of Christianity in midtown is quite visible by looking into the old churches and colleges established by Christian missionaries (Manickam 1977).

The emergence of a divided wall within this cemetery is alleged to have installed in the 1960s. Earlier, there was no clear-cut demarcation between Dalits and the upper-caste burial ground. This cemetery consists of one and a half acres of land. It is located on the left side of the warehouse flyover. This warehouse region is a highly populated and significant part of this city. The political context in which the eruption of the divided wall took place is considered being a significant phenomenon. It emphasized the nexus between caste, state actors, church authorities, and caste associations. This form of alliance seems to be common across the various castes. After independence, the Indian National Congress (INC) had ruled an extensive part of India; Tamil Nadu is no exception for the first two decades of this trend. During the 1960s, the *Pillai* and *Vellalar* castes had constructed the wall inside the cemetery at the warehouse strategically. These two castes were quite influential in the congress party during those times. Before the construction of this wall, dead bodies used to be buried based on familial ties and kinship patterns. Caste segregation of burying the dead bodies was already in practice without any concrete form of physical classification/markers.

The relationship between state powers, caste associations, and church authorities in dealing with the issues of the burial ground and notion of death needs to be analyzed in the framework of governmentality (conduct of action through political rationalities) and pastoral counter-conducts. The death rituals vary substantially among Hindus and Christians. Anthropological analyses of death rituals among Hindus are conceptually articulated in Jonathan Parry's work, and also they moved from the one tradition of scholarship such as Frazers (*The Golden* Bough) framework of analyzing death as mediation between myth, religion, mother rights (fertility and sexuality) – it concerned with Greek and Roman symbolisms to another tradition of scholarship such as Durkheim's pupil – Robert Hertz (1907) work on funerary cults of Malayo-Polynesian-speaking people. Jonathan's work focuses on the temporal aspects of death and ritual norms regarding household persons and the ascetic of Hindu communities, particularly in the socio-religious context of Benaras, Uttar Pradesh. The embedded mediation between cosmos, death, regeneration of life, and its ritual practices are pictured in his ethnographic narratives. His narration depicts the series of inversion between body, soul and cosmos (liberation of transcendent soul) based on Hindu mythologies and largely focuses on social order, the legitimation of authority concerning death rituals, and regeneration of life (1982).

We can draw inference from this work that legitimation of authority is confined to religious sanctions of social order in approaching the dynamics of death rituals. Therefore, Christian death rituals and their attributions of caste discrimination can be looked at in the frame of religious syncretism and relativizing complex exchange between the notion of time and space. However, the overarching relationship between the dynamics of state and its apparatus with the aspects of meta-religious narrative or lived religion cannot be escaped so easily. The established scholarship on the relationship between anthropology and State needs to be taken into account for analyses of the field narratives. As Veena Das and Deborah Poole (2004) rightly observe:

> Our analytical and descriptive strategy was to distance ourselves from the entrenched image of the state as a rationalized administrative form of political organization that becomes weakened or less fully articulated along its territorial or social margins. Instead, we asked seminar participants to reflect on how the practices and politics of life in these areas shaped the political, regulatory, and disciplinary practices that constitute, somehow, the thing what we call "state".

The present ethnographic data inform a detailed narrative on the operational aspects of caste prejudices within church leadership as well in the apparatus of postcolonial State. This can be analyzed in the frame of political rationalities of governmentality (Rose 2007) and pastoral counter-conducts within the genealogy of Indian Christian religiosity.

All Souls' Day, Death Rituals, and Caste Rules

The "All Souls'Day" observed by the Catholic community pushes our attention away from the temporal to the spatial perspectives of death rituals. Hence, it sets the context in the modalities of the postcolonial frame along with the regional claims to encounter the question of democracy and secular state. The predicaments of geography cannot simply allude to the frame of ecological or environmental scholarship rather it needs to be approached historically (Papanna 2014). The relation between the domain of history and geography has to be kept intact for looking into the process of social transitions, not as derivative concepts but as an ingenious way of establishing claims and their context. A claim that an event of All Souls'Day conceptually differs from the Hindu way of observing death rituals can be justified when it is conceived only based on temporal aspects. However, approaching this ritual through spatial aspects complicates the entire edifice and also offers a fresh ground for analyzing social transition and brings the question of agency into the forays of conceptual vocabularies. It is, hence, observed that essentializing the aspects of caste need to be forged to deconstruct the elitist narratives on naturalizing aspects of caste and class in analyzing social transition

(Andre Beteille 1991: 25). This gauged approach need not be viewed in terms of opposition to modernity; rather, it strengthens the contours of historical claims to annihilate caste or Dalit claims toward state apparatus to deepen the democracy and de-erase the invisibility of marginality and amplifies the protest voice in the mainstream academia (Robinson and Kujur 2010: 2) and longing for those possibilities.

The physical demarcation in the burial ground came into practice due to tensions that prevailed during the "All Souls'Day" festival. I quote what the field respondent says:

> upper caste and vellalars claimed that this wall is protection for their community. During the 'all souls' day' festival, Dalit teenagers and boys tend to burn firecrackers inside the cemetery and attempt to tease the upper caste girls who used to come for this festival. To protect this kind of activity, they had constructed this wall as RCMC trust members claim it. The land where the cemetery was located/stands belongs to government property in those days, the leading political members from Pillai and Vellalar caste made this property their land when they were politically influencial. During the 1960s, AGS Lourdusamy Pillai, F/o Adikalraja (EX M.P- he was a leading member in the congress party), when he became chairman of this midtownmunicipality. It is assumed that he informed his fellow caste people regarding the land details of the cemetery. Accordingly, they formed a trust called RCMC and land had sold to this group (Vellalar committee) at a very less amount. At this time, Bishop James Mando shah was in charge of this diocese.

The above narratives inform us that element of caste is not only present in Hindu death rituals but is also explicitly expressed and normalized in Christian rituals as well. The response of Dalit Christian activists in approaching these problems draws scholarly attention to understand the claim over "contested space".

Transformational Politics and Political Rationalities

To draw conceptual vocabularies from the Foucault paradigm offer critical insights to analyze the embedded aspects of caste prejudice within the institutional structure of Catholic Christians and the postcolonial Indian State. A body of scholarship on Dravidian politics in Tamil Nadu indicates the signals of transformational politics (Geetha and Rajadurai 1993) which are influenced by the critical reasons of enlightenment philosophy and foregrounding its discourse against the popular narrative of Hindu practices and it offers the political rationalities for non-Brahmin actors. However, the relationship between the Dravidian discourse and Dalit politics always constitutes a site of contestation in the gaze of existing scholarship and its discursive practices (Gorringe, 2005). The political rationalities of the postcolonial state carry an element of the residual substance of caste in governing the conduct of men both in personal space explicitly and implicitly/dishonestly in public spaces (Pandian 2002). These conceptual vocabularies explain the Dalit act of deconstructing the divided wall constructed in the warehouse cemetery at midtown. The respondent's deposition informs us that Dalit actors in midtown including Dalit priestsand Dalit Christian activists gathered in large numbers along with church authorities and attempted to demolish the divided caste wall in the year 1976. This event flared up the pride of upper castes who share the responsibilities/authorities in state apparatus and Catholic Christian institutions and diluted the converged effort of Dalit protest and their stakes in church property. The harsh realities of caste prejudice among Christian authorities can be inferred from this event and also the political rationalities of governmentality. The effects of power embedded in church authorities and state apparatus can be explained by referring to Foucault (2007) lectures,

> The Christian pastorate is not fundamentally or essentially characterized by the relationship to salvation, to the law, and the truth. The Christian pastorate is, rather, a form of power that, taking the problem of salvation in its general set of themes, inserts into this global, general relationship an entire economy and technique of the circulation, transfer, and reversal of merits, and this is its fundamental point. Similarly, with regard to the law, Christianity, the Christian pastorate, is not simply the instrument of the acceptance or generalization of the law, but rather, through an oblique relationship to the law, as it were, it establishes a kind of exhaustive, total, and permanent relationship of individual obedience. This is something quite different from the relationship to the law. And finally, if Christianity, the Christian pastor, teaches the truth, if he forces men, the sheep, to accept a certain truth, the Christian pastorate, is also absolutely innovative in establishing a structure, a technique of, at once, power, investigation, self-examination, and the examination of others, by which certain secret inner truth of the hidden soul, becomes the element through which the pastor's power is exercised, by which obedience is practiced and through which, precisely, the economy of merits and faults passes. It is not salvation, the law, and the truth but the new relationship of merits and faults, absolute obedience, and the production of hidden truths, which constitute, I think, what is essential and the originality and specificity of Christianity.

Here it can be argued that the "hidden truth" is nothing but the excess of caste capital and caste prejudice and the reproduction of it through the effects of pastoral power and artifacts of governmentality and political rationalities in the South Asian context. In contrast to the conventional interpretation of liberal instrumentalist state which assumes that government is seen as a process of authorized choice in response to identified collective needs, a recent scholarship has been informed through a frame of Michel Foucault's work of governmentality approach to look at the operational aspects of power and governance. Dean (1999:2) has observed that "there is no one governmentality paradigm". All the same, we can yet identify some of the major themes in the governmentality approach. Governing involves much more than the activities of government. As Miller and Rose (1990, 15) observe that political power (rationalities) is exercised through a multitude of agencies and techniques, some of which are only loosely associated with the executives and bureaucracies of the formal organs of state". Going further, the term is used "as a more general term for any calculated direction of human conduct"(Dean 1999: 3), with the concern as much with the questions about "how does the government govern us?" as with "how do we govern ourselves?" Attention thus comes to be focus on the ways of thinking and acting which render conduct governable – the "mentalities" or "rationalities" which underlie rule, the ways in which problems are discerned, expertise is recognized and mobilized, information is recorded and codified, participants are identified and organized, and codes of practice formed and promulgated.

The broad concern expressed as the form of governmentality approach need not necessarilytraverse the whole of the debate about governmentalityand political rationality but simply draw from it some constructs that seem helpful for the analysis of the activity under review and which also lends itself to a renewed logic of appraisal within political sociology. The constructs thatwe shall fix on as part of the governmentality framework are the following: problematizing, identities, technologies, and programs, and governing at a distance. These constructs, as served up here, have an analytical purpose. This is largely keeping with the point, underscored by Dean (1999:4), that "there is no one common way of using the intellectual tools produced by workers in this area".

Dalit Christian activists in approaching an apparatus of the state agency to resolve the issues of divided cemetery and caste discriminations within the Christian religiosity only produced a language of dissent primarily against upper-caste elites but never altered the material relations of caste equations. However, this chapter attempts to register these series of events as pastoral counter-conducts within the genealogy of Indian Christianity. It emphasizesthat power cannot be analyzed only through visible material terms but can also be looked into the invisible material expressions such as the cultural domain of symbolic representations as power and its effects. In this line of inquiry, we argue that the Dalit agency uses the modality of Christianity as a vehicle not only on the aspects of conversion but also in the dynamics of claiming democratic space and human rights and showcases the political economy of labor values and cultural imagination. Hence it is argued that the Dalit Christian resistance movement and dissent voice have immense potential to deepen the process of democracy within Christian religiosity, church leadership, and the apparatus of postcolonial State.

Conclusion

Narratives, avenues, content, forms, characters, and cultural meanings of social stigma often take the idea of "discrimination" for granted, and therefore, naturally tend to align with dominant narratives of polarity. The physical walls of discrimination we see today in the churchyards located in Tamil Nadu, South India, truly symbolize the institutionalized forms of discrimination in Indian Christianity and its religious discourse, wherein the marginalized are further victimized and have been subjected to new expressions of caste ideology earlier unknown to Indian caste politics as well as Indian Christianity. What is perhaps more distinctive about the forms of discrimination that Dalit Christians experience both inside and outside the church by their Christian brethren of upper-caste origin is that they are direct results of social stigma over their caste and social status. Groups who follow two different worldviews rather uniquely share these ideas of social stigma on Dalit Christians: caste Hindus and upper-caste Christians. This issue of divided churchyards only reinforces the significance of religion in the discourse of Dalit empowerment, as it remains one of the most contested domains to deal with in order to establish their anticaste, egalitarian, and democratic ideas among Indian Christian communities.

There is a need to look at these divided churchyards as an extension of caste geography and hence they become contested spaces wherein the equality of treatment after death is demanded. Entire rural India is largely organized around the idea of caste geography, based on the doctrine of purity and impurity, with visible and invisible boundaries that keep caste communities apart. The same logic is being extended to the churchyards to keep the dead bodies and gravestones apart on caste lines. Divided churchyards, therefore, provide us with a unique window to examine how politics of hegemony and accessibility get articulated in Indian Christianity on the avenues/locations that are collectively shared by Christian communities. In the face of the ongoing discriminatory practices of caste in Tamil Christianity, of which the divided churchyards arejust one form of many expressions, this chapter argues for the deepening of democratic and egalitarian ideas in Indian Christianity to counter such politics of hegemony and accessibility. Local church leadership has a vital role to play in restoring the faith of lower castes. An interventionist pitch may be required not toradically alter material transactions embedded in the church practices but identifying the problems and its programmatic solutions. It may evolve by embracing internal critique within Christian theology and accepting those solutions offered by them, and it's a long way to go. However, a lack of communitarian fraternity can be problematized or an embedded hierarchical form of caste system can be challenged through endorsing democratic forms of social practices by emulating not dominant world views but by acknowledging the world views of plural society andthat plural world views constitute democratic space ideally.

Notes

1 Within the frame of Christian theology, Giorgio Agamban (2011) analyzed power and government in the Western societies, and Zizek (2000) also claims for the 'authentic materialist subjectivity' embedded in Christianity and Psychoanalysis. However, Foucault's analyses offer a frame to understand "dissent" and operation of "resistance" in Indian context.
2 Nagaravoyil and Midtown are anonymous names for the place where we conducted field work during the month of December 2017 to February 2018 and February to April 2019, respectively.
3 Separate Churches and divided cemetery refer to the markers of caste symbols in Christian premises. It denotes that the existence of multiple churches and separate graveyard tend to be functioning based on caste lines. Unfortunately, it cannot even classify as upper caste versus Dalits Churches. Within the fold of Dalit churches too –access to resources, at some times, operationalized as *Paraiyar* versus *Arundhathiyar*. One could discern a pattern of multiple claims over church resources, specifically among the clusters of various caste groups.
4 Dalit Christian Liberation Movement is an organization that are vigilant about the plight of Dalit communities and forging multipronged struggle to enhance the conditions of Dalit communities within church institutions and apparatus of Indian state. And also demanding Scheduled Caste Status for Dalit Christians since its inception. Head office is located in Chennai and President is Dr. M Mary John. A few provinces/states have granted SC (Scheduled Caste) status to Dalit Christians by enacting bills in their respective Legislative Assemblies. Since this matter concerns the government of India (central government), these cases are currently pending with the Supreme Court of India.
5 Unmeipesum Athigaram and Uzhiyan are anonymous names for the persons whom we conducted in-depth interviews during the month of October 2017.
6 A narrative on caste and its complexity unravels its dynamics in common parlance (Public space). A tendency among the receptive agency spontaneously shifts a terrain towards the question of "nature" or "religion" which discourages the potential to highlight the production/reproduction of caste institution as a category of social inequality, contrary to above argument – this shift reaffirms the status-quo positions of globalized modern institutions (education, employment, financial, and corporate sectors) and force marginalized communities to accept that they are at the receiving end of unjust social spectrum and voice of rights discourse is curtailed.

References

Agamban, Giorgio. 2011. *The Kingdom and the Glory: For a Theological Genealogy of Economy and Government*. California: Stanford University Press.
Beteille, Andre. 1991. 'The Reproduction of Inequality: Occupation, Caste and Family', *Contributions to Indian Sociology*, 25(1): 25.
Chrulew, Matthew. 2014. 'Pastoral Counter-Conducts: Religious Resistance in Foucault's Genealogy of Christianity', *Critical Research on Religion*, 2(1): 55–65.
Das, Veena and Poole, Deeborah. 2004. 'State and its Margins: Comparative Ethnographies', in Veena Das and Deeborah Poole (eds), *Anthropology in the Margins of the State*, pp. 3–33. New Delhi: Oxford University Press.
Dean, Mitchell. 1999. *Governmentality: Power and Rule in Modern Society*. London: Sage.

Desai, A. R. 1956. 'Rural Sociology: Its Need in India', *Sociological Bulletin*, 5(1): 9–28.
Dumont, Louis. 1970. *Homo Hierarchicus: The Caste System and Its Implications*. Chicago: University of Chicago Press.
Forrester, Duncan. 1980. *Caste and Christianity: Attitudes and Policies on Caste of Anglo Saxon Protestant Missions in India*. London: Routledge.
Foucault, Michel. 2007. *Security, Territory and Population: Lectures at the College de France, 1977–1978*. New York: Palgrave Macmillan.
Geetha, V. and Rajadurai, S.V. 1993. 'Dalits and Non-Brahmin Consciousness in Colonial Tamil Nad', *Economic and Political Weekly*, 28 (39): 2091–2098.
Gorringe, Hugo. 2005. *Untouchable Citizens: Dalit Movements and Democratisation in Tamil Nadu*. New Delhi: Sage Publication.
Gupta, Dipankar. 2005. 'Whither the Indian Village: Culture and Agriculture in Rural India', *Economic and Political Weekly*, 40 (8): 751–758.
Guru, Gopal and Sarukkai, Sundar. 2012. *The Cracked Mirror: An Indian Debate on Experience and Theory*. New Delhi: Oxford University Press.
Jaspal, Rusi. 2011. 'Caste, Social Stigma and Identity Process', *Psychology and Developing Societies*, 23(1): 27–62.
Manickam, Sundararaj. 1977. *The Social setting of Christian Conversion in South India: The Impact of Wesleyan Methodist Missionaries on the Trichy-Tanjore Diocese with Special Reference to Harijan Communities of the Mass Movement Area 1820–1947*. Weisbaden Steiner: Beiträgezur Südasienforschung.
Miller, Peter and Rose, Nikolas. 1990. Governing Economic Life. *Economy and Society*, 19(1): 1–31.
Mocherla, Ashok Kumar. 2017. 'Contested Past and Complex Present: A Sociological Trajectory of Interaction between Caste and Christianity in India', *Papers on Ecclesiastical Law and Politics*, special volume: 127–142.
Mosse, David. 2012. *The Saint in the Banyan Tree: Christianity and Caste Society in India*. Berkeley: University of California Press.
Oddie, Jeffrey. 1995. *Hindu and Christian in South-East India: Aspects of Religious Continuity and Change, 1800–1900*.London: Routledge.
Pandian, M. S. S. 2002. 'One Step outside Modernity: Caste, Identity Politics and Public Sphere', *Economic and Political Weekly*, 37(18):1735–1741.
Papanna, Sudarshan. 2014. 'The Expanding City: Land Development and Urban Planning in Bangalore'. Unpublished Ph.D. dissertation, University of Hyderabad.
Parry, Jonathan. 1982. 'Sacrificial Death and Necrophageous Ascetic', in Maurice Bloch and Jonathan Parry (eds), *Death and the Regeneration of Life*, pp. 74–110. London: Cambridge University Press.
Roberts, Nathaniel. 2016. *To be Care for: The Power of Conversion and Foreignness of Belonging in an Indian Slum*. California: University of California Press.
Robinson, Rowena. 2010. 'Indian Christians: Trajectories of Development', in Gurpreet Mahajan and Surinder S. Jodhka (eds), *Religion, Communities and Development: Changing Contours of Politics and Policy in India*, pp. 151–172. New Delhi: Sage Publication.
Robinson, Rowena and Kujur, Joseph Marianus. 2010. 'Introduction', in Rowena Robinson and Joseph Marianus Kujur (eds), *Margins of Faith: Dalit and Tribal Christianity in India*. New Delhi: Sage Publications.
Rose, Nikolas. 2007. *Powers of Freedom: Reframing Political Thought*. Cambridge: Cambridge University Press.

Subramanian, Ajantha. 2009. *Shorelines: Space and Rights in South India*. California: Stanford University Press.
Subramanian, Ajantha. 2019. *Castes of Merit: Engineering Education in India*. Cambridge: Harvard University Press.
Viswanath, Rupa. 2014. *The Pariah Problem: Caste, Religion and Social in Modern India*. New York: Columbia University Press.
Webster, John. 2009. *Dalit Christians: A History*. Delhi: ISPCK
Zizek, S. 2000. *The Fragile Absolute: Or, Why is the Christian Legacy worth Fighting for?* New York: Verso.

Section IV

Everyday Life, Democratization, and Indian Christianity – Unfolding Prospects and Challenges

10 Prayer as an Instrument of Resistance

Contextualizing Prayer and Everyday Life of Dalit Christians in Kerala

P. Sanal Mohan

Introduction

Dalit Christians as a social group consists of Dalits from various caste backgrounds. However, as they are brought together as a religious community sharing a particular denominational rite, they assume themselves to be a community. It is also necessary here to consider the fact that because of denominational and liturgical differences, Dalit Christians might constitute different communities. However, the prevalence of caste among Christians in Kerala, just as in other parts of India, would make Dalit Christians a community irrespective of denominational differences. This idea of community draws heavily from the experiences of Dalit Christianity as a religion of the oppressed (Raboteau 2004). Additionally, the experiences of caste oppression suffered by Dalit Christians continue to be a resource used in articulating their historical consciousness. One might also argue that there is a political dimension inbuilt in it as it is inherently poised against caste oppression and domination. This chapter makes use of historical ethnography as a method in analyzing the religious experiences of Dalit Christians in Kerala foregrounding their prayers and everyday life. More importantly, it uses multiple registers of social life to articulate the arguments proposed. Therefore, it draws on a complex array of sources and methods. It also considers different Church denominations in different parts of Kerala. In this chapter, I analyze the significance of prayers in the everyday life of Dalit Christians of Kerala as prayers offered a particular language of internal deliberation. This chapter is divided into five sections. The first section introduces the central concern of this chapter, everyday life and prayers. This is followed by a discussion of specific aspects of the everyday life of slave castes. Dalit religion and Dalit Christianity form the subsequent sections. The final section, conclusion, would recapture the main problems discussed in the chapter.

Everyday life and Prayers

Everyday life is the site where meanings are produced and contested and transformed in society. Social science has a tradition of analyzing everyday life in which emphasis is laid on the question of everyday actions that are seen as performances or practices that cover a wide variety of actions (Goffman 2008; De Certeau 1988). Everyday life refers to the repetitive context in which people interact with others and engage in social relations. In other words, it is the site where life unfolds, meanings are created, and individuals carry out and participate in the production and consumption of things including food and the realization of other goals of life. In other words, the concerns of everyday life include almost all activities of human beings. It is in the context of everyday life that meanings are produced in social life. Language plays a very important role in everyday life as it enables transactions and articulations (De Certeau 1988: 1–14). In many ways, through the ordinary situations and actions, language gets transformed in the context of everyday life. This transformation of languages results from the ordinariness of the multiple contexts in which people use them. The insights derived from sociological analysis of the everyday life is extremely useful in understanding the everyday life of slave castes in Kerala before they joined missionary Churches in the 19th century and afterward as many facets of their everyday life began to change. In this chapter, I analyze prayers and everyday life of Dalit Christians in Kerala. Prayer practices have received greater attention from scholars studying religion and they have explored prayers and prayer practices following the debates in the area of practice theory (Giordan and Woodhead 2017; Genova 2015). What is of greater significance for my analysis of Dalit Christian prayers is the everyday unfolding of different prayer practices among individuals as well as societies. Scholars have also recognized the social dimension of prayers that develop in the everyday context (Harris 2006; Keane 2006, 2007). In the analysis of social practices, there is broader consensus among different theoretical traditions that practices eventually create the structure of society (Giddens 1977). Prayers as religious practices refer to both individual practices as well as social practices. In the Dalit Christian context, as they were being taught by the missionaries of the protestant missions in the Travancore region of Kerala against the threat of landlords, the social dimension of prayers become equally relevant as individual dimension (Hawksworth 1855: 477). From Marcel Mauss's point of view prayer is an activity which involves both belief and ritual at the same time. Prayers are oral religious rites that aim at modifying profane by conferring a sacred characteristic up on it (Genova 2015: 11).

Mauss further observed the original social character of prayer although subsequently it became individual in nature (Ibid 12). In recent research work, prayer has been described as a request, intercession, confession, praise, relationship, thanksgiving, meditation, rite or ceremony, and communication (Ibid 13). These features may be present simultaneously and they are not mutually exclusive. These aspects of prayer are very much present in prayers in their social as well as individual manifestation. As the ethnographic and archival data show, in the case of Dalit Christians too, it can be argued that all of these elements were present in different degrees like in many other contexts. However, in the course of my research, I have come across situations in which prayer was used to resist the caste violence. Therefore, I wish to propose another dimension of prayer, that is prayer as resistance (http://forums.ssrc.org/ndsp/2013/09/24/prayer-as-resistance/).

Although Christianity has a very long presence in Kerala, going back to the early Christian centuries, Dalits were not part of the traditional Church. However, there are references to a small group of Pulayas who joined the Catholic Church in the wake of Portuguese Catholic mission's work (Thekkedath 1988: 23). This small group and their Church were confined to the Cochin islands and did not spread to the interiors or the hinter land. But in the early 19th century, with the coming of the British missionary organizations such as the London Missionary Society (LMS) and the Church Missionary Society (CMS), this situation began to change (Hunt 1920: 191–206). Alongside them, missionary organizations such as the Salvation Army, Pentecostal Church among others, later began to work among the enslaved castes. (Committee 1998; Cook 2013). Therefore, it was from the mid-19th century that Christianity began to make inroads into the enslaved castes in Kerala in a substantial manner. Most accounts of the 19th century refer to the people of the enslaved castes as predominantly employed in the wetland and dry land farms of the upper-caste landlords, government, and temples. The history of their enslavement goes back to centuries, and there are historical documents that speak of enslaved castes belonging to AD 9th century (Varier and Veluthat 2014 114–15). From this period up to the 19th century, when the British missionaries encountered the slave castes, historical references to them prove the fact that they continued to remain as enslaved people in the agrarian sector. More importantly, they were also traded through Indian Ocean slave routes reaching Java, Sri Lanka, Cape Colony in South Africa, and other places (Van Rossum et al. 2020). Throughout the abovementioned historical periods, documents refer to them as slaves often bought and sold along with the land. As they are valued along with other properties of the landlords, the system of slavery prevailed in Kerala qualifies to be chattel slavery. It is in this larger historical context of slavery and oppression that missionaries intervened in the lives of the slave caste people transforming them. This situation demands a probe into the different aspects of the everyday life of enslaved castes including their religion. Before I analyze Dalit Christian prayers and prayer practices, I shall briefly analyze the salient aspects of their everyday life from the mid-19th century through the first half of the 20th century that showed remarkable continuity. More importantly, the same situation prevailed in the case of Dalits who did not join the missionary Churches. Further, I may suggest that many aspects of the everyday lives of the slave castes could be pushed back in time as we have some historical references to their enslaved social existence (Madhavan 2012).

Slave Caste's Everyday Life

The lives of slave caste men, women, and children were controlled by the landlords who exacted regular backbreaking work from them. Men, women, and children had to work hard from dawn to dusk and children's work went unpaid until they reached 15 (Hawksworth 1854; George 2015; Joseph 1938). The elderly who were not able to work and infants were left out. Most 19th-century sources refer to the fact that the elderly who were unable to work did not receive any support from the landlords, let alone the wages (Hawksworth 1854). The care of the infants remained a big issue as they were left in their hut along with the elders or under the care of older children (Nanu 1912: 85–86). There are several narratives of infants being kept in pits or left in the cradle made of rags hanging from the branches of trees. In some narratives, such infants die as they are eaten by colonies of ants or they experience other calamities leading to their death (Mohan 2015: 240–241).

In most wetland regions, they were engaged in the arduous task of cultivating rice. Rice cultivation is a labor-intensive activity that required large numbers of enslaved laborers to work during various seasons. John Hawksworth, who worked in Travancore from 1847 till his death in 1863, has noted that Pulayas were employed by their masters to do all the labor connected with the cultivation of rice. Their work involved long hours of toil amid the mud and water of the flooded rice fields often exposed to the full force of the torrential monsoon rains (Hawksworth 1854). The drudgery of deepening of the canals and water courses, and the repairing of their banks which is usually done with their hands without the help of any tools whatsoever, is also part of their day's work. Historical records of the nineteenth and early 20th century refer to the fact that men were forced to plough the fields along with draught animals as substitutes (Travancore and Cochin Diocesan Record 1905: 42–43). Ethnographic data collected through fieldwork refer to the fact that such practices were in vogue even in the early 20th century (Thuruthikkara 2015). In the context of dryland farming too, we come across reference to the labor of slaves. Another significant aspect of the slave labor is the extreme form of vigilance that prevailed that made it almost impossible for them to escape from the cruelties of the landlords. In both written and oral traditions, we come across examples of people escaping to wilderness and committing suicides to escape from slavery (Ibid).

The slave laborers were given two measures of rice as wages and it differed for both men and women. As the gender-based wage differences prevailed, women often ended up receiving less than what the men used to receive (Joseph 1938). Women received less than two measures of raw rice as wages. The slave laborers were given noon gruel in a hole in the ground in which plantain leaves were fixed to pour rice gruel into it. The laborers would scoop up rice and drink the rice water using spoons made of leaves of jackfruit tree. Surprisingly, this practice was found to continue in various parts of Kerala even in the 1960s. Although this work is hard and tiring, it is in this context of the work that the laborers would engage in communication among themselves.

No discussion of everyday life would be complete without a discussion on food, dress, nature of houses, water, fire, among other necessities of life. The 19th-century missionary sources have noted coarse food that the slave caste people used to eat. Although their labor was decisive for rice production, rice never formed a staple food item due to the high cost that they had to pay in spite of the fact that the laborers mostly received their wages in kind, rice. When they reach their little huts – homes – after the labor they must process the rice received as wages to prepare their evening gruel. Often enough, this would not be over before ten o'clock at night. And we may recall the fact that both children and the elderly people who stayed back their homes would have to wait for such a long time to get some food.

They had to save certain quantities of rice thus earned for future contingencies. Therefore, they had to eat a variety of leaves, roots, wild yams, taro, and other edible roots (Hawksworth, 1854). We also came across examples of people eating the fruits and nuts of wild jack tree (Anjili). In the course of my field work, many people have recalled the fact that older generations of people used to request the landlords for jackfruits in the summer. The fishes and oysters found in the water channels of the rice fields and streams often supplemented their nutrition requirements (George 2015). It has been noted that slave castes used to eat dead domestic animals (Nanu, 1912). Apparently, there was no tabu in eating the meat of dead cattle, though in some 19th-century missionary sources this is contested. There are instances of missionaries reporting that those slave castes who joined the missions discontinued such practices (Report on the Work in the Attingal District 1908: 11). However, if we go by 20th-century ethnographic data, it is quite possible to argue that Dalit Christians as well as other Dalits used to eat the meat of dead cows, buffalos etc. It has been observed that milk and milk products seldom entered their cuisine (Joseph 1938). As the slaves did not own land, it would have been difficult for most of them to cultivate necessary things to eat. Yet in the late 19th and early 20th centuries, we come across slave castes cultivating lands acquired through their own labor and selling their products in the market (Painter 1898; Bishop of Travancore and Cochin 1881). It may be noted that we do not have large numbers of such farmers who could really challenge the power of the landlords.

Dress is a powerful signifier of social position of individuals and communities. In caste society, there was control on the dress each social group were permitted to wear. Sources of information pertaining to the mode of dressing show that across communities, with an exception of Muslims, Christians and Brahmins, women did not cover the upper part of their body. Upper-caste men wore cloths and also kept another cloth on the upper part of the body. Lower-caste people, especially slave caste women did not cover the upper part of the body. Moreover, they did not have a spare cloth to change when they are back from the rice fields where they work knee deep in mud and water – transplanting, weeding – among other tasks. Many of them had to sleep wearing the wet clothes. It must be noted that the clothes they wore would reach only up to the knee (Joseph 1938; George 2015). Those who joined the missions did not have proper dress to attend the Church. It has been observed that many of them used tender spathe of the areca nut palm to cover their nakedness. Missionaries had observed that some of the slave castes did not wear any dress except leaves, and twigs around their loin.

Thanda Pulayas of Cochin wore grass around their waist for dress. There are references to the fact that the missionaries supplied them clothes. Even in the 1930s and 1940s in many parts of the Travancore region of Kerala, the Pulayas were never allowed to wear white clothes (George 2015). If they were able to buy new clothes, they had to soil it or blacken it rubbing against the bottom of cooking pots. During my field work, many Dalit Christians referred to the fact that they were never allowed to go to Church in the Sunday best (ibid). They had to wrap up their Sunday best in rags or small baskets that they used carry and change over in the Church compound. None of the sources of this period refer to them owning gold ornaments.

Although water sources were very abundant in Kerala, in many cases the slave castes had difficulties in accessing fresh drinking water sources, especially during the summer. But in places where sources of water were not near, the slave castes were not allowed to use the wells, often owned by the upper castes. On such occasions, the slave caste people had great difficulty in getting water. More importantly, water is imbued with meanings; water is carrier of purity in different religious traditions. In caste society, there was a control over water and sources of water. Among Christians, there is the powerful metaphor of "life-giving water" (John 4, 10).

Another significant aspect of everyday life which is fundamental for survival is the source of firewood for cooking. In the 19th and early 20th centuries, the slave castes used to lit their hearth with dry coconut leaves, fronds, dry coconut spathe, and dry bunches among others. It has been noted by some informants that it was difficult for the slave castes to get firewood and therefore they would use dry leaves of jack fruit tree and other trees (Kallumadayil, 2021). In wetland areas, products of coconut tree are most commonly used as firewood. Some of those living in the back waters have opined that they heard about people using driftwood collected in the monsoon season as firewood. Along with this, it has been observed that slave caste people used to burn outer husk of rice as fuel. One advantage of chaff and husk of rice is that they could preserve fire for the next evening in a situation where matchbox was not available. In certain households, hearth may not preserve fire; in such situations, women have to go to next house to get embers so that they can light their hearth.

Houses provide the space for meaning-making and new social imaginations, a space that make possible intergenerational continuity of societies. Mostly built by using poles and grass for thatch, these houses were erected with nondurable materials on six or four poles and situated on the outer bunds of the rice fields owned by the landlords. In most cases, they had to use bamboo poles and matted coconut leaves and fronds bought from the landlords or supplied by them. In the settlements of those living on the dryland farms, often they would use small branches of softwood trees, coconut fronds, and varieties of softwoods to erect these houses. Similarly, not many people of the slave castes could construct houses with even sunbaked bricks as it required some capital investment and also mud to make them. Such situations changed a bit with the coming of the missionaries who worked with the slave caste Christians. For example, in the report of 1938 that I have quoted, there is a reference to the fact that in North Travancore some of the former slave castes lived in houses with mud walls. Most of such houses had two rooms measuring 20 ft x 10 ft. One room was used as kitchen and other for all other purposes (Joseph, 1938). The architecture of the houses and the plan and layout of the houses are very important in understanding the process of meaning-making and imagination of a social group (Appadurai 2013). Alongside this, we may also need to think about the ideas of private life as reflected in the architecture of the house. Historically, most references to the houses of slave castes show that practically there existed no chance for a notion of private life to develop among them.

They never had any furniture or goods that are durable and valuable. However, in certain houses there were cheap wooden cots. Other things of everyday use included few mud pots, coconut shell spoons, one or two mats made of *Pandanus* leaves or grass, a grinding stone, and a wooden mortar and pestle for pounding rice. They also owned one or two sickles that were essential for harvesting and other works. In 1930s people used to have kerosene lamp made of tin. These were "the earthly possessions" of an average family. Same source refers to some households owning copper vessels and enameled plates. The use of such everyday things is crucial in understanding even the mentality of the people (Roche 2000).

Family is certainly the most significant institution that decides human relations. Family forms varied historically across castes in Kerala. While there have been lot of academic researches on matriliny and related issues that were problems of the dominant landlord castes, we did not come across much discussion on family forms among the slave castes. However, a discussion of everyday life and religion among the slave castes can't be accomplished without an understanding of their family structure. Most references to slave castes affirm the fact that people used to be bought and sold and that in such context people were referred to in kinship terms as father, mother, son, daughter, and wife. Therefore, what really prevailed was a nonstable, ephemeral family form that was subjected to the power of the landlords who could rip it apart. Yet, it is quite remarkable that the affective dimension of family and the emotions entangled in it were articulated in the oral tradition of the slave castes. However, in the case of those who joined the protestant missions, we may observe the gradual solidifying of the notion of Christian family that was patriarchal in nature. In spite of this, the CMS missionaries in Travancore lamented the fact that "among the Pulayas they were yet to see powerful father figures".

Dalit Religion

Dalit religion has emerged of late as a serious problem of academic enquiry, although it would be misleading to claim that it is of recent provenance (Dube 2020). Colonial ethnographers and census officials have grappled with the problem of Dalit religion and often expressed their highly partisan opinions about Dalit religious practices (Lee 2021). The missionaries of both the Protestant as well as the Catholic denominations, referred to the Dalit religion using very powerful expressions such as animism, superstition, sorcery, and devil worship among others (Hunt 1920). Among the slave castes in Kerala, a variety of religious practices flourished, a close analysis of them would show their significance in sustaining the lives of the slave caste people in the context of caste oppression and violence (Mateer 1883: 52). It is in this context that we need to understand the significance of ancestral worship. One's own parents and other ancestors were thought to continue to live with them even after their death. Therefore, they would help the surviving generation to face violence and other calamities. It is in this context that they imbued the ancestors with divine power, or they were thought to be the divine power to be worshiped. The ritual specialists among the slave castes developed a variety of practices to propitiate the departed souls so that they continue to bless the living generations. They would offer rice, puffed rice, beaten rice, and plantain in addition to toddy, chicken among others as offerings to the ancestors (ibid 53). In fact, to dethrone such a faith in the ancestors, it was necessary to have an idea of a more powerful god and associated religious practices. Elsewhere, I have referred to the religious practices of slave castes before they accepted Christianity as life-affirming practices in the context extreme of violence, torture and killing (Mohan 2015: 88). According to Talal Asad, "different kind of practice and discourse are intrinsic to the field in which religious representations (like any representation) acquire their identity and their truthfulness". He further argues that "the anthropological student of particular religions should therefore begin from this point, in a sense unpacking the comprehensive concept which he or she translates as "religion" into heterogenous elements according to its historical character" (1993: 54). I think this applies to Dalit religion as it is today talked about in social science research, emerging as a significant object of enquiry.

However, when Dalit religion is treated as a prehistory of Dalit Christianity or any other religion of Dalits, we do not understand the autonomous nature of their consciousness expressed through their religious practices.

Dalit Christianity

As I mentioned in the beginning, Dalits in thousands began to accept Christianity in Kerala only in the 19th century (Travancore and Cochin Mission 1912). It may be noted that it was mostly due the work of the Protestant missions such as the London Missionary Society and the Church Missionary Society in the princely Southern parts of Kerala and the Basel Mission in the British Malabar. Most of the Dalits belonged to the Pulaya, Paraya, and Kurava in the Southern Kerala and Cherumar, Nayadis, etc. in the North (Raina 1988). However, there were also numerically smaller communities such as the Thanda Pulayas, Aynavars, etc. In this chapter, I discuss more about the Pulayas, Parayas, and Kuravas than about other caste groups as the archives I rely on gives more materials on such caste groups. It does not mean that smaller communities are insignificant. In the mid-19th century, when the CMS started its work among the slave castes, the missionaries noted the fact that most of them were slave laborers owned by upper-caste Hindus and Syrian Christians (Matthan 1857: 13). Therefore, it was necessary that they were liberated as a precondition for laboring among them and ultimately winning over them for the missionary project. Equally important was the empathy that the missionaries felt for them. It was in this context that they petitioned the Travancore government in 1847 to initiate measures to liberate the enslaved humanity (The Petition 1847). Although the proclamation abolishing slavery was issued only in 1855, in the southern princely states of Travancore and Cochin, the CMS missionaries started their work among the slave caste Pulayas from 1850 onward and the first group of slaves were baptized in September 1854 in a hilly village named Kyppetta near Mallappally (Hawksworth 1855: 480). Subsequently, the CMS missionaries began to have many more such centers in Travancore where they brought together the slave caste people and began to teach them. Every day in the evening, after their work in the landlords' fields, the slave caste men, women, and children would assemble in what was famous as the slave schools. There, the missionaries and catechists would teach them scriptures, prayers, along with that they were also taught Malayalam alphabets. More emphasis was given to reading scriptures and learning prayers. There are graphic accounts of emotionally charged instances of slaves crying while they said the Lord's prayer (AH 1860: 95 Hunt 1920: 200).

It may be noted that portions of the scriptures were translated into Malayalam in the first decade of the 19th century and the complete Bible was translated in 1829. Soon, *The Book of Common Prayer* was also translated into Malayalam. However, until missionaries started teaching the slave castes as part of their mass movement work, in the early 1850s in the CMS areas, none of these texts would have reached the slave castes. It should be remembered that in traditional social order, there was a strict control over literacy and learning and, particularly, the untouchable slave castes were strictly forbidden from learning. It is important here to analyze further the meanings of the changed everyday practices of the slave castes. I have narrated the salient features of the everyday existence of the slave castes that were determined by the work in landlords' fields. With the coming of the missionaries, especially during the 1850s and 1860s, although those who joined the missions continued to be the laborers of the old masters even after abolition of slavery in 1855, the slaves entered the new disciplinary regime introduced by the missionaries. The main feature of it had been the evening prayers and learning at the slave school. Missionaries have noted that family prayers were new even to the traditional Syrian Christians (Hunt 1920: 72). In addition to this, slaves were instructed to have morning prayers in which mostly elders of the household would participate. However, it was very important that children also participated in the evening prayers. Likewise, we also read about small gatherings of people for prayer and fearing the landlords' men, they hurriedly finish the meeting and return to their settlements (Travancore and Cochin Diocesan Record 1905). I have also mentioned the importance of such meetings as the occasions when with the support of the missionaries they could buy oil to lit a lamp which was a big luxury for the slave castes (Mamen 1856). Light is very important as a practical thing and as a metaphor. We may recall what Jesus said about himself. "I am the light of the world. Whoever follows me will have the light of life and will never walk in darkness" (John 8:12). One may say that the occasions of prayer brought people together in light as against their conditions in their small houses where many of them did not have oil to lit a lamp. In the absence of lamp, they have to depend on the light from the hearth to carry out all chores. It is probable that they must have lit torches made of small bunches of dry coconut leaves for light.

It has been observed by the missionaries that the slave caste people always liked the small meetings in the slave churches where all of them could come together (Mamen 1858: 26–28). Obviously, it was for learning prayers and listening to the readings and participating in the worship. I consider it as a powerful indicator of the idea of collectivity or community that was impossible under slavery (Ibid). In the course of my field work as people narrated their social experiences, one important aspect recalled was this collective life in the slave congregations (George 2015). Alongside this in the Kottayam district, people recall another collective experience of seasonal migration to the great expanse of paddy fields in the back waters region, particularly during the harvest season. They stay there for the entire season of harvest lasting for months engaged in all sorts of related works staying in makeshift sheds. For the slave castes who had been on the brink of starvation during the lean season, the harvest season is a season of hope when everybody would get something in return for the backbreaking work and obviously it could be far more than the usual wage. So, there would be lot of joyous occasion for men, women, and children. What I want to emphasize here is the fact that the collective work of harvest season also offered the possibility of the humanity of the slave castes to flourish (Chirappad 2014).

Now, this sort of social collectivity brought together the laborers from both the Christian and non-Christian slave castes. It seems from the field work data that such interactions and particular communion of prayers of slave caste Christians helped spread the message of Christianity among the slave castes further. Most works in the rice fields of backwater region offered this possibility to Christian laborers to come together to sing and pray. Therefore, we come across an interesting example of prayers offering a possibility of community as against the oppressive system. Many of our informants described how people would pray while at work. One such narrative recalled the prayers of the workers who were returning after collecting mud blocks from the depth of the back waters. In the late night, they anchored the canoe in the back waters to pray. Likewise, people also recalled singing and praying as they return to their villages in canoes after harvest.

Now I wish to bring in certain other issues that are important as we consider prayers in everyday context. Although there are different forms of prayers depending on the cultural context, we may note here community prayers in which people participate as a group defying the landlord authority from mid-19th century onward. On many occasions, the slave schools and chapels were burnt down and slave caste Christians were severely punished for this obdurate decision (Hawksworth 1855: 480). Such retribution of the landlords continued even in the first half of the 20th century (Report of the Native Church 1910: 2–4).

Following the missionary practice of itinerancy, many catechists and pastors from the slave caste communities took to giving wayside sermons or giving sermons at the markets. This must have been a phenomenon of the late nineteenth and first half of the 20th century.

One important aspect to be noted in the context of the open sermons is the coming of modern Malayalam language to the slave castes through the reading of the scriptures and prayer books. The reading sessions and classes were regular in the slave schools from the early 1850s, and in 1857 itself, there was a report about a slave who could read scriptures to his own people gathered for prayer. It is quite likely that many slaves became well versed in reading. Similarly, those who listened to the readings picked up enough ideas and linguistic abilities to talk to the people gathered for prayer and worship. In the example given here, the slave who could read actually spoke about salvation through Jesus Christ (Church Missionary Record 1857: 127). As he was reading to men, his wife spoke to women. It may be noted that as early as 1857, we find the active involvement of slave caste women in the fledgling congregations. In fact, in the subsequent decades of the 19th century and the first half of the 20th century, the idea of salvation became very central to the social and religious imaginations of the slave caste Christians. In the context of their own religious and social movements, it is possible to observe substantial intellectual investment made by slave caste Christians in understanding and explaining the idea of salvation from their perspective (Mohan 2015). It is in this context that biblical phrases and metaphors found entry into the vocabulary of those from the slave castes who joined the missionary churches. It may be noted that language is thought to be the most important aspect of social life when problems of everyday life is discussed. In other words, everyday language of communication becomes very important here. Now, considering the social world of the slave castes, we may note that in the traditional social order their most significant expression and use of language could be seen in the manner in which they would compose work songs sung on different occasions of daily work. There used to be a number of work songs that both men and women used to sing. However, the same talent of composing and singing songs were harnessed for the worship and prayer at the slave school. In fact, the reports of the missionaries from the Mallapally village where the first "mass movement conversion" took place, recall the fact that the Corresponding Secretary of the Church Missionary Society in Madras

Rev. T.G. Ragland while on his visit to Travancore staying in the village parsonage listened to the slave caste men and women singing melodiously while working in the field. It shows the widespread nature of the usage of the work songs.

Listening to the scriptures and participation in prayers helped introduce the concept of redemptive history in the community. The notion of redemption here is connected with the Christian idea of redemption that the Gospels were able to communicate to the people who were brought under the missionary instruction. More importantly, the practice of baptism brings along with it the idea of death together with Christ as far as sin is concerned; resurrection along with Jesus Christ offers eternal life. Socially, this idea of redemption works in such a way that enslaved castes began to experience certain amount of freedom in their everyday life as redeemed by the savior. It is in this context that the redemptive history of salvation that Christianity offers had a fundamental transforming power on enslaved castes. In the early 20th century, this became far more explicit with their own religious movements enshrining the idea of salvation (Mohan, 2015: Nair, 2016:16). In a reported conversation that a missionary had with a group of slaves in the slave school, he "explained to them that they were all sinners, and that idolatry, sabbath breaking, and polygamy were sinful though they were not aware of it. Told them what Christ had done for men to deliver them from sin". Responding to another person who was more attentive to the missionary than others, who asked the missionary if it was too late for him to serve God, as he had been serving Satan and living in all manner of sins, the missionary explained the examples of a penitent thief and that of the prodigal son. In the report of the missionary, Rev. K. Koshi for the quarter ending 30 September 1856, we come across the narrative of "A Converted Thief", where he talks about a Pulaya convert who stopped stealing rice for survival as he realized such practices as sin and became convinced about the promise of salvation. In these and similar examples, we observe the manner in which missionaries tried to intervene in the lives of the people to transform them. These were unfolding in the context of everyday life.

Throughout the late 19th century, there are references to people from the slave castes, particularly teachers of the slave schools moving from one place to another for teaching the slaves and organizing prayers and worship defying the restrictions on the use of public roads (Travancore and Cochin Mission 1912). One interesting aspect of the missionary work was itinerancy that included sermons and prayers on the wayside. One perceptive missionary had observed in 1873 that the Christians from the slave castes perhaps thought more of their advances as citizens than as simple Christians with the result that some of them became "cheeky and self-assertive". The same source talks about their resolve to seek remedies through litigation as they are supported by "European Missionaries and higher caste brethren". Certainly, not everyone of the higher caste brethren supported them as the subsequent history of the CMS in Kottayam testifies. Further, it is to be noted that they were "willing any longer to be deprived of the use of public roads" (Collins 1873: 182). In fact, this was something that the Dalit Christians used to their advantage from late 19th century onward when they began to develop their own religious groups such as South India Gospel Association in 1895 at Manganam near Kottayam by Chatham Puthur Yohannan. They used to organize their own prayer meetings and worship among other practices in which people of the Church used to participate.

Religious revivals taking place among Christians in Travancore was noted as a major phenomenon by the European missionaries. The first one was in 1873 and the last one was in 1906–1907 (CMS Mission in Travancore and Cochin 1915: 24). Although certain practices of the revival movements were antithetical to the perspectives of the CMS missionaries, they have noted the fact that such movements had powerful and lasting effects. Revival meetings were large events that attracted hundreds of people who expressed their desire to be saved. These were public events where preachers would address the gathering discussing Christian theological issues and giving sermons. After the first meeting 587 people were baptized. These revivals could be traced to the preaching of missionaries, both European and Indian who used to visit Travancore (ibid).

With the coming of other missionary organizations such as the Salvation Army in 1896 and the Pentecostal movement in 1918, many more Dalits joined these Churches (Committee 1988: 137–151; Cook 2013; 103–155). Both these movements had prayer meetings and public sermons attended by thousands of people (ibid). Many of their pastors would give wayside sermons and later started conventions of their churches drawing in thousands of people. There were also smaller prayer meetings. These conventions became popular events attracting large crowd of people listening to sermons. In fact, in the course of the ethnographic field work, we could listen to the histories of such conventions by exclusive Dalit Churches one of which became a major event from at least 1949 onward. This convention became popular as Kariamplavu convention in Pathanamthitta district of Kerala organized by the Pentecostal Church named World Mission Evangelism (Perumpetty 1999: 160–163). The significance of these prayer meetings, sermons, choirs, and conventions lies in the fact that they were taking place at a time when there were lot of restrictions placed on the oppressed slave castes when they forayed into public space. Elsewhere, I have referred to the space thus created as subaltern counterpublics borrowing the concept from Nancy Frazer (Mohan 2019; Frazer 1990).

As the examples discussed so far were pertaining to Dalit Christians of Protestant Churches, it would be interesting to consider here the experiences of Dalits in Catholic Church in Kerala. While in the CMS Churches, the Dalits were in a majority but dominated by a minority of dominant-caste Syrian Christians, the situation in the Catholic Church was absolute domination of Syrian Christians. Yet, in the Southern native state of Travancore, thousands of Dalits joined the Catholic Church due to the work of European

Catholic missionaries as well as native priests of different orders. However, it is quite well known today that Dalits in Catholic church continues to be dominated by Syrian Christians. The often-repeated example of the work of Syrian Christian priests who worked among Pulayas of Nedumkunnam further east to Kottayam is tainted by the caste power they articulated. The Priest instructed the Pulayas that they would remain Pulayas even as they were becoming Christians to which the Pulayas replied that they would not aspire the status of the Syrian Christians and that they only need to "learn the Vedam" (Kathanar 2000: 10). Learning scriptures assumed significance in the imagination of the Pulayas who joined the Catholic Church. Yet, it was impossible as even the Syrian Christian Catholics were not reading the Bible unlike the Protestants. Dalit Christians who joined the Catholic Church were taught Apostolic Creed and the Lord's Prayer. They were also taught the significance of sacraments and leading a life observing the sacraments. In many villages of Travancore where the Syrian Catholics had an upper hand, they began to work among the slave castes and won many to the Catholic faith. Unlike what we saw in the case of the Protestant Churches, it was very difficult to identify Dalit Catholics evolving as a significant social group within the Church. There are a few vernacular histories authored by Dalit Christians that deal with this situation (Kozhuvanal 2006). Although caste slavery was a definite form of domination prevailing throughout the 19th century even after the formal abolition of slavery, in many rural areas, those Dalits who joined the Catholic Church continued to be slaves of the Syrian Christian landlords (Kozhuvanal: 19–20). In spite of this, one may find instances of prayer in the families offering a new and different world view to the people. In the midst of continuing oppression and sufferings, those Dalits who joined the Catholic Church remained as a different community. Religious practices including prayers that were said on different occasions were decisive in demarcating the community. For example, Kozhuvanal observed that traditional Christians taught the holy Biblical messages and stories and ideas in a very attractive manner accompanying sometimes performance enabled the sprouting of expectations in the hearts of the poor unlearned people (ibid 12).

I wish to analyze further the interface of Dalits and Catholic Church in a mission field in the Malabar region where historically dominant-caste Syrian Christians were absent. Famous as the Chirakkal Mission north of Kannur, where in 1937, Italian Catholic missionaries began their work. It was in 1937 that the first missionary Fr. Peter Caironi SJ arrived and started what was famously known as the Pulaya Mission (Taffarel 1950: 110).

He had a few other colleagues, all of them Italian Jesuits who along with Fr. Caironi worked tirelessly among the Pulayas (Cherumars) of Malabar who were living as chattels historically serving the masters, both Muslim and Hindu. The work of Jesuit mission was a pathbreaking one as far as the north Malabar region was concerned. There were also a congregation of Italian missionary nuns who were actively involved in a medical mission that Fr. Caironi had started. Like other mission centers, here too we find substantial social and economic changes as there was an emphasis on education in the work of Fr. Caironi. In addition to this, there were concerted efforts by the missionaries to help the oppressed Pulayas to buy land and be independent of the landlords. At the moment, I am not going into the details of the socioeconomic changes that the mission brought about in the late colonial period. Nevertheless, I wish to refer to the religious practices including prayers that were introduced by the missionaries. Like any other missionaries, the Jesuit missionaries too emphasized the need for prayers; they instructed their people that it was prayer that was the source of support of all the missionary labor among them and that the people should lead a prayerful life. In the Catholic faith it was absolutely important to pray the Holy Rosary beseeching the intercession of Mother Mary. Missionaries used to give rosary to people and teach them all the prayers. They instructed the people to have daily evening prayers at home when everybody returns after a day's hard labor. Another instruction was to attend the Holy Mass regularly. They used to have prayer meetings and blessings in homes and the people used to carry all the sacred objects for the prayer including scaffoldings to be used to make an altar (Taffarel 1950: 110) The significance of this practice lies in the fact that the house of the most despised people could be transformed into a sacred space. Blessing would also indicate the sacredness that the Pulaya bodies could be imbued with. During the family prayers, blessings take place in the families after the rosary that has the potential to instill the notion of the sacred in each member of the family. It may be noted that the Brahmanical Hinduism had represented them as polluting beings and that they were beyond any redemption. Their social and spiritual selves were put under erasure and they were not thought to be human beings. It is in this context that the Jesuits recognized them as human beings which had a redemptive effect on the people. I wish to emphasize the fact that prayer became an instrument to resist the power of the dominant castes.

In the context of Chirakkal Mission in the Kannur district, one could say that the community of Catholic Dalits could really resist the landlord oppression as they were demarcated as a community. Needless to say, the missionary intervention was the most decisive thing that brought about this change. Alongside this, it should also be emphasized that the leadership in the Churches was provided by Dalits themselves as against the experiences of Dalits in the Southern part of Kerala where they were dominated by the Syrian Christians.

Another leading missionary, Rev. Fr. Joseph Taffarel SJ, of the Chirakkal mission in 1959, began his work among Dalit Christian migrant peasants and agricultural laborers who migrated from the Travancore region to the eastern hills of Kannur district in Malabar namely, Kottukappara. The representatives of Dalit Christians visited him at Tellicherry, under the leadership of Paulose Kannalikkattil, one of the community elders, and requested the missionary Fr. Taffarel to help them as they were facing violence from Syrian Christians in the wake of the right-wing mobilization against the first communist ministry of Kerala in 1959. They have already left the St. Thomas Church, Karikkottakkari which was under the Syro-Malabar Catholic diocese of Tellicherry where they were also members. As the Dalit Christians were without Church membership, they used to assemble in their own houses for prayers. Mobilizing themselves against the violence of Syrian Christians, all the decisions of the community mobilizations were preceded by prayers. Such meetings used to begin and end with prayers. There was a Dalit Christian elder in the community, namely, Elanjimattathil Ouseph, who was well versed in all Catholic prayers, and people reverentially referred to him as, Achan (Father). He was a revered figure in the Dalit Christian community, and even Syrian Christians used to invite him to lead prayers on certain occasions when the services of their own people were not available. Known for his knowledge of the Bible and prayer books and being adept at extempore prayers, he was able to provide religious leadership to the community of Dalit Christians on all special occasions and gatherings. On the day of the visit of the missionary, all Dalit Christians of the village assembled in a decorated shed by the road side, where Fr. Taffarel celebrated the Holy Mass and held a short meeting afterward. Immediately after this, they had a meeting at the house of a Dalit Christian, named Devasia Padikaprampil as they thought it was not wise to discuss matters in the open as their decisions would reach their opponents, the Syrian Christians. In the course of the meeting, the visiting missionary asked them about their requirements. In response, an elderly woman said that all their young men were threatened by those who claim to be traditional Christians. She said she feared these young men would be killed by the adversaries and that they could not even walk on the road. Another person, Varkey Padikaparampil, replied that they needed a secure place where they can safely pray the Lord's Prayer and response prayer, Hail Mary Mother of God without being afraid of caste violence by the Syrian Christians. Subsequently, the missionary, Fr. Taffarel, established a Catholic Church at Kottukappara in 1962. Without going into the details of the history of the Catholic mission in the village, I wish to emphasize the significance of prayer in the resistance to caste violence. Fr. Taffarel appointed one of his trusted catechists, PR Louis, to teach the people of the new church, Our Lady of Lourdes, prayers and the Bible. In due course, he could train selected people of the new church as catechists and readers. Louis was also interested especially in teaching the children and molding their character as recalled by some of the informants. The foregoing discussion would underline what I argue as the anticaste thrust of Dalit Christianity. More importantly, many examples discussed above would show prayer as resistance (Mathew, 2017; Varghese, 2021).

I have already referred to the historic events of the translation of the Bible and the Book of Common Prayer by the Protestant missionaries based in Travancore and the gradual percolation of the translated texts. While it is a fact that initially it was circulated among the literate section of society both Christian and non-Christian communities, it reached the Dalit communities very late as they were not part of the missionary labor and they were illiterate. However, the situation began to change once the missionaries started their labor among the enslaved castes. In the CMS areas of Travancore, they began to teach the slave castes from the late 1840s but picked up momentum in 1852. I have already referred to the examples of slaves reading scriptures which happened in 1857 and they belonged to Tiruvalla mission. This situation demands an analysis of the significance of books, through which the written word and modern Malayalam reached the slave castes. Additionally, there emerges the question of translating the Biblical concepts and categories making the slave caste Christians to appropriate a different vocabulary to articulate their ideas. In the small evening gatherings, the slave caste people could listen to Biblical narratives that they themselves translated in their local context. As a result of it, they were able to see themselves in a new light. In other words, they were able to use the conceptual language derived from the Bible and prayers to articulate their own experiences. Once they were able to read, they started evening prayers, and reading scriptures at home. Following the testimonies provided by the local people and reported by the missionaries, we may observe the changing soundscape of the settlements of the slave castes where the passers-by heard the sound of prayers and reading instead of the sounds of drunken bouts. The missionaries used the Biblical concepts creating what JDY Peel in the African context referred to as "transgression" where in Parables of Jesus "were used to reach up to sublime truths". It actually refers to ideas, practices, and events of quotidian life being suddenly transgressed to create new meaning by signifying Biblical connotation. According to Peel, this transgression is a normal practice of "sermons of all churches" (Peel 2000: 162). Likewise, he also refers to the notion of transvaluation which refers to the fact that many instances of everyday life could be valued differently providing it with an elevated meaning. An often-repeated example in the missionary reports is that of death narratives. In many such narratives, we read about the peaceful death of the person who joined the missionary Church while those who have not joined the mission died a hopeless death as the life ends at the grave. In other words, those who have been baptized die in peace believing that there is a life after death, and they would be rewarded by the Lord as they have had repented for their sins committed. Such instances have been interpreted as transvaluations (Ibid). As it happened in the history of Christian missions, in Kerala too we find the unfolding of a redemptive history that became very central to the concerns of Dalits.

Conclusion

Prayers have played a pivotal role in forming Dalit Christian community in Kerala. However, it is important to observe that due to denominational differences, such a monolithic community may not be realized in actual practice. Yet, one could see very interesting formations of communities across the denominational divides. I have identified certain aspects of the everyday life of slave castes historically in order to show how some of those aspects changed with the coming of missionary Christianity and the new practices it introduced. Although we do not find substantial changes in the everyday work of the slave castes, there is an open admission by the landlords that Christian slaves became hardworking and truthful. This actually shows certain changes in the moral economy that prevailed in Kerala with regard to the slave castes. Missionaries as well as the others have observed that the practice of stealing has been stopped. This probably had a severe effect on the conditions of the slave castes as they stole for survival if at all they did so. More importantly, the landlords did not undergo any moral torment seeing the plight of the slaves that would have created a better economic condition for the slaves. Until the first half of the 20th century, we do not see the situations of slave castes undergoing radical transformation. Yet, some of them could own small pieces of land by the early decades of the 20th century. As I have pointed out, there were exceptional persons who became successful peasants amid all sorts of violence and opposition. From the archival and ethnographic information, I argue that in rural areas of Kerala in the early 20th century structural violence continued creating open violence on everyday basis. Similarly, we do not see much changes in the economic conditions if we compare the 1854 interviews of the missionary Hawksworth with two Travancore slaves, and the report of PC Joseph published in 1938. The ethnographic interview of Mariam George, who was born in 1920s, corroborates the information found in the 1938 study I had quoted. However, in the case of the Church Missionary Society, there were some efforts to support the slave castes who joined the mission by helping them to acquire land. In many places, people cleared lands and sought the help of the missionaries to register such lands for them. One may observe some marginal improvements in the huts of the people. May be some could construct huts with half walls of mud or sunbaked bricks. More importantly, the meaning of such houses changed as they were redesignated as sacred spaces with the coming of the missionaries. This was evident in the prayers that were said in the evening and morning. Alongside this, there were designated places to keep the Bible, or portions of scriptures. It could be a place underneath the thatch or hung from the roof to protect it from termites. My argument is that prayer and prayer practices redesignated the huts of the slave castes as sacred spaces. Probably, the missionary intervention prohibited certain social practices such as polygamy and polyandry, consumption of foods such as the meat of the dead animals. However, we are not sure how the larger question of availability of food was addressed. Yet, the missionaries conveyed a particular idea of desirable food. There are lot of references to the manner in which children, both boys and girls, are to be brought up. They were concerned with a bright future for the young as against their everyday condition I have discussed in the early part of this chapter.

There was a remarkable understanding and redefining of slave caste body making it as a sacred one not just by introducing new sartorial culture of white dress, but the fact that men, women, and children went to the slave churches and schools in the mid-19th century and continued to do so in thousands in the decades to follow, challenging the restrictions in accessing public space in Kerala. This was in a sense the effect of recasting of slave body as sacred. New notions of family introduced by missionaries were also important in redefining the individual and social selves. Dalit Christianity accomplished these changes as it functioned even under severe domination as a religion of the oppressed. Through prayer, Dalit Christians, therefore, challenged the established structures of domination to democratize both Christianity and public space in Kerala.

References

Anonymous. 1905. 'Jubilee celebration at Chelakompu'. *Travancore and Cochin Diocesan Record Vol. XV May. No.3.*
Appadurai, Arjun. 2013. *The Future as a Cultural Fact. Essays on the Global Condition.* London: Verso.
Asad, Talal. 1993. *Genealogies of Religion: Discipline and reasons of Power in Christianity and Islam.* Baltimore: The Johns Hopkins University Press.
Bishop of Travancore and Cochin. 1881. 'The Trichur Report', Church Missionary Society Archives, University of Birmingham.
Bishop of Travancore and Cochin to Mr. Durand dated Feb 20, 1912, Travancore and Cochin Mission 1912. G2/I5/0 1912 Document No. 7 Church Missionary Society Archives University of Birmingham.
Chirappad, Patrose. 2014. Interview in Mathew, Peter. *Interviews with Dalit Christian Elders of Kottukappara, Karikkottakkari and Parakkappara.* Unpublished Manuscript.
Church Missionary Record No. 5, May 1857 Vol XXIV, p. 127 Church Missionary Society Archives University of Birmingham.
Collins, Richard. 1873. *Missionary Enterprise in the East with Especial Reference to the Syrian Christians of Malabar and the Results of Modern Missions.* London: Henry S. King.
Cook, Robert F. 2013. *Apostolic Achievements in South India: Autobiography.* Trichur: Robert F. Cook Centennial Celebrations.
De Certeau, Michel. 1988. *The Practice of Everyday Life.* Berkeley: University of California Press.
Dube, Saurabh. 2020. 'Anthropological Archives Dalit religion Redux,' *Economic and Political Weekly.* Vol. LV. No. 34. pp 42–48.
Frazer, Nancy. 1990. 'Rethinking the Public Sphere: A Contribution to the Critique of Actually Existing Democracy,' *Social Text* No. 25/26 pp. 56–80 accessed on 09/10/2013 17: 51.
Genova, Carlo. 2015. 'Prayer as Practice: An Interpretive Proposal', in Giordan, Giuseppe and Woodhead, Linda (eds) *A Sociology of Prayer.* Ashgate: Surrey.
George, Mariam. 2015. 'Interviews', in Mathew, Peter (ed) *Interviews with Dalit Christian Elders of Kottukappara, Karikkotakkari and Parakkappara.* Unpublished manuscript.
Goffman, Erving. 1959. *The Presentation of Self in Everyday life.* New York: Anchor Books.

AH. 1860. *Day of Dawn in Travancore: A Brief Account of the Manners and Customs of the People and the Effects there Being made for their Improvement.* Kottayam: CMS Press.

Hawksworth, John. 1854. 'Questions by a Missionary Answers by Travancore Slaves Taught in a School of the CM Society'. Manuscript true copy of the original, C 12/07/24. Archives University of Birmingham.

Hawksworth, John 1855. In the *Church Missionary Register* 1855. P. 480.

Hunt, W. S. 1920. *The Anglican Church in Travancore and Cochin 1816–1916.* Kottayam: Church Missionary Society Press.

John (4, 10.) 1976a. 'The Gospel According to John' in *Good News Bible. Today's English Version.* The Bible Societies. Collins/Fontana p. 123.

John (8, 12.) 1976b. 'The Gospel According to John' in *Good News Bible. Today's English Version.* The Bible Societies. Collins/Fontana p. 123.

Joseph, P. C. 1938. *The Economic and Social Environment of the Church in North Travancore and Cochin.* Travancore: CMS College Kottayam.

Kallumadayil, Babu 2021 Interview. At Vadakara, Kottayam on 16/09/2021.

Kathanar, Palakunnel Mathai Mariam. 2000. *Palakunnel Valyachante Nalagamam Diary,* Changanacherry: Palakunnel Mathai Mariam Kathanar Death Centenary Committee.

Kozhuvanal, Kunjukutty. 2006. *Anickadau Adimajanathayum Lekhu Charithravum.* Anickadu: Indian Education Development Charitable Society.

Lee, Joel. 2021. *Deceptive Majority: Dalits, Hinduism, and Underground Religion.* Cambridge: Cambridge University Press.

Madhavan, K. S. 2012. *'Primary Producing Groups in Early and Early Medieval Kerala: Production Process and Historical Roots of Transition to Castes (300–1300 CE)'* Unpublished Ph.D. dissertation, University of Calicut.

Mamen, Oomen. 1856. 'Another Prayer Meeting'. Council of World Mission Archives School of Oriental and African Studies University of London.

Mamen, Oomen. 1858. 'Journal for half year ending June 30, 1858' Council of World Mission Archives School of Oriental and African Studies University of London. pp. 26–28.

Mateer, Samuel. 1883. *Native Life in Travancore.* London: WH Allen & Co.

Mathew, Peter. 2017.(ed.), *Interviews with Dalit Christian Elders of Kottukappara, Karikkotakkari and Parakkappara.* Unpublished manuscript.

Matthan, George. 1857. Letter to Rev. JH Osmaston January 22, 1857 G2 I5/L4 195–31 p. 13. 'Church Missionary Society' Archives University of Birmingham.

Mohan, P. Sanal 2013. "Prayer as Resistance." in *Reverberations: New Directions in the Study of Prayers.* https://forums.ssrc.org/ndsp/2013/09/24/prayer-as-resistance/

Mohan, P. Sanal. 2015. *Modernity of Slavery: Struggles Against caste Inequality in Colonial Kerala.* New Delhi: Oxford University Press.

Nair, Janaki 2016. Textbook Controversies and the Demand for a Past: Public Lives of Indian History, *History Workshop Journal.* doi: 10.1093/hwj/dbw023, accessed on August 29, 2016.

Nanu, T. S. 1912. 'The Work in Ponkunnam' *Travancore and Cochin Diocesan Record* Vol. XXII August 1912, No 4.

Painter, A. F. 1898. 'An Outcaste: A Son of God'. *Church Missionary Gleaner,* 1(289)

Peel, J. D. Y. 2000. *Religious Encounter and the Making of the Yoruba.* Bloomington: Indiana University Press.

Perumpetty, Skaria Vijoy. 1999. *Pastor CS Mathew 'Mochanathinte Suryamugham'. (A brief Life Story of Pastor CS Mathew)*. Kariamplave: WME State Council.
Raboteau, Albert J. 2004. *Slave Religion: The "Invisible Institution" in the Antebellum South*. New York: Oxford University Press.
Raina, C. R. 1988. 'Basel Mission and Social Change in Malabar'. Unpublished MPhil dissertation, University of Calicut.
'Report of the Native Church Missionary Association, Travancore and Cochin for the year 1904 Presented to the Provincial Council', March 3, 1910, Kottayam, CMS Press p. 2–4. Church Missionary Society Archives, University of Birmingham.
'Report on the Work in the Attingal District 1908'. Council of World Mission Archives, School of Oriental and African Studies, University of London, 1908.
Roche, Daniel. 2000. *A History of Everyday Things*. Cambridge: Cambridge University Press.
Taffarel, Joseph Fr. S. J. 1950. *Jottings of a Poor Missionary*. Calicut.
The CMS Mission in Travancore and Cochin. 1915. London Church Missionary Society. Salisbury Square.
The History Writing Committee, 1988. *Kerala Raksha Sainya Charithram. Porattathinte Nooru Varshangal (1896–1996). History of The Salvation Army in Kerala*. Trivandrum: The Salvation Army Territorial Headquarters.
'The Petition of British Missionaries in Travancore to the HH the Raja 1847'. Box No 5. Jacket E March 26. Council of World Mission Archives, School of Oriental and African Studies, University of London, n.d.
The Travancore and Cochin Diocesan Record Vol. XV. No. 3, May 1905.
Thekkedath, Joseph. 1988. *History of Christianity in India, Vol II From the Middle of the Sixteenth to the End of the Seventeenth Century (1542–1700)*. Bangalore: Church History Association of India.
Thuruthikkara, Devasia. 2015. 'Interview' in Mathew, Peter (ed) *Interviews with Dalit Christian Elders of Kottukappara, Karikkotakkari and Parakkappara*. Unpublished manuscript.
Travancore and Cochin Mission 1912. G2/I5/0 1912 *Church Missionary Society Archives*, University of Birmingham.
Varghese, Jestin T. 2021. *"Forms of Caste and Dalit Life in the Churches of Kerala. An Ethnographic Study"*, Unpublished PhD Dissertation, Mahatma Gandhi University, Kottayam.
Varier, Raghava M. R. and Kesavan, Veluthat. 2013. *Tharisappally Pattayam*. Kottayam: National Book Stall.

11 Via Food Ways

Challenging Ideas of Christian Equality and Democratization

Miriam Benteler

Introduction

In continuation of the article *Food, Memory, Community: Kerala as Both "Indian Ocean" Zone and as Agricultural Homeland* by Fillipo and Caroline Osella (2008), which deals with the food habits among Muslim and Hindu communities in different settings in Kerala, this chapter in a first step takes a closer look at the Latin Catholic community in central coastal Kerala, their diet and serving practices, and, via this, their concepts of hierarchy and equality. In a second step, the concepts of equality and hierarchy in Christian thought and practice are set in relation to ideas of Christianity and democratization.

Why approach the topic of Christianity and democratization via food ways? Osella and Osella, who encourage "ethnographers to pay closer attention to local imaginings of food" (2008: 171), compare two very different settings and contexts in their article and are aware of the distortion this might affect in some aspects: an urban Muslim majority and a rural Hindu majority and their food habits are in focus. Nevertheless, the authors argue that one "can justifiably name 'Hindu' and 'Muslim' food practices" (2008: 171) – and, I would add, Christian food habits, or, to be more precise, Latin Catholic food habits. These mentioned (regional) religious communities have different ideas and concepts about food items, preparation as well as about serving and eating practices. The food habits and serving practices of the Latin Catholics show, on the one hand, striking similarities, on the other hand, striking differences to their Hindu neighbors, that is, on the one hand, the nonrelevance of the considerations of purity and impurity in the community, and on the other hand, the valuation of hierarchy, which is prevalent in many other contexts as well. Thus, taking food and serving practices as a starting point, the chapter sets hierarchical structures observable among the Latin Catholics in relation to the generally emphasized Christian idea(l) of equality. Following, it questions the idea of Christians or Christianity's apparent closeness to democratization, which is based on the idea of the prevalence of egalitarian principles in Christian belief. Thereby, it also examines the relation between lived religion and believed religion.

Another reason is that food is highly political and politicized, especially so in India. Referring to the parallel existence of different food habits, from vegetarianism to various forms of meat eating in different castes and communities in India, Kancha Ilaiah states in his article on "Beef, BJP and Food Rights of People" (1996): "Indian society has been co-existing with all these [food] practices and must be allowed to do so" (1996: 1445). He points out that beef-eating is in no way a "minority phenomenon", a food habit of Christians and Muslims, as the BJP claims. On the contrary, meat is an essential part of the food many different Hindu castes consume. His discussions, focusing on the beef-ban ideology of the BJP, thus shows how food and eating is used by political parties in India. A politization and polarization of food and eating habits is here instrumentalized to build up resentments and differences between religious communities to challenge and destroy India's "unity in diversity" (cf. Dumont). Food is thus not only political on a global level with its undemocratic food systems, which are, for example, characterized by control of the global seed sector by transnational agribusinesses. It is also very political on a national level. Against the background of the beef-ban discourses described by Ilaiah, it becomes obvious why Caroline Osella's giving-up of vegetarianism while living among Muslims in India (see below) becomes a political statement against nationalist, antiminority political aspirations (while vegetarianism in Europe is often a political statement regarding animal rights and the climate crisis). The food ways of the Latin Catholics certainly express the community's identity and delimitation to other communities. But it is, as will be shown in the following pages, not used in the coastal community to promote equality and/or democratization.

The Latin Catholics

In his study on the Christian involvement in the independent movement, Geoffrey Oddie (2001) points to the Indian Christians' heterogeneity. Christians were not only geographically unevenly distributed in India but differed also in many other respects such as language, literacy and education, economic position, caste, class, denomination, urban and rural backgrounds, and Western-educated or without or little Western contact. Therefore, they did not have a common identity or form a common group (2001: 349). This has not changed, and the Christian heterogeneity has certainly to be kept in mind when talking about Christians in India today, about Christianity and democratization – and, certainly, also when talking about food and food practices.

The Latin Catholics, on whose ethnography I base my account, constitute one of the manifold Christian communities in the South Indian state of Kerala. In the 16th century, Portuguese missionaries who arrived with traders from Europe converted predominately lower fishing castes in the coastal region of Kerala and other parts of South India. Due to their former liturgical language and distinction from the long-established Syrian Christians, these

Roman Catholics are known as Latins or Latin Catholics – *latinkaar* in Malayalam. Fieldwork was carried out in a large coastal village in the Ernakulam District of Central Kerala. It is a non-nucleated village, whose borders are hard to make out (2001: 36,209 inhabitants in the Grama Panchayat Chellanam). The Latin Catholics make up about 70–80% of the population and certainly constitute the dominant community of the village due to their numerical as well as economic, educational, and social strength (Srinivas 1967; Dumont 1980: 160–163). The members of different Pentecostal denominations and different Hindu castes, namely Gaudha Saarasvatha Brahmans (belonging to one family only), Kudumbi, Izhava, and members of a scheduled caste, also inhabit the area (for more details, see Benteler 2014).

Latin Catholics – Diet and Serving, Impurity, and Hierarchy

Rice and fish, which Osella and Osella call the "base diet of Kerala" (2008: 170), are also the two main food items, which the Latin Catholics consume. A meal lacking one of these components is considered incomplete and not making someone full. Thus, rice is eaten (and demanded) three times a day in many, if not most families, while others prepare certain breakfast dishes such as *puttu* or *appam* or buy them from small restaurants at the roadside (the main ingredient of these dishes being rice powder).

Fish is expected to be part of every meal, be it as fish curry or fried fish. Vegetable curries are not regarded as an adequate substitute for fish and are often absent or constitute a minor part of the meal. About a meal with three or four different vegetable curries, one might hear people say that "nothing is there to eat", whereas a meal with only one fish curry to go with the rice will rarely be the subject of complaint. If there is no fish, the gravy of a fish curry may help to get at least the taste of it. Other seafood, such as prawns, crabs, and mussels may replace fish – certain vegetable curries can be "upgraded" by adding small prawns. Fish and other sea food (caught in the sea or backwaters) is purchased from small local markets (mainly by men) or from (male or female) fish vendors going by scooter, cycling, or walking from house to house.

Meat is an accepted substitute for fish, but is usually only cooked on Sundays or at feast days. Chicken and beef are the most common kinds of meat people in the village consume. Beef can be purchased especially on Saturdays and Sundays from small open stalls on the roadside or from nearby inland places. Chicken can be bought from some houses in the village or inland villages.

What is true for food in everyday life is especially true for food in the context of functions/celebrations: a feast without meat or fish is unimaginable for the Latin Catholics. Thus, a standard dish served at festive functions such as baptisms, engagements, or weddings, is *biriyani* – a dish consisting of basmati rice, which is cooked with spices (cinnamon, cardamom, and cloves) and mixed with vegetable oil and ghee and small vegetable pieces, nuts, and raisins. It is served with chicken or beef pieces and dished up with lemon pickle and onion salad (*kacchambar*). An alternative is the so-called "dishes" (which are more costly): *appam* or bread with (fish or meat) stew, followed by rice with different vegetable curries, meat, fish, and pickles. At evenings before a function, *kutal*, a curry made of intestines, is usually prepared and served with rice.

Nowadays, only some people follow the fasting requirements during the Christian Lenten seasons before Easter and Christmas and do not consume meat, fish, eggs, and milk during these periods. Meat and fish are thus also cooked and served at celebrations during Lenten times. Good Friday – as the climax of the Lenten season – is, however, a fasting day, and all Latin Catholics avoid the consumption of fish and meat. In accordance with this, the only celebrations at which vegetarian meals are an absolute must are the meals served after a funeral and on the seventh day after a death, the entire week being one of fasting for the family of the deceased. After a funeral, the simple meal, which is cooked in neighboring houses and served to the guests, is fully vegetarian and usually consists of rice and different vegetable curries. The meal on the seventh day after a death – a ceremony of commemoration, celebrated with a mass and meal afterward – is usually served on banana leaves. It consists of rice and a number of particular vegetables curries and concludes with a sweet gruel, eaten together with mashed bananas and pappadam, a crispy pancake. Known as *sadhya* or, in reference to the items it closes with, as *pappadam, pazham, paysam*, it is the same meal, which is served at all ritual functions among Hindus in the area. It is, however, said, that people today tend to celebrate the seventh day after a death on smaller scale, with relatively few guests, while the 30th day after death is celebrated on grander scale instead, with a larger number of guests: nonvegetarian food is allowed at the later occasion.

Meat Eating and Latin Catholics

It has hopefully become obvious that the Latin Catholics are noticeably meat eating, and very much stress their nonvegetarian attitude. While Caroline Osella gave up her vegetarianism among the Kozhikode Muslims as a kind of political statement (2008: 9), I give up mine when I am in Kerala – it would just cause too much irritation and incomprehension among Latin Catholics there. In the village, there is only one vegetarian caste, and vegetarianism is not at all propagated by the other Hindu castes of the area, but seemingly rather in decline in everyday life. The explicit antivegetarianism of the Latin Catholics, among whom meals containing meat are the standard, is, however, exceptional. (For Goa, Rowena Robinson points out that Christian converts who avoided meat, had to fear the Inquisition for adhering to Hindu beliefs such as adoring the cow (1998).) It also becomes obvious that the consumption or nonconsumption of seafood and meat marks happy and unhappy occasions among the Latin Catholics: happy occasions need to go along with food containing meat. Sad occasions, in contrast, demand vegetarian food. Vegetarian food is to be understood in relation to the Catholic notion of repentance, renunciation, and sorrow and is therefore deeply connected with Christian ideas: it is to be consumed during Lenten Seasons or after a death has occurred. In accordance with this, marriages as first and foremost occasions of happiness are not to be held during Lenten Seasons as well as after a death in the family. Vegetarian food thus indicates sadness and renunciation and at certain points even bodily weakness – a person considered too thin might, for example, be suspected not to eat meat (c. Osella and Osella 2008: 180, reporting about non-Brahmins refusing to eat in Brahmin restaurants, since the food is supposed not to give strength). Ilaiah confirms this attitude regarding vegetarianism, stating: "If a guest is served with vegetarian food, it is considered a humiliation. Among many castes and communities there are jokes that ridicule vegetarianism" (1996: 1445).

Consuming vegetarian food shows that something is out of order, be it due to a death in the family, a special event in the church (e.g., the passion of Christ), or, more trivial, the (temporary) absence of the husband, who is in many families responsible for the purchasing of fish and meat. In contrast, meat and fish are usually associated with happiness and festivity, and supposed to give strength: these items should thus neither be missing in everyday life nor at festive occasions. Fish and meat eating, and especially the consumption of beef, are thus not at all considered to cause impurity, and, accordingly, vegetarian food is not associated with purity. In general, the ideas of purity and pollution are nearly absent among the Latin Catholics. Eating from each other's plates is, for example, also not considered problematic. This differs considerably from the concepts of purity of their Hindu neighbors. It is among the Hindu castes, except the Brahmans, usual to consume fish and partially meat, including beef, in everyday life. But – and this is different in other parts of India – all these castes consume and offer to their guests only vegetarian food at all ritual functions and religious ceremonies, that is, on all occasions when ritual purity is important (cf. also Osella and Osella 2008: 182).

Serving Practices and Hospitality

While the Latin Catholics' disregard of ideas of purity and pollution sets them apart from their Hindu neighbors in the realm of food, serving practices are rather similar.

In the family context, social hierarchies are observed when food is consumed and gender as well as age distinctions are of great relevance. Usually, the wife serves her husband during meals. Only when he has finished or when it has been assured that the husband has had enough, the wife starts eating the remaining food. If elder family members, for example, the husband's parents or elder brothers, are present, they will be served first, and others will not eat before they have started eating. People will not even sit down until male elders have taken a seat. Younger children, however, are often served beforehand, and then do not hesitate to order both of their parents around, while small children are often fed while they crawl or walk around. It is not at all common that the whole family eats together. Hospitality is very important among the Latin Catholics and guests mostly receive special preparations of food. Since purity is not relevant, it is unproblematic to invite non-family members and even strangers to one's house (cf. Osella and Osella 2008: 193 on hospitality among Hindus). When guests are present, the guests are always served first when they eat in the company of a senior family member. Most of the time, however, they will eat alone, the hosts being busy serving the guests (sometimes even a male family member, doubling the honor), who remain standing at the table to serve food to the guests. Guests are thus not only honored by the preparation and offering of special food items, but also by the serving practice, which is a sign of respect. One could even see the hierarchical relation of husband and wife mirrored in the relation of guest and host.

As in the Hindu context described by Osella and Osella, the "guest-host hierarchal etiquette demands that guests should express reluctance to eat, should be served (guests should never serve themselves, but should have their needs anticipated), should be seated at a table and attended by standing womenfolk, and should eat silently and speedily" (2008: 194). At festive occasions, people tend to sit in long lines, mostly men with men, women with women, or in family groups, order the serving men about, and eat without much conversation. This is the case during marriage functions, but also during the banquet held by the main festival sponsor during the church festival. It is in striking contrast to the description of the Muslim context by Osella and Osella: here, eating together with the guests simultaneously (though in gender-specific rooms) emphasizes an idea of equality:

> Sitting to eat in a line or a circle; sitting in single-sex or mixed groups; eating in relays according to social hierarchy or together, simultaneously; serving oneself or been served; expressing relish or diffidence in eating food cooked by non-kin: all these are bodily indications of community affiliation and a community-specific vision of human relationships – as egalitarian or hierarchical, status as marked primarily by age and caste or by gender, outsiders as dangerous or to be welcomed.
> (2008: 196)

The Latin Catholics and the Value of Hierarchy

In the realm of food, one finds hierarchy in an everyday-life context and in a deeply embodied form, in the full sense of the word (Bourdieu 2003: 94; Osella and Osella 2008: 4, talking about an "embodied food memory", 173–174). However, the hierarchical structures revealed in the realm of food are present in many other contexts as well, also in more "formal" ones. They can thus certainly not be attributed to the "impressions of the ethnographer" (Pfeffer 2004: 382). They are to be found in quite "diverse manifestations" (Dumont 1977: 20) such as kinship practice and kinship terminology, gender and age relations, gift exchange or membership in different Christian communities and subcommunities, or in the pompous church festivals of the Latin Catholics in coastal Kerala, which show distinctly hierarchical structures and thinking.[1]

If one takes a closer look, for example, at the kinship terminology, one can see that the terminology of the Latin Catholics differs considerably from a so-called Dravidian terminology. However, the hierarchical nature of the terminology is immediately visible. The terminology of the Latin Catholics shows, for example, a strong hierarchical distinction of age, especially in ego's generation: different terms are used for elder brothers and sisters and for younger brothers and sisters in the terminology of reference. Accordingly, in the terminology of address, younger siblings are called by name and elder siblings by kinship terms. Kinship practice confirms the hierarchical nature in the relation of younger and elder kin, which are characterized by respect and obedience (cf. Benteler 2014: 58–62, 215–216).

On the level of the Latin Catholic community as such, one can observe that the Latin Catholics of the coastal area are divided into hierarchically ordered subcommunities, the so-called 500s and 700s, belonging to different parishes and different dioceses. They are traditionally associated with different occupations, and the 500s are considered lower in status than the 700s. Until quite recently, these subcommunities were strictly endogamous. Furthermore, the Latin Catholics are attributed a certain rank in relation to the different Hindu castes in the area and thus have a, albeit ambiguous, position in the local caste hierarchy (cf. Benteler 2014: 65–94, 195–198).

Contrary to the views of Fuller (1976: 64), hierarchy can thus be seen as continuous among the Latin Catholics: it is relevant in the relation between different castes and communities as well as within the Catholic community: hierarchy pervades/encompasses the whole of social live and is obviously valued in the community, as in Indian society in general – Vitebsky (2020, viii) speaks of the "hierarchical and totalising nature of Indian society", and the Latin Catholics are certainly a part of this society (Benteler 2014), because they share the value of hierarchy with society at large.

At the same time, the idea of impurity plays next to no role in the community (cf. ideas of purity and pollution do not exist, or in a limited or weakened form (cf. Fuller 1976: 64; Dumont 1980: 201–202; Robinson 1998: 84)), as it becomes obvious in the context of food, but also in many other contexts, such as, for example, birth and death. Hierarchy thus lacks the "ritual justification" (Mocherla 2020: 70, 81) among the Latin Catholics, but, nevertheless, exists and is valued. The Latin Catholics can be seen, to quote Vitebsky again, as one example for the "almost infinite variety in what people do with the distinctive elements which the Indian cultural universe does provide" (2020: viii, see also Ilaiah 1996: 1445), a universe characterized by principles of hierarchy and holism (2020: viii).

Politics and Religion, Christianity, and Democratization

As food, religion is political. In her article, "'God is not a democrat'. Pentecostalism and democratisation in Nigeria" (1995), Ruth Marshall points out that the "churches first concern is not politics" (1995: 241). Nevertheless, though religion (mostly) focuses on the "transcendental and the eternal realm", as Ashok Kumar Mocherla and James Ponniah point out in their introduction, religion "operates on the mundane terrain" as well (this volume). Religion and politics are intertwined in many ways: religion works on the political level, conveys political statements, and influences politics in different ways – and vice versa (cf. Vitebsky ix). This happens on very different levels, from the local level to the national level, and in very different contexts. Mocherla, for example, shows that religious celebrations among the Lutherans in Andhra Pradesh cannot be separated from the political context, but need to be seen as conveying religious as well as sociopolitical messages (2020: 78). Similarly, Latin Catholics narrated that the sponsoring of the grand church festivals and the election of the sponsor(s) was in the past used to play out rivalries and powers between landowners (Benteler 2014: 168). Mocherla also emphasizes how communism, by raising caste consciousness among the Dalits, facilitated conversion to Christianity in Andhra Pradesh (2020: 68).

In direct relation to the processes of democratization, Oddie (2001), concentrating on the level of national politics, relates how Christianity or Christians operated in the context of India's process of democratization and discusses the part Christian nationalists played in the Indian national movement. Certainly, the Christian interest in political affairs did not end with independence. That the Catholic Bishop conference as well as bishops of different states in India asked the Catholic electors to vote for or vote not for certain parties in the national elections via statements to be read in the church is another example of post-independence direct influence of religious leaders on political events (Sundar 2012: 6). However, Aparna Sundar also emphasizes that the church was not always directly involved in politics, as in these cases, but often acted through social activism. This is exemplified in Sushil J. Aaron's article in the volume "Evangelical Christianity and Democracy in Asia" (2009). Aaron points out that he is explicitly not concerned with "electoral politics", but rather with developments on a micro level. He shows how specific Christian communities – Evangelical Christian groups in the tribal context of Gujarat – are linked to the processes of democratization: "social effects of a certain stand of Indian evangelicalism provide[s] *adivasis* greater opportunities and create political possibility by fostering collective identity and community organisation" (2009: 87). This especially happened when the evangelical community in question changed its agenda from "evangelism alone" to "evangelism and development" (2009: 103) by formulating the goal to enable and empower the Christianized groups to take political action in the future (2009: 103).

Equality, Hierarchy, Christianity, and Democracy

While the food the Latin Catholics consume in everyday life is similar to that of their Hindu neighbors, the food served for festive occasions differs in that it should contain meat and/or fish. These differences are due to the distinction, not between pollution and purity but between meat-eating and vegetarian food, which is associated with happiness and sorrow, respectively. The serving practice, however, shows that hierarchical structures exist in the Latin Catholic community, as among their Hindu neighbors. What is observable in the realm of food is observable in other areas, too. It challenges the quickly drawn equation of Christianity, equality, and democratization, which is discussed below.

This discussion on the issues of Christianity and democratization focuses neither on a historical level nor on a micro level as the study of food practices might suggest and neither on the direct influence via political statements nor on the indirect influence via social activism. The focus is thus not on the historical process of democratization in India, the part Christians played in it (or did not play in it) or on the ongoing process of democratization today. I would rather examine the view that Christian religious and spiritual ideas seem to favor the processes of democratization, as is apparently often assumed, at least implicitly (cf. Anderson 2009: 17–45).

Undoubtedly, equality is one of the cornerstones of democracy, since "democracy is a system for ensuring control over such decision making by all members of the association, *considered as equals*. It is a system of collective decision making, in other words, which embodies the twin principles or ideals of popular control and political *equality*" (Beetham, 1995: 61–62, emphasis added). Certainly, the Indian constitution secures all people of India "equality of status and opportunity" in its preamble, and the right of equality as a fundamental right, denying discrimination on grounds of religion, race, caste, sex, place of birth or any of them (Part III, Fundamental rights).

Like democracy, Christianity is generally associated with equality.[2] The thought that people are equal and preach and practice "egalitarian principles" and see "each individual [as] [...] an image of God with dignity and importance", as John Thattumkal, former bishop of Kochi diocese, writes in his book *Caste and the Catholic church in India* seems to be embedded in Christian thought, and in Indian Christian thought as well. He stresses "to be Christian in India, as anywhere else, [...] means to belong to a community that does not recognize caste distinctions among its members, that does not tolerate [the] caste system, and that encourages its members to live in freedom, equality and fraternity" (1984: 23) – only to add that "the Church in India is far from being a casteless community, which the very core of its faith and teachings demands" (1984: 272).

The idea that Christianity, based on egalitarian principles and Christians, adhering to these principles, supports democracy and the processes of democratization, seems plausible on the first sight and under the assumption that the mentioned "translation" from theory to practice, from believed religion to lived religion, really took place in the history of Indian Christianity. In fact, there are few to deny (Appadurai 1986, 1988; cf. also Klausen 1968; Busby 2000) that hierarchy or concepts of caste have had their impact on religious practices in India, too, and the examination of the realm of food only confirms the valuation of hierarchy among the Latin Catholics as an Indian Christian community (especially in comparison to the urban Muslim group examined in the article by Osella and Osella (2008)). Titles such as *Comparison: are there castes among non-Hindus and outside India?* (Dumont 1980), *Kerala Christians and the Caste System* (Fuller 1976), *Caste Stratification among the Roman Catholics of Goa* (D'Costa 1977), *Caste and Castelessness among South Indian Christians* (Caplan 1980) or *South Indian Christians, Purity/Impurity, and the Caste System: Death rituals in a Tamil Roman Catholic Community* (Mosse 1996) confirm the interest in the question of the relation of caste and Christianity. The studies all interpret caste and hierarchy as an important part of Christian practice in India. Dumont concludes: "[a]dherence to a monotheistic and egalitarian religion is not enough, even after several generations, to lead to the disappearance of the fundamental attitude on which the caste system is based" (1980: 205).

This is consistent with the view that conversion is "not a rupture, but [...] an ongoing process in which some earlier cultural ideas and practices might be suppressed but others survive to inform the trajectory of the local form of Christianity into the future" (Angelova 2020: 130). The contrast between what "religion professes" and what "religion practices" is obvious in this context. It is also inherent in the speech by Vedanayagam Samuel Azariah, founder of the Indian Missionary Society (IMS) and later bishop of Dornakal. During the World Missionary Conference at Edinburgh in 1910, he "asked the West not to send missionaries, but friends, commenting that the missionaries were good at promising thrones in heaven but never offered converts chairs in their drawing rooms" (Stanley 2009: 123–125, cited after Doss 2018: 256). The mentioned "thrones in heaven" point to another interesting aspect: the fact that the Christian idea of equality is (originally) an equality in relation to God, and in relation to God only and by no means excluded or excludes societal hierarchy: The Christian equality is, basically, an outworldly equality and the wordly equality is actually considered theologically irrelevant in relation to the former (Lexikon für Theologie und Kirche 1995: 738–739). However, this outworldly equality has constantly been reinterpreted and is, it seems, today predominantly equated with equality in general, also in the church itself. Ayyar for example, nearly 100 years ago points out: "According to the conception of the followers of Christianity all are equal and devoid of any difference in social status. This fact is observed more in its violation than in its observance" (1926: 277).

The idea of equality is certainly also the basis of social activism, Aaron and Surpana mention. Jeffrey Hayne reminds us of the fact that "religions are creative and constantly changing; consequently, their relation with democratisation and democracy can also change over time" (2020) – the religion-democracy relation is "a dynamic affair" (Anderson 2009; Sundar 2012: 16). However, not only religions and their relation to democracy are creative and constantly changing but also perceptions of religious ideas are subject to change: religion or religious concepts experience different readings in different times and from different perspectives, too, as the shift of meaning from equality to God to equality in general proofs. In addition, if we talk about the influence of caste concepts and hierarchical thinking on Christianity in India, we should not forget to look at the place of hierarchy in Christian thought in general, on its implications and on changing perceptions. After a survey of literatures related to the Christian concepts of equality, it seems that it has constantly been underrated that hierarchy too has always been a basic aspect of Christian thought (Fuller 1976: 65, cf. also Robinson 1998: 88–89), while the notion of egalitarianism in Christian thought has often been overemphasized and, in the Indian context, contrasted to hierarchical caste society. Fuller thus writes:

> One problem can be dealt with immediately: the apparent contradiction between Hindu hierarchy and Christian egalitarianism. The significance of this contradiction can be greatly exaggerated. Although certain forms of Christian teaching have, at various times, given some prominence to egalitarianism, it is historically the case that its dogma has not emphasised this aspect and that hierarchy [...] has been a constant and fundamental element in Christian thought.
>
> (1976: 65)

The image of the "chain of being" or the believers as part of the "mystical body of Christ", evoking the idea of a hierarchically ordered whole, exemplify this statement. For example, the "great chain of being", a concept of importance from antiquity to the 19th century (Lovejoy 1936), orders all beings hierarchically, including human beings. In the model of the mystical body of Christ, human beings constitute different parts of the body. These are not equal, but stand in a hierarchical relation to each other: the head, for example, is superior to the other parts (cf. Bell and Weinstein 1982; Robinson 1993: 79). Furthermore, Christianity has always adapted itself perfectly well to hierarchical societies, for example, the feudal society in Europe (cf. Robinson 1994: 98). We thus find an interesting mixture of religious beliefs and religious practices, of Christian ideas of equality and equality in relation to God, of hierarchical Christian concepts, and the valuation of hierarchy among Christian communities in India today and its manifestation in different contexts of the life and practice of Christian communities, such as the Latin Catholics.

Conclusion

The Latin Catholics are noticeably meat eating and very much stress their nonvegetarian attitude. They follow nearly no dietary restrictions and the (non)consumption of seafood and meat marks (un)happy occasions rather than pure or impure situations. Food items thus form a very important part of the Latin Catholics' diet and are connected to concepts of strength, happiness, and sorrow. While their diet, especially at ritual occasions, distinguishes the Latin Catholics considerably from their Hindu neighbors, it is striking that the serving practices and hospitality of the two communities are very similar. Among the Latin Catholics, for example, the wife serves her husband during meals and eats the leftovers, as in the Hindu context. Among many others, the context of food is an example for the valuation of hierarchy in the Latin Catholic community. A look at Christian concepts shows that hierarchy can not only be seen as the impact of caste society but also has roots in Christian thought, too. In contrast, equality is not valued and practiced in the Latin Catholic community; it plays an inferior role. And if we again look to Christian idea of equality, we see that Christian equality is, basically, equality in relation to God. The above cited studies show that on the micro level as on the macro level and on the regional level as on the national level, Christians are and were involved in the processes of democratization in India and by different means actively promoted and promoted democratization. That Christianity is especially apt to initiate democratization processes due to its egalitarian principles and practice cannot be confirmed: the idea of Christian equality, on which this assumption is usually based, constitutes, in different respects and seen from different angles, a rather shaky foundation for this argument. To be Christian in India can mean, but does not necessarily mean, to belong to a community that "encourages its members to live in freedom, equality and fraternity" (Thattumkal 1984: 23), that encourages democratization.

Notes

1 Knut M. Rio and Olaf H. Smedal note that "in social sciences it is becoming increasingly difficult to even think hierarchical relationships and holism in Dumont's terms – and even more so to make our audiences believe in them" (2009: 2).
2 In his article, Oddie mentions the founding of Christian ashrams from the 1920s onward, which were based on the "ideas that they would demonstrate the social equality implicit in Christian teaching, including equality between races, so conspicuously absent in Indo-European relations elsewhere" (2001: 354).

References

Aaron, Sushil J. 2009. 'Emulating Azariah: Evangelicals and Social Change in the Dangs', in David Halloran Lumsdaine (ed.), *Evangelical Christianity and Democracy in Asia*, pp. 87–123. Oxford, New York: Oxford University Press.

Alexander, K.C. 1977. 'The Problem of Caste in the Christian Churches of Kerala', in Harjinder Singh (ed.), *Caste among Non-Hindus in India*, pp. 50–65. Delhi: National Publishing House.
Anderson, John. 2009. *Christianity and Democratisation: From Pious Subjects to Critical Participants*. Manchester: Manchester University Press.
Appadurai, Arjun. 1988. 'Putting Hierarchy in its Place', *Cultural Anthropology*, 3,1: 36–49.
Appadurai, Arjun. 1986. 'Is Homo Hierarchicus?', *American Ethnologist*, 13,4: 745–761.
Ayyar, L. K. Ananthakrishna 1926. *Anthropology of the Syrian Christians*. Ernakulam: Cochin Government Press.
Benteler, Miriam. 2014. *Shared Values. Hierarchy and Affinity in a Latin Catholic Community of South India*. Delhi: Manohar Publishers.
Bell, Rudolph M. and Weinstein, Donald. 1982. *Saints and Society: The Two Worlds of Western Christendom 1000–1700*. Chicago: University of Chicago Press.
Beetham, David. 1995. 'Problems of Democratic Consolidation', in Paul Gifford (ed.), *The Christian Churches and the Democratisation of Africa*, pp. 61–74. Leiden, New York, Köln: E.J. Brill.
Bourdieu, Pierre. 2003 [French 1972]. *Outline of a Theory of Practice*. Cambridge, New York: Cambridge University Press.
Busby, Cecilia. 2000. *The Performance of Gender: An Anthropology of Everyday Life in a South Indian Fishing Village*. London: The Athlone Press.
Caplan, Lionel. 1980. 'Caste and Castelessness among South Indian Christians', *Contributions to Indian Sociology*, 14(2): 213–238.
Doss, M. Christhu. 2018. 'Indian Christians and the Making of Composite Culture in South India', *South Asia Research*, 38(3): 247–267.
Dumont, Louis. 1980 [French 1966]. *Homo Hierarchicus. The Caste System and Its Implications*. London, Chicago: The University of Chicago Press.
Dumont, Louis. 1977. *From Mandeville to Marx. The Genesis and Triumph of Economic Ideology*. Chicago, London: The University of Chicago Press.
Fuller, Chris J. 1976. 'Kerala Christians and the Caste System', *Man*, 2, 53–70.
Ilaiah, Kancha. 1996. 'Beef, BJP and Food Rights of People', *Economical and Political Weekly*, 31, 24, 1445.
Klausen, Arne Martin. 1968. *Kerala Fishermen and the Indo-Norwegian Pilot Project*. Oslo: Universitetsforlaget, London: Allen & Unwin.
Lovejoy, Arthur O. 1936. *The Great Chain of Being. A Study of the History of An Idea*. New York: Harper & Brothers.
Lexikon für Theologie und Kirche. 1995. *Gleichheit*, Freiburg, Basel: Herder, 738– 741.
Mocherla, Ashok Kumar. 2020. 'Communism and the Cross: A Caste-Class-Trajectory of Religious Conversion in South India' in Peter Berger and Sarbeswar Sahoo (eds), *Godroads: Modalities of Conversion in India*, pp.68–84. Cambridge: Cambridge University Press.
Marshall, Ruth. 1995. '"God is not a Democrat": Pentecostalism and Democratisation in Nigeria' in Paul Gifford (ed.), *The Christian Churches and the Democratisation of Africa*, pp. 239–260. Leiden, New York, Köln: E.J. Brill.
Mosse, David. 1996. 'South Indian Christians, Purity/Impurity, and the Caste System: Death Rituals in a Tamil Roman Catholic Community', *Journal of the Royal Anthropological Institute*, 2(3): 461–483.

Oddie, Geoffrey A. 2001. 'Indian Christians and National Identity, 1870–1947', *Journal of Religious History*, 25: 346–366.
Osella, Caroline, 2008. 'Introduction', in *South Asia: Journal of South Asian Studies*, 31,1, 1–9.
Osella, Caroline and Osella, Filippo. 2008. 'Food, memory, community: Kerala as both 'Indian Ocean' zone and as agricultural homeland', in *South Asia: Journal of South Asian Studies*, 31,1, 170–198.
Pfeffer, Georg, 2004. 'Order in tribal Middle Indian "kinship"', *Anthropos* 99, 381–409.
Robinson, Rowena. 1998. *Conversion, Continuity and Change: Lived Christianity in Southern Goa*. New Delhi: Sage Publications.
Rio, Knut M. and Smedal, Olaf H. 2009. 'Hierarchy and its alternatives. An introduction to movements of totalization and detotalization', in Knut M. Rio and Olaf H. Smedal, *Hierarchy. Persistence and Transformation in Social Formations* (eds.), New York, Oxford: Berghahn Books, 1–63.
Sundar, Aparna. 2012. 'Thinking beyond Secularism: The Catholic Church and Political Practice in Rural South India', *South Asia Multidisciplinary Academic Journal*.
Srinivas, M.N. 1967 [1955]. 'The social system of a Mysore village', in McKim Marriott (ed.), *Village India. Studies in the Little Community*, pp. 1–35. Chicago, London: The University of Chicago Press,
Thattumkal, John. 1984. *Caste and the Catholic Church in India: A Historico-Juridical Study on the Nature of the Caste System and its Implications in the Catholic Church of India*. Cochin: Santa Cruz Press.

12 Naming the Unspoken

Domestic Violence and the Church*

Bharathi Nuthalapati

Introduction

Patriarchy, hierarchy, and gender discrimination engender violence against women, thereby negating their rights and human dignity. Power and control are the means through which violence is perpetrated on women in the domestic spaces (Chapman: 2014). Violence is antithetical to democratization, which is modelled on the principles of equality, empowerment, and justice (Alexander & Welzel: 2011; Dobbins et al.: 2007). Christianity affirms the values of justice, equality, and the inherent value and worth of a human being. The lived experiences of Christian women, who are victims of domestic violence, render a contrary reality, and church, as an institution, adheres to the societal norms of patriarchy and gender discrimination. The church's teaching on hierarchy within the family, and its indifference to this endemic problem, not only make its a corroborator in this violence but also hinders the process of empowering Christian women to realize their intrinsic value and worth as equal beings. The chapter intends to demonstrate how a woman's life is controlled and violated by those who are supposed to be her custodians – her partner and her church.

From the time she was an unborn fetus to the time she is confined to her grave, the life of a woman is marred with violence. Her body, her very person is defined by vulnerability. In India, she is praised as the goddess, deity, protector, the epitome of creation, and the sustainer of life (Dhruvarajan 1989; Ghadially 1988; Sharma 1995). She is also a property, a servant, and a slave who is devoid of any rights (Altekar 1959; Bose: 2000). Women's bodies are the site on which the honor and dignity of the nation, tribe, caste, and family are enshrined (Gadially 1988; Thapan 1997). Violation of their bodies is what entails the final victory of the enemy. They are the pawns in the game of the politics of power and control (Chapman: 2014; Agarwal: 1995).

Violence against women has been one of the hot issues in India after the gang rape of the Delhi girl who came to be called as Nirbhaya.[1] However, as

---

* This unpublished article is a modified version of a paper presented in a seminar at Union Biblical Seminary, Pune.

DOI: 10.4324/9781003426035-17

the print and electronic media began to report these cases on a daily basis, as if they are common happenings, rape also lost its severity. Today's news pages could be printed with the ink of the blood of the women who are being raped, murdered, attacked with acid, molested, and shamed, not to mention the domestic violence that goes on behind the closed doors in the places they call home.

We are living in a society where a naked Jain Baba, Tarun Sagar,[2] taught the legislative assembly of Haryana the meaning of Dharma and politics. He said,

> Rajniti par dharam ka ankush zaroori hai. Dharam pati hai, rajneeti patni. Har pati ki yeh duty hoti hai apni patni ko samrakshan de. Har patni ka dharam hota hai ki woh pati ke anushasan ko sweekar kare. Agar rajneeti par dharam ka ankush na ho toh woh magan-mast haathi ki tarah... ho jaati hai (The control of dharma over politics is essential. Dharma is the husband, politics is the wife. It is the duty of every husband to protect his wife. It is the duty of every wife to accept the discipline of her husband. If there is no control of dharma over politics, it will be like an elephant out of control).
>
> (Sandhu: 2016)

These words mirror the status and dignity of women in India.

Methodology

I have adopted the feminist historiographical method, especially the qualitative method with emphasis on the category of personal experience. Experiences or the subjective factor did not constitute a part of the dominant history. Feminist science must concern itself on the totality of society bringing relationships to light which previously remained in darkness. That is when we speak of women we must speak of men, and when we speak of poverty, we must speak of wealth and so on. We must speak of both for one condition the other. Maria Mies rightly puts that experience "denotes the sum of the processes which individuals or groups have gone through in the production of their lives: It denotes their reality, their history" (1991: 66). Though all women cannot be brought under one single basket, the commonalities are more than they appear to be. It is observed, "Despite of all cultural manifestations, all women share a common affectedness, that there are not only differences but also commonalties between two groups of women" (Mies 1991: 79). "'Affectedness' refers to the victim and object status of oppressed, humiliated, exploited beings who have become the target of violence and repression. That is to say, they have been directly affected at one time by aggression, injustice, discrimination. They are victims" (Ibid). Thus, by entering the subjectivity of their experiences by reading the tone, attitudes, feelings, and consciousness, the reality of the situation is analyzed. Entering the silences, it is tried to fill the blank spaces and unearth the influences, values, and ideas, which undergird their experiences.

Apart from the written sources on the topic, this research is done over a period of one year in 2016. The area of research is from the two Telugu speaking states of Andhra Pradesh and Telangana. Most of the women I spoke to are from independent churches, where the pastors of the church are quite influential in the lives of and the teaching they imparted to the women. The churches are hierarchical in structure with the pastor as the sole authority and women are given minimum importance. I found it difficult to trace these women who would come up to share their stories. It was through mutual friends and contacts that I was able to reach them. Only after developing a relationship and confidence with these women that they openly shared their issues. It was always a one-on-one conversation over a period of time both physically and virtually, with no structured interviews. Though they were willing to share their distress, some declined permission to use their stories in the chapter. While some felt embarrassed and shy, another saw the situation as a passing one and she believed that God would rectify it, and it is an issue of faith and patient waiting on the Lord. Though others did give permission, three of them willingly shared their stories with the intention that this would enlighten others and be of help to the Church at large.

The names of the women are not mentioned in order to protect their identity. Facts stated in quotations are expressions of different individuals. I have also refrained from using the term "victims" because it deprives them of their individual identity as women. It should be pointed out, however, that they come from various streams in the society and the church. Most of them are postgraduates, professionals, homemakers, working women, women in ministry and domestic workers. As mentioned earlier, all are "Affected" and carry the wounds and scars of their "affectedness". All of them are grounded in their Christian faith which is the anchor and the driving force of their lives. The chapter intends to bring out the voices of the women who were victims of domestic violence and to let their pain and trauma be heard. Making these women visible and their voices heard becomes emancipative and furthers the process of democratization of the church.

"Domestic violence is the number one health threat to women and accounts for more deaths than automobile accidents, muggings, and rapes combined" (Schlueter 1996: 254). According to a survey conducted in 2006 by the World Health Organization, intimate personal violence statistics around the world varied from 15% in Yokohama, Japan to 71% in Ethiopia (Marshall: 2006). Domestic violence is a major public health crisis in the United States. today. One in four women in the United States are victims of domestic violence. During the COVID-19 pandemic when men are confined to their houses, there was a rapid increase in domestic violence across the globe. This increase is called by the UN as "shadow pandemic" (Guidorzi: 2020). The United Nations Women has launched a shadow pandemic awareness campaign. Phumzile Mlambo-Ngcuka, former Executive Director of UN Women said: "Even before the pandemic, violence against women was one of the most widespread violations of human rights. Since lockdown restrictions, domestic violence has multiplied, spreading across the world in a shadow pandemic" (unwomen.org).

In a 2018 survey conducted by Reuters foundation, India was ranked as "the world's most dangerous country for women" (Banka: 2020). As per the report of the Crime Records Bureau,

> A total of 4,05,861 cases of crime against women were registered during 2019, showing an increase of 7.3% over 2018 (3,78,236 cases). [Table – 3A.1] ii. Majority of cases under crime against women under IPC were registered under 'Cruelty by Husband or His Relatives' (30.9%) followed by 'Assault on Women with Intent to Outrage her Modesty' (21.8%), 'Kidnapping & Abduction of Women' (17.9%), and 'Rape' (7.9%). The crime rate registered per lakh women population is 62.4 in 2019 in comparison with 58.8 in 2018. http://ncrb.gov.inCII2019 (accessed on 26 January 2021)

According to India's National Commission for Women, during the period from March to May 2020, India has recorded the highest number of domestic violence cases in the past ten years. This is not to mention all the cases that are not reported due to the lack of access during the lockdown. Even in normal days as per National Family Health Survey (NFHS) 2015–2016, "roughly 77% of women who experienced domestic violence didn't ever mention it to anyone and even less than 1% of the women actually sought help from the police" (Banka: 2020).

Defining Domestic Violence

The United States Justice department defines domestic violence as

> a pattern of abusive behavior in any relationship that is used by one partner to gain or maintain power and control over another intimate partner. Domestic violence can be physical, sexual, emotional, economic, or psychological actions or threats of actions that influence another person. This includes any behaviors that intimidate, manipulate, humiliate, isolate, frighten, terrorize, coerce, threaten, blame, hurt, injure, or wound someone. https://www.justice.gov/ovw/domestic-violence (accessed on 27 January 2021)

Often, these forms of violence occur together. It is important to note that while some may tend to minimize the consequences of emotional or psychological violence, research suggests it may have more profound consequences than physical violence alone (Ramsay 2006: 28; Kalokhe et al.: 2015).

Culture and religion play a vital role in the functioning of the society and family. They give the core meaning to their existence. Religion has a total sway on the life of an Indian woman. Patriarchy, of course, is the controlling force and foundation on which the life of a woman stands. The self-understanding and mindset of an Indian woman (here I use Indian because the "ideal woman" image is the same irrespective of the religious background) is based on the system and the ideological underpinnings she was structured into. Her dignity and identity lie in maintaining this self (imposed)-construct, thereby making her both the custodian and victim (for it is a prescribed and proscribed construct of patriarchy) of the system.

According to the Hindu scriptures, which also came to be the accepted ideology of the patriarchal system in India, women do not possess an independent identity apart from men. According to the teaching of Manu, "Though destitute of virtue, or seeking pleasure (elsewhere) or devoid of good qualities, (yet) a husband must be constantly worshipped by a faithful wife …If a wife obeys her husband, she will for that (reason alone) be exalted to heaven" (Manusmriti V: 154–155). "Day and night women must be kept in dependence by the males of the family…her father protects her in her childhood, her husband protects her in her youth and her son protects her in her old age. A woman is never fit for independence" (Manusmriti V: 145). Men were even given the right to abuse women if they breach the code of conduct even in a trivial way. Tulasidas, a Hindi poet, writes, "An animal, a rustic, a drum and a woman all require beating" (Madhurima 1996: 19).

Though this appears to be a religious teaching, this ideology was culturally ingrained into the psyche of Indian men and women. Thus, gender relationships are markedly unequal and hierarchical. In Christianity too, the words of St. Augustine echo similar understanding of treating women and about violence. He argues that "wives should view their husbands as their lords, and if they would submit utterly to their husbands' authority they would not be beaten. If they were abused, it was their own fault for going against their earthly lord" (Tracy 2007: 586).

The church which exists in such a cultural context spontaneously adhered to similar Christian teachings which was also a global phenomenon. The church traditions which are structured on the strong patriarchal ideology do not view domestic violence as an issue to be considered. Though there is no statistical evidence of the number of battered women in the churches today, it is considered as a normal practice. In 2017, the Australian Broadcasting Corporation had published a series of articles on the issue of domestic violence in the church. Researchers Julia Baird and Hayley Gleeson report that, "church is not just failing to sufficiently address domestic violence, it is both enabling and concealing it" (2018). Shane Clifton observes that the authors "provide evidence that certain Christian perspectives about masculinity and femininity have exacerbated the problem of violence faced by too many women" (2018: 72). According to a study in Britain, one in four churchgoers has experienced domestic abuse in their current relationship. In another report, clergy wives confess of abuse. They share their experiences that, "after committing their lives to supporting their husband's ministry, each had been forced to leave after decades of emotional, financial and sexual abuse which had left them depressed, fearful and, for some, suicidal" (Baird & Gleeson: 2018). They also claim that the church knew about the abuse and did little to help them. Though there are no statistics of domestic abuse of Christian women in India, the situation in the Indian church appears to be even more bizarre as there is no platform for the battered women to share their plight and claim their dignity as human beings, as the guardians of the church itself are at times the corroborators and even perpetrators of violence.

Why Domestic Violence

In a patriarchal system of hierarchal power relationships, the place of a man is always superior and he carries the power to control and regulate the activities of women who are considered not as individuals with equal rights, but as property of the owner. While patriarchy creates an environment for domination and control, not all men involve in domestic abuse. So, it is widely agreed that multiple factors are involved in male violence against women. Alcoholism appears to be a major factor in their violent behavior. There are "biological (differences in brain structure, brain functioning, and hormones), intrapsychic (personality disorders, attachment disorders), and social construct (childhood experiences of violence) factors in men's violence against women" (Tracy 2007: 579). Most of the batterers refuse to take responsibility and justify their actions of abuse blaming the women for provoking them. They also believe that society is unfairly persecuting them for their actions. According to Dr. Barnett "batterers often feel justified in battering because they were reared in an environment – whether a family or neighbourhood – where violence was accepted as a proper method for solving problems or enforcing the rules. Between 40% and 70% of batterers in clinical samples have been exposed to abuse in childhood". http://www.villagelife.org. (accessed on 29 January 2021). It is also observed that they are characteristically insecure and have a low sense of self-esteem. These insecurities may induce a need for power and control, and they feel entitled to use violence to achieve or fulfill this need. Jealousy and possessiveness are other factors that provoke abusive behavior. When these men are exposed to fundamentalist Christian teachings of male superiority, headship, fixed gendered roles, and female inferior status, they feel doubly reinforced to justify and persist in their violent behavior. Gender discrimination by parents in the family is another cause in India. Because of the male preference and the inferior status given to girls at home, boys internalize that they are superior and believe they can treat women the way they like.

Dowry Demand, Domestic Violence, and Indian Christians

Domestic violence is generally viewed as physical battering or sexual abuse by a husband toward his wife. In reality, however, it manifests in different ways that are way beyond the normal expectations. Most of the women who are abused find it difficult to verbalize their experiences. One of the reasons is that they feel exposed. It is with a sense of shame and reticence, shedding their ego that a woman opens up to the reality of her life. She is also afraid of the response of others, even her own family, including her mother. Only when a woman realizes that she could not contain it any longer, she reveals her plight.

Economic factor appears to be one of the reasons for abuse in some families. Demand for money and property from the girl is a common phenomenon in Indian family system, not to mention the dowry deaths that occur almost every day. The use of the money given by the bride's family differs in each context (Caplan 1984; Kalokhe et al.: 2015). Transfer of property was the main bone of contention in one family. From the third day of the marriage onward, the husband began to harass his wife verbally, which later led to physical abuse. As long as the wife was earning, she was allowed to stay with the family. When she lost her job, she was blatantly sent back to search for one. Even when she was working and earning, she was not given proper food. "They (husband's family) did not give me proper food. I used to feel like eating raw vegetables. Such was my craving for food". For another woman, "I was treated well as long as the money my parents sent lasted. After that I was not given food". By denying the basic necessities, they try to pressurize the family to give in to their demands for more money.[3] For one homemaker, the husband, who earns, would remind the wife that she is eating off his earnings. "You are eating because I am giving you food". Even as she was eating, he would say such words humiliating to the extent that she could not consume any more. These were educated Christian men treating educated Christian women. By depriving the basic needs, they are, in fact, violating the human rights of these women.

Verbal and psychological abuse is another form of violence which is the most devastating and depressing experience of all. Verbal abuse makes them feel dehumanized, worthless, rejected, and disgraced. Common terms used by the women to explain their feelings were "crushed", "tortured", and "humiliated". One of the women explains, "Verbal abuse is like murdering the person. It goes all the way through out your life. Those words keep coming back and they kill you every day. In physical abuse we forget the pain, this continues to dig at you all the time". Most of them confess, "those words cannot be repeated". "Morning when I see his face those abusive words hit my face. It is very difficult to forget" avers one wife. Though she has not experienced physical abuse, one wife expresses,

> Having experienced indifference, withdrawal, mostly listening to correction and criticism of me and my family all through, I felt stifled and came to a position where I could not even answer properly. Once when

there was an occasion to express who I was for him, my husband did not even utter a word about me. I felt publicly humiliated and rejected and it only confirmed that I as an individual, a person or as a wife do not mean anything to him.

Verbal and psychological harassment runs deeper than physical abuse. It silences the woman, deprives them of their self-worth, and plunges them into deep throes of self-pity and self-doubt.

Physical abuse like beating, slapping, shoving, and other forms of sexual violence is a common phenomenon in domestic violence. One woman narrates,

> The first time I was physically abused, I felt like dying, I wished that I would die. As the battering intensified, I was pushed out of the house, I was forced to fulfill his desires, was beaten almost every day with some pretext or the other. I had to sleep in the corridor or in the bathroom at nights because he used to lock me out of the house. I was verbally abused with the vilest words name calling me as barren and bitch. I had contracted diseases because of him and my health deteriorated very badly. Finally, when I discovered that he had an extra marital relationship, he beat me so rudely he began banging my head to the wall. The neighbors (owners of the house) intervened, took me to their house, kept me for a day and called my family saying that he would kill me if they do not rescue her. They said they do not want their house to be a place of murder. It was then my family sent a driver to fetch me home. I left everything behind and went home as I was.

The inducing of torture systemically by the state or an individual seems to have a similar purpose and outcome. According to Scarry,

> The torturer seeks to substantiate a fiction of power—to make a world, usually connected to the state—through the alteration of the body of the tortured. Torturing the body serves the further purpose of altering, or if necessary, destroying the imagination or voice of the tortured. The point is to produce pain to the extent that the voice of the tortured and, therefore, the world of the tortured no longer oppose the fictive power of the state, as represented by the torturer. The tortured body and silenced voice thus make the power 'real'.
>
> (Cooey 1995: 29)

Physical violence not only silences the person but also hurls them into such deep despair that life itself loses its meaning and vigor. Life is not worth living for them. One woman confesses "When I am battered most of the time I felt like consuming poison. In fact, at one point, I tried to poison my children and myself but luckily my son who was a toddler then, hit the glass and spilt it off. But at the same time, I think God is there he is watching. I should not do this which is against God. He will take care. I keep wavering between these two feelings most of the time". Explaining what physical abuse does to the psyche of a woman, Paula M. Cooey writes,

> The body carries the marks of its violation in the memory of the sensations of violation long after visible bruises, cuts, and scars have healed (in the case of battering) and long after the sensations of forced arousal or entry have disappeared (in the case of sexual abuse). This memory, even when not always intentionally present to consciousness, plays a central role in generating and perpetuating enduring feelings of shame, misplaced guilt, humiliation, suppressed rage, depression and worthlessness that become pervasive and destructive if not addressed by providing alternative positive ways for a survivor to experience or perceive her or his own physicality. Even once a victim of abuse has escaped the abuse and confronted the memories of abuse, identity itself is still a problem.
>
> (1995: 34)

The corollary to the physical and psychological abuses for these women is the loss of their health. Domestic violence is the number one public health crisis in the United States. In India, talking about domestic violence is a taboo and women, men, and healthcare professionals do not recognize it to be the cause of ill health in women. Even wounds incurred due to physical violence are reported as accidents. Most of the women were diagnosed with diseases related to psychosomatic problems. Many of them attempt suicides and some are dying because of the consequences of prolonged physical and psychological abuses. Some of those, who I spoke to, are physically suffering due to the ill health contracted through this violence. Their level of despondency could be understood when one woman says, "We have to die like this".

Kinship and Social Environment

Domestic violence is a deep social problem. According to the last exhaustive family survey done by the Indian government, more than 54% of men and 51% of women said it was okay for a man to beat his wife if she disrespected her in-laws, neglected her home or children, or even over something as trivial as putting less or more salt in the food (Pandey: 2014). In other words, it is not a problem at all. However, when a woman comes out openly against the issue, then the society turns it head accusing and mocking at her. Socially, the first place that these women encounter humiliation is at hands of the husband's family and also from the natal family. Most of the time the husband's family are also partners, perpetrators, or instigators of violence. Anne Ganley says, abused women "not only have to fight the abuser to keep sanity and safety, they also have to fight the community who want to blame them and put them down" (Schlueter 1996: 257). For some of these women, the worst opposition came from their own families. They were sent back again and again saying that after marriage their place is with the husband and not with the natal family, knowing fully well that they were being abused. A woman states, "I was treated like a servant by my family". Another mourns, "I was asked to go back to my abusive and unfaithful husband". Usually, the natal family would be supportive initially but later they also look down upon them. Societal pressures of honor and shame play a vital role in treating their own kin. A woman asserts, "Not that I cannot live without a husband but it is the fear of the scorn from society that keeps me from leaving him and to live with him". Women do not reveal their identity as separated women or single women, but tell others at their workplaces that their husbands are working abroad. The sense of fear and shame haunts these women even as they figure out their identity and go about with their daily life.

Children as Silent Sufferers

Children are the silent sufferers and victims in this crisis. They become confused to process the violence and the abuse they witness and endure in their tender age. Their pain was described as affliction, which is more intense than suffering. "Affliction" is pain which scars all dimensions of a person's life. Affliction is an extreme condition which leaves its victims powerless and with no escape. It is stated that "Affliction permeates the soul and affects one's future direction, one's destiny and one's hope" (Collis 2009: 342). Rossie Betty, an Australian, calls this as "Terrorism in the family". Children wrestle with multiple experiences, like bitterness, despair, compassion, hopelessness, and to some extent a sense of justice.

A daughter of one of the women told her mother, "You have been living in this hell for so long and now we are also living in this hell. You are taking all this, if it is me I would (gestured by crossing her hands to her neck and showed the ceiling fan to the mother) (implying) have hanged myself". When an eight-year-old son stood up to the father questioning him as to why he beat his mother, (for no obvious reason the father slapped the mother in front of him), the mother says, "the child was so angry he was shaking, and it became my turn to pacify him". One adult son shared that he could not understand his father, "he is a hopeless husband but a good father. I feel so helpless". When a father began verbally abusing the mother by name calling, a five-year-old girl told him "That is not mummy it is you". Even as infants, children carry the pain of their parents. I noticed an infant who was about six months old playing as her mother was talking. After some time when the mother was explaining something in tears, the baby stopped playing, watched her mother intently, and began tearing up. Children share the lives of their parents.

Imagine what goes into the tender hearts and minds of these children who were supposed to have experienced that love and security, had to stand up for the rights of a parent. It is said that, "The loss of this care and the security of family relationships associated with it appear to create an emptiness and a silence which results from the isolation caused by unspeakable events" (Collis 2009: 343).

These children eventually become both the victims and perpetrators of domestic violence when they grow up. Boys witnessing domestic violence, for example, are twice as likely to become abusers themselves. Some will repeat the patterns of violent behavior they learned as children as they mature into adults. Others will perform poorly in school, suffer with depression, fearfulness, anxiety, sleeplessness, antisocial behavior, and/or become aggressive. According to an UN report on gender in 2012, "It is shown that the children who witness domestic violence are more likely to perpetrate or accept family violence when they are adults thus perpetuating control, patriarchy and disrespect for women in a family" (Raj: 2016).

Why Do These Christian Women Bear with the Abuse?

The teachings of the church set the standards for women regarding their faith and life. Any deviation from this internalized value system would be deemed sacrilegious and warrants a life in hell. Thus, "Religious women are less likely to leave, are more likely to believe the abuser's promise to change his violent ways .... and commonly express guilt—that they have failed their families and God in not being able to make the marriage work" (Nason-Clark 2004:304). Griffin and Maples suggest that abused Christian women are strongly influenced by their beliefs and value systems and these values may be a powerful force in their decision to remain in an abusive marriage where their safety and that of their children may be at risk (McMullin et al. 2015: 114). This is very true with the women I spoke to. One of them who had been in this abusive relationship for the past three decades says, "Women have to endure this for in the end God will recompense for all the suffering we have undergone. God is just, someday, somehow, he will bring justice. But as believers we cannot go for divorce". She further quotes 1Peter 2.19, 20 and argues that she is bearing all this for God's sake and for testimony. "All this she (a woman) bears and she has to bear for Christ and because of Christ. It is only because of God that a believer in Christ endures the violence, the rejection and pain inflicted by the husband". Even after going through so much of pain where their lives were also at stake, some women strongly believe that God would not allow more than what one could bear (1 Cor 10.13).

Some of these women also appear to live in denial by convincing themselves and attributing the violent behavior of men to Satan's strategy to destroy the families. By doing so, they exonerate men of their sin and become perpetrators of violence. Moreover, "there are explicit religious notions that make it especially difficult for religious victims to see the full extent of their suffering or to sound out the call for help. Paramount among these are Christian notions of forgiveness and women's identity with Jesus the Sacrificial Lamb". Spiritualizing the real problems mitigates the seriousness of the issue, thereby disempowering women and making them live in denial. "Pastors are inclined to see the problem primarily in spiritual terms and to simplify the psychological familial and social complexities involved" (Alsdurf & Jim 1987: 9). Having internalized this kind of teaching in the churches, women find themselves in a cauldron of conflicting ideals and reality. They stoop to a level of resignation where they do not have a ray of hope. One of them confers, "No one can change some one (men) who does things wantonly. The Law is not Just. Moral values are dwindling in the churches. There are pastors, elders and leaders who are abusive. So where can a woman go. She has to die like this thinking that God is our Judge". These words speak volumes of the state of the woman. A sense of hopelessness and helplessness echoes through those words in a way consigning her to her fate.

On the contrary, only one woman spoke that domestic violence was against God. She stood up against the violence and sought for justice through the court. She says,

> I was bound to my faith. I stood for what is right. A family should be like this and these are the family values .... all that I kept aside. What is right in Christ I should do it. I will not listen to anyone I will only listen to the Lord. I was alone but the Lord was there with me. As a husband my husband is not doing anything for me, God you as my husband should do for me. You stand for me. I took everything to the Lord in prayer. The church has to understand the correct teaching of Christ.

When women stand for this kind of assertion and faith in God's justice meted through human agency, there is hope for women and for the church.

Response of the Church

The teaching in the churches is primarily geared toward the submission of women in family and about the headship of the husband. Rod Buxton says that

> Victims who find their way to the sanctuary seeking help may find a double-edged sword where the people of the church are loving and caring but the church is not a safe place to talk about problems of domestic Violence: it is a taboo subject.
>
> (2000: 53)

Even when the life of a woman was at risk, divorce was taught as sin against God by some pastors. Moreover, the onus of keeping the family together is more on women than on men. Any dysfunction in the family is attributed to the behavior or failure of women in preserving the unity of the family. "Almost without exception they [pastors] focus their energies on getting the woman—not the man—to change. The message often communicated to the battered woman is that she is not welcome in the church family unless she stays with her abusive husband and takes the burden of responsibility for change upon herself" (Alsdurf & Jim 1987: 10).

Women confide that Church or pastor is the last place for them to seek help. We know pastors who are abusive and justify their behavior quoting scriptures. It is a common and accepted behavior for the pastors and the congregation and thus it is not treated as an issue or a problem in the church. One congregant says, "When I approached the pastor, he was initially kind and supportive. But later he started preaching that, women should be submissive and divorce is against God's will. Moreover, he started looking down upon me and asked if I would marry again after divorce". Another wife laments, "when I became sick because of the prolonged abuse, my pastor husband said I became sick because of my sin". Most of the pastors give the simplistic answer asking women to obey and pray. When a battered woman approached the wife of the head of a Church about the abuse, she categorically stated, "Beating is wrong. But if you want your family, according to scripture you should submit and bear. That is the only answer I have". This is how the church responded to these women. The plight of the wives of the pastors was even worse, for they could not share their situation to anyone for fear of tarnishing the reputation of the pastor and, thereby, become a hindrance to the ministry. Even after confessing they are living in abusive relationship, pastors' wives refused to see it realistically and expressed that they believe that God would change things and so they would wait for that day expectantly because God is just.

Once they come to know about the situation, the congregation members also treat abused women differently. While some distance themselves, others try to be sympathetic and some question them on their face about the problem. It is very rare that they accept them as they are. Only in one woman's case her experience was different. She said the pastor and the congregation were very supportive. "They never treated me differently, they even helped me out when I was sick and took care of me. My pastor encouraged me to look and depend on God alone and told prayer is the only refuge I have. He asked me not to look at people, even him, but God alone". Thus, it is the belief and the attitude of the leadership and the congregation in the church that renders the issue as inconsequential and a matter in the process of democratization of the church.

The Role of the Church

Church, as a community and as the guardian of its flock, has utterly failed in its responsibility in protecting the victims from the dehumanizing effects of domestic violence. She continues to maintain the "Holy hush" about the violence. By doing so, she stands as a culprit in perpetuating domestic violence and is in need to repent and redeem herself from the sin of promoting violence. By tolerating such violence and by keeping silent, the Church is colluding with the oppressor and the abuser. This is an affront to the Love and Justice of God embodied in Jesus Christ.

In order to bring about change in the domestic front, and thereby in her own life, Church should teach about the dignity, worth, and value of an individual as a human being created in the image of God and that both men and women are equal. And in reality, the Church should confront the patriarchal notions of male superiority and dominance by treating her women with integrity, dignity, and worth. Before teaching divorce as sin, the Church should first teach about adhering to the marital covenant and vows made before God. It is the abuser who had breached the covenant and vows to love, trust, and cherish and not the one who is running for the safety and protection of her life and their children's life. Domestic violence rejects God's intention for the integrity of embodied life and relational commitments. The responsibility of the community (church) lies "in helping to assure the integrity of the marriage vows".

The pastors should be trained about human rights and justice, and where to seek help when these are violated and how to help the victim in need practically. They should help the congregation realize domestic violence is not just the problem of women, but it actually lies with men and how they have to cope with it. Women fellowships should also learn to affirm their own dignity and promote equality in their home in treating their children. They should be equipped to help their sisters in need, by forming support groups to the victims and survivors. Awareness should be created about the women's rights to the congregation and the legal support and constitutional laws regarding the violence against women by conducting workshops and seminars. Children should be taught about gender equality and help change their patriarchal mindset by helping them treat their sisters with respect and dignity.

The community is also accountable in seeking justice for the injured one (Mat 18:15–20).

> It is in fact a great support when survivors of violence feel the congregations' support not only as compassion that validates their loss and pain as wrong, but as encouragement to resist the dehumanizing effects of such violence, and as support to seek healing and justice. When congregations incarnate in this way God's fierce tenderness, survivors of violence will suffer far less spiritual and emotional damage, for they will benefit from the redemptive witness of the faith community. The congregation also will benefit from taking responsibility clearly to embody God's compassionate resistance to the dehumanizing effects of intimate violence.
> (Ramsay 2006:37)

From the above discussion, it is obvious that patriarchal culture in the society empowers men to discriminate, violate, and control women. It is the belief system and mindset of both men and women in Christianity that in a way endorses and perpetuates violence in the domestic spaces. The Church's teaching of male headship in the family and the subordination of women, or teachings of gender inequality, reinforces Christian men's behavior in abusing their women. Women, on the other hand, endure the abuse as part of their faith to submit and invoke God's judgement as the answer. Realistically, however, religious or Church's sanction of gender inequality and violence in domestic spaces impinge on each other, thereby curtailing the process of democratization in both spheres. Churches could open up to some of these measures in order to bring about change in her own outlook and the behavior of the believers. Thus, domestic violence should no longer be a personal issue, but an issue of human rights, justice, gender equality and faith in the church.

Notes

1 On 16 December 2012, a 23-year-old physiotherapy student was raped by five men, and a minor on a private bus in New Delhi, who later died from her injuries. Later, she was named Nirbhaya, which means fearless, in order to conceal the identity of a rape victim. https://en.wikipedia.org/wiki/2012_Delhi_gang_rape_and_murder
2 Tarun Sagar was a Jain monk and a religious leader.
3 Cycle of Abuse – Those who have worked with battered women describe a three-stage cycle through which an abusive relationship travels. The first phase is one of tension building. There is a gradual escalation of irritation over such issues as finances or children. Minor battering incidents occur, such as verbal tirades, throwing objects, or temper tantrums. The man becomes oppressive, jealous, and possessive, and the woman attempts to cope by calming him to prevent a major incident. As time goes on, the man increases his brutality and smothering behavior, employing psychological humiliation and verbal harangues. The woman, exhausted from trying to keep equilibrium, withdraws more from the batterer, in order not to ignite an explosion. He begins to move more oppressively toward her, looking for expressions of her anger, misinterpreting her every move, and hovering so close that she feels suffocated. The tension reaches an extreme. Phase two is that of the acute violent incident, the uncontrollable discharge of the tensions that have built up during the first phase. The batterer's attacks are more serious and his rage is out of control. The woman is unable to predict the kind of violence that will occur. Now the situation lies completely in the man's control; the woman has ceased to be able to manipulate his behavior. His anger and greater strength render her powerless. This is the stage at which injuries are inflicted. Only the batterer can end this phase; all the woman can do is to find a safe place to hide. Movement into a third phase is marked by kindness and contrite behavior on the part of the batterer. It is a period of calmness; the tension, built up through the first phase and released during the second phase, gone. The batterer behaves in a charming and loving manner, becoming reasonable and assuring the woman that she will not again have to suffer such an incident. He is usually sorry for his actions and often showers her with gifts and attention. And she wants to believe that she will no longer have to endure abuse.

Linda Day 2000. "Rhetoric and Domestic Violence in Ezekiel 16" in *Biblical Interpretation* 8 (3) 215.

References

Agarwal, Purshottam. 1995. 'Savarkar, Surat and Draupadi: legitimizing Rape as a Political Weapon'. in Tanika Sarkar & Urvasi Butalia, (ed.). *Women and the Hindu Right: A Collection of Essays*, New Delhi: Kali for Women.

Alexander, Amy C. & Christian Welzel. 2011. 'Empowering Women: The Role of Emancipative Beliefs,' *European Sociological Review*, 27(3) 364–384.
Alsdurf, Phyllis and Jim. 1987. 'Wife Abuse and the Christian Home,' *Daughters of Sarah*, July August.
Altekar, A.S. 1959.*The Position of Women in Hindu Civilization*. Delhi: Motilal Banarasidass.
Baird, Julia with Hayley Gleeson. 2018. '"Submit to your Husbands": Women told to Endure Domestic Violence in the Name of God.' *ABC News*, 22nd October. http://www.abc.net.au/news/2017-07-18/domestic-violence-church-submit-to-husbands/8652028
Banka, Shrey. 2020. 'Domestic Violence in India: Has Anything Changed in Patriarchy?' *Counter Currents*, 25th December. http://www.countercurrents.org
Buxton, Rod. 2000. "Domestic Violence in the Church: "There is an Elephant in the Sanctuary and No-One is Talking about It. The Results of a Manitoba Survey. In Διδασκαλία, Fall.
Caplan, Lionel. 1984. 'Bridegroom Price in Urban India: Class, Caste and 'Dowry Evil' among Christians in Madras', *Man*, 19, (2) 216–233.
Chapman, Jean. 2014. 'Violence against Women in Democratic India: Let's Talk Misogyny'. *Social Scientist*, 42 (9/10) 49–61.
Clifton, Shane. 2018. 'Spirit, Submission, Power, and Abuse: A Response to Teaching on Female Submission and the Scourge of Domestic Violence.' *St Mark's Review* 243.
Collis, Sue M. 2009. The Analysis of Young People's Experiences of Domestic Violence: Spiritual and Emotional Journeys through Suffering, *International Journal of Children's Spirituality*, 14(4).
Cooey, Paula M. 1995.Re-Membering the Body: A Theological Resource for Resisting Domestic Violence, *Theology and Sexuality* (3)
"Crime in India 2019," National Crime Records Bureau, Ministry of Home Affairs. http://ncrb.gov.in CII 2019, "Crime in India", vol1, p. xii https://www.justice.gov/ovw/domestic-violence
Day, Linda. 2000. Rhetoric and Domestic Violence in Ezekiel 16' *Biblical Interpretation*, 8 (3).
Dhruvarajan, Vanaja. 1989. *Hindu Women and the power of Ideology*. New Delhi: Visthar Publications.
Dobbins, James, Seth G. Jones, Keith Crane and Beth Cole DeGrasse. 2007. *The Beginner's Guide to Nation-Building*, RAND Corporation Stable. http://www.jstor.com/stable/10.7249/mg557srf.17
Guidorzi, Brianna. 2020. 'The Shadow Pandemic: Addressing Gender – based Violence (GBV) During Covid-19' In: Padraig Carmody, Gerard McCann, Clodagh Colleran, Ciara O'Halloran. (ed.) *Covid-19 in the Global South: Impacts and Responses*, Bristol University Press.
Gupta, Samjukta Gombrich. 2000. 'The Godess, Women and their Rituals Hinduism' in Mandrakanta Bose, (ed) *Faces of the Feminine in Ancient, Medieval and Modern India*. New York: OUP.
Jim Witters, 'Men Who Beat Women Believe They Are Justified.' http://www.villagelife.org/news/archives/DV_coverstory/DV_menjustified.html
Kalokhe, Ameeta S. et al, 2015. 'How well does the World Health Organisation definition of domestic violence work for India' in *Plos One*. DOI:10.1371/journal.pone.0120909

Kumari, Ranjana. 1985.'Femaleness: The Hindu Perspective,' in *Religion and Society*, XXXII (2): 2–10.

Madhurima. 1996.*Violence Against Women: Dynamics of Conjugal Relations*, New Delhi: Gyan Publication House.

Marshall, Lucinda. 2006. 'Behind Closed Doors: The Invisibility of Domestic Violence,' *Counters Currents*, 20th October. http://www.countercurrents.org/gen-marshall201006.htm

McMullin, Steve et al. 2015. 'When Violence Hits the Religious Home: Raising Awareness about Domestic Violence in Seminaries and amongst Religious Leaders,' in *Journal of Pastoral Care & Counseling*, 69 (2).

Mies, Maria 1999. 'Women's Research or Feminist Research?: The Debate Surrounding Feminist Science and Methodology,' In: Mary Margaret Fonow & Judith, A.(ed.) *Cook Beyond Methodology: Feminist Scholarship as Lived Research*, Bloomington: Indiana University Press. 60–84.

Nason-Clark, Nancy. 2004. 'When Terror Strikes at Home: The Interface between Religion and Domestic Violence,' *Journal for the Scientific Study of Religion* 43(3).

Pandey, Geeta. 2014. '100 Women 2014: Violence at Home is India's Failing', 29th October. http://www.bbc.com/news/world-asia-india-29708612

Press Release: *UN women raise awareness of the shadow pandemic of violence against women during Covid-19*, May 27, 2020. unwomen.org

Raj, Pushkar. 2016 'What India Can Learn From Australia On Domestic Violence?' *Counter Currents*, 17th May, http://www.countercurrents.org/raj170516.htm

Ramsay, Nancy J. 2006. 'Confronting Family Violence and Its Spiritual Damage,' *Family Ministry* 20, (3).

Sandhu, Khushboo. 2016. 'A monk in nude, talks of Pakistan, female foeticide, duty of wife in Haryana Assembly.' *The Indian Express*, 27th August, http://indianexpress.com

Schlueter, Carol J. 1996. 'Creating a New Reality: No More Domestic Violence,' *Currents in Theology and Mission*, 23(4).

Sharma, R.P. 1995. *Women in Hindu Literature*, New Delhi: Gyan Pub House.

Tracy, Steven R. 2007. 'Patriarchy and Domestic Violence: Challenging Common Misconceptions' *Journal of Evangelical Theological Society* 50 (3).

Wadley, Susan. 1988. 'Women and the Hindu Tradition', in *Women in Indian Society*, ed, Rehana Ghadially, New Delhi: Sage Publications.

Afterword
Christianity, Democratization, and Indian Culture
Chad M. Bauman

It is an honor to have been asked to write a short afterword to this rich and important volume, to which many of the most sophisticated and impressive contemporary scholars of Indian Christianity have contributed. I am, at the same time, somewhat of an odd choice to write an afterword for a volume such as this. Though a scholar of Indian religions, and especially Indian Christianity, I am neither Indian nor a practitioner of Christianity. That said, and in ways that may perhaps become apparent in the prejudices I display below, my ethics remain largely guided by the servanthood of Christ and by the sermon on the mount, and in particular by the anti-empire, anti-hierarchical, anti-capitalist, and pacifist interpretation of the gospel emphasized by the Protestant Mennonites who raised and educated me. It is therefore as a cultural and religious outsider – knowledgeable about and sympathetic as I may be toward both Indian culture and religion – that I reflect and comment on the foregoing chapters.

As an outsider to Christianity who at the same time resonates with what this volume would frame as a radically "democratizing" reading of Christian scriptures, I find the antidemocratic and hierarchical actions of many contemporary Christians worldwide deeply concerning. These actions are nowhere more visible right now than in the United States, where the most vibrant and public Christian churches, that is, evangelical churches, are prominently (though obviously not universally) characterized by a self-serving political Machiavellianism and a more or less religious faith in the kind of unfettered, free-market capitalism that exploits and literally destroys human (and non-human) life. With regard to the American context, then, I share the same kind of disappointment in Christians expressed by YT Vinayaraj in this volume, when he notes that Indian Catholic bishops meeting India's Prime Minister advocated for their own interests, but failed to advocate for the poor and marginalized in society. And I am sympathetic, therefore, to the clearly normative approach of this book, which asserts both implicitly and explicitly that democratization is a good thing, both in society and in religious institutions, and, moreover, that a more democratic Christianity would be good not only for Christianity but also for the various nations in which Christianity is practiced and has a political voice.

One of the more intriguing aspects of this volume is the way it mixes methodologically ethical, social, and scientific descriptions with the emic perspectives of authors willing to make apodictic and somewhat generalizing assertions about what Christianity "is" or "should be". In reflecting on my own positionality and ethical commitments above, I have tried to situate myself in a similar space. However, that space is an ambiguous one that is in some ways difficult to inhabit. I will therefore organize my comments on the volume around three relatively broad questions that emerge, in a sense, from that ambiguity: 1) Does Indian Christianity foster democratization, and if so, what *kind of democratization*, 2) Can religious institutions outpace their own routinization (in the Weberian sense) to model something radically democratic, and 3) Supposing they can, is there any hope that *Indian Christianity* could alter *Indian* culture? In Conclusion, then, I will suggest some potentially fruitful lines of future inquiry.

Does Indian Christianity foster democratization, and if so, What Kind of Democratization?

Many of the volume's chapters share a presumption that the values of the Christian Gospel are emancipative and radically democratic in nature. Wilfred, for example, insists "the core values of the Gospel…are democratic in nature", and as I noted above, I was raised to interpret the New Testament in similar ways. But from a social scientific perspective, as Wilfred himself knows, the Gospels are neither for nor against any ethic or political structure until they are interpreted by particular Christians in particular ways in particular contexts (many of which have produced radically antidemocratic ethics, such as those that justified slavery). Relying more on social scientific methods, Benteler's chapter makes the point bluntly by examining "the relation between lived religion and believed religion" to question the presumption of "Christianity's…closeness to democratisation".

The tension between these two perspectives animates many of the volume's chapters. Without irony, for example, Nuthalapati suggests in two successive sentences both that "Christianity affirms the values of justice, equality, and the inherent value and worth of a human being" *and* that "The lived experiences of Christian women, who are victims of domestic violence, render a contrary reality". Additionally, she later acknowledges that quite orthodox Christian teaching has for centuries supported patriarchal structures within the home, while promoting hierarchical gender roles that can be used to justify male-on-female domestic violence. Does Christianity promote democratization, then, or its inverse?

There is no question that Christianity has been used to motivate or at least justify and enable democratization in India and elsewhere. Indian Christians are rightfully revered for their historical and ongoing contribution to Indian education, healthcare, and human rights advocacy. Joseph's and Taneti's chapters in this volume highlight the contribution of Indian Christian *women* to that work particularly effectively. But Indian Christianity has also manifested thoroughly antidemocratic, hierarchical, and patriarchal impulses, and its dominant-caste adherents have often been inclined to separate themselves from and/or retain their privileges vis-à-vis Dalit Christians. As Walling's chapter puts it, "Lived-Christianity indeed seamlessly endorses unbiblical cultural practices without much critical assumptions". The issue isn't unique to *Indian* Christianity, as Nuthalapati notes: Christian teaching from St. Paul, St. Augustine, and others forward until today established hierarchies between men and women that have sometimes been used to justify and/or cause Christian women to tolerate and submit to domestic violence. Is it really true, then, that *as an institution*, Indian Christianity can foster democratization? That question is related to the second one about institutionalization discussed below.

Before turning to the matter of institutionalization, however, we must also ask *what kind of democratization* does Indian Christianity foster (when it fosters democratization)? In this volume, democratization is presented implicitly as a singular noun. But just as we have learned to speak of multiple "secularisms", we should, it seems, expect democratization to take on different forms in different contexts. Indian Christian human rights workers have often been accused of importing to India a particularly western, and therefore, culturally inappropriate understanding of human rights. And it bears mentioning that with the prominent exception of MM. Thomas, the theorists most regularly and prominently cited by the volume's authors to describe what they mean by democratization both within Christianity and in general (Jürgen Habermas, Giorgo Agamben, Alain Badiou, Richard Horsley, Michael Hardt, Antonio Negri, Joerg Rieger, Peter van der Veer, Andre Beteille, Antonio Gramsci, Erving Goffman, Michel de Certeau, Anthony Giddens, Marcel Mauss, Pierre Bourdieu, etc.) are overwhelmingly western. I have recently argued (Bauman 2020) that Indian Christians' promotion of what are perceived by critics as "western" forms of modernity (of which advocacy for democratization is a part) is in itself part of the explanation for why Christians are so frequently (and increasingly) harassed and targeted in acts of majoritarian violence. We must acknowledge, of course, that resistance to these putatively "western" forms of modernization and democratization within India serves the interests of those (particularly dominant-caste communities) privileged by the status quo, and that the claims that Indian Christians are promoting westernization may be at least in part a red herring. Still, in the context of centuries-long Indian Christian efforts to articulate an appropriately acculturated form of the faith, it is worth asking, apart from its efforts to eliminate caste prejudice, is there anything particularly *Indian* about the democratization that Indian Christianity fosters? If so, what? If not, might Indian Christians be able to articulate a distinctly Indian program of democratization? Might they gain broader cultural purchase by framing their democratization efforts in more thoroughly Indian terms?

Can Religious Institutions Outpace their Own Routinization?

As mentioned above, the bureaucratization/rationalization entailed in manifesting a religious community institutionally often runs counter to the processes of democratization. As Max Weber (1947) asserted long ago, while the charismatic religious founder's vision might be transgressive, emancipative, and radically anomic, the institutionalization (or "routinization") of that vision by the founder's followers generally tames it, while systemically entrenching the privileges of dominant communities. Victor Turner's (1995) description of oscillating periods of "communitas" and "structure" mirror Weber's cycles of "charisma" and "routinization". And within Christianity, many (including Wilfred, in this volume) have noted the biblical tension between the prophetic (aligned with "charisma" and "communitas") and the royal or priestly (aligned with "routinization" and "structure"). This tension is also manifest, as Vinayarajan points out in his chapter, in the socio-political disparity between early and post-Constantinian Christianity. Is it possible, then, for the Christian church as a religious *institution* to contribute to democratization? Reinhold Niebuhr famously suggested it is not, in both the pages and the title of his *Moral Man, Immoral Society*.

The issue seems particularly salient in the Catholic Church. It is worth noting that most of the volume's authors center Indian Catholicism in their chapters, and not surprisingly those working from an emic Catholic perspective bemoan the thoroughly bureaucratic and hierarchical nature of the Catholic Church. Many of the chapters of the volume, like Murugun and Mocherla's, highlight "counter-conducts", spaces of emancipatory or democratic world-making within the Catholic Church. Still – and here I may be exposing the latent bias of my upbringing, which is one of the reasons I acknowledged it at the outset – it is worth considering whether Protestant Christianity has a certain kind of advantage over Catholicism in this regard.

The endlessly schismatic nature of Protestantism creates regular opportunity for charismatic rupture, for prophetic critique, and for moments of communitas. Each new Protestant, and especially each new independent evangelical and Pentecostal preacher is a law, as it were, unto him or herself. Therein lies exceptional potential for undemocratic impulses to assert themselves, of course, but also for radical reimagining of human community. And the generally greater Protestant (especially evangelical and Pentecostal) impulse toward growth attunes many Protestant leaders to the needs of their parishioners in democratizing ways not required within the well-established and already large and powerful Roman Catholic Church. It is notable, in this regard, that in this volume the religious community lauded most admiringly for being "democratic and people-oriented" was the *Pentecostal* CCFM discussed by Sahoo and Ponniah. What would it mean for Catholics (or even for higher-church Indian Protestants with episcopal ecclesial structures) devoted to democratization as a principal *Christian* virtue to acknowledge that their own ecclesial structures present impediments to efforts of democratization,

Christianity, Democratization, and Indian Culture 245

many of which could be easily surmounted by abandoning Catholicism for more congregational forms of Protestantism?[1]

Can Indian Christianity Alter Indian culture?

Many of the chapters in the volume appear to presume that a more democratized Indian Christian church would further the democratization of India more broadly. It goes without saying that any form of democratizing, even if limited in scope, contributes to broader democratization at least somewhat, especially within the confines of the community where it occurs, and perhaps even beyond through the processes of osmosis. But should we perhaps temper expectations that Indian Christianity, in the current political climate, could have a significant impact beyond the boundaries of its own churches and social service organizations?

Before we can get to that more specific question, we need to consider a more general one: Does religion, on the whole, affect or merely reflect culture? The question is of course related to the previous discussion about routinization, since the routinization of religion inevitably involves the replication of certain kinds of socio-cultural stratification and hierarchy. But even more fundamentally, while religion is an element of culture, and though many unconsciously presume religion to play a significant role in the formation of culture, is it not the case that culture is the dominant partner in this pair?

Leila Ahmed (1992) has persuasively argued, for example, that the Quran and Islamic tradition more broadly could be interpreted in various ways with regard to gender relations and roles, and that while a more conservative reading became entrenched during and because of the "unquestioning androcentrism and misogyny" of the influential Abbasid period", "a reading by a less androcentric and less misogynistic society, one that gave greater ear to the ethical voice of the Quran, could have resulted in...the elaboration of laws that dealt equitably with women", and could thereby have "radically altered women's status in marriage", and in other arenas as well. While I do not doubt that religion can affect culture, my own orientation (and, it seems, Ahmed's as well) is a kind of Durkheimian one, which understands religions to function *primarily* (though not solely) as cultural systems that sacralize social norms and mores more forcefully than they create them (Durkheim 1995). And, of course, it bears mention, as Benteler notes in her chapter, that religious assertions of *spiritual* equality (among the genders or races, for example) do not necessarily prompt assertions or practices that promote *social* equality.

Is the democratization of Christianity, then, a leading or a trailing indicator? Murugun and Mocherla's chapter is instructive in this regard. Their chapter highlights Dalit Christian resistance to and rejection of caste prejudice within the church and frames it as a form of democratization. But Dalit efforts to assert their rights are of course often resisted by dominant-caste Christians, and have been for some time: In his chapter, for example, Mohan describes Dalit petitions to mid-twentieth century missionaries in Kerala for secure places where they could "safely pray the Lord's Prayer and response prayer, Hail Mary Mother of God... without being afraid of caste violence by the Syrian Christians". In Murugun and Mocherla's Tamil context,

> Dalit Christian activists in the recent past have strongly been challenging the caste prejudice within the Christian institutions and carved out a path to approach state agencies for their justice [by] facing court cases...Hence state becomes a pertinent pre-cursor to formulate Dalit Christian activist strategies for seeking justice.

Within the church. Here, then, we have a clear example of a situation in which those seeking democratization within the church not only did not democratize a broader society but also had to employ the legal/cultural resources already developed outside the church to further their democratizing goals. To what extent could we expect, then, that a thorough democratization of Indian Christianity is even possible in the absence of a broader Indian democratization?

Let us presume for the moment, however, that Indian Christianity could become thoroughly democratized in the absence of a prior democratization of Indian culture. If that were to happen, to what extent would the democratization of Indian Christianity impact Indian society more broadly? There are a number of reasons to presume that the ability of Indian Christianity to influence Indian society more generally is steadily declining.

First, and probably most importantly, the current political regime has successfully centered a certain form of political Hinduism and equally successfully marginalized all but the most compliant forms of Christian and Muslim religious communities. The centering of a particular brand of Hinduism as essential to the success of the nation has delegitimized the voice of religious others in the public sphere. As Patrick's chapter puts it, the result is the "taken-for-grantedness of the legitimacy of the religious presence or influence of the dominant or the numerical majority, while those of different others, especially of minority others, get vilified or antagonised". Framing most forms of Christianity and Islam as "foreign" faiths, and branding human rights talk as intrusive westernization or "sickularism", and bringing that critique from the margins to the mainstream, currently dominant political leaders have managed to neutralize the potentially prophetic or critical voice of Indian Christianity.[2] In this context, and additionally threatened with violence or a capricious, harassing use of the law – the incarceration and "judicial custody death of Fr. Stan Swamy" (as Vinayaraj puts it in his chapter) hangs like a dark cloud over this volume – many Christians in India have become cowed, learning to keep their heads down if they hope to carry on with some semblance of an ordinary life.

There are also, however, internal dynamics that play into the declining influence of Indian Christianity in Indian public life. As Patrick's chapter notes, while Indian Christians have been marginalized by others, they have also isolated themselves through "the exclusivist discourse of 'no salvation outside the church', embedded in both the Catholic ecclesiology and the

Protestant evangelical proclamation". Christians have also left themselves vulnerable to criticism because of their historical and continuing tendency to adopt the "manners, customs, food habits, and other cultural markers of the colonisers with whom Indian Christians...identified". Given the more inclusivist tendencies of the "Indic" religions (Hinduism, Buddhism, Jainism, etc.), these Indian Christian tendencies make it easier for critics to label them a foreign and threatening influence. Conversely, dominant-caste forms of Christianity such as those prevalent along the southwestern coast of India have tended to protect their privilege by assimilating to dominant-caste Hindu norms and politics, the price of which, *inter alia*, is the possibility of offering prophetic critique on behalf of the oppressed and marginalized. Unless the political situation in India changes drastically, then, and until Indian Christians discover a way to avoid the twin extremes of self-isolation and cultural conformity, it is difficult to see how a Christian prophetic model of democratization could contribute in truly substantial ways to a broader Indian cultural democratization.

By way of conclusion, let me offer some thoughts on how the work of this stimulating volume might be extended. First, and again exposing my latent religious biases, add more Protestantism. Protestant forms of Christianity manifest their own distinctive forms of both democratizing and anti-democratizing tendencies, of course. We should not turn a blind eye toward the latter. Still, what might Catholic Christians gain by considering the democratizing potential of Protestant Christians (and vice versa)? As noted above, at the very least, Protestant ecclesial structures (especially in their more congregational forms) seem better suited to democratization than the highly and enduringly hierarchical nature of the Catholic Church.

Pentecostalism is particularly intriguing in this regard. Much maligned for what critics consider their overly expressive worship, their obsession with spiritual gifts, their sometimes bombastic evangelism, and their schismatic tendencies, and justifiably criticized for their tendency to perpetuate gender hierarchies in the home and church (as noted by Abreu, SJ, in this volume), Pentecostal churches have at the same time proven their ability to reform human behavior, particularly – in study after study, including in the chapter by Sahoo and Ponniah – in regard to reforming Pentecostal men in ways that make them better (and more democratic) husbands and fathers. In addition, outside of some of its largest denominations, the schismatic, seeker-oriented tendencies of Pentecostalism produce ecclesial structures that are more horizontal and less vertical/hierarchical (at least in the relation of one religious leader to another) than most. If scholars and non-Pentecostal Christians committed to democratization were to remove their biases, they might they learn something from Pentecostal forms of Christianity?

Second, the work of this volume could be extended through more thorough ethnographic observation and sociological analyses. There appears to me a tendency in the volume to presume that Christian democratization projects have been successful and influential even outside of the church. Historically speaking, I think it is certainly safe to presume that Indian

Christians have played a somewhat influential role in the democratization of Indian culture more broadly. However, for reasons indicated above, I think it is important to be at least somewhat circumspect about the magnitude of that influence, both in historical and contemporary times. To understand that magnitude more fully, we will need to more carefully study not only Christian projects of democratization but also their *effects*.

When we read in Taneti's chapter, for example, that the work of female missionary doctors and Bible women has had a democratizing effect on Indian Christianity in the realm of gender, I find myself asking for the proof that these specific efforts have had an enduring effect, for example, in greater female literacy, health outcomes, and/or political power that *cannot be attributed to other factors*. Similarly, when we read in Mohan's chapter that Christian prayer has played a democratizing role by reconstituting the Dalit body, I find myself asking for the evidence that a *spiritually* reconstituted body results in *social* change as well. I do not doubt that evidence *could* be found. Such assertions are, however, difficult to establish without complicated and labor-intensive sociological and ethnographic analyses.

Finally, the work of this volume could be extended through analyses even more attuned to material, bodily, and ritual worlds. I say "even more" because of the fact that several chapters were exemplary in this regard. Murugun and Mocherla, for example, attend carefully to the importance of democratizing *space itself*. Benteler examines the marking of hierarchy in Malayali foodways. And, Mohan asserts that ritual Christian prayer succeeded in sacralizing and thereby reconstituting the Dalit body, and hints of the reconstitution of the Dalit body and mind through changes in dress, comportment, and even diet.

These potentially fruitful lines of inquiry beg for greater investigation. By focusing on such things, we may come to discover how embodied performance (of religious and everyday rituals) can, to use the words of Catherine Bell (1998), "*create* [and, we should add, perpetuate, and alter] culture, authority, and transcendence". The perpetuation of both democratic and antidemocratic cultures is no purely intellectual matter. It succeeds, in addition, through the performance of everyday rituals. Cultures are "ingested" (Bourdieu 1984) through foodways, organized through space, and imprinted upon the body in gestures and dress. By attending more clearly to the performative, the bodily, and the material, we may not only achieve a more sophisticated analysis of culture, but may also discover more wholistic and effective ways to promote democratization.

Notes

1 The point is not, of course, to suggest that Protestantism is inherently more democratized than Catholicism. The American situation (where Catholic hierarchy seems to moderate Catholic politics while denominationally unfettered Evangelical churches are increasingly dominated by the kinds of antidemocratizing efforts described above) is adequate to discourage such overgeneralizing.

2 In so doing, these political leaders guard their own privilege in much the same way that conservative politicians in the United States guard theirs (and that of their predominantly white constituents) by branding any attempt to reckon with racist history or racial disparity "reverse racism", or branding attempts to give greater advantage to the disadvantaged "socialism."

References

Ahmed, Leila. *Women and Gender in Islam: Historical Roots of a Modern Debate.* New Haven: Yale University Press, 1992.

Bauman, Chad. *Anti-Christian Violence in India: History, Theory, Interpretation.* Ithaca, NY: Cornell University Press, 2020.

Bell, Catherine. "Performance." In *Critical Terms for Religious Studies*, edited by Mark C. Taylor, 205–224. Chicago: University of Chicago Press. 1998.

Bourdieu, Pierre. *Distinction: A Social Critique of the Judgement of Taste.* Translated by Richard Nice. Cambridge: Harvard University Press, 1984.

Durkheim, Emile. *The Elementary Forms of Religious Life.* Translated by Karen E. Fields. New York: The Free Press, 1995.

Turner, Victor Witter. *The Ritual Process: Structure and Anti-Structure.* The Lewis Henry Morgan Lectures; 1966. New York: Aldine de Gruyter, 1995.

Weber, Max. *The Theory of Social and Economic Organizations.* Translated by A.M. Henderson and Talcott Parsons. New York: The Free Press, 1947.

Index

Pages in **bold** refer to tables and pages followed by n refer to notes.

Aaron, Sushil J. 137, 217
Abraham, Kochurani 109, 120n17
Abraham, S. 133
Abreu S. J., Savio 21, 91–104
Achila 163, 166n24
Adivasi Hindus 141
Adivasis 16, 145–146
Agamben, Giorgio 20, 67, 69–70, 73
Agape Fellowship Church 134
agency and autonomy 129
Ahmed, Leila 245
AICC 18
Aierer clan 157–159, **158**
Ajungla 165, 167n38
Akbar 57
All India Catholic Union (AIUC) 46
All India Women's Conference 86
Ambedkar 1, 14, 31, 41, 67
American Baptist missionaries 82
American Lutheran missionaries 86–87
Andhra Pradesh 77, 226
Anglo-American scholarship xvi
anticonversion laws 72
Archbishop of Goa 92
Arendt 14
Aristotle 35
Arokiaraj, Cosmon 42
Arundhathiyar Christians 173
Augustine's theory of two cities 34
Aynavars 196

backwardness 132, 150n2
Badiou, Alain 68
baptism 92, 104n2
baptismal equality 41
Baptist Church in Nagaland 159

Baptist denomination of protestant Christians 163, 166n25
Baptist World Alliance (BWA) 159
Barro, R. 14
Basileia vision of Jesus 111, 121n27
Bauman, Chad M. 241–249
Bayly, Susan 57, 91–92
"Beef and Food Rights of People 211
believed Christianity 154
Bell, Catherine 248
below the poverty line (BPL) 139–140
Benteler, Miriam 24, 210–221, 242, 245, 248
Berger, P. L. 5
Berryman, Philip 39
Beschi, Joseph Constantine 57
Beteille, Andre 156, 162
Bethel Fellowship 134
Beyer, Peter 3
bhajan mandalis 139
Bhil in Rajasthan: attention of missionaries 133; *Billu/Villu* 131–132; criminal tribe 132, 150n1; female literacy 132–133; growth of pentecostalism 133–135; poverty 132; religious system 132; state as Scheduled Tribes 131; tribal groups 132
Bhopa 136
biblewomen 77, 80–84, 88
biopolitics of sovereign state and people 67, 74n1
bishops of South India 40
BJP 72, 211
Boggs, Kate 80
Bollen, Kenneth A. 7
Book of Common Prayer 197

Bower, Marion 81
Brahmin dissenters 86
British rule 43

Caironi, Peter Fr. S.J. 202–203
Calvary Covenant Fellowship Mission (CCFM) 22, 129–131
Campbell, Thomas V. 84
Carman, John 79
Casanova, J. 7
caste: geography 168–182; hierarchy 168; ideology 168
Catholic: community 46, 92; of Cuncolim 92; ecclesiology 36; missionaries 33, 43; nuns 22; Oriental Churches 39; sisters 112
The Catholic Bishops of India 44
Catholic Charismatic movement 94
Catholic Charismatic Renewal (CCR) in Goa 21; chairpersons of GST 96; classical Pentecostal movement 93; demography of 95–97; *see also* Catholic Charismatics in Goa; emerging Pentecostal Churches 93; feminine nature of 96; Mapusa group 94, 96; Merces group 95; origin and history of Pentecostalism 93; women participation in *see* Catholic Charismatic women
Catholic Charismatics in Goa: age-wise distribution of 96, 97; gender-wise occupation of 97, 98; marital status of 96, 97
Catholic Charismatic women: Ms. Alzira Antao 98–100; Ms. Flory Rodrigues 100–103
Catholic Charity 145, 150n8
Catholic Church 130, 177, 244; absence of democratization in 31; checks and balances of 38–39; clergy and laity 33, 38; Dalits–Partners in making of 40–41; democracy and democratization in 32–33; democratization and credibility 35–36; democratization as mission 43; inclusion and affirmation of Dalits 41–43; minority 44–45; participatory structures by Vatican II 36–39; Pentecostalism within 94; power, money and influence 39–40; priesthood 93, 104n4; scriptures and tradition 34–35; suspicion of Indian Democracy 43–44

Catholic Church–Pius IX 32
Catholic Indian Association 46, 48n4
Catholicism 43, 103
Catholic laity 43–44
catholic nuns in India 21–22, 106, 108, 112, 116–118; *see also* Catholic Women Religious in India; in democratic process 111; in empowerment of domestic workers 114; promoting education and empowerment 111–113
Catholic Women Religious in India 107–108; advocating social justice and human rights 113–114; challenges before 108–111; democratizing theology 114–115; ethos of effectiveness 117; impact of 117; obstacles and limitations 117–118; voice in the Church and Society 115–116
CCFM and democratic development: decentralizing leadership 135–136; empowering bhil women, equality and dignity 137–138; idea of development 135; promoting partnership in community development 138–139; rationalizing/modernizing religion 136–137
Chari/Longkumer clan 157
Charismatic Konkani retreats 99
Cherumar 196
Chintamani, C. Y. 15
Christian: bishops 73; church as religious *institution* 244; egalitarianism 220; food habits 210; *see also* Latin Catholics, food ways of; idea of equality 210, 218–221, 221n2
Christian communities xvi, 47, 66, 77, 88, 108; of earliest centuries 33–34; governance of 35
Christianity xvi, 67, 130; anthropology of xvii; and democratization 210, 218; genealogy of 171; idea of democratization 164; organizations and associations 172; in South Rajasthan 133–134
Christianity in Odisha: Christianity and social transformation in Kandhamal 142–143; Christianity, Panos, and development 141–142; Christian organizations and minority rights 146–148; Kondha–Pano dynamics 139–141

252 Index

Christian/Latin Catholic food habits *see* Latin Catholics
Christian leadership training 136
Christian minorities 131
Christian missionaries 21, 84, 131, 133
Christian organizations 138, 141–142, 146–148; *see also* Jana Vikas
Christian Panos 141–142, 144
Christian scriptures 241
Christian social democracy 21–22, 106, 111, 113, 116, 121n37
Christian theology 115, 182, 183n1
Church: authority 39; as coming community 69–70, 73; de-imperialization of 67; as democratic and egalitarian community 66; democratic community in India today 72–73; denominations 189; and empire 19, 68–69; as new humanity 70–72; in Vatican II 35
Church Missionary Society (CMS) 191, 195–196, 199, 201
Church's Auxiliary for social action (CASA) 16–17, 19
Citizen Amendment Act (CAA) 72
citizenship rights 129
civil society 20, 66
clan, land ownership and church affiliation **158**; clans in Yimti 157–159; nokzenketer 157
Clay, John 87
clericalism 67
Cochin 40, 191, 194, 196–197
Code of Canon Law 39
colonial political authority 4
coming community 70
communal violence 147
Conference of Religious India (CRI) 108
Confraria membership 92
Constitution of Democratic Republic of India 1
Convent education in India 113
Cooey, Paula M. 232
Council of Baptist Churches in Northeast India (CBCNEI) 159
Council of Jerusalem 38
Covenant Ministries 134
cross-cultural mission 134
Cucci, Giovanni 109, 120n19
cultural nationalism 66
Curran, Charles 36

Dahl 7
Dalit(s) 37, 39, 47, 146; anti-nationals 72; articulations 169; autonomous (political) subjects 129; Bible woman 83; candidates 170–171; Catholics 40–42, 48, 202; Christian activists 246; Christians 141; Christian students 170–171; communities 48, 77; conversion of outcaste 40; human rights of 146–147; issue of inclusion and representation 41–43; leadership and 40; Panos 141; population 131; of Rajasthan 129; in South India, marginalization of 174; and tribals 129, 147; women 78, 88; worship goddesses 78
Dalit Christianity in Kerala: Chirakkal Mission in Kannur district 203; Christian missions 205; CMS missionaries in Travancore 195, 197, 201; Dalit Churches 201; Devasia Padikaprampil, house of 204; dominant-caste Syrian Christians 201–202, 204; idea of redemption 200; Kottukappara 203; Malayalam 197, 199; Protestant Churches 201–202; Protestant missions 196, 204; Pulaya Mission 202; Pulayas (Cherumars) of Malabar 202; Pulayas, Parayas and Kuravas 196–197; slave castes 197–198; St. Thomas Church, Karikkottakkari 204; Tellicherry 203–204
Dalit Christian Liberation Movement 172, 183n4
Dalit Christians 174–176, 182; in Kandhamal 130
Dalit Christians in Kerala: Christianity *see* Dalit Christianity in Kerala; everyday life and prayers 189–191; religion 195–196; religious experiences of 189; slave caste's everyday life 191–195
Deleuze, Gill 67
Delhi gang rape case 138–139
democracy 3; in age of empire 67; Catholic Suspicion of Indian 43–44; Christianity and Indian discursive 56–59; and Christian public theology 59–63; diversity 34–35; equality 218; freedom and 43; high-intensity 31; idea of xvi; instruments of 72; liberal 52–55; low-intensity 31; power, money and 39–40; public spheres and participatory 55–56; resistance to 33; substantive 129

Index   253

democratic citizenship xvi–xvii
democratic ecclesiology 67
democratic society xvii
democratic values 130; in Church 32, 35; of inclusion 41
democratization 2–3, 78; in Church 40; and credibility 35–36; as mission 43; "Third Wave" of 43
democratizing theology 114–115
de Nobili, Robert 57
Dewey 14
discipleship of equals 35
divided church: becoming democratizing space 162–164; and lived christianity 160–161; united church democratizing village 164–165; of Yimti village *see* Yimti village
D'Lima, Hazel 108, 119n11
domestic violence: affectedness 226; alcoholism 229; cases of crime against women 227; children as silent sufferers and victims 233–234; Christian women bearing with abuse 234–235; dharma and politics 225; dowry demand 230; faith in God's justice 235; gender discrimination 229; kinship and social environment 232–233; patriarchy 229; physical violence 231–232; response of Church 235–236; role of Church 236–238; torturing body 231; UN as "shadow pandemic" 226–227; United States Justice department 227–229; verbal and psychological abuse 230–231; victims 225–226, 235
dominant caste 156
Doorenspleet, Renske 7
Dr. Barnett 229
Dumont, Louis 168
Durkheim 14

ecclesial communities 47
Ecclesia of the Multitude 68
Elanjimattathil, Ouseph 204
empire 66; church and 68–69; economy of suicide 72; Kyriarchal model of 68; logic of 67, 72
The End of History 52
Evangelical Christianity 78
"Evangelical Christianity and Democracy 217
Evangelical fellowship of India (EFI) 16–18

Evangelical Fellowship of India Commission on Relief (EFICOR) 16–17, 19
evil spirits and good spirits 136–137
Ezhavas 15

Feminization of Culture 77
feudal system 33
Filadelfia Bible College (FBC) 134–135
Filadelfia Fellowship Churches of India 134
Filadelfia Fellowship Mission 135
focus group discussion (FGD) 146
formal democracy 129
Foucault, Michel 101, 171
friendship evangelism 136
Friere, Paulo 109, 120n18
Fr. James D'Souza 94
Fr. J. M. Dupont 142–143
Fr. Philippe Richard 142
Fr. Richard Vas 147
Fr Stan Lourdusamy 45
Fr. Stan Swamy 66, 72
Fr. Unmeipesum Athigaram 170
Frykenberg, Robert Eric 11
Fuller, Chris J. 216

Gandhi 52, 154
Ganley, Anne 232
gender discrimination and violence 138
George, Mariam 206
Germany 44
Gibson, J. L. 5
Goadby, John 142
Goa Service Team (GST) 94–96
gospel 35, 111, 133–134, 139; in Rajasthan 135; values of 31–32
Goyal, B. R. 15
Gram Sabha 145–146
Griffin 234
G. Udaygiri 142
Guntur 85

Habermas' idea of public sphere 20
Hail Mary Mother of God 204, 246
Harijans 156
Haynes, J. 220
Hefner, R.W. 138
hegemony: common sense 153; of dominant ideology 153; practices 165
Henriques, Henrique 57
Hertz, Robert 177
Hibbert-Ware, George 87

Hill, William 142
Hindu(s) 130; castes 212; epics 79; gods and goddesses 132; hierarchy 220; Jagannath cult, Rajasthan 131; Kandhos 144; Kondhs 141; mythologies 79, 177; neighbors 210, 214, 218, 221; Rajput ideology 131
Hindutva 17, 61, 66
holistic development 138
Hollenweger, Walter 102
Holy Communion 163, 166n26
Holy Mass 203
Holy Rosary 203
Holy spirit 99, 137–138
Holy Thursday liturgy in Rome 93
Holy woman 99–100
Horsley, Richard 68
Huntington, Samuel 43

IBVM nuns 113
India: "Emergency" 44; religious traditions of 1
Indian Catholic bishops 241
Indian Catholic Church 19–20, 47
Indian Catholic community 47–48
Indian Catholicism: contribution of 46; democracy and democratization 32–34; and democratic challenges of today 44–47; democratic openings of Vatican II 36; hierarchical legacy of 35; inherent difficulties 36–37; question of democracy 31; revival of 47
Indian Christian agencies 16
Indian Christian engagement: economic and social inequalities 16–17; with gender and caste inequalities 10–13; human rights and 17–19
Indian Christian institutions 168
Indian Christianity 1, 182; alter Indian culture 245–248; ambiguity 242; caste inequalities and subaltern social movements 12–13; and categorical inequalities 9–10; democratization of 2–3, 91; foster democratization 242–243; Foucauldian analysis 168; idea of "affectedness" 24; idea of democratization 6–7; Indian modernity and dialectics 51–52; institutionalization/routinization 244–245; internal challenges 2; preached by 2; religion and democracy 4–6; religion, state and democratization 7–9

Indian Currents 46
Indian National Congress (INC) 177
Indianness of Indian Christianity 4
Indian Pentecostal Church of God (IPC) 102
Indian polity 31
Indian society 1–2; caste structure of 32; education and knowledge inequality in 14–16
Indian village committee 37
Indian weekly 31
India's National Commission for Women 227
indigenous congregation 107
Indira Gandhi 44
infant mortality (IMR) rate in Rajasthan 133
institutionalization/routinization 244–245
Integrated Child Development Service (ICDS) 143

Jaffrelot, Christophe 51, 58
Jana Vikas: cooperatives 143; empowerment of women 145–146; governance and rights 145; Government and 143; Peace Committees 144; SHGs 143–144, 146; vision and mission 145
Jan Vikas in Nuagaon 130
Jaspal, Rusi 174
Jennings, Theodore W. 68
Jesus Christ 60, 72, 199–200, 236
Jesus' cross 71
John, Antony 42
John, Mary 43
Jones, Kenneth W 12
Joseph, P.C. 206
Joseph, Pushpa 21, 106–123, 242
Joshua, Chegudi Dhanamma 85

Kandhamal region 130–131; population in 140; supplying Meriah 140–141
Kannalikkattil, Paulose 203
Kappen, Sebastian 67
Kaveri river 177
Kerala Christianity *see* Dalit Christianity in Kerala, Dalit Christians in Kerala
Keralam 40
Kerala missionaries 134
Kerr, Isabel 83
Kim, Sebastian 13
knowledge inequalities 14–16

Koinonia: in Christ 71; and New Humanity 70
Kondh tribe 139
Konkani Charismatic movement in Goa 99–100, 103
Kooiman, Dick 10
Kotra/*kalapani* 132
Kottayam 198, 200–202
Kozhikode Muslims 213
Kozhuvanal, Kunjukutty 202
Kugler, Anna S. 80, 85
Kumuti community in Raikia 141

Lal, Vinay 61
Latin America 6, 39, 43–44
Latin Catholics: anti-vegetarianism of 213; base diet of Kerala 212; Christian communities in Kerala 211–212; Christian heterogeneity 211; community 210, 216, 218, 221; diet and serving, impurity and hierarchy 212–213, 221; equality, hierarchy, Christianity and democracy 218–220; food habits and serving practices of 210; food ways of 211; meat eating and 213–214; processes of democratization 217; religion and politics 217; serving practices and hospitality 214–215; and value of hierarchy 215–216; vegetarian food 214
Leclercq, Jean 34
legislative assembly of Haryana 225
Lemtors clan 157–158, **158**
Leonard, John 86
Lewis 156
liberal democracy 52–55, 67
Linger clan 157–158, **158**
Lipset, S. M. 14
liturgical theology 67
lived Christianity 153–154
London Missionary Society (LMS) 82, 191, 196
Lord Jesus Christ 70–71
Louis, P.R. 204
Lourdusamy, S. 42
Lukose, W. 134
Lutheran missionaries 81

Madras Presidency 86
Maharajah of Pithapuram 86
Maharajah of Vizianagaram 86
Mahatma Gandhi 43

Mallapally village 199
Maples 234
Marshall, Ruth 217
Marshman, Joshua 15
Marx 67, 154
Mathews, Thomas 133–134
Medical School for Women in Vellore 85
Meriah sacrifice 140–141
messianic community 69, 72
messianic politics 70
Mies, Maria 225
Mill, J.S. 14
Missionary Medical School for Women 85
Mission Hospital in Guntur 85
Mlambo-Ngcuka, Phumzile 227
Mocherla, Ashok Kumar xvi, 1–25, 168–183, 217, 244–246, 248
Mohan, P. Sanal 23, 189–207, 245, 248
Mohanty, R.K. 140, 146
Moorshead Memorial Christian Hospital 143
Moral Man, Immoral Society 244
Moses, Karra Mary 85
Mosse, D. 92
Mouffe, Chantal 70
Mrs. Phyllis Dias 94, 96
Ms. Alzira Antao 95, 98–100
Ms. Flory Rodrigues 95, 100–103
Mudhaliar Catholic Christians 173
Mundadan, A. M. 57
Mungdang 163–164, 166n29
Muniz, Teresa 94–95
Munson, Arley 88

Nagaland 156; 1649 churches in 159, 166n13; attainment of 162; council of churches in 164; villages in 159
Nagaland Baptist Churches Council (NBCC) 159
Nagaravoyil in Northern Tamil Nadu 169, 173, 183n2; Agaram and Thenpennai caste-based discriminations 172–174
Naga society: class formation in 162; as egalitarian society 162
Naga tribes 155
Naidu Christians 173
National Council of Churches in India (NCCI) 19
National Family Health Survey (NFHS) 227

Native Missionary Movement 135
Nayadis 196
Nayars 10
Nellore 15, 82
neo-Pentecostal churches 135
Neoplatonism 34
Neura Church 99
New Frontiers International (NFI) Church 102, 104n11
New Testament 35
New Testament model 103
New Year prayer 138–139
Niebuhr, Reinhold 244
non-Christians in Rajasthan and Odisha 130
Non-Timber Forest Products (NTFP) 140
Northeast India (NEI) 23, 153, 160; borders 155; and Nagaland 156; study of villages in 154; village context 154–155
Northeast India Committee on Relief and Development (NEICORD) 16–17, 19
North-East Indian Catholicism 37
Nuthalapati, Bharathi 224–238

Occupy Religion 68
Oddie, Geoffrey A. 211, 217
Old Testament 34
Oommen, T. K. 12–13
Orissa Human Development report 143
OROSA 18
ORSSA 143, 147–148
Osella, Caroline 210–211, 213, 219
Osella, Filippo 210, 212, 219
Ozuku clan 157–159, **158**

Palli Sabha 145–146
Palliyogam 39
Panchayat Raj institution (PRI) 145–146, 148
Panjim 95
Papacy 67
Papaioannou, E. 14
Paraiyar Christians 173
Paraiyar Hindu 173
Parekh, Bhikhu 53
Parish Pastoral Council of Merces 101
Parry, Jonathan 177
participatory and consultative bodies 36–39
pastoral counter-conducts 168
Pastor Manohar Kala 135

Patrick, Gnana 51–64, 246
Paul, D. 68–70
Paul, Nilanjana 113
Peel, J. D. Y. 205
Pentecostal CCFM 244
Pentecostal-Charismatic Christianity in Goa 92
Pentecostal-Charismatic movement: gender paradox 101; history of 95, 103; as protest movement in Church 91
Pentecostal Church 129–130, 201
Pentecostal groups 134
Pentecostalism 91, 93–94, 102; among Bhils, growth of 133–135
Pentecostal missionaries 134–135
Pentecostal organizations 134
Pentecostals 133
Philippines 44
Pillai and Vellalar castes 177
Pinto, Ambrose 15–16
Plato 14
Plutschau, Henry 15
Podipara, Pacid J. 57
political ecclesiology 70
political Hinduism 246
Pongen clan 157–158, **158**
Ponniah, J. xvi, 1–25, 129–150, 217, 244, 247
Pope Francis 93, 108
Pope John XXIII 33
Pope Paul VI 33
Porter, Edward 82
Posnett, Charles W. 83
post-Constantinian Christianity 244
Premram, M. R. 23, 168–183, 244–246, 248
Protestant Christians 77, 247
Protestant missionaries 33, 81–82, 84, 241
Pseudo-Dionysius 34
public spheres: Christianity and Indian discursive 56–59; participatory democracy and 55–56
public theology 19–20
Pulaya Mission 202
Pulayas 15
putu 159, 166n17

radical ecclesiology 67, 70–71, 73
Rajahmundry 85
Rajasthan Pentecostal Church 134–135
Raj, Devasagaya 42
Ramakrishna, V. 15, 87

Ranyard, Ellen 82
Rawls, John 55
Reddy 173
Redemptoris Missio 107, 119n6
Reformed missionaries in Chittoor 87
religion 2, 72; functional role of 3; performative role of 3
Reuters foundation, India 227
Rev. K. Koshi 200
Rev. T.G. Ragland 200
Rieger, Joerg 68
Robinson, Rowena xvii
Roman Catholics 142, 212; *see also* Latin Catholics
Rousseau 14
Roy, Arundhati 72
Rueben, Martha 82

Sadtler, Amy S. 80
Sagar, Tarun 225, 238n2
Sahoo, S. 22, 129–150, 244, 247
Sustainable Development 146
Samanir 159, 166n16
Scarry 231
Schade, Agnes I. 80
Scheduled Tribes (STs) 131, 155
Schussler Fiorenza, Elizabeth 68
scriptures and tradition 34–35
Scudder, Ida 84
self-help groups (SHGs) 130
self-serving political Machiavellianism 241
Sempo clan 158, **158**
Sen, Amartya 14
Shaivite tradition 79
Shanars 10
Shyamlal 133
secularism 246
Siourounis, G. 14
slave castes 191–195, 197–198
social democracy 1
social ontology 70
Social Sciences and Humanities 2
spiritual warfare 137
Spivak, Gayatri 109
Srinivas, M.N. 154
Sr. Nirmalini Nazareth AC 108, 119n9
Sr. Noella D'Souza, MCJ 108
State of Democracy in South Asia (SDSA) 32
St Cyprian 38
Stirrat, R. L. 100
St. John Lateran basilica 93
Subramanian, Ajantha 176

Sullivan, John 15
Sundar, Aparna 217
Sunday schools 164, 167n32
Sustainable Livelihood enhancement 146
The Synod on Justice 36
Syrian Christians 40, 197, 201–202, 204
Syro-Malabar and Syro-Malankara 39

Taffarel, Joseph Fr. S. J. 203–204
Tamil Christianity 168; all souls' day, death rituals and caste rules 178–179; caste geography in India 172–173; caste-wise division of village 173–174; discrimination and divided churchyards in Tamil Nadu 176–178; social stigma in religious domains 174–176; sociology of caste stigma in India 172–174; transformational politics and political rationalities 179–181
Tamil Nadu 182; Nagaravoyil and Midtown of 169, 183n2; Sripuram village in 154; wall of discrimination and divided churchyards in 176–178
Taneti, James Elisha 21, 77–88, 242, 248
Tanjore 15
Telangana 77, 226
Telugu Christianity 77; bible women 80–84; *see also* Telugu women; women in local cultures 77–80
Telugu women 77; bible women, with bible in hand 81–84; health workers, agents of healing 84–86; schoolteachers, empowering literacy 86–88; and Western missionaries 80–81
Temsu 160–161, 166n19
Thanda Pulayas of Cochin 194, 196
Thenpennai village 173
theology: new community 71; of *oikoumene* 68; of state and democracy 71
Thomas, M.M. 20; messianic community 72; participatory democracy/radical ecclesiology 70–71; theology of humanization 71; theology of state and democracy 71
Thorat, Sukhdeo 54
Timor-Leste 44
Tracy, David 62
Travancore 177, 195, 197, 204–206
tribal groups 132

tribal population 131
trustee system 38–39
Turner, Victor Witter 244
Tzudo clan 157–158, **158**

Udaipur 133–134, 136, 139
umbrella church 135–136
UNDP, Odisha Human Development Report 139

Varkey Padikaparampil 204
Vatican II: democratic openings of 36; directives of 37; new participatory structures 36–37
Vattamattam, S. 67
victims 225–226, 235
village-core and village-periphery 172
village Swaraj 154, 165n4
Vinayaraj, Y. T. 20, 66–74, 241, 244
violence 224; domestic *see* domestic violence; Nirbhaya, Delhi girl 224, 238n1; patriarchy, hierarchy and gender discrimination 224
Visakhapatnam 82
Vitebsky 216

Walling, Wati 23, 153–167, 243
Ward, William 15

Weber, Max 154, 244
Welzel, Christian 2
Wesley, Mary 82
Wesley, Peter 82
Wilfred, Felix 19, 31–49, 242
Wilkinson, Abiatha 142
Wilkinson, Paul 12
Williams, Rhys H. 94
women 47; Bhil 137–138; as Bible women 21; Dalits, tribals and 147; diverse group of 106, 118n1; lived experiences of 224; violence against 138, 145, 224, 227, 229, 237; *see also* domestic violence
World Mission Evangelism 201

Xalxo, Pallavi 108, 119n11

Yimti village: division of church 160–162, 165; historical practice of usury in 154, 165n2; lived Christianity in 153–154, 162, 164; social fabric of 161; tzuktem as customary practice of usury 161–162, 164, 166n21

Ziegenbalg, Bartholomaeus 15, 57
Zuzarte, Cletus 108, 119n11